*Teaching Music
in the Secondary Schools*

Of related interest:

Hoffer, A Concise Introduction to Music Listening, Fourth Edition

Hoffer, The Understanding of Music, Sixth Edition

Allvin, Basic Musicianship: An Introduction to Music Fundamentals with Computer Assistance

Dallin, Foundations in Music Theory: With Programmed Exercises, Second Edition

Duckworth, A Creative Approach to Music Fundamentals, Third Edition

Lindeman/Hackett, MusicLab: An Introduction to the Fundamentals of Music

Martin, Basic Concepts in Music, Second Edition

McKay/McKay, Fundamentals of Western Music

Nelson/Christensen, Foundations of Music: A Computer-Assisted Introduction

Irwin, Playing the Piano

Lindeman, PianoLab: An Introduction to Class Piano

Lindsley, Fundamentals of Singing for Voice Classes

Robinson, Basic Piano for Adults

Stanton, Steps to Singing for Voice Classes, Third Edition

Anderson/Lawrence, Integrating Music into the Classroom, Second Edition

Hoffer, Introduction to Music Education

Irwin/Nelson, The Teacher, the Child, and Music

Nye et al., Singing with Children, Second Edition

Swanson, Music in the Education of Children, Fourth Edition

Fourth Edition

Teaching Music in the Secondary Schools

Charles R. Hoffer
University of Florida

WADSWORTH PUBLISHING COMPANY
Belmont, California   A Division of Wadsworth, Inc.

Music Editor: Suzanna Brabant
Editorial Assistant: Andrea Varni
Production Editor: Angela Mann
Managing Designer: Donna Davis
Print Buyer: Barbara Britton
Designer: Wendy Calmenson
Copy Editor: Margaret Moore
Compositor: GGS
Cover: Donna Davis
Cover Photos: Top to bottom, © 1989 Nita Winter,
    © 1989 Nita Winter, Patricia Hollander
Gross/Stock, Boston.

Printed in the United States of America   85

1 2 3 4 5 6 7 8 9 10—95 94 93 92 91

Library of Congress Cataloging in Publication Data

Hoffer, Charles R.
    Teaching music in the secondary schools / Charles R. Hoffer.—
4th ed.
        p.   cm.
    Includes bibliographical references and index.
    ISBN 0-534-14136-6
    1. School music—Instruction and study.   I. Title.
MT1.H73   1991
780′.71′273—dc20   90-12430
                                                    CIP
                                                    MN

To my mother and father

BRIEF CONTENTS

Chapter 1   So You're Going to Teach Music 1
Chapter 2   The Music Teacher 8

Part 1   WHY TEACH MUSIC? 27
Chapter 3   The Reasons for Music in the Schools 29

Part 2   WHAT: THE SUBJECT MATTER OF MUSIC 47
Chapter 4   The Music Curriculum 49

Part 3   HOW: THE METHODS OF TEACHING MUSIC 75
Chapter 5   Psychology and Music Teaching 77
Chapter 6   Teaching General Music 94
Chapter 7   Teaching Music Appreciation, Fine Arts, and Theory Courses 117
Chapter 8   Teaching Performing Groups 139
Chapter 9   Teaching Musical Expression 177
Chapter 10   Achieving Accurate Intonation 198
Chapter 11   Teaching Teenage Singers 212
Chapter 12   Teaching Instrumental Music 238
Chapter 13   School Music Performances 268
Chapter 14   Computers in Music Education 292

Part 4   TO WHOM: THE STUDENTS 323
Chapter 15   Teenagers and Music 325
Chapter 16   Music Teaching and Student Discipline 342

Part 5   PLANS AND RESULTS 357
Chapter 17   Planning and Assessing Music Teaching 359
Chapter 18   The Music Education Profession 382
Appendix   The Music Code of Ethics 390
           Index 393

CONTENTS

Preface   xxi

Chapter 1   So You're Going to Teach Music   1

What Is Music?   2

What Is Teaching?   2

The Components of Music Teaching   3
 Why Have Music in the Schools?   3
 What Should Be Taught in Music?   4
 How Should Music Be Taught?   5
 To Whom Is Music Being Taught?   6
 What Are the Results?   7

Chapter 2   The Music Teacher   8

Personality and Ego   8
 The Importance of Being Yourself   10
 Human Qualities and Professional Competence   11
  Personal Efficiency   12
  Relations with Professional Colleagues   12

Professional Preparation   12
 Knowledge of Teaching Techniques   13
 Preprofessional Experiences   14
  Observations   14
  Student Teaching   15

The Music Teacher and the Community   16
 Professional Musicians   17
 Music Merchants   17
 Private Music Teachers   18

Community Organizations 19
The Community 19
Fund Raising and Parent Groups 19
School Administrators 21
Continued Growth and Self-Evaluation 21
MENC Professional Certification 22
Self-Improvement 22
Teacher Rating Forms 23
Playback of Classes 23
Supplementary Employment 24
Questions 24
Projects 25
Suggested Readings 25
References 25

PART 1   WHY TEACH MUSIC?   27

Chapter 3   *The Reasons for Music in the Schools 29*

Reasons for Considering Basic Goals 29

The Value of Music and the Fine Arts 31
What About Music Is Valued? 32
Aesthetic Experiences 33
Teaching for Aesthetic Awareness 34

Nonmusical Reasons for Music 36
Transfer to Other Subjects 37
Mental Health 38
Avocational Value 38

Students or the Subject? 39

Teachers and Educational Goals 39
Music Teachers and School Administrators 40
Public Relations 42
Questions 43
Suggested Readings 44
References 44

PART 2   WHAT: THE SUBJECT MATTER OF MUSIC   47

Chapter 4   *The Music Curriculum 49*

Learning in Music 49
Musical Syntax 50

Musical Works 51
Intellectual Understandings 51
  Concepts 51
  Way of Thinking 52
  Creative Process 53
Skills and Activities 53
Attitudes 55
Nonmusical Outcomes 56
Who Decides on Content? 56
  Guidelines for Selecting Music 57
    Educational 57
    Valid 58
    Fundamental 58
    Representative 59
    Contemporary 59
    Relevant 59
    Learnable 60
  Evaluating Music Works 60
  Popular Music 62
Areas of Study in the Music Curriculum 62
  Nonperforming Classes 63
  Performing Groups 64
  Enriching the Rehearsal 65
  Types of Performing Groups 66
    Small Ensembles 67
    Orchestras 67
    Marching Bands 68
    Jazz Bands and Swing Choirs 69
  Credit and Graduation Requirements 69
  Credit for Private Study 70
  Implementing the Curriculum 71
Questions 71
Projects 72
Suggested Readings 72
References 72

PART 3 HOW: THE METHODS OF TEACHING MUSIC 75

Chapter 5 *Psychology and Music Teaching* 77

Types of Learning 78
Maturation 79

Cognitive Learning 80
    Ways of Cognitive Learning 81
    Motivation 81
    Structure 82
    Sequence 84
    Reinforcement 84
    Intuition 85
    Other Aspects of Cognitive Learning 85
        Transfer 85
        Memory 86

Psychomotor Learning 88
    Distributed Practice 89
    Singleness of Concentration 90

Affective Learning 91

Applying Psychological Principles 91
Questions 92
References 93

Chapter 6 Teaching General Music 94
Status of General Music 94
    General Music in High Schools 95

Goals of General Music 97
    Skills 97
    Understandings 98
    Attitudes 98

The Teacher and General Music 99
    Characteristics of Successful Teaching 100
        Presents Definite Content 100
        Achieves Results Quickly 101
        Relates to Students 102
        Active Learning 103
        Builds on Student Maturity 105
        Contains Variety 105
    Individual and Class Instruction 105

Activities and Materials 106
    Singing 106
    Listening 111
    Creative Activities 112

Planning for General Music Classes 114
Projects 115
Suggested Readings 116
References 116

Chapter 7 Teaching Music Appreciation, Fine Arts, and Theory Courses 117

To Combine or Not to Combine? 118
 Conditions to Overcome 118
 Infusion of Arts in Other Areas 119

Music Appreciation 120
 Purpose and Problems 120
 Content 120
 Listening 121
 Methods of Teaching Listening 122
 Aesthetic Sensitivity and Understanding 126
 Recognition of Styles 127
 Introducing a New Work 128
 Testing 128
 Textbooks 129

Fine Arts and Humanities 129

Music Theory 131
 Content 132
 Keyboard Experience 133
 Ear Training 133
 Singing 135
 Creative Work 136
Questions 137
Projects 138
Suggested Readings 138
References 138

Chapter 8 Teaching Performing Groups 139

Being Prepared 139

Bringing Out Musical Qualities 140

Teaching Instrumental Music 140

Teaching Choral Music 143

Rehearsing School Groups 145
 Using Verbal Commentary 145
 Indicating Musical Entrances 146
 Isolating Trouble Spots 146
 Keeping All Students Occupied 147
 Reviewing Learned Music 148
 Critical Listening by Students 148
 Objective Listening by the Teacher 149
 Providing for Individual Attention 150
 Practicing Outside of Rehearsal 151

Saving Time 151
Pacing in Rehearsals 152

Developing Music Reading 155
Functional Music Reading 157
Counting Systems 157
Reading Patterns 159

Teaching Musical Understandings 161

Selecting Music for a Particular Group 167
General Considerations 167
Repetition 167
Length 167
Rhythm 167
Musicianship of Students 167
Quality of Music 167
Vocal Considerations 168
Text 168
Range 168
Tenor Part 168
Accompaniment 168
Dissonant Intervals 169
Number of Parts 169
Musical Arrangement 170
Instrumental Considerations 170
Key 170
Scalewise Runs 170
Range 170
Length of Difficult Passages 171
Musical Arrangement 171
Program Requirements 172
Finding Appropriate Music 172
Copyright Law 172
Adapting Music 174
Questions 175
Projects 175
Suggested Readings 175
References 176

Chapter 9   *Teaching Musical Expression*   177

Deciding on Interpretation 177
Performance Practices 178
Authenticity 178
Personal Judgment 179

Techniques of Teaching Interpretation 179
  Rhythm 180
  Blend 183
  Balance 185
  Dynamics 185
  Use of Amplification 188
  Sustained Tones 188
  Staccato 189
  Legato 190
  Phrasing 191
Interpreting Vocal Music 193
  Tone Color 193
  Humming 194
  Slurring 194
  Pronunciation of Foreign Languages 195
Musical Feeling and Technique 195
Questions 196
Projects 197
Suggested Readings 197

Chapter 10   Achieving Accurate Intonation 198
Intonation Illusions 198
Musical Inexperience 199
  Poor Listening Habits 199
  Lack of Coordination 199
  Lack of a Concept of Pitch 200
Poor Methods of Tone Production 200
Psychological Factors 201
Environmental Factors 202
Instrumental Intonation 202
  Wind Instrument Intonation 203
  String Intonation 204
  Procedures for Instrumental Music Class 205
Choral Intonation 206
  Range and Tessitura 206
  Tempo 207
  Modulations 207
  Intervals 207
  Lack of Ensemble 208
  Procedures for Vocal Music 208
Questions 210

Projects 210
Suggested Readings 211

Chapter 11   *Teaching Teenage Singers* 212

What Is Correct Singing? 213

Physical Actions for Correct Singing 214
    Correct Position 215
    Deep Breath 216
    Relaxed Throat 217
    Actions of Breath in Singing 217
    Resonance 218
    Teaching the Correct Physical Actions 218

Aural-Psychological Approach 219
    Style and Tone 219
    Range 220

Diction 221

Girls' Voices 224

Boys' Voices 224
    High Notes for Boys 224
    Voice Change 226

Classifying Voices in High School 229

Organizing for Choral Music Teaching 231
    What's in a Name? 231
    Group Size and Seating 232
    Selecting an Accompanist 233
    Use of the Piano 234

Memorizing Music 234
Questions 236
Projects 236
Suggested Readings 237
References 237

Chapter 12   *Teaching Instrumental Music* 238

Beginning Instrument Instruction 238
    Using Pre-Band Instruments 238
    Guiding Pupils 239
    Organizing the Beginning Class 240
    Beginning Instruction Books 241
    Teaching the Beginning Class 242
    Using Rote Procedures 243
    Stressing the Musical Qualities 244

Teaching Rhythm 245
Practicing 245

Need for Teaching Fundamental Skills 246

Fundamentals of Wind Instrument Performance 246
Breath Support 246
Basic Embouchure 248
Single-Reed Instruments 248
Double-Reed Instruments 249
Flute 249
Brass Instruments 250
Tonguing 251

Fundamentals of String Instrument Performance 253
Bowing 253
Left-Hand Techniques 254

Percussion 255

Instrumentation 255
Seating 257
Transferring Students to Other Instruments 258
Substituting Instruments 260

Equipment and Supplies 260

Preparation on the Score 262

Stage or Jazz Band 263

Marching Band Techniques 264

Musical Instrument Repair 264
Questions 265
Projects 265
Suggested Readings 266
References 267

Chapter 13   School Music Performances 268

Reasons for Performances 268

Guidelines for Performances 269

Planning for Successful Performances 272
School Assemblies 273
Informal Programs 273
Programs Outside of School 273
Adjusting to Performance Conditions 274
Planning the Program 276

Ways to Enhance the Program 277
Staging Vocal Music Programs 278

Types of Staging Activities 279
    Dancing 279
    Change of Dress 280
    Lighting 280
    Props and Scenery 280
    Actions 280
Limitations to Consider in Staging 281
    Size of the Stage 281
    Size of the Offstage Area 281
    Amount and Quality of Stage Equipment 281
    Practice Facilities 281
Staging Instrumental Music 281
    Dancing 281
    Scenery and Stage Setting 281
    Featuring Sections 282
    Musical Variety 282
    Vocal Soloists and Choral Groups 282

Business Aspects 282
    Printed Programs 283
    Tickets 284
    Publicity 285

Trips and Tours 286

Checklist for Program Planning 288
Questions 289
Projects 290
Suggested Readings 291

Chapter 14   Computers in Music Education 292

History of Computers in Music Education 292

Why Computers in Music Education? 293

Music Teachers and Computers 294

Definitions and Computer Jargon 295

Computer-Assisted Instruction in Music 296
    Writing Your Own Programs 297
    A Few Preliminary Programming Definitions 297
    A Few BASIC System Commands 297
    Some BASIC/Applesoft Program Commands 298
    Writing a Simple BASIC Program 298

Published Instructional Programs 300

Selected Computer-Assisted Music Instruction Programs
for the Apple Computer 301

Programs Available from *Micro Music Software*—Temporal
Acuity Products 301
Programs Available from Electronic Courseware Systems 304
Programs Available from Alfred Publishing Company 306

Musical Performance and Composition with Computers 307
MIDI—Musical Instrument Digital Interface 307
Sequencing 308
Converting Sequences to Notation 309
Notation and Composition 309

Music Programming Composition, and Printing Systems 309
Programs Available from *Micro-Music Software*—Temporal Acuity
Products 309
Programs Available from Passport Designs 310
Programs Available from Mark of the Unicorn 311
Program Available from CODA Music Software 311

Managerial Uses with Computers 311
Word Processing 312
Data Base 313
Sample Choral Music Data Base Fields or Categories 313
Spreadsheet 314
Word Processing Programs 314
Data Base and Spreadsheet Program 315
Programs Available from *Micro-Music Software*—Temporal Acuity
Products 315
Program Available from Electronic Courseware Systems 315

Other Technological Aids 316
Marching-Band Show Design with the Computer 316
Two Electronic Devices 316
Purchasing the "Right" Computer 316
Questions 318
Projects 318
Resources 318
Suggested Readings 319
References 320

PART 4   *TO WHOM: THE STUDENTS*   323

Chapter 15   Teenagers and Music 325
Teenage Problem Areas 325
Conditions Aggravating Adolescent Adjustment 326
The Culturally Disadvantaged Adolescent 327

The Teacher's Role in Adolescent Adjustment 328
Teenage Musical Development 329
Physical and Vocal Development 330

Motivating Teenagers 330
Group Motivation 331
Group Morale 334

The Teacher's Attitude 334

Securing Adequate Membership 337
Recruiting Boys 339
Working with Boys 340
Questions 340
References 341

Chapter 16   *Music Teaching and Student Discipline* 342

Discipline and Teaching 342

Developing Desirable Classroom Behavior 343
Special Suggestions for Music Teachers 348
Problem Areas for Music 349
Talking 349
Inability to Participate 350
Attendance 350
Other Problem Areas 351

Maintaining Classroom Control 351
Handling Minor Disturbances 351
Handling Persistent Rule Violators 352
Handling Serious Problems 353
Questions 354
Project 355
Suggested Readings 355
References 355

PART 5   PLANS AND RESULTS   357

Chapter 17   *Planning and Assessing Music Teaching* 359

Using Objectives 359

Planning 361
Need for Planning 361
Amount of Planning by Music Teachers 362
Aids in Planning 363
Planning for Different Types of Classes 363

Long-Range Planning 363
Unit Planning 364
Lesson Planning 365
Sample Lesson Plan for General Music 367
Planning for Rehearsals 369
Assessing 370
Ways of Assessing 370
Tests and Testing 371
Cognitive Tests 371
Psychomotor Tests 373
Affective Assessment 376
Grading Students 377
Questions 379
Projects 380
Suggested Readings 381

Chapter 18   The Music Education Profession 382
What Is a Profession? 383
The Profession in the Past 384
Concerns and Opportunities 385
The Future 387
References 389

Appendix   The Music Code of Ethics 390
I. Music Education 391
II. Entertainment 392

Index 393

PREFACE

This book is written for anyone who plans to teach or is now teaching music in the secondary schools. In a practical, thorough, and comprehensive way, it covers the things a music teacher should know and do to be effective. It helps prospective teachers explore and understand the challenges of what sometimes deceptively appears to be the simple job of teaching music.

The fourth edition of *Teaching Music in the Secondary Schools* differs in a number of important ways from its earlier editions.

First, a chapter has been added on the use of computers in music education. I wish to recognize the efforts of Russell L. Robinson of the University of Florida for playing the major role in developing this chapter.

Second, the order of the chapters, especially those dealing with general music, has been made more logical. The courses for the general students at the high school level follow the chapter on general music for the middle school students.

Third, the new edition emphasizes, in addition to the basic questions about teaching, important philosophical and professional matters. The opening chapter lays a foundation for the book, the second chapter deals with the characteristics and education of music teachers, and the final chapter discusses the music education profession.

Fourth, several chapters have been significantly improved to make them more up to date and more practical and useful to students:

Chapter 2 has a new section on the music teacher in the community, as well as an expanded discussion of fund raising and parent groups.

Chapter 4 has an expanded discussion on the role of activities in learning music and the implementation of the music curriculum.

Chapter 6 has a new section on general music courses at the high school level, in addition to the updating and improvement of the suggested materials.

Chapter 11 has a revised section on the boy's changing voice.

Chapter 18 has an improved discussion of the future of the music education profession.

Most of the chapters have been shortened, made more accessible for undergraduates, and updated as needed. Suggested readings in each chapter provide ready resources for further reading and research.

With all of these changes, the fourth edition retains several of the previous edition's most important features. It still emphasizes practical suggestions and realistic situations. It still tries, through clear and lively writing, to give as much as possible the "feel" of actual teaching. And it combines theoretical and practical considerations whenever possible, because each aspect is important and each influences the teaching of music.

I am grateful to the many people who encouraged and enlightened me in my efforts to be a teacher and writer. Citing a few names here would not be fair to the greater number who would not be mentioned. I can, therefore, only thank them as a group and hope that this is adequate. I do wish to acknowledge by name the reviewers of this edition: Curtis Funk, Wheaton College; Duane E. Johnson, Hastings College; Carolyn Livingston, University of Rhode Island; John Mitchell, Carnegie Mellon University; and Dan Shultz, Walla Walla College.

Charles R. Hoffer

CHAPTER 1

So You're Going to Teach Music

If you are preparing to teach music in the schools, you have chosen a profession that is interesting, challenging, and important. To begin with, it involves working with music in all its infinite variety of types and styles—and its beauty and enjoyment. There aren't many jobs in which a person can work with one of the arts; people who work with computers or sell auto parts or hold thousands of other jobs don't enjoy this privilege.

Then there are the students in the schools. Whatever else may be said about them, no one has accused them of failing to make things interesting and lively in classrooms. Students come in all shapes and sizes, and they have widely differing interests and abilities. A highly specific, "cookbook" aproach to teaching them music will often not be successful because of the great differences among them as individuals and the wide variations among the thousands of teaching situations across the United States. Imagination and intelligence need to be applied in coming up with ways to meet the challenges and opportunities these differences offer to every music teacher. For these reasons, among others, music teaching is not for the lazy or fainthearted.

In addition to being interesting and challenging, teaching music is an important field of work. For reasons that are described more fully in Chapter 3, music and the other fine arts should be included in the education of every student. They are far too important in people's lives for the schools to ignore.

Where do you start in learning how to teach this interesting, challenging, and important subject? A good way to begin is by making sure you have a clear idea of what the words *music* and *teach* really mean. Although their meaning may appear to be obvious, they both have implications that are basic to what music teachers should do. First, the word *music*.

WHAT IS MUSIC?

The nature of music may seem obvious, but is it? Is a crash of a cymbal or an eerie sound from a synthesizer music? Why is a boom from a bass drum considered musical and booms from other sources thought of as noise? The difference is not so much in the sounds themselves as in the context in which they are heard. If they appear in a planned sequence of sounds, then they become music; if not, they are just random noises. The key to the matter is organization. In fact, music is often defined as "organized sound."

The organizing of sounds in a span of time is something that human beings do. Music was not preordained by the cosmic laws of the universe and therefore something that people find. Music is created by humans for humans. It is a human activity, and it varies in the forms it takes as much as other human creations including language, clothing, and food.

The world of music is vast and complex. Not only does it include all the music that people have created—folk, symphonic, instrumental, vocal, electronic, rock—it also encompasses musical activities such as singing, listening, analyzing, and creating. In fact, music is both an *object* in terms of being composed or improvised works and a *process* in terms of the actions involved in producing or reproducing music.

The vastness of the world of music forces teachers to make choices about what to teach and how to teach it. Fortunately, the definition of music as organized sounds does offer a clue to the most important responsibility of music teachers: guiding students to understand, make, and appreciate organized sounds. The processes of performing and creating music often help in achieving this goal. For example, creating melodies helps students to understand better the organizing of sounds, and so does singing or playing melodies on a clarinet.

Sometimes teachers emphasize one aspect of music so much that other aspects are largely ignored. Some teachers, for example, concentrate so much on the techniques of singing, playing, or creating music that the students never get around to understanding where the activity fits into the world of music. In other cases, teachers devote so much attention to factual information that the students forget that music is an art form.

Successful music teaching requires a balanced view of music. Both musical objects and processes are needed, as is a variety in the type of music the students study. And both information and activities should be related to organized sound.

WHAT IS TEACHING?

Teaching is the organizing and guiding of the process in which students learn. Simply put, a teacher's role is to bring about the acquisition of information, understanding, and skills by the students. The way in which this role is accomplished can take a number of different forms. Sometimes it consists of providing the students with information, while at other times it involves setting up a learning situation and then stepping aside as the students work on their own. In some instances it means deciding on tasks for students to do individually, while in other cases it consists of leading a group in a unified effort such as singing a song. Whatever form the teaching takes, the essential characteristic is that the students learn. Results are what the process of teaching is all about, not the particular actions teachers take when working with students. The essential goal of teaching should not be confused with its different styles.

The definition of teaching as a process in which students learn also has implications for the attributes of teachers. Although a teacher may exhibit charm and good looks, lecture brilliantly, manage a classroom well, and use this or that method, if no learning takes place, he or she has not been successful as a teacher. In fact, occasionally (but not typically) a person who appears to violate the usual assumptions about what is needed to be a teacher turns out to be highly effective in getting students to learn. Teaching is so subtle and complex an endeavor that such a situation can happen every so often.

Teachers' jobs usually include duties in addition to leading the learning-teaching process—checking out instruments, taking attendance, keeping order in the classroom. Most of these duties are important and necessary, but they are not part of the process. A person can be a good manager of classrooms and still not be a good teacher.

THE COMPONENTS OF MUSIC TEACHING

What is included in this process called teaching? When all is said and done, it comes down to five simple but basic components that can be stated as questions: (1) *Why* have music in the schools? (2) *What* should be taught in the music class? (3) *How* will it be taught? (4) *To whom* will it be taught? (5) *What are the results?* Because these questions are the essential elements of teaching, they form the basic outline of this book. Each component is discussed in subsequent chapters, but first a brief introduction to each.

Why Have Music in the Schools?

The most basic question concerns why there are music classes in the schools and teachers to teach them. The answer to that question provides teachers with a sense of direction, and to some degree it affects the answers to the other four questions of "What?" "How?" "To whom?" and "With what results?" Teachers who lack a clear understanding of these questions are like rudderless ships floundering in the seas of education.

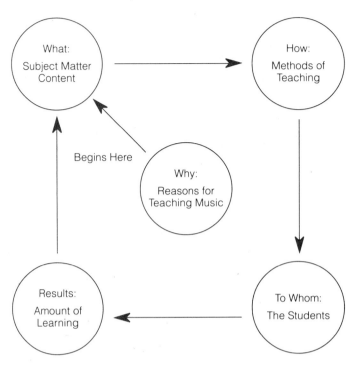

Figure 1.1　*Model of the Components of the Teaching Process*

Different answers to the question of "Why?" lead to different practical actions. For example, a teacher who sees school music primarily in terms of entertainment for the public teaches differently from a teacher who tries to give students a better understanding of music as organized sounds. These two teachers will choose different types of music, teach different skills and information, often use different methods, and evaluate their teaching and students differently.

Fortunately, it is not necessary to return to the question of "Why?" when thinking about every class or rehearsal. If you can express your reasons for teaching music with a reasonable degree of confidence, your answer can give direction and consistency to your teaching. However, it is a good idea to rethink from time to time the fundamental reasons for teaching music. Maturity, experience, and changed circumstances call for a periodic review of a person's views. The topic is too important to be decided once and for all at the age of twenty. Develop some solid answers now to the question of why music should be taught in schools, but don't "chisel your beliefs in stone."

What Should Be Taught in Music?

The question of the content of music classes deals with the "stuff" of music—musical works, facts, fingerings, patterns of sound, understanding of the process of creating music, interpretation, and similar things. It includes all types of information, skills, and attitudes, and it should light the spark of creativity and individual expression within the students.

Deciding what to teach is an enormously complex matter. As pointed out earlier, the world of music is huge, which makes choices about what to teach difficult. Other factors also contribute to the complexity of making these decisions, including practical considerations such as the musical background of the students, the amount of time available, the traditions of the community, the size of the class, and the amount and type of materials available.

It must also be remembered that students learn not only in music classes or under the guidance of teachers. After all, students spend only about 1000 of their 8736 hours each year in school, so it is not reasonable to credit or blame the school for everything students learn or know. The fact remains, however, that not much learning or understanding of music will usually take place without organized, competent instruction in school.

Unlike the question of "Why?" the matter of what to teach needs to be spelled out specifically for each lesson or class. It isn't enough merely to "put in time" in music. There should always be clearly stated objectives in terms of what the students are to learn.

How Should Music Be Taught?

The question of how music is taught focuses on the ways of organizing and structuring instruction, as well as selecting the manner of presentation. Some people who have never taught falsely assume that teaching is a job in which you merely stand up in front of the students and talk. If that were the case, teaching would indeed be easy! However, that is not the way it is, even if some experienced teachers make it look easy, just as a fine violinist makes the difficult passages of a concerto sound effortless.

The greater share of this book is devoted to the methods of teaching music. No claim is made that the suggestions presented in it are the only or even the best way to teach a particular aspect of music. So many variables are involved that nobody can point to any one way as the best for all situations. Although you can't expect a book to offer fixed answers in something as complex as teaching music, you should be given some useful and tested suggestions, which subsequent chapters do offer.

The suggestions in this book are geared to what is loosely called the "typical" school situation. Readers should realize, however, that there are almost no typical schools, and certainly each student is unique. The ideas presented apply to perhaps a solid majority of all teaching situations. As much as an author would like to, it is impossible to offer specific ideas on how to teach music in each of the thousands of schools in the United States.

The difficulty in specifying procedures for all situations is not characteristic of several other professions. For example, because nearly everyone's appendix is in approximately the same part of the body, surgeons can be taught a specific surgical procedure for its removal. Unfortunately, human behavior is much less consistent than human anatomy. Not all students have the same interests, musical background, and learning ability. For this reason, identical teaching procedures sometimes produce exactly opposite results in different classrooms, especially when different teachers are involved. Part of the challenge of teaching is being adaptable enough to meet a variety of situations.

Deciding on which methods are most appropriate for teaching specific material to a particular group of students is one of the challenges of teaching. Suppose that a teacher wishes to teach an alto section to sing a song with pleasing tone and accurate pitch. Assume further that it presents the teacher with no technical obstacles and the students are enjoyable to work with, offering the teacher few problems in guiding the class. The challenge comes in presenting the art of music so that it becomes meaningful to the students. How can the contour of the melodic line be impressed on students who may not know what the word *contour* means? How does a teacher make the singers conscious of the pitches and accurate when they sing them? Certainly not by merely telling them, "Watch your intonation!" How can the phrases of the song be presented so that the students will understand better the function of phrases in the song? These questions have just scratched the surface of the pedagogical matters that are involved in teaching the correct rendition of a part.

A sizable amount of information exists about learning and the conditions under which it takes place, but much remains unknown. This available information should be the "stuff" of music methods courses. Ideas on teaching change as new evidence becomes available from research and practical experience. For example, it was once believed that language reading should be introduced by teaching letters of the alphabet first, because words are made up of letters. When the alphabet had been learned, they were put into words and finally into sentences. This method (known as the ABC method) seems logical, but what is logical is not always the way people function. Today, teachers know that words are comprehended as a whole, not letter by letter. Without this knowledge and without training in how to use it, teachers would waste much time and introduce habits that students would have to break later. A fluent reading ability and a gracious way with children are not sufficient qualifications for teaching reading. The same is true of teaching music.

To Whom Is Music Being Taught?

Music is taught to someone, and the capabilities and motivation of the students are an essential component in the teaching process. Not only must teachers consider such obvious matters as the range of voices and previous musical knowledge, but they should also be aware of the probable use the students will make of what they learn. A seventh grade general music class and a high school orchestra may both study a Bach fugue, but each will approach the work in a different way and with a different degree of technical information.

The "To whom?" question calls for teachers to put themselves in the place of the students in order to recognize better their varied interests, needs, and backgrounds. Teachers must try to see the subject through the eyes of the pupils. This ability is needed not only to know how to adapt methods and materials but also to establish a teacher-class relationship that will encourage positive attitudes in the students. Students are often slow to distinguish between their feelings toward the teacher and their feelings toward the subject. And in a subject such as music, in which so much depends on feeling and perception, the students' attitudes are especially important. When the students realize that the teacher is sensitive to their interests, the relationship between pupils and teacher is greatly improved, and as a result more learning takes place.

What Are the Results?

The fifth component in the teaching process is finding out the results of a class or lesson. What do the students know or what are they able to do after the class that they did not know or do before? Exactly and precisely, what was accomplished?

Teachers cannot determine the amount of learning by trusting to luck or just by watching the students' facial expressions. Instead, what is needed is evidence in terms of what students can do as a result of the learning experience. The term *observable behavior* does of course not refer to classroom deportment, although there is some relationship between the quality of teaching and classroom conduct. Rather, it refers to specific learning revealed through the students' abilities to answer questions, to signal when a theme returns, to sing or play the third of a triad when asked, or to add an improvised phrase to a line of music.

Why? What? How? To whom? With what results? The answers to these questions are the essential parts of the process called teaching. If teachers fail to think through each one of these questions, they run the risk of producing educational failures marked by wasted time and lost opportunities for learning. Teaching is similar in this respect to getting an airplane off the ground. If any important part is missing or not working, the plane will not take off. Because educational failures are less dramatic and less immediately visible than airplanes failing to become airborne, some teachers are able to hold their jobs without thinking carefully about what they are doing. Only their students are the losers. Sometimes the material is too difficult, too easy, or meaningless; sometimes the hours spent in music classes add up to little additional knowledge or skills for the students; sometimes teachers and classes wander, not knowing what they are trying to accomplish or if they have learned anything. When any of these situations occurs, the lack of learning can correctly be called an "educational failure."

The five questions discussed in this chapter provide an approach for thinking and learning about teaching. They also give focus to thoughts that would otherwise be a formless blob in one's mind. Analyzing and understanding the teaching process are the first steps in becoming a good teacher.

CHAPTER 2

The Music Teacher

Are people born with the ability to teach music well, or do they become good teachers by hard work and self-improvement? What characteristics do most good music teachers possess? Where do preprofessional experiences and student teaching fit into the training of teachers? These and other questions are concerned with the type of persons music teachers should be, the skills and knowledge they need to have, and the ways they can continue to improve their ability to teach after they get a job. Because music programs can be no stronger than the people who teach them, the quality of music teachers is vitally important.

PERSONALITY AND EGO

The research and writings on the topic of the personality of good teachers have tended to reaffirm what nearly everyone already knows: Warm, friendly, understanding teachers are more effective than those who aren't; businesslike and organized teachers are more effective than teachers who are careless and disorganized; and imaginative and enthusiastic teachers surpass in effectiveness those who are routine and dull. One writer concludes that a good teacher is "held to embody most human virtues along with a great many qualities more frequently attributed to divinity" (Stephens, 1963, p. 59).

A few points can be stated with confidence, however, about the personality of successful music teachers. They should be adults in the fullest sense of the word, and they should be conscious of the needs and feelings of others. The whims and idiosyncrasies of an "artistic" temperament have no place in the schools.

It does seem that music teachers are susceptible to greater ego involvement in their work than are most other teachers. It may be that the "leader" role that many music teachers have as part of their jobs attracts people with greater ego

FUNKY WINKERBEAN   **Tom Batiuk**

Funky Winkerbean by Tom Batiuk. © 1977 *Field Enterprises, Inc. Courtesy of Field Newspaper Syndicate.*

needs. It could be that the circumstances of the job tend to encourage a heightened sense of personal involvement; as someone has pointed out, the applause of an audience is "heady wine." It may be that some music teachers would rather be performers. Whatever the reasons, many music teachers tend to view their work as an extension of themselves. For example, a number of times the author has heard music teachers almost boastfully relate how the choir or band "fell apart" after they left a particular teaching position. Some teachers work hard with students who have ability because they help bring recognition to the teacher, but they have little time for the less talented students. The situation pictured in the comic strip on this page in which the teacher draws attention to himself or herself has actually happened in football programs and yearbooks; only the size of director's face was less prominent.

Music teachers need to face the fact that the pressures of ego involvement will be present throughout their teaching career. What they need to do—and do often—is remind themselves that the role of teacher is one in which you gain satisfaction through observing the learning of your pupils. Music exists in the schools for the benefit of the students, not for the aggrandizement of teachers. The *Final Report* of the Teacher Education Commission of the Music Educators National Conference (MENC) makes the point clearly: "The ego-satisfaction of the music student in college is often gained through personal performance whereas that of the music educator is gained largely from creating opportunities for students' music expression" (MENC, 1972, p. 5).

The preceding paragraph about where the satisfactions in teaching are found may sound like a teacher's role is one of self-sacrifice. That would not be the correct conclusion. It is not so much a sacrifice of ego and self as it is a different way of achieving satisfaction. When you teach so that the students learn something they would not have learned without your efforts, that is truly gratifying. There is something deeply satisfying about knowing that you make a difference in the lives of people, especially young people. Such satisfactions can hardly be thought of as making a sacrifice; far from it. They are much more rewarding than a career devoted to beating out someone for better chairs in an orchestra or solo parts in oratorios. When all is said and done, there is a lot more enjoyment in doing something for others than in worrying so much about oneself, and such activity carries with it its own type of ego satisfaction.

The grooming and appearance of teachers is a subject that has occasionally produced heated discussions, but it probably has little effect on the students' learning *as long as it does not distract from or interfere with the respect and confidence the students have in the teacher*. It is everyone's right as a citizen to wear any hairdo or clothing style they wish. But if a person's appearance causes the students to look upon the teacher as a freak or egoist, then it is simply not worth the loss of learning that results. Each college and each school has its own standards, both written and unwritten, on this matter. New teachers and student teachers should find out what those expectations are and abide by them. In most cases, common sense is a reliable guide for personal appearance.

The speaking voice of teachers should be pleasing, and, more important, it should carry a quality of decisiveness. During student teaching the complaint is sometimes leveled at a novice teacher that his or her voice cannot be heard in the back of the room. This problem usually disappears as the beginning teacher gains confidence and experience and makes an effort to improve in this area.

In the final analysis there is a quality beyond personality, grooming, and voice: a sense of commitment to being a good teacher. David Ausubel, the noted educational psychologist, has written: "Perhaps the most important personality characteristic of a teacher ... [is] ... the extent of the teacher's personal commitment to the intellectual development of students.... It determines in large measure whether he will expend the necessary effort to teach for real gains in the intellectual growth of pupils or will merely go through the formal motions of teaching" (1968, p. 412). Myron Brenton is more blunt about it: "The best teachers wear a large invisible button that reads, 'I give a damn' " (1970, p. 40).

The Importance of Being Yourself

When authors or groups write about what teachers should be like, they are presenting an ideal or model, not a set of minimum competencies that must be met. They realize that teachers are human beings and that no one can fulfill every suggested quality. The reason that all the qualities are mentioned is to make readers aware of what is desirable in a music teacher.

Every one of us has strong and weak points in terms of being a teacher. It is obvious that we should utilize our strengths to the fullest in order to compensate for our weaker points. With some teachers their strength is their ability to play piano, with others it is an ability to inspire students, and with others it is their knowledge of music and their intelligence. Each person develops different ways to fulfill the role of teacher.

Many young teachers who have studied under a dynamic, extroverted individual or observed such a person in full swing at a workshop may have wondered, "Is it necessary for me to have that kind of personality to be successful?" Extroversion does not guarantee a teacher's ability to convey ideas and teach effectively. Suppose a teacher puts on a red shirt and conducts groups something like a cheerleader. At first that would probably grab the attention of the students, but what about the fiftieth or hundredth class? What was once attention grabbing could become pretty annoying. And what does the red-shirted teacher do *then* to get attention?

Many good music teachers are not extroverts and would only look silly if they tried to be. Instead of extroversion what is needed is a quality of decisiveness, of knowing what is needed, and letting the students know that you are competent and in charge. Good teachers cannot be weak and timid. The way in which each individual achieves this quality of competence depends on his or her unique personality, but it must be achieved, especially when teaching in the secondary schools. Two conditions can help achieve the impression of competence: (1) a firm belief that what you are teaching is worth the students' knowing and (2) the confidence that arises from understanding what you are about as a teacher. Beyond these basic understandings the quality of decisiveness (not aggressiveness—there is a difference) is something that many future teachers must work on and develop through experience and training.

Human Qualities and Professional Competence

It is easy to point out that teachers should be sensible, fair, decisive, and interested in the students' learning. But how do these attributes relate to the ability of teachers to work with people, something that is central to teaching? Here are some thoughts on the question:

- Music educators, like all teachers, need to be ever growing in their outlook on the work and on their students. They continue to learn until they retire from teaching. They look for and consider new ideas carefully, and they are not afraid to try different approaches to old problems.

- They relate well to other human beings, especially their students. They empathize with their students and colleagues. They can relate to people of differing cultural backgrounds.

- They can relate the subject matter of music to other academic disciplines, especially the other arts. They see music as a part of the larger culture.

- They understand their role as teacher. They gain satisfaction, not from receiving personal attention but rather from seeing growth and success in their students. They realize that they need to lead and inspire their students, but they also realize they should not dominate the class or rehearsal room.

- They are musician-teachers. They realize that they fail their students if they don't teach them musical skills and understandings, as well as favorable attitudes toward music. They seek out a variety of music for study and performance, and they value the music for its expressive qualities.

Personal Efficiency.   Proper planning requires personal efficiency and organization. Unless teachers have these qualities, both they and their students are apt to find themselves in a state of confusion. Music teachers have been known to forget to order chairs or risers for a performance, to lose their own music, to fail to keep track of uniform and instrument numbers (or worse yet, money from ticket sales!), and to wait to the last moment to prepare a program for a concert. What excitement these fumblings create! But when confusion reigns, the educational results are reduced. Musicians, along with almost everyone else, may dislike "administrivia"; but trivial or not, details must not be neglected.

Relations with Professional Colleagues.   In some instances, a music program is hampered because of poor relationships between music teachers and the people with whom they work. For example, if a teacher is personally disagreeable, the school guidance counselors may be hesitant about encouraging students to enroll in music courses. Some instrumental music teachers consider themselves to be in competition with choral music teachers, and vice versa. Not only do the two factions fail to work together, but occasionally the teacher of one group belittles the other in an attempt to build up his or her group. Such friction undermines the total music program and is a waste of emotional energy for the teachers, to say nothing about its unethical qualities.

Music teachers sometimes overlook the school clerical and custodial staff, or they feel superior to them and let those feelings show. A successful music program depends on the assistance of the nonteaching staff, but thoughtless music teachers occasionally take this help for granted and fail to acknowledge it in any way.

Music teachers need to take an active interest in school activities. They cannot say on the one hand that music is an integral part of the curriculum and then shy away from serving on schoolwide curriculum committees because they feel that music is a "special" area. Nor should they display little interest in the fate of the football team or the winter play, especially if they want the support of the physical education and drama departments for the music program.

PROFESSIONAL PREPARATION

Virtually every state has developed a set of minimum requirements for the certification of music teachers. In most cases, these are only minimums and are far below the amount of training that is desirable for preparing competent music teachers. Usually these requirements are stated in terms of credit hours for various courses or areas of study.

Some preparation in both vocal and instrumental music is valuable in music-teacher education programs. Not only is this requirement musically and philosophically desirable, it is also a practical necessity for many teachers. Beginning teachers most often have dual responsibilities, because they are likely to work in school systems too small to warrant hiring specialists for each of the various areas of music, and because the new person sometimes gets the odds and ends that the teachers already in the system have left behind.

There is another reason for a broad undergraduate preparation. Suppose that it could be determined just what you needed to know to be a music teacher, and you were given only those courses. That situation would be like buying only the amount of blanket needed to cover you at night. You would lie on your back with your hands at your side as your tailored blanket pattern was traced and then cut. Yes, this procedure would save blanket material, but a problem would come up if you wanted to change positions as you slept, because you would have no cover for any other position. A narrow teacher-education program provides little "cover" for different positions in music education and inhibits growth in the profession. As an undergraduate it is impossible to be able to predict exactly what will be useful to you ten or twenty years from now.

The concept of preparing music teachers for all grades, kindergarten through grade 12, is certainly justified. The vast majority of jobs available to music teachers involve teaching on more than one level.

Knowledge of Teaching Techniques

Good teachers know how to teach what their students are to learn. For example, if a band plays a passage in a staccato style, how does the teacher get the idea of staccato over to the players so that they can execute it correctly? Without knowing how to do this, the teacher must resort to pleading, "Now, make those notes *short!*" This procedure is all right as a beginning, but experienced teachers know that just telling the students to play short notes is not enough to teach staccato, except for a few short notes that might happen by trial and error.

Teachers should have in mind numerous examples, analogies; and explanations for use in teaching. They cannot stop a class, run to their desks, and thumb through a book to find this technique or that bit of information. Whenever possible, music teachers should anticipate the problems that might be encountered in a certain piece. If a work requires staccato playing, they can review various ideas for playing staccato (it's not the same on every instrument) prior to presenting the piece to the group.

In teaching a performing group, teachers should teach their students to do more than execute the printed music symbols and follow the conductor's gestures. Singing and playing can easily become mechanical, so that the students make music in a parrotlike fashion without any understanding of what they are doing. Playing and singing are fine, but they are only a part of music education. Students should also be taught something about the style, harmony, form, rhythmic structure, and composers of the more substantial works the group performs. Specific techniques for doing so are presented in Chapter 8.

Preprofessional Experiences

Observations.   Many states and colleges require that future teachers have contacts with schools and students prior to the student-teaching experience. These contacts are called by a variety of names, with "field experiences" perhaps being the one most commonly used. The purpose of field experiences is to encourage future teachers to think about and be aware of school situations well before the last semester of the undergraduate preparation, when student teaching is usually taken. In fact, some colleges and states specify contacts with schools beginning in the freshman year, and sometimes the observation of disabled or minority children is also stipulated.

Usually field experiences take place in a variety of school situations so that future teachers gain a perspective of the total music curriculum. Many of them are for one time only in any one school or with any one teacher. Occasionally a small-project type of teaching is done in conjunction with a music methods class, such as when a committee of three students develops and teaches a lesson on playing the autoharp to a third grade classroom.

The usefulness of these pre-student-teaching experiences depends to a great extent on the attitude of the future teachers. If they look upon them as just putting in time to fulfill a requirement, then they probably will receive the minimum benefit from them. On the other hand, if they go into school situations and try to analyze the teaching process (*not* the teacher as a person) and learn from what they see, they can benefit a great deal from these experiences.

And what should future teachers attempt to analyze as they observe school music classes? The teaching process as described in Chapter 1. (Surprised?) Because these experiences present only a limited time to observe a teacher, and because there is an ethical question about future teachers attempting in an hour or two to guess the motivation of a teacher, the five questions presented in Chapter 1 should probably be reduced to four for purposes of the observation experiences. For each class, then, the observing students should answer these questions:

1.   What was the teacher trying to have the students learn?
2.   What methods did the teacher employ to help the students learn?
3.   What appeared to be the musical background and interests of the students?
4.   What were the observable results of the instruction?

In addition, student observers will find it useful to notice how the teacher managed some of the routine matters of teaching. Such matters include the setup of the room, the distribution of music, the promptness with which the class is started and conducted, the assignment of seats for the students, and the manner in which attendance is taken. In no sense are such actions equal in importance to the amount of learning that takes place, but they can affect the educational results and are therefore worth observing.

Student Teaching.   Student teaching has three purposes. First, it provides the future teacher with the opportunity to observe and work with an established, successful teacher. A student teacher in a real sense is an apprentice to an experienced teacher. This apprenticeship permits an intensive observation and testing experience that is considered essential in all teacher education programs. The cooperating teachers (the term often assigned to such teachers) are selected because they are considered to be better than average. The cooperating teacher accepts student teachers largely out of a sense of professional commitment, not to make his or her job easier or to gain extra income.*

The second purpose of student teaching is to provide a guided induction into teaching. Student teachers can move step by step into situations structured by cooperating teachers; consequently, student teachers are not just pushed into jobs in which they must either sink or swim.

The third purpose of student teaching is to establish the fact that the student teacher can in fact teach. A prospective employer wants to know, "How did this person do when in front of a classroom?" A good college record and good character recommendations are fine, but there is no better test of teaching ability than actually teaching in a "real life" situation.

It helps if you are clear on what everyone's role is in the student-teaching situation. Your role as student teacher has already been pointed out: an apprentice. It is an in-between situation. You will be a teacher, but yet not quite. You will be closer in age to the students than their teacher, but you are expected to act like a teacher, not a student or an intermediary between the class and the teacher. The students know that you are a student teacher and that after a while you won't be around anymore. They also suspect that you won't have a lot to say about their final grades or their seats in the clarinet section. In a real sense, the position of student teacher is one of a "guest" or "temporary resident." You will be working with someone else's classes in a school in which you are not a permanent employee. You will not be in a position to make significant decisions without the approval of the cooperating teacher, to fill out requisitions unless the supervising teacher approves them, or to negotiate a different schedule for music classes.

Yet you will be a teacher. By that time you will have had much specialized training for what you are doing. Your role will be that of teacher, and you will be expected to show up promptly each day school is in session. You will be allowed some initiative in what is taught, but such undertakings should be cleared with the cooperating teacher ahead of time.

The role of a cooperating teacher is that of mentor to the student teacher. A mentor is one who guides, offers constructive help, and answers questions. Offering suggestions for improvement is part of that process, as are commendations for assignments that are done well. Student teachers need not agree with every suggestion they receive, but the cooperating teachers' thoughts should be given careful consideration and in most cases given a try. In addition, the cooperating teacher

---

*The stipend for supervising a student teacher is only a token payment, if there is any at all.

is responsible for a report to the college about your teaching and usually is asked to write a letter of recommendation. For all of these reasons the usefulness of the student-teaching experience depends very much on the cooperating teacher.

College supervisors usually do not have a major role in the student-teaching situation. This situation is so for one simple reason: The number of times they can visit a student teacher is usually limited. Even if three of five visits are possible, these usually last for only a couple of classes. The college supervisor's role consists more of making the initial placement and then serving as a coordinator between the college and the cooperating teacher. If important problems arise in the student-teaching situation, then the college supervisor's role becomes very significant. Also, if a college supervisor has observed your teaching, he or she can write a letter of recommendation for you that is more credible than letters from other professors because it can report on your teaching.

The amount and type of teaching that a student teacher undertakes depends on the cooperating teacher's opinion of the particular needs of the program. Usually the first week or so is spent observing and learning about the situation. Gradually the student teacher is given more responsibility. Often this initial responsibility consists of working with individuals or small groups and doing menial chores such as passing out books, moving chairs, and typing tests. After a while the student teacher is given entire classes and eventually most of the cooperating teacher's schedule.

For student teachers who demonstrate initiative, optimism, and a willingness to learn, the student teacher experience is most rewarding.

THE MUSIC TEACHER AND THE COMMUNITY

There is more to being a music teacher than meeting classes and managing supplies and student grades. In addition to teaching, all music teachers must devote a small amount of time—perhaps one hour a week—to educating others about the purpose and values of music in the schools. Music educators understand the value of having music in the school curriculum, but most people do not. It is not that they don't want music in the schools; rather, it is that they are uninformed about its value in schools. Therefore when money is short, support is "soft."

Furthermore, uninformed persons tend to look for the wrong things in forming opinions about the music program in their local schools. A win at a contest, even one of little importance, is often misconstrued into thinking that the schools have a fine total music program. In addition, almost all opinions are formed from hearing or seeing performance groups, which tends to put most of the attention on them. These groups often involve only 10 or 15 percent of the student body. As a result, music for the other 85 percent of the students is largely forgotten.

What should music educators do to build better public understanding? The answer to that question depends on the situation and the teacher's abilities and interests. It may mean writing an annual report to the principal on the school's needs and plans in the area of music. It may mean making public performances more like "informances," in which an effort is made to educate the audience about music and music education. It may mean trying to get the band boosters to think of themselves as "music boosters" by supporting the addition of another teacher in orchestra and general music. It may mean taking time to work with the school guidance counselors to avoid scheduling conflicts. A more complete listing of ideas for informing others about music education is contained in the MENC publication *Beyond the Classroom: Informing Others.*

Part of the task of informing others about school music and developing their support lies in reaching particular groups of people in the community.

Professional Musicians

School music programs are affected by the other music activities and interests in the community. A city or town with an active musical life helps the school music program, and, in turn, effective school music programs contribute to the level of the arts in communities. For these reasons music educators should promote musical activities in the community. Also, music teachers should work to bring professional performers into the schools. To the extent possible, in-school performances by professional performers and the educational concerts should be jointly planned ventures between the school music teachers and the performers. The benefits are greater when such cooperation takes place.

Attempts have been made to define the "turf" or domain of professional musicians and of school groups. In 1947 the MENC, the American Association of School Administrators, and the American Federation of Musicians drew up a comprehensive Code of Ethics that specifies which activities are the domain of school music groups and which should be left to professional musicians. The code has been reaffirmed every seven years since 1947. All music educators should be familiar with and abide by the provisions of the code. It is presented in the appendix.

Music Merchants

Contacts between music teachers and music merchants should also be conducted ethically. Because music teachers are employed by the public, and therefore should treat everyone equally, they should not accept personal favors or commissions from merchants. The acceptance of gratuities has a way of obligating the teacher and gives the appearance of favoritism. The choice of store and purchases made should be determined solely on the basis of the quality of goods and services in relation to the cost. When purchases amount to $100 or more, it is wise (and usually required by law or school regulation) that bids be secured. Competitive bidding encourages the best price from the merchants and provides proof that business transactions are handled fairly and openly.

An especially delicate situation exists when there are a small number of local

music merchants whose prices and services are not as good as those of merchants from neighboring communities. In such cases, music teachers should make all pertinent information available to the students and their parents, but they should make no recommendations about merchants. When this practice is followed, the responsibility for which merchant is selected becomes a matter for the individual family, not the music teacher. The same policy should be followed with regard to brands of instruments. Instrumental music teachers should make a list of acceptable brands and types available. Unacceptable brands need not be listed.

Private Music Teachers

The same practice should be followed with regard to music teachers' recommendations of private instructors. Never should the work of an incompetent private teacher be deprecated publicly; that person should simply not be recommended. Whenever possible, music teachers should provide interested parents with the names of more than one competent private teacher.

The level of the school music program can be advanced considerably by the efforts of good private music teachers. This is especially important in the case of instrumental students who have progressed beyond intermediate levels. Because few instrumental teachers know the advanced techniques on more than one or two instruments, the progress of the school band or orchestra depends in part on the availability of private instruction.

Community Organizations

Community service clubs and organizations, and especially a local arts council, should not be ignored. Service clubs sometimes provide scholarship help to enable worthy music students to study, and they also contribute travel monies on occasion. These groups also are a good means of getting information about the music program to the public. The arts council represents a ready-made group that supports the arts, and such support can be valuable if the music program faces financial cutbacks.

The Community

The most useful contacts music teachers have with the public are the parents of the students. Information should be supplied to the parents periodically about the activities and goals of the music program. Slide shows, videotapes, and brochures can be prepared explaining the program. In some instances, parent support groups have been of great help in furthering high school performing groups, especially bands. Over time, music teachers should steer the interests of such organizations toward the entire music program, not just one segment of it.

For a number of years in March the MENC has led a nationwide effort to promote music in the schools; it is called Music in Our Schools Month. Not only does the MENC national office supply prepared materials and posters, it also secures some national publicity for school music. Teachers are encouraged to secure proclamations from mayors and state organizations from governors. Such proclamations provide favorable publicity for school music and let everyone know that music education is indeed alive and well. When music teachers have taken advantage of the Music in Our Schools Month through special performances and programs, they have reported positive results in terms of the public's response.

Parents look to music teachers for guidance when their child is contemplating a career in music. School guidance counselors may also be involved in such matters, but their knowledge about music is usually limited. To assist students who are considering music teaching and other music careers, the MENC has prepared materials on careers in music.

Fund Raising and Parent Groups

Each year it seems that the amount of money raised outside the school budget for music groups grows a bit larger. One survey revealed that two out of every three dollars spent for high school bands comes from nonbudget sources (*The Instrumentalist,* 1989, pp. 15–17). Even at the elementary and middle school levels the figure is nearly one out of every three dollars, and there is little justification for private funding in such schools. Casual observation of the many candy sales and car washes throughout America confirms the data in the survey.

There is a positive side to this situation. In some schools, funds are woefully inadequate for the purchase of necessary equipment and materials, which is a deplorable situation where it exists. Furthermore, in a number of schools the funds raised have meant the difference between an anemic and a thriving band or choral group.

There is, however, a large negative side to the fund-raising situation in music education. The drawbacks include:

1. Fund-raising efforts often take class or rehearsal time.

2. Not only do fund-raising efforts take teaching time, they require energy as well. Many music teachers devote more effort to money-making activities than they should—and they know it. Because they became teachers to teach, not raise money, most music educators gain little professional satisfaction from such efforts. Feelings of "burnout" are thereby encouraged.

3. Someone needs to raise the funds. The usual answer, one found in three out of every four high schools, is the booster group, which is mostly composed of parents of the students in the particular musical organization (*The Instrumentalist,* 1989, pp. 15–17). While such groups can do much for music education, they generally confine their efforts to only the band or choral group that includes their children. The rest of the students and their music education are, for the most part, ignored.

4. Not only do people ignore the rest of the music program, they also often make the mistake of thinking that the music groups with booster organizations are the entire music program. The large amount of fund raising that is going on is giving music education some real public relations problems. It is diverting attention away from the education students receive in music to activities similar to those found in other youth groups, both within and outside the schools.

5. The situation has encouraged the formation of businesses to help in raising funds. These businesses provide plans and products to sell, which in one sense helps. But they also tend to promote more and better money-making activities; they aggravate the situation.

6. An important part of the fund-raising problem is the use of the funds raised. Years ago, the funds were well spent on instruments and uniforms. Today, those funds go for nonscholastic trips of doubtful educational value. Some teachers claim (and they are probably right) that a trip serves to recruit students and build group morale. These are certainly desirable results, but are they worth the price in terms of money, effort, and public image? And can't group morale be built and student recruitment accomplishd in other ways? One would think so.

7. A major drawback to fund raising is that many school administrators and school board members are very willing to let music support itself financially. The funds saved from the music program can then be used for other worthwhile areas of the curriculum. The effect of all this is that many music teachers have unwittingly almost taken their programs out of the school budget!

8. Even more serious is the "message" that is projected by allowing music ed-

ucation to be largely supported by fund raising: Music is not really a curricular subject; it isn't in the mainstream of the curriculum. Such a result is logical, even if it isn't desirable. When music teachers act like they are conducting an extracurricular activity, their subject is soon treated accordingly. In some communities it is difficult to avoid giving the impression that the school music program is a kind of publicly supported entertainment service.

Improvement in the funding situation will require much thoughtful effort. It means working in four areas: (1) Get the booster organizations to support the *total* school music program. (2) Make sure that trips are truly educational and not excessively expensive. (3) If fund raising must be done to have a vital music program, then it should have reasonable limits in terms of the time and effort required. (4) Secure adequate funding for music in the school budget. This requires persistent effort to educate school administrators, board members, and others about values and purposes of music education.

The stakes are high in the struggle for adequate funds. In a real sense, it is for the "soul" of music education. Is music education primarily for the education of the students or for the entertainment of the community? Should it have educational substance or is it mainly glitz and tinsel? The way music education programs are funded provides an important answer to that question.

School Administrators

Clearly the matter of promoting the music curriculum with school boards and administrators is of great importance. A special section is devoted to this topic in Chapter 3.

CONTINUED GROWTH AND SELF-EVALUATION

Continued professional development of music teachers after graduation from college is necessary for several reasons. If you graduate from college at the age of twenty-two, you have forty-three years remaining before you reach the age of sixty-five, which is the most common mandatory retirement age for school teachers. Think of it, forty-three years! This is a very long time just to think about, but it is an even longer time to remain fresh, vital, and interesting. Without continued growth, teachers run the risk of repeating one year's experience forty-three times rather than improving with each year of experience. No one should want to be "in a rut" for an entire career.

What can teachers do to continue growing professionally? The most obvious means, and one required in most states before permanent certification can be attained, is to continue study at the graduate level during summers or evenings.

MENC Professional Certification

A more meaningful form of certification is the Professional Certification program instituted by MENC in 1990. This program is designed for teachers with eight or more years of experience who have demonstrated continuing growth as music educators and success in teaching. Applicants for Professional Certification are asked to document their professional activities and provide letters of recommendation from administrators and other music teachers. In addition, those applying for the second level of the program must supply a videotape of their teaching prepared according to a carefully spelled out set of directions. The certification is renewable every five years.

The Professional Certification program is an important means of identifying experienced teachers who demonstrate success in teaching music. Teachers so recognized are publicly singled out as being significantly above average, which should help them in terms of employment and self-esteem. The profession of music education will benefit from the encouragement the program provides teachers for continued improvement and the focus it places on the act of teaching, in contrast to the attention given contest results for teachers of performing groups at the secondary school level.

Other means of professional growth include the reading of journals and their reports of research. Teachers should be aware of the results of studies of music teaching and of practices in music education. Research results are reported at MENC meetings and in its publications. Music teachers should not be satisfied with answering the question "Does this teaching procedure work?" In addition, they should ask, "Would another procedure work better?" Being satisfied with something just because it happens to work is like being content to spend a lifetime hopping about on one leg. Undoubtedly hopping works, but there is a more efficient way to get around; it's called walking.

Self-Improvement

Even after taking advantage of every opportunity and graduating from a good music education program, beginning teachers should realize that they must still teach themselves to teach well. No course or series of courses, no professor, no book, no college can impart enough information about the particular school, its students, and its unique nature to train teachers fully for the job they will undertake. Teachers finally must succeed or fail on their own. They must look objectively at themselves and improve on their own work.

Fortunately, there are some guidelines for going about the process of evaluating your own teaching. They are presented in Chapter 17 on evaluation. That chapter is not nearly as concerned with grading pupils as it is with improving instruction. Basically the idea is to decide when planning the lesson or class what it is that the students should be able to do as a result of the instruction. They may be able to answer certain questions, or play certain notes, or tell when a modulation has taken place, or demonstrate similar actions related to what they were taught. Such observable actions aid teachers by letting them know which portions of a lesson seem to have been learned by most of the students and which were not learned so well. Then knowing that, a teacher can do a better job of planning for the next class.

Although self-evaluation has the obvious disadvantage of being somewhat subjective, it is the only practical means open to most music teachers. For one thing, self-evaluation is a continuous process. It is not something that occurs once or twice a semester; it should go on in one form or another during every class. For another thing, it is done with full knowledge of what one is trying to teach and of the total school situation.

Evaluations by outsiders are of limited usefulness. School administrators seldom know much about music. Visits by school principals to classrooms often bring forth comments about things other than the learning of music—"The students seemed to enjoy the class" and similar statements. Even adjudicators at contests, who are competent in music, are listening to the performance of a few prepared works with no knowledge of the school situation. School music supervisors can offer the best critiques for teachers. However, their time available for such work is limited, and many school districts do not have music supervisors.

Teacher Rating Forms

The use of forms for evaluating teachers is a standard at the college level for professors seeking promotion or tenure, but such forms are not found often in the schools. Even at the college level, rating forms are of limited value. The ratings given are only partly the result of the instructor's actions. For example, instructors of required classes for freshmen and sophomores seldom rate as high as do instructors of junior- and senior-level courses in the students' major area. Rating forms seem to work best with mature students; they are of little worth in elementary and middle schools. The other problem with teacher rating forms is that the responses must be only general reactions about the teacher. A general statement that one is or is not a good teacher is not very helpful in improving instruction. The use of specific objectives and the evaluation of teaching in terms of the students' learning of those objectives is a more valid and useful way of analyzing instruction than is a teacher rating form.

Playback of Classes

Another specific means of self-evaluation is the use of a videotape or tape recorder. Some teachers make a recording of their classes or rehearsals. Before the next class with the same group, they listen to the tape and evaluate what they hear. The recordings serve two purposes: They allow a more leisurely and thoughtful study of what the class has done, and they enable teachers to evaluate their own efforts in teaching the class or rehearsal. In analyzing a tape for self-evaluation purposes, teachers can ask themselves these questions:

1. Were there unnecessary delays and wasted time?
2. Were the points on which I corrected the group those that needed attention?
3. Did my suggestions to the group result in improvements?
4. Were my statements clear and decisive?
5. Did I repeat certain words and phrases—such as "OK?" "You know," "Right"— so frequently that they became annoying?
6. Was the pace of the class about right?
7. Were there relaxing breaks in the rehearsal or class routine—a little humor or something done just for the pleasure of it?
8. Specifically, what was accomplished in the class?
9. Did I encourage the students to discover and learn some points for themselves, or did I direct every action?

Supplementary Employment

Some teachers undermine their effectiveness by assuming workloads that would frighten Superman or Wonder Woman. Many teachers are hard-pressed financially, especially those who are supporting a family, and outside work such as teaching private lessons or directing a church choir may be necessary. The problem is that teaching is already a full-time job, and beginning teachers find that the duties connected with it consume all of their time and energy. They must consider the ethical and practical considerations of how much outside work they can do.

One important music educator of the first half of this century used to schedule one night a week that he spent at home reading, practicing, or in other ways improving himself professionally. His example should be copied by all music teachers.

No one has ever achieved the status of "perfect teacher." Teachers are human. However, each teacher's unique strengths and weaknesses give him or her a distinctive way of teaching. Such individuality is desirable and can be developed along with the requisites of sensitive musicianship and personal maturity. Music teachers need to relate their educational efforts to the efforts of other professionals in music and in education, and to inform the community about what happens in school music classes. Finally, teachers must look objectively at their work throughout their careers if they are to achieve their potential as teachers of music.

Questions   1. Think of two good school music teachers you have had and of two that you felt were not as good. What in their personalities and teaching methods made them successful or unsuccessful?

2. Being as objective as you can be, do some self-examination of your own personality and how it relates to teaching music. What are your strong points? What needs improvement?

3. Think of a community that you know well. If there are professional musicians in it, what efforts are made to promote coordinated efforts between them and the school music teachers? What is the relationship between private music teachers and the school music teachers? Between music teachers and music merchants?

4. Suppose that you are responsible for planning a set of slides to explain the music program to parent groups. How many pictures would you use, and what would they depict? What would you say to accompany the pictures?

5. During your first year in a new job, you take your musical instrument to a local music store for repair. As you pick it up, the merchant says, "Forget the bill. It's on the house." Should you accept this favor? Why or why not?

Projects 1. Make a video or audio recording of yourself teaching a segment of a music methods class or a class in the schools. If this cannot be arranged, record yourself teaching a lesson to a fellow student on your major instrument or in singing. Evaluate the effectiveness of what you said, the amount of talking you did, the pertinence of your comments about the student's work, and the general pace of your teaching.

2. Visit two identical classes (high school bands, fifth grade general music, and so on) in two different schools. Evaluate the comparative musical maturity of the students, their musical ability, equipment, schedule, and other factors. Make a list of the areas in which the two classes differ.

Suggested Readings

Beyond the Classroom: Informing Others. Reston, Va.: Music Educators National Conference, 1987.

Hoffer, Charles R. "Informing Others about Music Education." *Music Educators Journal,* 74, no. 8 (April 1988), p. 30.

Music Teacher Education: Partnership and Process. Reston, Va.: Music Educators National Conference, 1987.

References

Ausubel, David. *Educational Psychology.* New York: Holt, Rinehart & Winston, 1968.

Brenton, Myron. *What's Happened to Teacher?* New York: Avon Books, 1970.

Music Educators National Conference. *Teacher Education in Music: Final Report.* Reston, Va.: MENC, 1972.

Stephens, J. M. "Traits of Successful Teachers: Men or Angels?" *Theory into Practice,* II, no. 2 (April 1963).

The Instrumentalist, Vol. 44, no. 1 (August 1989).

PART 1

Why Teach Music?

The first major question to answer before preparing to teach is "Why should students learn music?" The answer to this question is the foundation on which successful teaching rests. No one should assume the role of teacher without a carefully considered and logical answer to this question. Because it is fundamental, the question "Why?" is the first aspect of music teaching discussed in some depth in this book.

CHAPTER 3

The Reasons for Music in the Schools

Many music teachers don't want to be bothered with fundamental questions about why music should be a part of the school curriculum. Why not just go ahead and do a good job of teaching and leave the philosophical questions to college professors? There are at least four reasons why every teacher needs to think through such matters for himself or herself.

REASONS FOR CONSIDERING BASIC GOALS

First of all, teachers cannot avoid taking positions on the question of "Why is music being taught in the schools?" through things they do and decisions they make when teaching.

> *John Marsh believes that the main purpose of music in the schools is to entertain audiences. He selects music for its audience appeal and then drills the performers on it. His students gain very little understanding of how the music is organized or of the meaning of the texts of the songs. Only the best students are selected for the performing groups; the average students are ignored.*

By his actions John Marsh has provided a clear statement of his beliefs about music in the schools. The correctness of his opinions is not the issue here. The point is that through what he does he reveals a philosophy—a set of beliefs—about music education.

Second, there is a need to "sell" music in the schools. Most of the time the problem is not one of coping with obvious and deliberate doubts about the value of music instruction. Very few people are opposed to having music in the schools. Rather, teachers have to do some convincing so that more staff can be added when needed, schedule conflicts can be worked out, and sufficient money can be budgeted for supplies and equipment.

> *Sandra Petrocelli, teacher of general music at South Middle School, has discovered that the number of sections of seventh grade general music will be reduced and each class will be 50 percent larger than it was last year. Sandra realizes that she needs to convince the school administration of the importance of realistic class sizes for general music classes and that the employment of another teacher for a couple of periods each day is a good use of school funds.*

If Sandra Petrocelli is to make a case for reasonable-sized classes, she must first know what should be accomplished in the classes and then make clear the probable effect of class size on student learning. In most school situations, by the way, it must be the music teachers who need to educate the school administrators on the nature and needs of the music program, a need that was pointed out in the previous chapter. Many districts do not have music supervisors, which is unfortunate, so the responsibility cannot be left to someone else. Even in districts with supervisors, often the intraschool solutions to problems such as scheduling and room assignments are left up to the teachers who teach in the building. More is said about how to educate administrators and the public later in this chapter.

Third, for their own sake teachers need to be clear on what they are trying to accomplish.

> *Marian Knowles is tired. It's been a hard day; nothing has seemed to go right. The classes have been talkative, and their singing dull and often flat. As an added disappointment, she has just realized that she has used up most of the money in the budget for new music, with none of the music for the spring concert purchased yet.*
>
> *As she drops into a chair in the teachers' lounge after school, a veteran teacher notices her dejected air and says, "Don't worry so much, Marian. Why work so hard? After all, who wants to be the best teacher in the graveyard?" Marian wonders, "Is it really worth all the work and worry?"*

Marian Knowles had better be able to answer the question about why teaching music is worth it, if for no other reason than to keep her sense of perspective. If she can, she will be a happier and more effective teacher.

Fourth, teachers need to be clear about their goals in order to be consistent.

> *Last fall was Neil Gorton's first year as band director at St. Marks. He was anxious to have a prize-winning marching band, so he enrolled anyone who would carry an instrument or flag. He worked hard on the corps style of marching, with its careful attention to the one show to be used for many performances. The results were only mixed. Some of the better musicians became unhappy with the limited type of music and quit, but a few other students were motivated to join the band. Other, more experienced bands won the contests that St. Marks entered, but at least Neil could talk about winning "next year."*

At the end of the marching season, he realized that he didn't need many of the students who were enrolled. In order to have a good concert band, he tried to convince the less able players to drop out for a semester (to return next fall, of course). Also, he made rigorous demands for extra rehearsals and caustic remarks in the hope that the less able students would quit. The band members became indifferent to the band and to Neil, and a couple of good players dropped out.

In March, prodded by his conscience and some talks with the principal, Neil changed to a more pleasant approach and showed more interest in his students as persons. But the time was late. The students did not quickly forget the way things had been over the past few months. His more relaxed attitude initially produced more talking and fooling around. After a month the behavior improved, and the band made an effort to prepare for the spring concert. As the year closes, Neil wonders what he will do next fall when he again wants to enter marching contests. He feels torn between a desire to create a public image as a "winner" and an interest in teaching music to his students.

Neil Gorton's wobbling sense of direction is making him miserable, and it is keeping him from doing anything well. He must make a choice of goals and then stick consistently to them, so that the actions he takes in October will not undo what he wants to accomplish in February.

At first glance, thinking about the basic goals of music in the schools may seem impractical, but in a real sense such efforts may be the most practical thing teachers can do. Wandering about with no sense of direction is wasteful, impractical, and frustrating.

THE VALUE OF MUSIC AND THE FINE ARTS

You may have noticed that the heading for this section includes music and the fine arts. At the basic, general level the same points can be made for each of the fine arts. The differences among them lie in the medium of expression. Music is organized sound, painting is organized shapes and colors on a two-dimensional surface, and dance involves both form and movement in a span of time. While the arts are not identical, especially in terms of the technical factors present in each, they have the same basic reasons for existence and for being included in the school curriculum.

It is not difficult to establish the point that music and fine arts are important in human life. It can be done in several ways. One way is to assemble data on the amount of money people spend for instruments, recordings, and sound-reproducing equipment. Also, the number of people attending concerts in the United States each year is truly impressive; it is larger than the number who attend sports events such as major league baseball and college football. Also, millions of Americans play musical instruments and sing in church choirs.

Another way is to point out the fact that music is present in every area of the world, even among the remote aborigines in Australia. It has been present in every historical era since the dawn of civilization. The walls of Egyptian buildings picture people playing instruments and singing, and the Bible tells how David soothed King Saul with his music. Clearly, there must be something important about an activity when it is so pervasive today and in the past. Music is not just another pastime like roller skating or macrame.

More than logic and objective data are available to music educators in seeking support for music in the schools. Most people, when they hear a group of children sing or young people play their instruments, have a good feeling about it. Intuitively they sense—correctly—that making music is a constructive, worthwhile thing for children and teenagers to do. Usually they can't say exactly why they feel this way, but that is not necessary. If this feeling that music is good for school students is true of most people, it is especially true of persons involved with education and, of course, parents. For years music educators have observed the enthusiasm of parents for the music events in which their children are involved, even if the music is not particularly well performed.

The objective evidence about the important place of music in life can be combined with good feelings people have for music and school students in order to present a stronger case for music. This approach might be called, for lack of a better name, the "let's not cheat the kids" approach. For many years the most successful fund raiser for the local arts fund in one community was a businessman who called on other businessmen and said something like this: "Look, you and I don't know much about the arts, but do you want the young people of this community to grow up as ignorant about art and music as we are?" His choice of words is clearly not recommended for music educators, but he was correct in his essential approach, and he was very effective.

It is on the demonstrable and intuited significance of music in people's lives that music educators should build their case when communicating with school administrators and the public about why music should be included in the schools, a topic discussed more fully on page 40. Although objective, logical evidence does not (unfortunately) always carry the day in education and other areas of life, having the facts on your side is a much more useful and stronger position than not having them.

What About Music Is Valued?

The question of why music and the fine arts are important to people is usually not a particularly interesting one to nonmusicians. They are not won over by assertions like "music is a tonal analogue of emotive life" (Langer, 1953, p. 27). In fact, the matter is not of much interest to many music teachers, but it should be, because it has quite a bit to say about what music teachers should teach and how they should teach it.

There are a number of different theories about why the arts are valuable to people, but they are more nearly intellectual guesses than they are established facts. One view, perhaps best represented by the twentieth-century American writers on philosophy and aesthetics John Dewey and Susanne Langer, holds that in the arts humans reexperience in a roundabout way feelings associated with life, and through them they gain insight into subjective reality. Others, such as the nineteenth-century philosopher Arthur Schopenhauer, maintain that music is "transfigured Nature" transcending the world and revealing the realm of the ultimate Will (God) (Schopenhauer, 1896, p. 333). And there are other views. As profound as these theories are, it seems probable that no single explanation can account for the workings of the human mind, especially when doing something as complex as listening to music. It is important to remember, however, that the lack of agreement among aestheticians and philosophers about why the arts are valuable does not alter the fact that they make a fundamental and important contribution to the quality of human life; on that point there is wide agreement.

Essentially the arts represent an important difference between existing and living. Animals exist in the sense that they manage to survive; that's their objective in existing. Humans live; they attempt to make life interesting, rewarding, and satisfying. Humans are not content merely to get by, to survive. Music, painting, and dance all enrich life and bring to it their special meanings and provide an avenue of expression. People admire the shifting surf, the color of a sky at sunset, and the beauty of a flower. They also create objects that they can contemplate and with which they can enrich their lives. For example, although a large cardboard box could serve as a nightstand by your bed and it would cost nothing, you would rather have a wooden table or stand with a little bit of grace and beauty. This compulsion of humans to reach beyond their immediate, practical needs is not just a nice luxury; it is an essential quality of being human.

Aesthetic Experiences

The arts involve an aspect of human experience called *aesthetic,* a word that is often heard and seen in writings on music education. For about two decades now music educators have been exhorted to emphasize the aesthetic aspects of music, to make youngsters aesthetically sensitive, and to involve themselves in aesthetic education. Fine; but what does the word *aesthetic* mean? What makes an aesthetic experience different from ordinary experiences like eating a hamburger or going to class?

One basic difference between aesthetic and ordinary experiences is the nonpractical nature of aesthetic experiences. They are valued for the insight, satisfaction, and enjoyment they provide, not for any practical benefits. Looking at a bowl of fruit (a scene frequently painted by artists) is aesthetic when you contemplate the color and shape of the pieces of fruit; it is nonaesthetic when you are thinking about how the fruit reminds you that you are hungry. An aesthetic experience is an end in itself; it is done only for the value of doing it.

A second characteristic of an aesthetic experience is that both intellect and emotion are involved. When you look at a painting aesthetically, you are consciously aware of considering thoughtfully its shapes, lines, and colors. That is the intellectual part. At the same time, you are reacting to what you see; you have feelings about the painting, even if it is abstract art. Seldom are these reactions so strong that you start laughing or crying, but you react to some degree; your feelings are involved.

Because intellectual contemplation is required, recreational activities like playing tennis and purely physical sensations such as standing under a cold shower are not considered aesthetic. Neither are purely intellectual efforts such as working multiplication problems, although even in that case a reaction is often involved, as when you see $3 \times 9 = 28$.

A third characteristic of aesthetic experiences is the fact that they are experiences. You cannot tell someone else about a painting or a musical work and expect that person to derive the same amount of enjoyment from the work as you did. In fact, telling about a piece of music or a drama seems to ruin it. For this reason aesthetic experiences have no answers, as do problems in a math class. Listening to the last minute of Beethoven's Fifth Symphony is not the "answer" to that symphony. Anyone who tries doing that will be cheating himself or herself out of the aesthetic enjoyment that the symphony provides.

A fourth characteristic of aesthetic experiences is a focusing of attention on the object being contemplated. This centering of attention is on the object as an object and not on a task to be accomplished, such as hitting the ball out of the infield in a baseball game. When you listen to a song aesthetically, you concentrate on its musical qualities and how they enhance the text, not just on the message of the words or the singer's appearance.

Where does the notion of beauty enter into the discussion of aesthetic experiences? In one sense it doesn't enter in very much. Not all aesthetic experiences need be beautiful in the usual sense of the word. Hundreds of works of art ranging from Stravinsky's *The Rite of Spring* to the Ashcan school of painting of Edward Hopper and George Bellows have demonstrated that the aesthetic and the beautiful are two different considerations.

Pointing out what an aesthetic experience is *not* may help to clarify further what it *is*. The opposite of *aesthetic* is not *ugly* or *unpleasant* but rather might be thought of as *anesthetic*—no feeling, no life, nothing. Perhaps the clearest example of "anesthetic" behavior that comes to mind happened one day while I was observing a rather bad junior high school band rehearsal. A sousaphone player was talking to one of the drummers when the director started up the band without waiting for players who were not paying attention. After a few moments the young sousaphone player realized that he should be playing along with the others. Although he didn't know where or why, he swung the mouthpiece to his mouth and started blatting away without any sense of what was happening musically.

Teaching for Aesthetic Awareness

The example of the boy playing the sousaphone without any idea of what he was doing points out an important obligation of all music teachers: Teach for an awareness of the aesthetic properties in the music. Precisely what does that mean?

Should the sousaphone player have known facts about the composer of the piece and its stylistic characteristics? That would have been nice, but such information is not aesthetic. Should he have been taught about the technical features of the music? Nothing wrong at all in learning analytical skills, but they are not aesthetic either. Should he have known how to play the correct notes at the right time? That would have been valuable, too, but it isn't aesthetic. Rather, the properties of the music that can cause aesthetic experiences include such aspects as the rise and fall of the melodic lines, the greater and lesser tensions in the chord progressions, the timbres caused by the various instrumental combinations, the repeating or developing of melodic and rhythmic ideas, and the changing dynamic levels. Those and similar points are the aesthetic features of music that students need to be taught to notice.

Perceiving music aesthetically is a complex human action that has two aspects. One aspect consists of cognitive processes such as identifying, comparing, analyzing, and classifying. In general, these processes are objective, and they can be practiced, tested, and taught. The other aspect consists of feelings, which are, of course, subjective. Feelings and reactions can only be hinted at in words, and they cannot be analyzed, tested, or taught in any direct way. Therefore, teachers must devote their efforts to what is teachable and encourage and hope for aesthetic reactions. Teachers can only set up situations in which reactions can happen, much as one might set up the pins in a bowling alley in the hope that the bowler will knock them down.

To teach the more objective aspects of aesthetic experience, teachers can draw the students' attention to the properties in the music either through asking questions or sometimes telling about them. The teacher of the band in which the sousaphone player was a member might have asked him such questions as these: "How should the smooth melodic line affect the way you play your accompanying bass part?" (The student would need to think about the relation between his part and the melody.) "When the piece changes from major to minor at letter G, how does that change seem to affect the quality of the music?" (The student would have to listen and think about the quality of the music.) "Do you have a fragment of the melodic line in your part a couple of measures after letter E?" (The student would need to compare his part with the melodic line.) "Where should you take a breath in the passage after letter C?" (The student would be encouraged to think about phrasing and its effect on the music.) "In the first four measures of the melody at letter D, which is the most important note?" (The student would need to consider the relationship among the notes of the melody and which one seems most significant to it.) Hundreds of such questions can be raised about the qualities of any work of music.

The teaching for an awareness of the aesthetic qualities in a piece of music can take place concurrently with learning to play or sing the music, as well as with the learning of some information about the piece. It is not necessary to neglect one aspect of music to learn another. Traditionally music teachers have taught performing skills and a little bit of information about the music, but not nearly often enough have they drawn attention to the qualities of the music. This is too bad, because aesthetic experiences are the "payoff" for being involved in the arts; they are what the arts are all about. Therefore, music teachers should make the teaching for aesthetic awareness as important a goal as the learning of skills and information.

On the basis of educational priorities, John Marsh's main goal of entertaining audiences (p. 29) can be faulted. He is giving his students a limited education in music, one confined to performing a certain type of music in an attractive way. Any awareness that his students gain of the aesthetic qualities of the music they sing will be on their own initiative and ability. Some additional weaknesses in John Marsh's goals will be discussed in Chapter 4 on the music curriculum.

From the points that have been presented in these pages, it is evident that the reason why music and the other fine arts are important does have something. to say about what teachers should do when they stand in front of music classes. The reasons why music is valuable to human beings may not be fully appreciated by nonmusicians, but they are an important guide to music teachers.

NONMUSICAL REASONS FOR MUSIC

Music has a long tradition of being included in schools for reasons such as citizenship, character development, team spirit, and health benefits. Plato in his *Republic* cites the need for music in the education of every citizen. His reasons were based on the ancient Greek idea of *ethos*—the belief that each mode promoted certain qualities of character in a person. Music was also much more broadly conceived in his day and included aspects of poetry and physical education. Since music was closely allied with mathematics during the Middle Ages, music was taught in the medieval universities partly because scholars were fascinated with the acoustical ratios of musical sounds. They wondered if the ratios might reveal secrets about the universe. During other periods of history, music was included in the curriculum primarily because a knowledge of music was a mark of an educated person. In 1837, when Lowell Mason was given permission to begin music in the Boston schools, the subject was justified because it contributed to reading and speech and provided "a recreation, yet not a dissipation of the mind— a respite, yet not a relaxation—its office would thus be to restore the jaded energies, and send back the scholars with invigorated powers to other more laborious duties" (Birge, 1966, p. 43).

The practical benefits of music were still being stressed through the era of the Seven Cardinal Principles of Education and the progressive education movement during the first half of the twentieth century. As late as 1941 such eminent music educators as Peter Dykema and Karl Gehrkens were emphasizing nonmusical outcomes with their philosophy that "the teacher teaches children through the medium of music" (1941, pp. 380–81). The clear implication was that music is included in the schools to achieve some goal greater than itself.

Not until the 1950s did music educators begin publicly to question the validity of statements about music's usefulness in promoting nonmusical goals. There were three reasons for their doubts. One was the lack of research demonstrating that music classes influence students to become better citizens or healthier individuals. Granted, music does not encourage poor citizenship, immoral behavior, or failing health. However, claims that "it doesn't hurt people" are not very convincing when it comes to getting music in the school curriculum.

A second factor that weakened the traditional utilitarian claims for music was the realization that other curricular and extracurricular activities can do the job better. Courses in history and government are more pertinent to citizenship than are music courses, and physical education is more beneficial than music for health and physical fitness. If school administrators wish to strengthen these areas, they are not likely to select the music program as the means of achieving such ends.

A third reason for the change was the awareness that music and the fine arts are significant and valuable in their own right. Just as biology and history teachers do not claim to teach something "through the medium of biology or history," music educators realize that their subject is valid too. Unsupported claims for nonmusical outcomes only make them appear weak, illogical, and uncertain about the value of their subject. Today most music educators agree that music is an area of study that is equal in worth to other subjects of the curriculum.

The interest in the nonmusical values of music has never completely been abandoned, however, and renewed interest in them has been seen in recent years with the faddish interest in which hemisphere of the brain processes musical sounds. Happily, music can be two things at the same time. It can be an art filled with aesthetic qualities, and it can serve as a means of nonmusical ends such as leisure-time diversion, emotional release, and social activity. In any case these nonmusical values merit further discussion.

Transfer to Other Subjects

If you study one subject, and what you learn in that subject contributes to your understanding of a second subject, transfer of learning has taken place. Does instruction in music transfer to other areas of the curriculum? If so, which areas, and how much? Unfortunately, the research on the topic of transfer is limited, and some of what has been done is suspect in quality. Almost all the studies of transfer have been done in elementary schools; little can be said about transfer at the secondary school level. It appears that a program infused with study and activity in the arts contributes to a better attitude toward school. A better attitude, in turn, results in more learning and less absenteeism on the part of the students (Boyle and Lathrop, 1973, p. 42). The area holding the greatest prospects for transfer from music appears to be language arts and reading. Music also helps with certain types of speech problems, especially stuttering (Graham, 1975, p. 35).

After a thorough review of the available research on transfer, Karen I. Wolff concludes:

> *The weight of evidence gleaned from the research leads one to believe that there may be measurable effects of music education on the development of cognitive skills and understanding. This seems to be true for both general transfer, i.e., "learning how to learn," and specific transfer. Specific transfer is particularly apparent in its effect on performance in the language arts (Wolff, 1978, p. 19).*

Mental Health

The old belief was that music has the power to "soothe the savage breast." That may be an overstatement, but music therapy has demonstrated that music can affect human behavior and aid mental health. It may be that music allows for the venting of emotions in a socially acceptable way. Young people have for years said that music helps them when they are "feeling low" and contributes to a sense of well-being.

Once upon a time music was promoted with slogans such as "A boy who blows a horn will never blow a safe." Although guiding adolescent behavior is far more complex than that statement indicates, it does suggest that there are some psychological benefits for students who study music.

Avocational Value

While the average life expectancy has been increasing, the average workweek has been decreasing. These facts mean that more time for leisure is available. Music is an important avocational activity in many countries, including the United States. The American Symphony Orchestra League's listing of community orchestras contains over 1400 entries, and there are thousands of church choirs and other amateur choral groups. An even greater numer of people listen to music. For these reasons the training for intelligent listening is an important challenge for music educators.

Two significant points should be kept in mind about the nonmusical outcomes of music instruction:

1. *There are valid and supportable reasons for including music in the elementary school curriculum, apart from any nonmusical benefits.* The nonmusical benefits can be thought of as "bonuses" for instruction that the schools should be offering anyway. The place of music in the schools does not depend on them, but its position may be stronger because of them.

2. *There is little a teacher can do directly to make these transfer, psychological, and avocational benefits happen.* The self-image of students, their social and psychological needs, and their choice of what to do with their leisure time are all influenced by circumstances over which teachers have little control. Teachers cannot use a teaching procedure that ensures any nonmusical benefits,

although good teaching can help create a situation in which they are more likely to happen.

STUDENTS OR THE SUBJECT?

The fact that students can learn the subject of music while gaining personal and social benefits should lay to rest a longstanding but false dilemma: Should teachers teach the subject *or* the students? They should teach both; it is not an either-or proposition. Students are not helped if they are left ignorant about what they are supposed to learn, no matter what their personal problems may be. On the other hand, teachers cannot ignore the fact that they teach human beings. They need to be flexible and sensitive to the students' needs so that they can do the best possible job of teaching.

TEACHERS AND EDUCATIONAL GOALS

Teachers have both opportunities and limitations in determining the goals in public education. They must accept the broad goals endorsed by the society and its educational system. Teachers who act contrary to these goals reduce the total effectiveness of the schools, to say nothing of possibly losing their jobs. For instance, teachers cannot ignore the many for the benefit of the few or teach the violent overthrow of the government without detracting from the results the schools seek to achieve. These broad mandates apply to music teachers just as much as they do to other teachers. Music is a specialized area of study, but so are other school subjects. Specialization is not a grounds for exemption in this matter.

The educational mandates guiding teachers are broad and general. They are something like the directions a passenger gives a taxi driver. The rider gives the destination, but decisions about the best way to get there are the driver's, because he or she is the "expert" in getting around that city. There are some general restrictions, such as not hitting other cars and not driving on the sidewalk, that the passenger doesn't need to state specifically. Taxi drivers, like teachers, make the detailed decisions about the process of reaching the destination and implement them as intelligently and efficiently as possible.

Who finally decides what the specific objectives are for music classes—administrators, boards of education, governmental agencies, or teachers? The forces that affect educational goals and objectives are diverse and often conflicting. States authorize local school boards to oversee education, and school boards then employ administrators to guide the daily efforts of education. But the matter does not stop there. Teachers can also influence decisions within school systems. Because administrators rarely know as much about each subject matter area as the teachers who are specialized in an area, they must depend on the music faculty members for guidance and leadership concerning the music program. Then after considering the other needs in the school system, they will try to render a fair and equitable decision about how fully the recommendations of the music teachers can be implemented. Unless administrators are informed by the music faculty members about what is needed, they will assume that the present situation is satisfactory and will tend to continue it. Thus the need for music teachers to inform school administrators.

The detailed, within-class decisions are the responsibility of each teacher. There is no way for administrators to oversee such matters. There simply isn't time for them to look over the shoulder of every teacher, and (except for music supervisors) they lack the knowledge of music to make specialized decisions. Very few school administrators know the correct embouchure for the French horn or what the Kodály-Curwen hand signs are!

Music Teachers and School Administrators

Music teachers tend to place much importance on the quality and amount of support provided music programs by school administrators. (Many school administrators feel that the powers attributed to them by teachers are exaggerated, however.) It is true that school administrators can have a significant effect on the success of a music program. Sometimes teachers have devoted much attention to their teaching but forgotten to work with the school administration so that conditions exist in which music can be taught effectively.

If, as hoped, music teachers do communicate with school administrators about the music program, what do they say that is (1) understandable and meaningful to nonmusicians and (2) true? Part of the answer to the first question was given earlier in this chapter on pages 31–32. Music teachers must build a solid case for music on (1) its significant place in American society and (2) the administrators' positive intuitive feelings about music and children. Important as these points are, they are only the first step.

The second essential point is that music needs to be taught in school in a systematic way by trained personnel. As in the case of mathematics and language skills, when music moves beyond the rudimentary level of singing a few simple songs, it exceeds the teaching capabilities of most families. There is too much to learn that is too complex for the family to teach. That is one reason virtually all societies have found it necessary to establish a system of schools. Although there would be some music in America without music instruction in the schools, the amount and type of music would be only a shadow of the subject as we know it. Young people would be truly limited in their knowledge and understanding of music, the point on which the successful fund raiser mentioned on page 32 built his appeal. In no way can radio disc jockeys and record players adequately replace music teachers.

People who know music only superficially usually regard it as a recreational activity. And it is true that music is often merely a pastime. However, there is a big difference between singing a song around a campfire for fun and singing a song to gain a greater understanding of its musical properties. One is recreation, while the other is education. For these reasons music teachers must make the point that music is a subject requiring consideration and esteem equal to what is given other school subjects. If this point is made, music teachers are of course obligated to teach children and young people music and not just consider music classes as an entertaining pastime.

Many times music has been sold to the public and school administrations for its public relations value. This is where the "true" criterion mentioned earlier for communicating with administrators comes in. Sometimes an administrator has been urged to buy a certain instrument because the band needs it to look good on the football field or to win a higher rating at contest time, and not because the instrument will help students learn more adequately how the music should sound. The "we don't want to be shown up" argument is not a valid one; administrators should not be urged to do the right thing for the wrong reasons.

Often school administrators have been given the nonmusical benefits of music as the reason for including music in the schools. As was mentioned earlier in this chapter, such reasons are shaky, and many school administrators know it. They know, for example, if improvement in reading is the goal, it is better to add more time or teachers for reading than to increase the amount of attention given music, even if music instruction does contribute to reading skill.

A brief example of how one teacher dealt with the school administration can serve as a successful example of communicating with administrators.

Margaret Coppock teaches strings in several Centerton schools. For a number of years it was clear that strings were not faring well when it came to enrolling beginning instrumental students for the classes in the sixth grade. The band teachers recruited intensively through the use of their jazz bands, and the attraction of the shiny instruments and vibrant music presented tough competition for the gentler sound of violins and cellos. Margaret became convinced that Centerton should follow the practice of a number of other school districts of offering string instruction one year earlier than instruction was offered for the winds. The other full-time string teacher in the district was supportive but not interested in working on the idea, so she proceeded on her own.

Although the school administration had not asked for ideas for improving the music program, Margaret prepared a proposal in writing for the administration in which she spelled out the requested change and the reasons why it was desirable and needed. The first pages of the proposal presented a brief statement of what the string program was trying to accomplish and why strings are a necessary part of the total music curriculum. Then the suggested improvements were described, including how instruments could be secured and the amount of additional instructional time that would be needed. The response to her proposal was a polite letter from the superintendent indicating interest in the idea but expressing regrets that funds did not permit instituting the change for the coming year.

The next year Margaret sent a slightly revised version of the proposal to the administration, with about the same results. The proposal was prepared and sent a third year, again with about the same response.

There was no music supervisor in the Centerton district, and so one year the administration asked that a committee of music teachers be formed to formulate suggestions for program improvement. The idea of starting strings a year ahead of the winds was proposed by Margaret to this committee. After about a year and a half of meeting sporadically, the committee developed a list of recommendations, of which the string proposal was one. Margaret's earlier proposal was touched up and served as documentation in the committee report. After several months the administration decided to move ahead with the idea, and the following fall string instruction was offered to fifth graders for the first time.

Her efforts did not end there. During the first year she and the new string teacher believed that a massed performance of all the fifth grade string players in the district was necessary to demonstrate the success of the program. A performance was scheduled (and starting time moved ahead thirty minutes to accommodate the superintendent) for early April. Preparing for the performance was quite a bit of work, and the musical results were modest, but the large group performing some simple music reasonably well established an image of success in the audience's mind. Figures on enrollment and attrition were also presented to the administration after the first year.

No two cases are the same, of course, but certain facts about this example merit attention. First, the teacher communicated with the administrators, even when such information was not specifically requested; she didn't wait for their invitation before presenting a needed improvement in the program. Second, the teacher persisted in seeking the improvement. It is not enough to make a point once and then forget about it. Sometimes it takes several years to convince the administration that a change is needed. Third, it helps a great deal if the music faculty can make its recommendations in a unified manner. A group statement has more impact than do an individual's views, although an individual is better than no one speaking up at all. The idea became a reality after it achieved group endorsement. Fourth, it is not possible in this case to determine what influenced the administration to adopt the idea. In a sense it doesn't really matter, but such knowledge might have been useful to teachers in presenting proposals in the future. Probably there was not just one cause, because such matters are usually complex ones. Fifth, the requests, by both the teacher and the committee, were organized, well thought out, and put in writing. When these steps are followed, the proposal being made to the administration is presented in the best possible manner. Sixth, the efforts at informing the administration continued even after the new program had been instituted.

Public Relations

Music teachers should also attempt to generate more understanding of and support for the music program among members of the community. There are several means for doing so. One of the most effective is the students themselves. Their interest and favorable attitude toward their music experiences can do much to encourage support among parents and relatives. For this reason there is a relationship between effective music teaching and the support of the program among a portion of the public.

Another avenue of contact with the public is through newspaper stories, radio spots, and the like. The details of a press release will not catch the attention of every reader, but many people notice and remember that something appeared in the newspaper about the school music program. The use of photographs helps draw attention to the story. Not every item given newspapers is printed. Their space needs differ from day to day, and so one can never be sure how much of a story will be published. Newspapers like stories written from a newsy "angle," not just another concert announcement. The material should be written as a news story and provide the essential who-what-where-when information.

Some school districts prepare an attractive brochure about the music program. Such brochures should be economical in the amount of text they carry and liberal in the number of attractive photographs. Sometimes a question-and-answer format is effective in such publications. For example, a question such as "Does the school rent instruments to students who wish to begin taking lessons?" offers the chance to provide readers with information about the availability of instruments.

Speaking appearances by music teachers and performances by school groups before organizations such as the PTA and Rotary are other accesses to the public.

Strong, articulate teacher guidance is vital in establishing an effective music curriculum. To provide guidance, teachers themselves must know why music should be included in the curriculum of the schools. Then they need to educate the school administration and the public about the merits of school music instruction.

Questions   1.   Is John Marsh's devotion to entertainment (p. 29) as the main goal of his performing groups defensible in terms of music education? Why or why not?

2.   Suppose that you are Sandra Petrocelli (p. 30). What points would you make to the school administration for reasonable class sizes?

3.   This chapter stressed that the main reason for teaching music in the schools is to give students an understanding of its aesthetic qualities. Is this goal also the primary function in art education? English? History? Extracurricular activities such as scouts and interscholastic athletics? If the reasons are not the same, in what ways are they different?

4.   Assume that you are asked to give a fifteen-minute talk to a local service club on the school music program. How would you explain in simple, practical terms the goals of aesthetic sensitivity? Or would you just ignore the subject and talk about the more obvious features of the program?

5.   How consistent with the objectives of education in America are the following statements by music teachers?
    (a)   "You can't make a silk purse out of a sow's ear. No use straining yourself over a kid who just doesn't have talent."
    (b)   "I've got one of the best positions in the state. Three fine junior highs feeding me well-trained players, and I use the best of them."

(c) "I know that not many youngsters take choral music. But if the few I have get a good music education, then it will have been worth it."

(d) "I don't care how poor or lacking in talent they are, I'm determined to teach them as much as possible about music and what makes it tick."

Suggested Readings

Meyer, Leonard B. *Emotion and Meaning in Music.* Chicago: University of Chicago Press, 1956.

———. *Music, the Arts, and Ideas.* Chicago: University of Chicago Press, 1967.

Reimer, Bennett. *A Philosophy of Music Education.* 2nd ed. Englewood Cliffs, N.J.: Prentice-Hall, 1989.

References

Birge, Edward Bailey. *The History of Public School Music in the United States.* Reston, Va.: Music Educators National Conference, 1966.

Boyle, J. David, and Robert L. Lathrop. "The IMPACT Experience: An Evaluation." *Music Educators Journal,* 59, no. 5 (January 1973).

Dykema, Peter W., and Karl Gehrkens. *The Teaching and Administration of High School Music.* Evanston, Ill.: Summy-Birchard, 1941.

Graham, Richard M., comp. *Music for the Exceptional Child.* Reston, Va.: Music Educators National Conference, 1975.

Langer, Susanne K. *Feeling and Form.* New York: Charles Scribner's, 1953.

Schopenhauer, Arthur. *The World as Will and Idea.* 4th ed., Vol. I. Trans. R. B. Haldane and J. Kemp. London: Kegan, Paul, Trench, Trubner, 1896.

Wolff, Karen I. "The Nonmusical Outcomes of Music Education: A Review of the Literature." Council for Research in Music Education Bulletin no. 55 (Summer 1978).

PART 2

What: The Subject Matter of Music

What should students learn about music? Are some areas of music more important than others? On what basis are decisions about the subject matter of music classes made? Should there be a common content for all students? These questions are part of the major component of the teaching process—the concern for what is taught and learned in music classes and rehearsals. Such questions are discussed in Chapter 4.

Unless course content is thought through carefully, teachers can waste much of the limited time available for music in the schools, and the students can end up with a superficial acquaintance with music. Or they come away with a lopsided, distorted idea of the subject. ◆

CHAPTER 4

The Music Curriculum

Music teachers are largely responsible for the content of the music classes they teach. In many school situations there is no districtwide plan or course of study that teachers are expected to follow, and where such plans do exist, they are the products of committees made up mostly of teachers. Furthermore, many state and school district curriculum guides are not very specific, a fact that gives teachers much latitude in and responsibility for what is taught.

Often, it seems, discussions of curriculum and course content make one feel like the sorcerer's apprentice, who, desperately trying to stop the broom from carrying buckets of water, grabs an ax and chops the broom into pieces, only to see each new piece begin carrying water. When curricular topics are examined, each idea and its ramifications seem to multiply, and before long the topic is cluttered with questions about ends and means, goals, content, methods, skills, concepts, maturation, and countless other interrelated topics. So that this chapter is kept within manageable proportions, it is confined largely to subject matter content. What is being discussed is content—the "stuff" taught in music classes—not methods. A distinction between them needs to be kept in mind to avoid confusing *what* is taught with the *way* it is taught.

LEARNING IN MUSIC

The chorus at Middlebury High School is singing the black spiritual "There Is a Balm in Gilead." What should the students be learning from singing this beautiful song? At least five things:

1. patterns of musical sounds—the syntax of music
2. the song as a work of music

3. understandings about musical processes and organization

4. skills in performing and listening to music

5. attitudes about the particular piece and about music in general

Each of these five outcomes of learning merits further discussion.

Musical Syntax

If music is organized sound, as it was defined in Chapter 1, then a sense of organization and patterns of sounds is absolutely required for a person to hear the sounds as music. Otherwise, they are just a random jumble, as when a cat walks on the keys of a piano.

The analogy between language and music is not a perfect one, but in a number of ways they are much alike. When learning language, children find out that "runs big slowly dog black the" is not an understandable pattern. They need similar learning in music, except with musical sounds, of course. Apparently a sense of syntax in language, and probably in music as well, is developed through experience with speaking and listening. Children enter school with several years' experience in hearing and speaking words. Then only after they have had much practice and experience with spoken language are they given the visual symbols for the words they already know aurally.

There is another similarity between language and music. Research studies indicate that the learning of syntax and the pronunciation of words develop early in life (Penfield and Roberts, 1959, pp. 240–55). By the time a child is ten years old, the ability for such learning begins to decrease. For this reason it is very important that children in the primary grades of elementary school be given many opportunities for gaining a sense of musical syntax and learning to be accurate in singing pitch.

It is easy to overlook the importance of learning the syntax of music. (Actually, throughout the world and history there have been a multitude of different syntaxes that were considered music by someone, but American children first should learn Western "common practice" syntax.) This is true because syntax is sensed and is not so easily testable. Also, its acquisition is gradual, at least by the age when children enter elementary school. In fact, all of us are still improving our sense of syntax for the types of music with which we are still involved. At our "mature" stage of experience in music, the increments of improvement in our syntactical sense are very small, but we are still improving.

The syntax of music is probably the first type of learning that students should acquire in music, because without it the other four areas of learning won't mean much. Syntax alone can carry a person quite a distance in the world of music. For example, most of the early jazz musicians had little formal training and could not read music, yet their great intuitive sense for musical patterns more than compensated for these limitations. However, they were limited in what they knew about music, and music educators would not want their students today to be similarly restricted in what they know and can do in music.

Musical Works

The amount of music created throughout the world over the past couple of thousand years is massive beyond comprehension. Not only is there art music ranging from the 3800 works by Telemann to the 1600 trouvère and troubadour melodies to Haydn's 104 symphonies, but there are also thousands and thousands of works of folk music and popular songs. No one, even the most avid listener to music, could in an entire lifetime hear each work even once. And the amount of music increases each day.

One of the things students should learn in music classes is where a particular piece of music fits into the world of music. In the case of "There Is a Balm in Gilead," the singers should acquire some understanding of the text, melodic characteristics, social setting, and similar information about this work and other black spirituals, as well as other types of black music. It is not enough just to sing a song; the singers should also know something about it as a piece of music.

A difficult problem for teachers is the selection of music. With the time available for music instruction in schools so limited, teachers can barely skim the surface of the deep waters of available music. Therefore, some hard decisions must be made, and many fine works of music simply have to be left out. Some suggestions for making the necessary choices are presented later in this chapter.

Intellectual Understandings

The intellectual understandings of music involve the formation of concepts about music, the manner of thinking about music, and some knowledge of the process of creating music. Of the three, concept formation seems to be the most important.

Concepts. The dictionary definition of *concept* is useful in understanding what concepts are and how they are formed: "the resultant of a generalizing mental operation; a generic mental image abstracted from percepts." Concepts, then, are generalizations about phenomena.

Some concepts such as music are broad in scope, while others such as phrase are more specific. The structuring of concepts of differing comprehensiveness is somewhat like the system of classification used in biology—phylum, genus, species, and so on. In music there are conceptual ideas about melody, harmony, form, rhythm, and so forth. Subconcepts of melody include ideas about contour, motive, theme, expression, and so on. And each of these subconcepts can be divided further into more specific categories.

A concept is not the same as its verbal symbol or definition; in fact, a concept can exist without a verbal symbol. A definition is merely the assignment of a verbal "handle" to something already formed in the mind. It is more accurate, for example, to think of the generalized quality of "dogness" as the concept rather than the more specific word *dog.*

People form concepts as they notice similarities and differences among objects and in the process organize and classify them. For example, they form a concept of dogness as animals with four legs and one tail, with an ability to bark and an acute sense of smell, but unable to climb trees or see in the dark, and with all the other features that make up the quality of dogness. Without previous experience with animals, definitions ("A dog is . . .") and factual statements ("Dogs can bark . . .") are largely meaningless. A concept must first exist on which to affix the verbal symbol. What this means is that teachers are limited to establishing situations in which the students can form the desired concepts. The generalizing process essential for concept formation must happen within each student's mind; it cannot be accomplished by outside forces. Like the sense of musical syntax, concepts are refined somewhat with each experience. Concepts are never learned once and for all.

The reason that teachers should be interested in concept formation is that concepts facilitate the ability to think. The fact that words are mental tools as well as a means of communication is well established (Shibutani, 1961, pp. 187–91). Students who have no concept of melody are seriously impaired in their ability to think about, understand, and appreciate melodies. Furthermore, because concepts are generalized ideas, they are far more versatile and flexible than specific ideas. The concept of melody can be applied in all kinds of pieces of music, but the melody to "There Is a Balm in Gilead" is specific to only that one piece of music. A third virtue of conceptual learning is that basic, general ideas are remembered much better than specific facts, a point that is cited again in Chapter 5.

Way of Thinking. Every field of study—science, history, music—has its mode of thinking, its way of looking at things. A physicist, for example, is interested in the physical properties of sounds; a social scientist is interested in the effect of sounds on human behavior; a musician is interested in how sounds are manipulated and the tonal effects and compositions that can be created with them. Part of what students should learn in school is to think as scientists in a science class, as social scientists in a social science class, and as musicians in a music class. Appropriate thinking and mental approach is as much a part of the subject as is the factual information associated with it.

And how does musicianlike thinking differ from other thinking? If you question the proverbial "man on the street" about his views on music, the chances are that you will find that he thinks of music as something for accompanying other activities—whistling songs while painting a fence and playing music on the car radio while driving to work. Almost never will he talk about music as an object for careful consideration by itself. On the other hand, musicians value organized sounds; they think that the way Mozart put sounds together in the last movement of his Symphony No. 41 is pretty impressive. In fact, they don't want distractions like painting a fence while listening to the *Jupiter* Symphony. Also, musicians analyze the sounds they listen to; they are interested in figuring out what Mozart did with the sounds. Because they value sounds and analyze them, musicians enjoy music more and know more about it than do most nonmusicians.

Creative Process.   Learning in music should not be confined to the re-creation of what others have done. At a level consistent with their musical development, students should engage in creating music through composition and/or improvisation. Creative activity is valuable because it requires students to think about how sounds are manipulated, which is a central feature of the way musicians think. It also educates students about the process of creating music, including its mental trial and error and just plain hard work. In addition, creative activities allow students to explore their own music potential and in that sense to know themselves better.

As valuable as creative activities are for students in learning music, they are only a part of the subject. Students should not be confined to only those works that they themselves create, any more than they should be limited to works that someone else has created.

Skills and Activities

The words *skills* and *activities* are not synonymous. Skills refer to physical activities such as vibrato on the violin, tonguing the clarinet, and sight singing. Some music classes have the acquisition of skills as a major part of their content. This fact is true of the instrumental music classes and of private instruction in singing or on an instrument. Other music classes include some learning of skills.

Activities are actions that the students engage in as a means of learning. Other things being equal, students who sing a song are more likely to understand and appreciate the song than are students who just listen to it, especially if the students have not had much musical experience. For example, when English teachers want their students to understand drama, they have them read a play and discuss its purpose, literature, and technical production. To increase their understanding of certain points, English teachers may have the students act out a portion of a play in the classroom. The activity furthers learning about drama, just as activities in music can aid learning in music.

Activities, however, cannot substitute for subject matter content. Singing one song after another, class after class, does not contribute much to the students' understanding of music or their aesthetic sensitivity. At one time, music programs in the elementary schools were described entirely in terms of activities: singing, playing instruments, rhythmic movement, reading, creating, and listening. Although it may seem like hairsplitting, these were activities, not subject matter content. It would have been more accurate to say what students learned through the activity of singing or listening. The goal of music education is not just to do something in music. Rather, it is to educate students in music, and it happens that this education is often furthered through the use of appropriate activities.

The division of the subject matter content of music into activities and outcomes, or any other system of categorizing the topic, is, of course, somewhat artificial. A musical experience is a complex, unitary experience in which most of the categories are involved at the same time. When students sing or play pieces

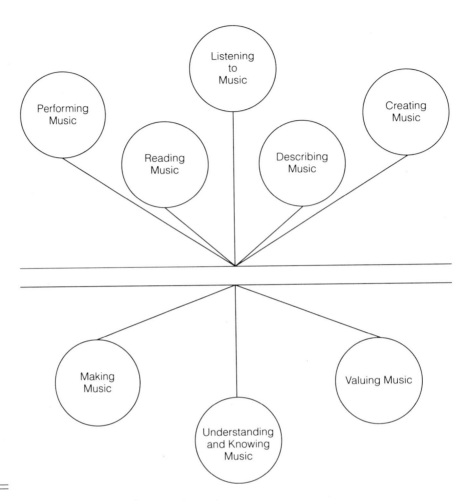

Figure 4.1 *The various aspects of content in music.*

of music, they are usually strengthening their concept about music, gaining some information about it, improving their skill at performing it, and affecting how they feel about the piece in particular and music in general. The extent to which each of these results is achieved depends partly on what the teacher chooses to emphasize. Sometimes music teachers concentrate so much on one category of outcomes that little is accomplished in other categories. Effective music instruction avoids this pitfall. It strikes a reasonable balance among the making, understanding, and valuing of music, regardless of the level or type of class.

Figure 4.1 is a representation of the various aspects of content in music. The horizontal lines through the middle of the figure marks the distinction between activities and outcomes. The activities of performing, listening, creating, reading, and describing or analyzing are related through connecting lines to each other and to making, understanding and knowing, and valuing music.

Attitudes

How a person feels about what he or she knows is important. This statement is probably truer for music than for the traditional academic subjects. All of us use the ability to read and write daily, regardless of whether or not we enjoyed reading and writing when we were taught them in school. Nearly everyone needs to balance checkbooks and compute income taxes regardless of how he or she felt about arithmetic in school. Not so with music. People who don't like music can refrain from buying recordings and attending concerts. If forced to listen to music in the supermarket, they can psychologically "tune it out." Much of the ultimate success of music instruction depends on how the students feel about the subject after the classes are over. And students do acquire attitudes about the subject whether or not teachers realize it. The question is not "Will the students form feelings about music?" but rather "What feelings will they develop?"

What influences the attitudes people adopt? Some generalizations can be offered in terms of tendencies, but no rules can be stated that people invariably follow. One generalization concerns familiarity. If there be truth in the statement "I know what I like," there is also truth in the words "I like what I know." Social scientists have discovered this fact in a variety of situations ranging from people to words to pictures (Freedman, Carlsmith, and Sears, 1970, pp. 71–72). Music teachers can support this finding also. Many teachers have found that a good musical work that was not liked when it was introduced to the students gradually became well liked.

People tend to like things that are similar to what they already know and like. A person who likes Broadway musicals can more easily acquire a favorable attitude toward art music than can a rock-ribbed lover of country music.

People are influenced by the person who is suggesting a change. A teacher who is liked is more effective in changing attitudes than one who isn't. Part of reason for this tendency lies in the fact that the students have a pleasant association with the subject when they like the teacher. And the associations people make with music can influence their attitude toward it.

Attitudes are also influenced by what one's friends and peers think, and this is especially true of students in the secondary schools. If all your friends like a particular piece of music, the chances are greatly increased that you will like it, too. This is so partly because you respect and like your friends, partly because you don't want the friction involved in disagreeing with them, and partly because you tend to "go with the flow" of their feelings as you perceive them.

The family has a significant influence on children's attitudes. If the parents listen to symphonies on their record-playing equipment or tapes, the chances are much greater that the children will end up listening to that type of music when they are mature.

Attitudes and knowledge are complementary. People cannot have intelligent reactions to something they don't know. If asked, "Do you like aardvarks?" they will probably answer, "I don't know." So a teacher's first task is to remove ignorance so that at the least there can be intelligent preferences and at the best there can be what educator-philosopher Harry Broudy refers to as "enlightened cherishing" (1968, p. 13). Few people, including music teachers, enjoy all types of music equally well. Being educated about something does not mean that you must like it. Rather, education offers the opportunity to make intelligent choices.

Some practical actions that music teachers can take to encourage positive attitudes on the part of their students include the following:

1. Seize every opportunity to make students familiar with the music that it is hoped they will learn to like.

2. Avoid direct attempts to teach an attitude; for example, don't say, "This is a great piece of music that you ought to like." Attitudes are in a sense "caught" in a more indirect way, including observing how other people react.

3. Make the learning of music as pleasant and positive an experience as possible. True, a few students will tolerate very negative experiences and still like music. However, the great majority of students try to avoid such situations, and in doing so, they avoid music. If a classroom is a situation with constant pressure, carping by the teacher, and little feeling of success, few positive attitudes will be engendered.

4. Try to have the students enjoy a feeling of success in music. People like better the activities they believe they do well. For example, if you throw many gutter balls when bowling, you will avoid bowling whenever possible; if your average is over 200, you will seek chances to demonstrate your bowling skills—and in the process become even better at bowling.

Nonmusical Outcomes

Nonmusical benefits also result from the study of music. For instance, a student may derive emotional release from singing a song. Whether or not such a release happens depends primarily on the inclinations of the particular individual and not on any direct action of the teacher, as was pointed out in the preceding chapter. As long as the classroom atmosphere is not repressive, emotional release and other nonmusical outcomes can happen as by-products of the class.

WHO DECIDES ON CONTENT?

In recent years a number of writers on education have advocated changing the role of the teacher from one of a leader in the learning process to one of helper. The concept of the teacher as leader connotes making decisions about what is to be learned, although the view of the teacher as helper means, for some advocates at least, giving the students a great deal of choice about what they will learn and when they will learn it. The term used by some educational writers for teachers assuming the helper role is not teacher but rather facilitator, enabler, or similar words.

The theoretical case for the helper role is quite interesting and attractive. Some students do learn better when left to pursue their own interests. However, in the area of music there are some practical problems with allowing the students the dominant voice in deciding what they will learn. If the music specialist can visit each elementary school classroom only twice a week for a total of fifty or sixty minutes (a typical schedule), then time is a very valuable commodity. It is nearly impossible to permit much time for exploring what the students may want to do or to devote much attention to the variety of topics they might select. Also, seldom does an entire class decide on the same thing to do, so large-group activities such as singing songs are greatly reduced, if not eliminated.

There is an even more serious problem with student-selected content. People can make intelligent choices only about things they know. Students rarely decide to study something about which they know little or nothing, and the result is a severe limitation in their education. Their music study becomes a perpetuation of what they already know, which is usually what they hear on the radio or the latest record hits. Such a situation violates an important guideline to be suggested shortly, one that says students should learn things in music classes that they do not know or would not learn without instruction.

It is not being "authoritarian" or "dominating" to realize that teachers who have a college degree in music know more about music than does the average fourteen-year-old. Furthermore, it does not seem unreasonable to use this much greater knowledge of the subject to render most of the decisions about the educational needs of the students in music. These decisions will, of course, be more effective if they take into consideration the interests and backgrounds of the students. Considering the interests of the students is important in achieving the best teaching. That is not the same, however, as turning over most of the curricular decisions to them.

Guidelines for Selecting Music

Because time is limited for music instruction, teachers must make some difficult decisions about what to teach. In doing so, they may consult students and parents and consider their wishes. Even when this is done, however, teachers have to make choices. The following guidelines may help in doing this.

Educational. The first guideline sounds like a simple one: The students should gain information, skills, or attitudes that they did not have prior to the class or course and probably would not acquire without instruction in school. This idea seems basic to any educational undertaking. Without it, education becomes merely baby-sitting or a recreation program.

While the guideline is a simple but important one, it has sometimes not been followed, for a number of reasons. Some teachers have felt that the effort to teach something would not be worth it, or that it would not make any difference to the students, or that there is not really anything to learn in music. Whatever the reason, the students were the losers. Here is how Raymond Lopez puts the matter:

> As soon as you can establish rapport, then you can introduce Brahms and Wagner. You don't have to stoop to "all they can sing is pop." In one school, all they were doing was drivel, in any old way. There was no attempt to organize it. The kids could just as well have been walking down the street—and maybe that's what we're preparing them for. We say that we are preparing the student for the world of reality. But shouldn't we always be struggling for enrichment? Why not acquaint the kids with those in the stream of time who have created outstanding music? I have heard a teacher say, "Why give them that stuff (a great composer's music)? They've never heard it. They'll never know it, and it won't make any difference to them." If I had had teachers like that maybe today I wouldn't know the difference. My teachers exposed me to the greats in music and that enriched my life. I'm better off for those teachers (Music Educators Journal, 1970, p. 96).

One practical question for the criterion of being educational is, "What would the students learn about music if they had no instruction in school?" Is there some music and information about music that, like riding a bicycle, would probably be learned without a music teacher? The music that can be learned outside of school can be left to others and other subject matter content can be taught in the schools.

Valid.   Music is an established academic discipline, a recognized field of knowledge and study. Teachers should ask themselves, "Is what is being taught a legitimate portion of the field of music? Would most trained musicians (performers, musicologists, teachers) recognize and accept this content as a part of the field?" For example, a few teachers of violin with elementary school children use a kind of notation in which notes are identified not by pitch but by the name of the string and fingering: A1, D3, and so on. The system cannot indicate relative pitch, note values, or sharps and flats. It must be unlearned as the students progress. No music theorist, symphony musician, or musicologist uses this system in studying or playing music. Therefore, it is not valid in the field of music.

The call for validity is a logical one. Why teach something under the name of music that is not really part of the field of music? It is neither logical nor honest to transform a subject, even in the hope of aiding learning.

Fundamental.   Closely related to validity of content is the belief that students should learn the basic ideas of the subject, not just factual minutiae. Knowing the keys of the thirty-two Beethoven piano sonatas is not as useful as understanding his development of themes and motives. When information is associated with a concept, it is useful, but memorizing insignificant facts is not effective learning. Fundamental ideas—tonality, development of themes, the 2:1 ratio in rhythmic notation, and the unity of words and music in art songs, to cite a few examples—are valuable because they are comprehensive and have wide application in music.

Representative. If the music curriculum is limited to only a few types or aspects of music, then the students are not being given a well-balanced education in music. The band director who has the band play one march after another and the general music teacher who spends all the class time working with the synthesizer are both guilty of shortchanging their students, because both are omitting many other important areas of music. Sometimes teachers give the students very little art music—music that contains a sophisticated handling of sounds. Their students continue to think of music only as a pastime or entertainment and are never introduced to the idea that music is an aesthetic, expressive human creation.

One way of checking out the representativeness of music selected is to take a piece of paper or a chalkboard and divide it into boxes according to categories. On the horizontal plane one might put style periods: pre-Renaissance, Renaissance, Baroque, Classical, Romantic, and Twentieth Century. On the vertical plane could be put types of music appropriate for the class, such as folk songs, show tunes, art songs, oratorio-opera, and religious works for a choral group. Making a mark in the appropriate category for each piece of music provides a good picture of the distribution of the music used.

Contemporary. The music and information taught in music classes should be up to date. This criterion refers not only to the date when composed but also to the style. Some works composed in the 1960s and 1970s are still in a style that is a century old. The main problem for teachers in this matter is the technical difficulty of many twentieth-century works. They would like to have the students sing or play them, but many times the music is too hard. It requires some searching, but contemporary works that are not technically so demanding can be found.

Relevant. The word *relevant* has been used in several ways in recent years. To some people it means those things vital for survival and living; to others it means topics that one happens to like or be interested in; and to others it means the relationship between a person and a given subject. It is in the third sense that the word is used here.

As mentioned in Chapter 3, sometimes the interests of the students and the requirements of valid subject matter have appeared to be in conflict. The pendulum has swung back and forth between these extremes several times in the rather short history of music education in America. Proponents of subject matter validity ask, "What good is a subject that has lost its integrity and character?" The advocates of relevance answer, "What good is a subject that seems meaningless and worthless to the students?" Both views have a fair claim for the attention of teachers, and the two positions need not be mutually exclusive.

Relevance is probably affected more by the method of teaching than by the content. Topics and subjects have little inherent relevance; people make things relevant. A topic that is important and interesting to one person couldn't matter less to another. Relevance results when a topic is given meaning through a teacher's attitude and skill in organizing the subject. Teachers need to teach so that the real content of music becomes relevant to the students. For example, figuring out minor scale patterns is not relevant to most students because it is not particularly helpful to them in understanding music. Achieving relevance is quite an assignment, but as the opening sentence of this book says, the job of teaching music well is not an easy one.

Learnable.　The music curriculum must be learnable by most of the students. It is useless to teach something for which they are not prepared. While the students' backgrounds and interests should be considered, these are not the only factors that teachers should think about. Teaching a piece of music that is of a suitable level of difficulty for the students should be determined in relation to the other guidelines, as well as to a host of practical matters such as amount of class time, books and materials, and performance obligations. A good teacher can build on the interests the students already have without abandoning the subject. If students seem uninterested in a topic, perhaps another approach to it is called for instead of giving up on it entirely.

Some of the guidelines presented here may appear to be contradictory, and to a degree this is so. The need to offer substantive instruction seems to work against the idea of relevancy, and contemporary content appears to contradict the idea of representative samples of the subject. In the case of education versus relevancy, the solution lies in the proper methods of teaching. However, some of the time teachers need to strike a balance in making curricular decisions between conflicting needs. None of the guidelines are absolute and overriding, which means that teachers have to account for a number of divergent factors in their teaching.

Evaluating Musical Works

It is nearly impossible to discuss the content of music classes without touching on the sometimes emotional and foggy question of the quality of musical works. Is there a difference, or is it simply a matter of what a person happens to like? The answer is that there are differences, but they are difficult to state in words. A few points can be stated, however:

1. Because music is a human creation done in a particular cultural setting, there are no universal criteria for evaluating musical works. For example, it is impossible to claim that Japanese piece of music is superior or inferior to a Mozart piano sonata. Each should be considered within its own cultural context.

2. The purpose or type of music should be considered in evaluating works. Some music is not intended to be listened to intently (film music, hymns, most popular songs, and so on) and should not be evaluated in terms of concert music. And the opposite is true; music written for careful listening should not be evaluated in terms of its usefulness around a campfire or for social dancing.

3. Works of music do not fall into neat categories: great, incompetent, OK. Instead, they seem to exist on a continuum ranging from very simple to very complex.

4. Judgments can seldom be made on the basis of the technical features of the music—the amount of syncopation, range and contour of the melody, percentage of tonic chords, and so on. Most attempts at identifying technical characteristics of "good" music ended up excluding some works generally considered to be of good quality.

5. It appears likely that some judgments can be made in comparing the quality of similar works. Briefly, the music considered to be of better quality provides listeners with a greater challenge and variety as it progresses in ways generally expected of music; less significant music is less challenging and more obvious. This theory of music quality is developed fully in the writings of Leonard B. Meyer (1967) and others.

In addition to considering the greater complexity of music that Meyer and others cite, what practical questions can teachers ask to gain a clearer idea of the quality of works they are considering using? Here are some practical, intuitive criteria that may be applied. They will not provide conclusive or final answers to the quality of a musical work, but at least they can serve as a starting point.

1. Does the work seem to stick with you after you are away from it for a few minutes, or is it forgettable?

2. Does the work seem to "wear well" over the days of rehearsal, or do you become tired of it easily? Quality works have something about them that can stand—indeed almost seem to require—working with them time and again. Each time you find something in the music that you had not noticed before.

3. In the case of a work that has been around for a generation or so, has it "stood the test" of time? For example, there is a quality in the marches of John Philip Sousa that people find interesting nearly a century after many of them were composed, and that quality has not been found in many other marches. Time has a way of sorting out what is of better quality.

4. The content of the music series books has been subjected to careful evaluation by the books' authors. The fact that a song is included in these books means that it has passed a screening process. An attempt is made in these books to offer a wide variety of good music. The contest lists for high school bands, orchestras, and choral groups often contain selections of high quality. The quality of these lists is not consistent, however.

5. If you have a choice between a work by a recognized composer and one you have never heard of, it is wiser to stay with the known composer. Bach, Brahms, and Bartok are not esteemed names in the world of music because they had clever managers or because someone proclaimed their music to be good. Rather, musicians over the years have found that their music possesses

qualities that make it stand out in the world of music. Such recognition should influence teachers in deciding which pieces of music to study in their music classes.

Popular Music

What do the curriculum selection guidelines and considerations of musical quality indicate for the use of popular music in school music classes? They seem to say to music teachers, "Certainly, use some popular music, but don't make it the main course on the musical menu. Most of it is not as worthy of careful study as most works of art music, but the matter of musical quality is not the only factor that should affect your choice of music."

There are two reasons why popular music is justified in school music classes. One is to help develop the students' interest in the class. The other is to use popular music as a vehicle for the study of aspects of music—rhythmic patterns, phrases, melodic style, and so on. Teachers need to be selective about which popular songs to use, because some are more useful than others. Students can often assist in making choices of popular works.

Most music teachers do not look down their noses at popular music, but there are probably a few who do. Such an attitude is quickly picked up by the students, and they resent it just as much as you would if someone said your musical preferences were inferior. Haughty attitudes must be avoided! Some music teachers who had quite a bit of experience with playing in popular groups while in high school or college may feel they are up to date on popular music. Well, the field changes very fast, and almost all teachers are somewhat "behind" on popular music. Their students notice it, even if they don't. Fortunately, teachers need not be up to the minute in order to make effective use of popular music in their classes.

AREAS OF STUDY IN THE MUSIC CURRICULUM

Because music requires specialized abilities and training, music teachers often confine their attention to a limited area of the total program—band, strings, choral, general music. It is natural for each teacher to think of his or her specialty first and to be less concerned about the rest of the music program. However, all music teachers need to support each other's area of the curriculum, for a number of reasons. First, essentially the same subject is being taught. Second, other educators tend to look at the total program when they consider the effectiveness of the faculty and the curriculum. Third, the various parts of the music program can benefit each other. For example, a good general music course aids in the development of audiences for the school performing groups.

In some school situations, talented students have been caught in a tug-of-war between two music teachers, each of whom wanted the students in their program.

In other cases there was no organized curriculum for students to follow if they wished to prepare for becoming music majors in college; the "course of study" was the particular teacher and his or her performing organization. Neither factionalism nor a myopic view of the field helps the music program or the students.

Music courses in the secondary schools have traditionally been classified as either "performing groups" (band, orchestra, and choral groups) or "classes" (general music, theory, music appreciation). The distinction has some justification, because the two types of course normally approach music differently—one by performing and the other with books, tests, and discussions. In the elementary schools, the music classes rarely perform for the public. The distinct differences between "performing groups" and "classes" may not be the best situation in terms of what the students need, but it is well established.

Music classes that do not perform for the public have both profited and suffered from a lack of attention. Because their work is seldom displayed, teachers feel freer about having the students learn whatever seems most worthwhile. However, for the same reason nonperforming classes have often been neglected and the first to be hurt if the budget becomes tight.

The attention given the music education program needs to be spread equitably among the various levels and courses. The allocation of funds is important in accomplishing this goal, but even more important is the attention the teachers give the various portions of their teaching assignments. Some teachers work very carefully with their performing organizations, but their general music classes are examples of thoughtless improvisation. Music teachers should reject the temptation to devote much attention to those portions of the music program that the public sees and to shortchange the rest of their classes.

A balanced music program is spelled out in some detail in the 1986 MENC publication *The School Music Program: Description and Standards,* Second Edition. Part of the publication offers specific standards for the curriculum, staff, scheduling, facilities, and materials in terms of both a "basic program" and a "quality program." It is the most complete statement of specific aspects of the music curriculum available.

Nonperforming Classes

Most of the music instruction in elementary schools is of a nonperformance nature. While the children usually engage in some music-making activities, they are not usually preparing for public performances. Only the elective choral groups at the upper grades in elementary school are organized as performing groups. Beginning instrumental classes may perform once or twice a year for the parents, but little attention is devoted to any other type of public performances.

In the middle and junior high schools, the general music classes are populated by students not in a performing group. Some music (sometimes only a quarter of a year) is usually required of sixth and seventh graders. Starting with eighth grade, music becomes usually an elective subject. Some individual work is incorporated into many general music classes.

At the high school level there are only a limited number of small nonperforming classes, usually theory and appreciation types of courses.

The distinction between performance and nonperformance classes need not be so definite. There is no reason why the nonperforming classes cannot perform occasionally. In one school, for example, the theory class presented some of the better student compositions in a concert. In other schools, the general music classes perform as a massed chorus once a year.

Performing Groups

Performing groups overwhelm the nonperformance classes at the high school level. The most recent figures for secondary schools show about 1,600,000 students were enrolled in band, 1,700,000 in choral groups, and 193,000 in orchestra (Osterndorf and Horn, 1976, pp. 214–219). In contrast, only 64,000 were enrolled in theory courses and 192,000 in music appreciation, which in some cases was probably general music. The data are clear on one point: About 95 percent of all music enrollments in high schools are in performing organizations.

Some historical background is needed to understand why secondary school music has become so performance-oriented. The great leap forward in secondary school enrollments occurred between the years of 1910 and 1940. During that period a person's chances of attending high school increased from one in ten to three in four (Department of Health, Education, and Welfare, 1970, p. 49). This increase meant that many of the students going to high school were not college-bound, so a greater variety of courses was needed in the curriculum. Also, attitudes changed somewhat about the values of studying subjects other than the traditional academic ones. Because school music at the secondary level expanded rapidly, there were few teachers trained to teach music at the secondary school level. Therefore, schools often turned to professional musicians, a trend that was greatly boosted by the unemployment of the early 1930s. These former professional musicians, naturally, worked with their performing groups in much the same way as a director of a professional organization. The period when the band or choir met was called a "rehearsal," and the purpose of the band or choir was to present polished and perfected performances. The teacher was designated the "director," a term more familiar to professional musicians. So music became the only curricular area in which "directors" conducted "rehearsals" instead of teachers teaching classes.

Many of the professional musicians who entered the teaching field made valuable contributions to music education. Even today the limited opportunities for making a living as a performer have turned many persons toward teaching in the schools. Common interests bind the professional musicians and music educators together, and the teaching profession needs capable and sensitive musicians. What should be realized, however, is that whatever is good for a professional organization is not always right for a school performing group. Because the two groups exist for different purposes, they should be conducted and taught differently.

There are several good reasons for continuing performing groups in the secondary school curriculum. One is that students learn by doing and experiencing. Students who go through the effort of learning their parts and rehearsing with the group know a musical work much more thoroughly than students who only listened to it. Many a student who had an initial lack of interest in a piece of music has ended up liking it after working on it and learning what it offers musically.

Another point in favor of performing groups is that they are well suited to meeting teenage needs for recognition and activity. In most of their other school courses the students sit passively. Music is one area in which they can truly participate. Preparing music for a performance motivates them, as well as offers them a chance for some recognition.

A third point in favor of performing groups is that they are well established in the school curriculum. One should be careful about criticizing success. Teachers are trained in teaching performing groups and materials are available. Before discarding such achievements, something of greater value should be found to replace them.

What appears to be needed in the future is (1) a building up of the nonperformance courses and (2) an evolution (not a revolution) toward more educationally valid performing groups.

Enriching the Rehearsal

What is the educational limitation of most performing organizations? Their efforts are usually devoted entirely to learning to sing or play. Performing music is fine— up to a point. However, there is more to an education in music than fingering notes and following a conductor. Many students in performing groups have little musical or intellectual understanding of what they are doing; they are getting a lopsided education in music.

A few teachers of performing groups have tried to teach more than the correct performance of the notes. Sometimes, however, their efforts are not presented with enough consistency or depth to make a difference. A few off-the-cuff remarks about historical circumstances or theoretical features of a work are fine for educated musicians, but most school students do not have the musical background to learn from a scattershot approach. It is easy for a teacher to believe that because the group was told once about the continuo line in Baroque music, the students now understand the significance of that information. A couple of questions on a quiz will usually dispel such a pleasant notion.

How can teachers give their performing groups a music education beyond only technical skills? They can do so best by setting aside a *small* amount of class time to enrich and supplement the regular rehearsal. Because the members of the group already know something about music, are interested in the subject, and can also perform *and* study it, a small effort by the teacher can reap large educational dividends. If there seems to be no time for anything except preparing music for performances, then the group has too many performance commitments, or the music is too difficult, or it is being overrehearsed. In any case, studies indicate that some time can be taken from rehearsals for learning about music without adversely affecting the performance level of the group (Gebhardt, 1973, pp. 71–72).

While specific suggestions for enriching the rehearsals of performing organizations are presented on pages 161–166, two general suggestions can be offered here. One is that teachers plan for a two-year period. Music is virtually the only subject in the curriculum in which students at different levels of training are in the same class. Although this contributes to the quality of performance, it creates difficulties in organizing instruction. The teachers of performing groups run the risk of boring the second-year students by covering material they already know or bewildering the first-year students by omitting necessary prerequisite information. Basic information should probably be reviewed each year, but plans need to be made to avoid repeating other material each year.

The other suggestion is that the teachers of performing organizations select music to suit educational as well as performance needs. Some pieces should be chosen for public performance, some for just reading through, and some selected so that the students can perform or listen to a work of a particular type or one containing a particular musical feature. The planning should also include books, videotapes, and recordings in addition to music.

What is the usual student reaction to enriching the rehearsal periods of performing groups? Probably the word *cautious* best describes it. For years the students have been given the idea that all they do in a performing group is play or sing. At first they may seem indifferent to additional learning, although this has not been the experience of most teachers who have made a real effort to enrich the learning of their performing groups. Any lack of enthusiasm from the students may be explained by one of the following reasons: (1) The students may not understand the relationship between what they are studying and what they are performing in rehearsal. (2) It is easier to just play or sing and not be bothered with thinking and remembering. (3) Students are usually quick to realize that such study may involve work outside of rehearsal and tests, neither of which they particularly like. However, if performing groups are to be curricular subjects on an equal academic footing with other courses in the school curriculum, a comparable effort is required from the students.

Naturally, if the enriching activities are poorly taught, they will not be beneficial or successful. Dull twenty-minute lectures on hemiola and the rote memorization of intervals are likely to alienate all except the most ardent scholars.

Types of Performing Groups

Not all secondary school students can profit equally from music instruction. Students want and need music that is suited to their abilities and interests. When enough enrollment permits, groups at different levels of ability should be offered. There can be a choir for the more interested and talented students, and a chorus for the less able and interested. The same idea holds true for instrumental groups. Such an arrangement is consistent with the democratic tenet of equal opportunity.

Teachers should guard against slighting the less talented group. The education given students in a chorus is just as important as the education given the students in the top choir; only the level at which the learning takes place is different.

Small Ensembles. A weakness of music education at the secondary school level is its overemphasis on large ensembles. Most music educators realize that performing in small ensembles is a valuable experience for students. They gain independence by being the only performer on a part, and small ensemble work engenders interest and good musicianship. In addition, there is a rich literature for combinations involving strings and groups such as woodwind quintets and brass ensembles.

At least three factors discourage small ensembles in the schools. To begin with, it is hard to work up much public enthusiasm for a woodwind quintet or horn trio, which is not true for bands or choral groups. Second, the time that teachers can devote to small ensembles is limited. Their schedules are filled with classes and large ensemble rehearsals. Few school systems can afford to hire a teacher for classes of four or five students. Third, the amount of time available to students for small ensembles is limited. Very few students have time in their school schedules for more than one music class per day, and that class usually is a large ensemble. Most small ensembles are formed for purposes of performing at a contest, and they meet only a few times with a teacher.

These problems do not erase the fact that small ensemble experience is highly desirable. Music teachers should encourage and plan for it as much as possible. Some teachers arrange for several small ensembles to rehearse at the same time in adjacent rooms so that they can circulate among the groups. In some situations, the better performers can form an ensemble. Because they learn their parts more quickly than the other students, they can be excused from large ensemble rehearsal once or twice a week to rehearse small ensemble music.

Orchestras. For a variety of reasons, orchestras have been far surpassed in enrollment by bands. This is a most unfortunate situation, for two reasons. First, the orchestral literature is vastly richer than that for bands. Except for some contemporary works, bands must play pieces written strictly for the educational market or transcriptions, which are not usually as effective as the original works. The wind band is slowly acquiring some good contemporary literature of its own, and possibly in fifty years the problem of good literature will not be so serious. Second, the playing opportunities after high school for interested amateurs lie overwhelmingly in orchestras, which use only a limited number of winds. The existence of well over a thousand community orchestras was mentioned earlier in this book, and most of them would like to have more string players.

When speaking candidly, many band directors give three reasons for not offering string instruction: (1) It might take potentially good players away from the band. The result would be two mediocre groups instead of one good organization. (2) There is no one competent enough to teach strings in the district. (3) The band director has no time for additional classes. The first reason may have some truth to it in school districts with enrollments of less than 1000 for grades 7 through 12. However, some small districts have a good band and a good orchestra. The excuse of a lack of string teaching ability is not valid. Band directors who are clarinet players do not hesitate teaching brass instruments, at least at the beginning and intermediate levels.

The matter of teacher time must be faced. It is not possible to get something for nothing. Fortunately, string instruments cost about the same as wind instruments, and often they can be rented from music merchants, in which cases an investment by the school district is not required. During the first year or two in which a string program is started, only a small amount of additional teacher time is needed. When the program reaches to all grades, the program adds about one-fourth to one-third as much instructional time as the winds require.

Marching Bands. The marching band has commendable features. It is good public relations for the music department. Many people see the band only at a football game or street parade, and that is their only contact with the school music program. Its members achieve recognition, school spirit is fostered, and good feelings are generated all around as the colorful groups parade by. What could anyone have against something that gives so many people harmless enjoyment and impresses them favorably with the school music program?

The problem is that in some communities the marching band dominates the music program in the school district; in some high schools the marching band has become almost the entire music program. In such instances the result is a narrow music education for a small number of students and just about no music education for the vast majority of the students.

The problem has been intensified over the past twenty years in many places because of the growth of marching band contests and the increasing popularity of the corps style of marching. Aside from its technical features, the corps style bands usually learn only one show each year that they perform for every appearance. Clearly this one show provides the students with a very restricted musical experience. Many of the appearances are at marching band contests, with some bands entering five or more contests each fall. The evaluation of bands at these contests is largely on nonmusical factors, and a correlation has been observed by many people between the size of the group (band members and auxiliary units) and the ratings received. One study of high school bands uncovered the fact that many of the students liked the competition and potential recognition but realized that they learned much more in a concert band. Even many of the directors of successful contest bands freely admitted that the experience has little to do with music education (Rogers, 1982, p. 83). The values claimed for the marching activity, both at contests and at football games, were the promotion of the band and character building and recognition for the students, reasons which hark back to the topic of the nonmusical values of music discussed in Chapter 3.

What can music educators who teach bands do about the situation? In most American communities today, the marching band is so much a part of the scene that it is unrealistic to suggest that it be discontinued, and probably that would not be a good idea anyway. Teachers can begin by bringing the attention devoted to the marching band into proportion with that given other aspects of the music program. In some cases this adjustment may mean reducing (over a period of a couple years) the number of marching appearances or contests entered. It may mean simplifying the marching shows in terms of the routines the students are expected to learn. Truthfully, most football fans cannot tell the difference between a complicated and a simple band show (or maybe they don't care). A third action that will make the teachers' lives a little easier is to have someone else oversee the auxiliary units—flag bearers, rifle corps, pom-pom unit, and so on. Other teachers or people in the community can work with these groups, and music teachers will have more time for teaching music, which is what they were trained to do.

Jazz Bands and Swing Choirs.   Should "specialized" performing groups such as jazz bands, madrigal singers, and swing choirs be included in the secondary school curriculum on the same basis as band, orchestra, choir, and general music? Certainly such groups should be offered when possible, but in most cases they should be operated as adjuncts to the larger groups. That is, jazz band membership should be made available only to the members of the concert band or to those who have been members for two or more years. If this condition is not made, a student's musical education is limited by his or her premature selection of one specialized area before becoming educated to some degree about a larger world of music.

In some schools such specialized groups have received most of the attention of the teacher and the public, and the larger group has been neglected. For example, one prestigious suburban high school let its concert band deteriorate noticeably while a steel band was receiving most of the director's attention.

Credit and Graduation Requirements

If music is to be a curricular course, then music classes should meet during the school day as do classes in every other academic field. If they are forced to meet outside the regular school hours, they become extracurricular, like basketball and cheerleading. Some music activities seem to be possibilities for extracurricular status, among them pep band, musicals (which often involve several departments in the school), marching band if it includes a number of auxiliary units, and the like. However, concert band, orchestra, large choral ensembles, and the more academic music courses certainly merit status as curricular subjects.

At the high school level, credit should be offered for music study on the same basis as it is offered for all other subjects in the curriculum. This means one full unit of credit per year for all music courses meeting five days a week and requiring outside preparation. Half credit simply means that music is considered by the school to be half as valuable to the students as other courses. Two excuses are given for allowing only half credit (or less) for music in some schools. One is that no textbook or homework is involved. Music teachers can answer this excuse by noting the need for individual practice in performing groups and the homework required in nonperforming classes. If the performing group can be made into a more educational situation, as was urged in the preceding chapter, then a better case can be made for offering full credit for it.

The second reason sometimes given for less credit for music is this: Because students from several grades are combined in the same class, and because a student in a performing group takes the same course for several years, not enough learning takes place after the first year. This view shows a lack of understanding of the conceptual way in which music learning takes place, but on the surface it appears logical and therefore deserves an answer. Part of that answer involves pointing out the gradual acquisition of concepts in music. And part of it comes from the fact that over the years students assume positions of leadership. As a freshman Joe Green was a hesitant second violinist, but in his senior year he is concertmaster and responsible for leading the section.

Most students do not need credits in music for high school graduation. Most of the students who are now in music classes would probably enroll even if no credit were offered. The concern here is for equality and prestige for both students and teachers. The claim that music is as important as other subjects in the curriculum is weakened if the school supports the subject with only half as much credit. Also, when the students work hard and improve in skills and knowledge, they can hardly be blamed for resenting the implication that so little is thought of their efforts.

Virtually all schools have graduation requirements that are spelled out in detail. A minimum number of credits is specified for English, social science, mathematics, science, foreign languages, and electives, as well as other such non-credit requirements as physical education, which sometimes includes a swimming test. What is often missing is any mention of the fine arts. The requirements tacitly say, "The fine arts are not an essential part of a high school graduate's education."

In recent years many states and school districts have added a fine arts requirement to their high school graduation requirements. Such a requirement has the effect of placing the fine arts on an equal status with the other areas of the curriculum and draws attention to the significant place of the arts in society. As Chapter 6 points out, if music teachers take advantage of the opportunity, the requirement could bring many students into music who are currently not involved with it.

Credit is a two-sided affair. If the school fulfills its obligation by granting full credit for music, then the music teachers must fulfill their obligation by providing courses worthy of receiving credit. Whatever is taught should have substance and be more than a pastime.

Credit for Private Study

Although private study is not usually supervised by school music teachers, school systems in about thirty states can arrange for credit to be given for it in a program formulated by the state department of education. Again the credit is seldom needed by the student for graduation, but it does give music study additional status and places such study on a student's record for colleges to consider. These programs vary somewhat in the way they are organized, but most of them require approval by the state department of education for a list of approved teachers and the grading process. In some cases only study on piano, voice, violin, and other such instruments is allowed for credit.

Implementing the Curriculum

The best laid curricular plans are of little value if they are not implemented. Plans are only pieces of paper until teachers bring them to life—and teachers need time to teach and students need books, equipment, and satisfactory facilities in which to learn music.

Although these topics are generally beyond the scope of this book, teachers should know that the MENC has published a valuable aid in the development and implementation of school music programs: *The School Music Program: Description and Standards,* the second edition of which was published in 1986. This publication represents a type of consensus in the music education profession about what is needed for successful music instruction in terms of time, staff, materials, and facilities. It is not just the opinion of a few music educators; it was developed by a MENC committee in consultation with several hundred music educators. This means that its recommendations carry the imprint of the profession, and that endorsement can be helpful to teachers in supporting their requests for time and materials.

A quality music curriculum results not only from drawing up a list of courses but also from providing a varied and quality program of music education. Deciding what to teach requires thoughtful attention to subject matter validity, relevance, and the selection of music. Most important, music teachers should realize that they are teaching a subject and that in their classes students should learn music, both as an academic area and as an art.

Questions

1. Should a performing group hear and study musical works that it does not perform for the public? Why or why not?

2. What are some characteristics of musicianlike thinking?

3. What are the purposes of music activities in music classes?

4. What does the term *subject matter validity* mean? What does the term *relevance* mean?

5. On what basis do Meyer and some other scholars make value judgments about musical works?

6. Why is it especially important that strings and orchestra be part of the music program in school districts with enough students?

7. What does the word *syntax* refer to? Why is it important that students recognize it?

8. Why is creative activity important in music education?

Projects
1. Select three musical works that might be included in the repertoire of a performing group. Decide what you could teach the students about music as the group learns each work.

2. Select a book designed for use in a general music class and evaluate its content according to the guidelines suggested on pages 57–62.

3. Select three songs or other musical works and evaluate them for their music quality.

4. Secure a curriculum guide or course of study for a music course. Evaluate it in terms of the suggested guidelines on pages 57–60.

5. Using your main performance medium (band, orchestra, choral), plan an eight-week course of study. Indicate the music you plan to use and what you specifically plan to teach through and with the music.

Suggested Readings
Ernst, Karl D., and Charles L. Gary, eds. *Music in General Education*. Reston, Va.: Music Educators National Conference, 1965.

Klotman, Robert H. *The School Music Administrator and Supervisor: Catalysts for Change in Music Education*. Englewood Cliffs, N.J.: Prentice-Hall, 1973. Chapter 4.

Music Educators National Conference. *The School Music Program: Description and Standards*. 2nd ed. Reston, Va.: MENC, 1986.

Reimer, Bennett. *A Philosophy of Music Education*. 2nd ed. Englewood Cliffs, N.J.: Prentice-Hall, 1989. Chapters 8 and 9.

References
Broudy, Harry S. "The Case for Aesthetic Education." In *Documentary Report of the Tanglewood Symposium*, edited by Robert A. Choate. Reston, Va.: Music Educators National Conference, 1968.

Department of Health, Education, and Welfare. *Digest of Educational Statistics*. Washington, D.C.: U.S. Government Printing Office, 1970.

Freedman, Jonathan L., J. Merrill Carlsmith, and David O. Sears. *Social Psychology*. Englewood Cliffs, N.J.: Prentice-Hall, 1970.

Gebhardt, Larry. "The Development and Testing of an Integrated Course of Study Providing for the Acquisition of Musical Knowledge and Skills by Students in a Junior High School Band." D.M.E. dissertation, Indiana University, 1973.

Meyer, Leonard B. *Music, the Arts, and Ideas*. Chicago: University of Chicago Press, 1967. Chapter 2.

Music Educators Journal, 56, no. 5 (January 1970).

National Center for Educational Statistics. *Course Offerings and Enrollments in the Arts and Humanities at the Secondary School Level*. Washington, D.C.: U.S. Government Printing Office, 1984.

Osterndorf, Logan C., and Paul J. Horn. *Course Offerings, Enrollments, and Curriculum Practices in Public Secondary Schools, 1972–73.* Washington, D.C.: U.S. Government Printing Office, 1976.

Penfield, Wilder, and Tamar Roberts. *Speech and Brain—Mechanisms.* Princeton, N.J.: Princeton University Press, 1959.

Rogers, George L. "Attitudes of High School Band Directors, Band Members, Parents, and Principals toward Marching Band Contests." D.M.E. dissertation, Indiana University, 1982.

Shibutani, Tamotsu. *Society and Personality.* Englewood Cliffs, N.J.: Prentice-Hall, 1961.

PART 3

How: The Methods of Teaching Music

How to teach music is the third and largest area covered in this book. Chapter 5 begins the section with a discussion of basic psychological principles for teaching music. Many of the specific actions teachers should take in teaching can be developed from the fundamental generalizations presented in that chapter. For example, students will remember more if, near the conclusion of the class, the teacher reviews the material presented earlier in the class period. Although one could make up a number of rules (for example, "Review all factual lessons within one half hour of presentation"), if teachers understand the principles of how the human mind retains information, they can apply this information to teaching a wide variety of topics in many different situations. A general understanding is more adaptable and is therefore more useful than a specific fact. Besides, one usually remembers basic ideas better than isolated specifics—another fundamental principle about the retention of information.

Chapter 6 deals specifically with the middle and high school general music classes. Here, as in much of the content of the remaining chapters, the suggestions presented are based on the principles discussed in Chapter 5.

Chapter 7 not only covers teaching theory and music appreciation but also discusses the humanities and fine arts courses as well.

Chapter 8 covers the rehearsal and teaching of performing groups.

Because the same basic information is valid for both choral and instrumental groups, the two types of musical organizations are considered together, with a few exceptions.

Chapter 9 covers teaching musicianship and interpretation in musical performance; Chapter 10 treats intonation. In these chapters, choral and instrumental music are also discussed together.

Chapter 11 is devoted to teaching singing, including the important topic of voice change in boys. Chapter 12 is the instrumental counterpart of Chapter 11 and includes basic playing techniques of families of instruments.

Because public performances are an integral part of secondary school music, an entire chapter, Chapter 13, is devoted to the topic.

Because computers have shown so much potential in helping music teachers in their work, Chapter 14 is devoted to the topic. It presents the use of computers and related equipment not only in teaching music but also in helping manage music libraries, budgets, and similar obligations.

CHAPTER 5

Psychology and Music Teaching

Below is a true-false quiz containing some common-sense beliefs about learning music. It can be an interesting springboard to a comparison between what everyone "knows" about teaching and what research into the learning process reveals. The answers to the questions are disclosed at various points in the chapter. Prior to reading the chapter, you may wish to try your luck at the quiz.

T   F   1. There is a best way to teach a new work to a group, and the prospective teacher should learn and use that method.

T   F   2. In learning new music, a performing group should first get the notes right and then work on interpretation.

T   F   3. Students learn better when they understand the reason for what they are doing.

T   F   4. Children in elementary school can learn the basic points of a subject if it is properly structured for them by a teacher.

T   F   5. The most effective way to correct the performance of a particular rhythmic figure is for the teacher to tell the students how to do it.

T   F   6. Thinking, especially in solving difficult mental problems, is a skill that is developed through practice in much the same way that physical exercise builds muscles.

T   F   7. General ideas are usually remembered better than particular facts.

T   F   8. If you want to learn to play a Mozart sonata, you will get better results if you practice it for two hours on each of the last two days before your lesson than if you work on it for thirty minutes for the six days preceding your lesson.

T   F   9. If a performing group cannot get a passage right, the students should go over it again and again until they can do it correctly.

T   F   10. Because people remember so little of what they learn in school, teachers should concentrate on seeing that the students enjoy music, whether learning takes place or not.

Although there is a little truth in each of the ten items on the quiz, seven are false. Which are correct and which are incorrect is not the point at this moment. What matters now is that each answer calls for an assumption about how music is best learned. Just as teachers reveal their beliefs about the purposes of school through their actions (see Chapter 3), teachers make decisions based on their fundamental beliefs about learning, whether they realize it or not. These basic principles have a strong bearing on what happens in music classes.

Virtually all students enrolled in teacher education programs are required to take a course in educational psychology, which is intended to provide basic information about the learning process. For one reason or another, many music education majors do not gain such information from the course. One reason may be that the points are not applied specifically to teaching music, something that this chapter will do. Whatever the reasons, an understanding of how students learn is essential in becoming a good teacher.

TYPES OF LEARNING

Learning is a many-sided word. It can refer to kinesthetic or psychomotor skills, as when a violinist learns to shift from first to third position. Learning also refers to memorizing information, such as the fact that A above middle C vibrates 440 times each second or that Mozart was a composer of the Classical period. Learning may also mean problem solving. For example, a student may have studied some impressionistic music and its phrasing. When presented with a work by Debussy that is unknown to him or her, the student is able to phrase it properly. Finally, a person has learned a piece of music when he or she can listen to it with understanding or play it and convey its aesthetic intent.

For these reasons there is no one correct way to teach music. The answer to question 1 is "false." The appropriate method depends on the situation, the students, and what the teacher wants the group to learn.

Recognizing the fact that learning involves different areas of human activity, Benjamin Bloom and others have developed hierarchies or taxonomies (a word referring to classifying something according to comprehensiveness) for two types of learning, or what they call "domains." The domain of information and understanding, which is called the *cognitive domain,* was devised first. The *affective domain,* which involves feelings and attitudes, came some years later. Although Bloom and his colleagues recognized the area of physical skills, or what is termed the *psychomotor domain,* they did not attempt to develop a taxonomy for it. Elizabeth Simpson has constructed a widely accepted taxonomy for this domain. Such taxonomies are useful to teachers because they offer a better understanding of educational objectives and the comprehensiveness of test items.

The taxonomies for the three domains are presented later in this chapter in conjunction with the discussion of each type of learning.

MATURATION

Over the last two decades psychology has shown renewed interest in the topic of student maturation or readiness. This interest in the topic is due largely to the influence of one man: Jean Piaget. Piaget spent most of his long life observing the growth and development processes of children, with his own children being his main subjects for a number of years. While he did not engage in an extensive program of experimental research, studies conducted by others dealing with music and other areas have tended to support his findings (Zimmerman, 1971, pp. 18–21). Although he saw cognitive growth as a continuum, Piaget divided it into four stages: The *sensorimotor* stage covers the years from birth to two; the *intuitive* or *preoperational* stage spans approximately the ages from two to seven; the *concrete operations* stage lasts from about age seven to eleven; and the *formal operations* stage includes the years from eleven to sixteen.

These general stages should be considered in making decisions about teaching music. For example, the concrete operations stage is especially suitable for beginning skill activities such as playing instruments and reading music, but it is not a good one for conceptualizing about types or styles of music. The choice of song material should be influenced by the concreteness of the text, as well as the length of the song and its pitch range.

The age of the students is only one factor to consider with regard to readiness. Other matters make a significant difference, especially the children's previous experience and training in music. Because of their previous education in music, some children in the second grade can do tasks that some fifth graders cannot do. Also, the intelligence and the motivation of the students make a difference. In some music classes the students are selected, and this fact can greatly affect the level at which the group operates. The point is that not all students of the same stage operate in the same way.

Making decisions about the readiness of a class for a particular musical activity is a tricky matter that must be learned from experience. Some help is provided by the music series books, and some districts have curriculum guides that provide some ideas. Teachers should present material that is challenging to the students but yet not so difficult that it frustrates them. Beginning teachers should have two or three pieces of music of differing difficulty ready as backup in case the first choice seems not to be suitable. Most new teachers just out of college should incline toward having the tasks of music be on the easy side for the students during the first few weeks of school.

COGNITIVE LEARNING

As mentioned earlier, the cognitive domain includes the learning of factual information and the gaining of intellectual understandings. Here is an abbreviated version of the taxonomy for it as devised by Bloom, with a musical example for each level (1956, pp. 201–207).

1. *knowledge:* the ability to recall specific items of information without regard to the understanding of it (for example, naming notes on the bass clef)

2. *comprehension:* the ability to grasp the meaning of the material, including interpretation, translation, and prediction (for example, understanding the function of the tonic chord in tonal music)

3. *application:* the ability to use material in new situations (for example, finding the tonic chord in a number of different pieces of music)

4. *analysis:* the ability to divide material into component parts so that the underlying structure is understood (for example, describing the factors in a piece of music that characterize it as romantic in style)

5. *synthesis:* the ability to put parts together to form a new understanding through new structures or patterns (for example, the development of a new description of the effect of chromaticism in Wagner's music)

6. *evaluation:* the ability to judge the value of material for a given purpose (for example, the ranking of Wagner's music dramas in terms of their use of the characteristics of romanticism)

In addition to these six levels, Bloom and his associates divided each level into several subcategories. However, the particulars of each level in the taxonomy are not nearly as significant as the general idea of the increasing comprehensiveness and complexity with each level. The taxonomy should not be interpreted to mean that the lower levels are of less value than the upper levels. Some knowledge and facts are needed, just as comprehension, analysis, and evaluation are needed. What teachers should avoid is emphasizing any one level while ignoring the others.

The call for encouraging students to think at the higher levels of the cognitive taxonomy has been given special attention in recent years under the rubric of "critical thinking." Some applications of the ideas of critical thinking have been applied to music teaching, especially in the MENC publication *Dimensions of Musical Thinking.*

Ways of Cognitive Learning

Psychologists do not agree on how learning in the cognitive domain happens. Some psychologists, often referred to as "neobehaviorists," believe that a person learns one bit of information after another in response to various stimuli. Eventually these bits of learning add up to form larger ideas and concepts. Another group of psychologists, often designated as "cognitivists," believes that learning consists more of grasping the "large picture" in moments of insight and that isolated bits of information are useless. There are several reasons for these two differing viewpoints: too much theorizing and not enough practical research, different testing situations, and differing ideas about what learning is. In recent years psychologists and educators have realized that both positions have merit and that people actually learn in both ways. Individual items of information are examined, but at the same time a person's mental processes organize that information into a meaningful pattern.

For this reason music teachers should consider both approaches in sequencing material that is to be learned. If a song is being learned, the teacher should help the students understand its text and general mood. At the same time, the teacher may need to correct a missed final consonant or an out-of-tune C sharp. Generally the answer to question 2 is "false." The right notes (particular items) and the proper interpretation (whole) are learned at about the same time. Certainly there should be no lengthy separation between them.

The issue of how students learn cognitive information is not the only topic of interest to educational psychologists, of course. Several other topics such as motivation, structure, sequence, reinforcement, and intuition have been studied, and the psychological insights that have been uncovered merit the attention of music educators.

Motivation

Teachers should build on the fact that most students have a built-in curiosity and desire to be competent in what they undertake. Although they may not act like it at times, they really do not want to be ignorant or to fail to learn. A number of researchers have observed this natural curiosity even among the higher animals. In one experiment a monkey worked at a complicated metal lock for ten straight hours. The experiment was terminated because the experimenter grew tired; the monkey was still going strong (Stolz, Wienckowskik, and Brown, 1975, pp. 1027–48). In another experiment, the researcher made a small peephole in a screen to watch a monkey. The peephole, however, soon attracted the monkey's attention, and when the experimenter tried to see through the hole, all he saw was the eye of the monkey looking at him from the other side of the hole!

Students seem to be motivated the most when they are presented with a modest challenge. To use an analogy from the world of athletic competition, you would not find the high-jump bar set at 1 foot very challenging; nor would it be set at 6 feet. You realize that in no way can you jump that high, so you would not be motivated in trying this impossible task. Teachers should set the "height" of the task at a level just a bit higher than what the students have done previously. For example, a band that can play grade 4 music without undue effort should be challenged with a grade 5 work.

Learning and motivation are aided if the students understand the purpose of what they are doing. Therefore, the answer to question 3 is "true." It is not enough for a teacher to expect students to learn "on faith." If the beginning violinists are told to maintain a straight left wrist, they should be shown how this practice helps them finger notes on the G string better, how it aids them in using the firm tip of the fingers on the strings, and how it allows for easier shifting to higher positions. The teacher of general music classes faces the same requirement. The class may have a project of filling twelve water glasses, one for each semitone. The teacher sees the point of this activity as an exercise in understanding pitch and tuning. The students need also to understand the purpose of the activity. It helps if the teacher can relate the water glass activity with singing in tune by saying, "Remember the water glasses we tuned yesterday? What happened when we got to a point where we needed just a little more or a little less water? We had to listen and work very carefully, didn't we? Listen to the pitch of your singing in the same careful way you did then."

Part of the process of challenging students is not only spelling out the objectives for what they are doing but also offering some criteria for learning. The more concrete and specific these objectives and criteria are, the better it is for the students. The objective may be the identification of songs from looking at the music, with the level of successfully completing the activity being to get three out of five correct. Students at all ages appreciate such specific conditions.

Structure

Perhaps the most important obligation of teachers is to teach the basic and fundamental ideas—the structure—of the subject. Every area of the curriculum, music included, has its basic knowledge and way of thinking, as was pointed out in Chapter 4. Probably the most frequently cited view of Jerome Bruner, the noted psychologist, is the belief that any given subject or area of knowledge can be structured so that it can be transmitted to and understood by almost all students (1966, p. 44). But this statement does not mean, for example, that an elementary school student can fully master the elements of tone row compositions. Rather, it means that the basic ideas of tone row music can be learned *if* presented in a simple enough fashion. As a result of such teaching a student would be able to discuss tone row music in a manner that a music theorist or composer would find recognizable. The answer to question 4 in the quiz is "true"; children can learn the fundamental ideas of a subject.

There is a certain progression in the way in which children acquire understandings. The first step in the sequence is in terms of action, which Bruner terms "enactive." The idea that actions and experiences are the basis for ideas and knowledge goes back at least as far as the seventeenth-century essayist John Locke:

> *Let us then suppose the mind to be, as we say, white paper, void of all characters, without any ideas; how comes it to be so furnished? . . . To this I answer, in one word, from experience. . . . I find I am absolutely dependent upon experience for the ideas I can have and the manner in which I can have them (in Russell, 1891, p. 35).*

What this means is that students learn about the beat in music by feeling it, not by memorizing a definition of it. Therefore, the answer to question 5 about the teaching of a rhythmic figure is "false." Talking about rhythm is not an effective way to teach it.

Two qualifications are necessary to make the experiences and actions effective. First, the experience must be of the right kind. A student can easily do the wrong thing—hold an instrument incorrectly, for instance. Second, the experience must be instructional. Not all learning experiences are equally instructional. Some require more time and effort than they may be worth. What is needed is to do significant activities correctly and not just to do something for the sake of activity.

Actions and experiences are especially important for children in elementary school, but they are also valuable for teenagers and adults. For example, holding a string instrument is best accomplished with a few words and the teacher showing the student. In fact, much learning takes place through students mimicking a teacher or other students. Although rote imitation and mimicking have sometimes been looked down on because they are not particularly intellectual ways of doing things, the amount of learning that takes place that way is enormous. Everyone learns to talk, sing songs, and perform most bodily motions by copying others.

Several important music educators have realized this fact and have developed ways of teaching based on it. One is the noted violin teacher Shinichi Suzuki. His pedagogical methods call for the students to listen to pieces of music many times prior to attempting to play them. Not only does this method present an aural model for students to copy in terms of phrasing, tone, and style, but it also appears to aid them in overcoming some of the technical problems encountered in playing. Hugh Tracey, an authority on African music, has described how time after time he has seen an African father teach his young son to drum by reaching around him from behind and guiding the boy's hands (1975).

The next step in Bruner's structure is the representation of ideas on a pictorial or "iconic" level. Teachers who use figures such as □ ○ □ to represent ABA form are using such a mode or representation.

The third and final step is symbol representation, which is primarily through language. Language makes for greater efficiency in acquiring information and also helps people to think more compactly.

As useful as language is, teachers should avoid overteaching by using more words or materials than are necessary for the students to learn. Concise summaries are more likely to be effective than are complex presentations, because complexity has a way of obscuring the main point. Good teaching (and textbook writing) should simplify and synthesize material to make it more easily understood.

Sequence

Teaching involves guiding learners through an appropriate sequence of activities related to learning the subject. The sequence in which the aspects of the topic are presented often determines whether or not the students will learn; they may successfully learn something when presented in one sequence and fail to learn if presented in a different sequence. Bruner feels that the sequence of progressing from activity to representation to symbolization is probably the best general sequence for learning. The progression in teaching music is probably one of moving from experience to symbolization, as is represented in the old dictum for learning to read music, "Ear it before you eye it." Sequencing should also involve presenting challenges to the students. If learning is to continue, students need to be motivated throughout the process, not just given one motivational boost at the beginning.

Reinforcement

Most psychologists agree that reinforcement or feedback is required in learning, because students need to know how they are doing. Not only do they need to know this; they learn best when they are given feedback soon after the completion of the effort at learning. If such information is provided before the learning task is completed, it can confuse the learners; if it comes long after the task is done, the learners may find it of little value because they have gone on to other things.

Reinforcement should be given in terms the learners understand. For example, if a child is trying to tap out rhythmic patterns, the feedback of this active type of learning should not be given in verbal explanations. A tapped version of the correct pattern should be provided so it can be compared with what the student did.

The word *reinforcement* can call up thoughts of rewarding correct answers with pieces of candy, merit points, words of praise, or other types of extrinsic motivation. Sometimes rewards are given to reinforce learning, especially to encourage proper behavior in class under the rubric of "behavior modification," which is briefly described in Chapter 16 in conjunction with managing the classroom. The use of extrinsic rewards is usually successful under some short-term circumstances, but it is questionable over a long period of time. A student should not expect to be rewarded for each bit of learning in each subject year after year. (One could conceivably grow very tired of M&M's or begin not to believe the teacher's favorable comments!) Rather, the goal of education is self-sufficiency in which the students are not dependent on reinforcement by teachers. The "reward" then becomes what is gained from the learning activity.

Intuition

There are times when teachers should challenge students to use their intuitive sense and make what is sometimes called a "perceptive leap" in attempting to discover a relationship or pattern. The elementary school music teacher might say: "The first section of the piece we just listened to was rather fast and somewhat loud; the third section was even more loud and just as fast. But the second section was quiet and smooth. Can you think of a reason why the composer might have made the second section different?" It is hoped that the students would come to a conclusion about the need for contrast in the music.

As valuable as these perceptive leaps and techniques of "discovery learning" are, they are not suitable for many learning situations. Such learning requires much time and skill on the part of the teacher. What seem to be most useful for student discovery are basic principles that account for important aspects of the subject. Asking students to assume the responsibility for some of what they learn requires teachers who are bright and flexible and who have a thorough knowledge of the subject. Such teaching also demands patience on the part of the teachers. When it is successful, however, the time and effort are well worth it in terms of what the students gain from the experience.

Part of the success of having students make perceptive leaps and discover things for themselves stems from the fact that it involves them in the learning process. When students are involved, they usually learn better.

Other Aspects of Cognitive Learning

In addition to the basic points just presented, two other areas of cognitive learning merit some attention. These are the matter of transfer from one subject matter area to another and the factors that encourage students to remember what they have learned.

Transfer. Transfer occurs when something learned in one area is applied to another area. For example, the idea of transfer can be traced back to the ancient Greeks, who believed that one's mind was disciplined by schooling. They thought that the mind was like a muscle that must be exercised until it became strong; then it could learn just about any new material. This idea, sometimes called "formal discipline," went unchallenged until nearly the turn of the twentieth century. The results of research dating back to William James, E. L. Thorndike, and Charles Judd demonstrate that the automatic transfer does not happen to any great extent. Therefore, the answer to question 6 is definitely "false."

What does research indicate about transfer? First, there is no such thing as *automatic* transfer. Second, transfer depends on the degree of similarity between the two areas involved. For example, studying the historical development of musical notation will not improve the students' understanding of Brahms's music, but studying Liszt's techniques of theme transformation will, because Brahms also uses theme transformation extensively.

Teachers can teach for a greater transfer of what is being taught. If the students play a particular rhythmic pattern by rote, they may not do much better on that pattern when it is encountered in another work. On the other hand, if teachers teach the students how to recognize aurally and visually the relationships among the note values, then what is learned has a greater chance of being applied to other situations.

Teachers should jog the students to think about other applications of what is being learned. One way to do so is by questioning. "How does the articulation in this piece compare with the articulation in the piece we just finished rehearsing?" "What kind of cadence occurs just before the tempo changes?" Too often students do not apply what they learned in music theory or literature classes to their performance of music. If they try to apply that knowledge to the music they perform, then more of it will transfer.

Memory.   Remembering what has been learned is a major goal of education. Sometimes the importance of remembering is down-graded by saying that all students do is "regurgitate facts." However, without memory we would live only on a level of instinct and impulse. The real issue should not be the merits of remembering but rather the value of what the students are taught and asked to retain. This is, of course, a curricular question, dealing with what is taught, not the way it is taught.

There are several ways in which remembering can be encouraged. One is to present the material in its best light so that its usefulness is apparent. People on a sinking ship will remember a set of instructions about finding their lifeboat much better than will the jovial passengers just sailing out of the harbor. While teachers can scarcely make what they teach seem to be of lifesaving importance, they can help the students see where it fits into the subject in particular and life in general. When students understand the purpose of the material to be learned— which is suggested elsewhere in this chapter—they will remember better.

Although the use of examinations is occasionally criticized, studying material for a test does aid in remembering. A test provides students with an immediate reason for learning. The criticism directed at "learning to pass a test" would be better aimed at *what* the students are tested on rather than at the practice of giving examinations.

Teachers can also urge the students to concentrate on the ideas of the material, not on isolated, detailed information. Broad, conceptual ideas are remembered best. A few years after having taken a course in chemistry, for example, most people will remember generally what atomic theory is but have forgotten the atomic weight of iron. The answer to question 7 is "true."

The quality of remembering is affected by the quality of the original learning experience. Often what is forgotten was never thoroughly learned in the first place. This fact does not justify going over the same material repeatedly, but it does

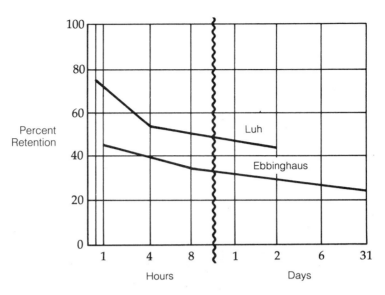

Figure 5.1   *Ebbinghaus curve of forgetting*

suggest the need for adequate clarity and comprehension when something is first taught.

Remembering is aided by the impact with which something is learned. This is one reason for using films and other visual aids in teaching. The more vivid the experience, the better it will be remembered. For example, placing key words in a lesson on the chalkboard does make a difference. One general music teacher played a fanfare on the piano and then announced in stentorian tones, "Today we will study *syncopation.*" If he did not overuse this gimmick, it grabbed the attention of the class and contributed to remembering.

Memory is aided when the students recognize a pattern. Nonsense material is much less likely to be retained, probably because it doesn't fit into a pattern. A series of numbers such as 1 11 12 5 14 2 8 7 is more difficult to remember than a series such as 1 5 2 6 3 7 4 8.

Finally, remembering is aided by frequent review. Most of what is forgotten fades soon after it is learned, usually within an hour. Hermann Ebbinghaus conducted the classic studies of memory, and from his research he plotted a "curve of forgetting." His curve has been confirmed by other psychologists, especially C. W. Luh, whose name appears in Figure 5.1 (1913, pp. 68–75). In practical terms, the forgetting curve indicates that the students will retain more if there is review at the conclusion of the class, in the next meeting of the class, and every so often after that.

The forgetting curve does *not* say that people forget 60 percent of whatever they learn. It's not that simple! Remembering depends on what is taught, how it is taught, the interests and abilities of the students, and much more. So the answer to question 10 is "false." Not only are concepts retained, but with good teaching methods many details and specific skills can also be remembered.

PSYCHOMOTOR LEARNING

An area or domain that psychologists have not given as much attention to as they have the cognitive and affective domains is that of psychomotor or skill learning. And it is an important domain to music educators, because much of what they teach involves skills such as playing or singing music, reading music notation, and hearing and notating aspects of music. In terms of the amount of attention given the three domains in school music instruction, psychomotor learning probably surpasses the cognitive and affective domains.

A taxonomy for the psychomotor domain has been devised by Elizabeth Simpson (1966) and is as follows:

1. *perception:* the awareness of the object and relationships through the use of the sense organs (for example, hearing and feeling the distance between the pitches of the major triad on the piano)

2. *set:* the readiness for an action (for example, learning the correct position for playing the cello)

3. *guided response:* the ability to execute an overt action under the guidance of a teacher (for example, playing the major scales on the piano during a lesson)

4. *mechanism:* the development of an automatic learned response (for example, when playing the piano, the maintaining of the Alberti bass pattern in the left hand while concentrating on the melody in the right hand)

5. *complex overt response:* the ability to execute a complex set of actions smoothly and efficiently (for example, playing a Beethoven piano sonata well)

6. *adaptation:* the ability to change the execution of actions to make them more suitable (for example, while playing piano in a piano trio, the adjusting of performance of the part to fit better with the other two players)

7. *origination:* the ability to develop new skills (for example, Franz Liszt's adapting the techniques he heard in Paganini's violin playing to piano compositions)

As with the taxonomies for the cognitive domain, the higher levels of the psychomotor taxonomy are marked by increasing complexity.

Psychomotor skills are especially interesting to teachers and psychologists for a number of reasons. One reason is the limited control of the mind over muscular functions. If the mind had to tell every muscle what to do for a simple action like walking, it would require several minutes to take one step. It has been calculated that 512 muscle settings are involved in striking just one key on the piano (LaBerge,

1981, p. 184). It is apparent, therefore, that much of the control over the muscles in carrying out the skill tasks comes from lower orders of the nervous system. While the mind may occasionally intervene—and is needed to start the muscular process going—other parts of the nervous system largely guide the many muscles involved.

Exactly how the muscles and nerves operate in executing an action is not fully known. Therefore, it is only partially clear how best to teach psychomotor learning. Some of the same guidelines that operated for learning in the cognitive and the affective domains seem to apply; for example, skills are learned in units or patterns, as they are in some cognitive learning (LaBerge, 1981, pp. 190–91). But other guidelines from those domains do not apply. However, some guidelines for learning skills can be offered that appear to help.

Distributed Practice

Educational psychologists have found that it is far more efficient to learn a skill in numerous short sessions than it is to learn the same thing in a few long sessions. Some psychologists refer to this principle as "distributed effort," others as "distributed practice" or "spaced practice." In a classic experiment by D. O. Lyon, the subjects learned stanzas of poetry (1914, pp. 85–91). When two stanzas were learned in one sitting, it required .38 of a minute per stanza. However, when one hundred stanzas were learned in one session, it took 3.85 minutes per stanza, ten times as long for each stanza! The significant figure here is the amount of time required per unit being learned. So it is many times more efficient to practice an instrument for one hour each day of the week than it is to practice seven hours in one day. More learning takes place in the first ten minutes of practice than takes place in the next ten, and with each additional amount of study there is a corresponding reduction in the amount learned. The answer to question 8 is "false."

There are several other reasons for encouraging distributed effort in teaching. First, fatigue and boredom set in during long practice sessions, and the desire to improve is diminished. Second, mistakes are more likely to be repeated in a long session and become fixed in the response pattern. Third, forgetting is a learning experience because it shows what elements have been inadequately learned. If there are additional practice sessions, these weaknesses can be overcome. Fourth, a person tends to resist immediate repetition of an act, and this resistance continues as the repetition continues. Fifth, incorrect acts are forgotten more quickly than correct ones, and spaced practice allows incorrect responses to be dropped.

Music teachers must realize that it is better to leave something unfinished and come back to it another day than it is to overwork it. Negative threats such as "We're going to stay on this until it's right" are not effective. On the other hand, distributed effort must not serve as a means of escape from hard work. Persistence is still vital to good teaching, but persistence should not be confused with dull repetition. The answer to question 9 is "false."

The maximum amount of time that should be spent on any one activity varies with the amount of concentration required, the age of the students, and their interest in the activity. Students can work for about ten to twenty minutes on a piece of music or on a musical topic in the general music class. In a drill activity, which may require more concentration, the time should be shorter.

Singleness of Concentration

People can concentrate on only one muscle activity at a time. When concentrating, they let the remainder of their actions continue without conscious thought. The necessity for singleness of attention raises problems of priority when one considers all that is involved in making music. Tone, words, notes, and style are all present together, yet an individual can think about only one aspect at a time. The answer lies in emphasizing different phases of the music at different times and in forming good habits quickly so that they become automatic responses as soon as possible.

Developing good habits in making music is much like learning to drive a car. When a person first begins to drive, he or she must consciously think of each step: turn the ignition key, release the brake, set the transmission, step on the accelerator, turn the steering wheel. Eventually these actions become automatic; people can simultaneously drive and carry on a conversation.

Although exaggerated for purposes of illustration, the following instructions are occasionally given to young violinists:

> *Hold the violin under your chin so that it points halfway between straight front and straight to the side. Keep your left elbow well under the violin and your left wrist straight; hold the neck of the instrument between the thumb and the index finger, like this; turn the left hand so that the little finger is nearest you.*
>
> *Now, the bow is held in the right hand with the thumb curved a bit so it touches the angle between the stick and the frog; lean your hand inward so the stick crosses under the index finger at the middle joint; the little finger regulates the balance and is curved so only the tip touches the top of the stick. The wrist is flexible but not flabby; the muscles of the bow arm are relaxed, just tense enough to move the bow properly. Now the bow is drawn at a 90-degree angle to the strings. Don't let the angle change as you approach the tip. Remember, you draw the bow gently across the string—don't scrape or bounce it.*

Then pointing to the music, the teacher says:

> *The note on the second space of the treble staff is A.*

If the student hasn't given up by now, the teacher may go on:

> *There are four beats in a measure. You know what beats are, don't you? Each note of this kind, with no stem and not filled in, gets four beats. Now we can figure out all the other note values mathematically.*

At least one thing can be said about this example of teaching, which violates the idea of experience as the basis for learning and can only bewilder most students: It is thorough.

AFFECTIVE LEARNING

The domain that includes the learning of attitudes and commitments is the affective domain. Bloom and his colleagues developed the following taxonomy for it (1964, pp. 176–85).

1. *receiving*: the willingness to pay attention (for example, being willing to listen to a musical work)

2. *responding*: the willingness to participate in an activity (for example, taking part in the singing of a song)

3. *valuing*: the placing of value on an object or activity (for example, buying a recording of a piece of music or checking it out of the record library)

4. *organization*: the bringing together of different values and resolving conflicts between them, and the building of a consistent value system (for example, a concern for the preserving of the music of other cultures, even though one does not fully understand or appreciate all other cultures)

5. *characterization by a value*: the maintenance of a system of values over a long period of time so that it is consistent, pervasive, and predictable (for example, consistently supporting music through attending music programs, buying recordings of music, and making contributions to the local symphony orchestra)

The main difference between this domain and the cognitive domain presented earlier in this chapter is the increasing attitude commitment rather than intellectual abstraction with each higher level.

APPLYING PSYCHOLOGICAL PRINCIPLES

The findings of psychology do not provide music teachers with step-by-step recipes for successful teaching. Rather, they supply the ground rules that teachers should follow. If teachers will evaluate their work according to these principles, their chances for effective teaching will be greatly improved. They can check their work out with questions such as these:

Was the lesson of reasonable difficulty for the students?

Did the students experience music or just hear words about it?

Were the aesthetic qualities of the music brought out?

Were the students involved in the learning activity?

Were the students given reasons for what they studied?

Did the students gain general understandings in addition to useful information?

Was the material presented in a way that encouraged remembering and transfer to other musical situations?

If the learning involved acquiring skills, was the effort distributed over a span of time? Was the students' attention focused on one aspect of the skill at a time?

Was the lesson presented so that it encouraged positive attitudes toward music?

These and other questions are also valuable in planning as well as in evaluation. When questions are based on solid psychological principles, they can guide teachers in how they should teach.

Questions

1. Arrange these cognitive activities in order from the most specific to the most comprehensive:
   (a) deciding what features of a work make it more suitable for flute than violin
   (b) knowing that Franz Schubert was born in 1797
   (c) arranging an organ work for brass choir
   (d) being able to explain that an art song is a musical setting of a text for solo singer and piano

2. Suppose that a band director wanted to teach the band about the form of a march.
   (a) If he or she were a "neobehaviorist," what general steps might be followed?
   (b) If he or she were a "cognitivist," what general steps might be followed?

3. What principles of learning are expressed in the old saying in teaching music, "Ear it before you eye it"?

4. Describe five ways in which teachers can increase the chances that the students will remember what they have learned.

5. How can teachers increase the chances that learning in one area might transfer to another?

6. Arrange these psychomotor activities in order from the simplest to the most complex:
   (a) playing the violin with correct right- and left-hand position
   (b) concentrating on the phrasing of a melody while playing all the notes correctly
   (c) creating a new set of bowing exercises for violinists
   (d) playing a violin etude with all the notes correct

7. What is the principle of "distributed effort" or "spaced practice?" In which domain of learning does it apply?

8. Arrange these affective activities in order from the least to the most commitment or interest:

   (a) The general music class elects to watch a videotape on a piano competition instead of one on stock car racing.

   (b) The general music class members pay attention during a report on black spirituals and ask intelligent questions afterward.

   (c) The general music class members stay in their places and stop talking while a record is played, but many of them look out the window or daydream while doing so.

   (d) Some of the general music class members become so interested in music that they sign up for chorus in high school.

References

Bloom, Benjamin, et al. *Taxonomy of Educational Objectives. Handbook I: Cognitive Domain.* New York: David McKay, 1956.

Bloom, Benjamin, et al. *Taxonomy of Educational Objectives. Handbook II: Affective Domain.* New York: David McKay, 1964.

Bruner, Jerome S. *Toward a Theory of Instruction.* Cambridge, Mass.: Harvard University Press, 1966.

Ebbinghaus, Hermann. *Memory.* Trans. H. A. Ruger and C. E. Bussenius. New York: Teachers College, Columbia University, 1913.

LaBerge, David. "Perceptual and Motor Schemes in the Performance of Music Pitch." In *Documentary Report of the Ann Arbor Symposium: Applications of Psychology to the Teaching of Music.* Reston, Va.: Music Educators National Conference, 1981.

Lyon, D. O. "The Relation of Length of Material to Time Taken for Learning and the Optimum Distribution of Time." *Journal of Educational Psychology,* V, 1914.

Russell, J. E. *The Philosophy of John Locke,* extracts from *The Essay Concerning Human Understanding.* New York: Holt, Rinehart & Winston, 1891.

Simpson, Elizabeth. *The Classification of Educational Objectives, Psychomotor Domain.* Final Report. Urbana, Ill.: College of Education, University of Illinois, 1966.

Stolz, S. B., L. A. Wienckowskik, and B. S. Brown. "Behavior Modification: A Perspective on Critical Issues." *American Psychologist,* 30, no. 11, 1975.

Tracey, Hugh. Personal conversation, Mexico City, September 1975.

Zimmerman, Marilyn P. *The Musical Characteristics of Children.* Reston, Va.: Music Educators National Conference, 1971.

CHAPTER 6

Teaching General Music

For at least half a century educators have been trying to agree on what type of school is best for students between the ages of ten and fifteen. Seventh graders, for example, are included in any one of several grade arrangements: elementary schools containing grades 1–8, secondary schools containing grades 7–12, junior high schools containing grades 7–8 or 7–9, and middle schools containing grades 5–8 or 6–8.

Music educators have shown no more consistency than other educators in the naming and teaching of the music course for most of the students at this age. The term *general music* is widely applied to junior high and middle school nonperformance courses consisting of varied musical experiences, and the course is so defined in this book. Some general music courses are taught at the high school level, however, and the term is also applied by some music educators to the elementary school basic music program.

STATUS OF GENERAL MUSIC

The scheduling arrangements for general music classes differ widely. Some of these classes meet daily throughout the year; in some situations they meet daily for a block of time such as one semester or nine weeks. Some meet twice a week, and in a few cases they meet only once a week.

Whether or not the course is required also varies. Some schools require all students not in the instrumental music program to take general music in sixth and/or seventh grade, and others hardly require the course of anyone. Only occasionally are the students in music organizations included, which means that the more interested and able students are not in general music. Some schools group the students homogeneously according to academic ability, and this grouping carries over into music. Others have classes composed entirely of girls or boys. (The arrangement makes it easier to meet the special musical needs and interests of each sex.)

In some school systems the general music course in the junior high and middle schools is the first instruction in music the students receive from a music specialist. In other school systems, the students have a strong background in music because of the elementary school experiences.

American music education has an enviable record in terms of producing outstanding performing groups at the secondary school level, but its accomplishments in the teaching of general music classes in its secondary schools are not very impressive. Part of the reason for this discrepancy between performance and nonperformance courses lies in the interest music teachers have shown in the two areas. Some teachers consider the general music class as a feeder program for high school organizations. Others see it as a recreational period in which it doesn't matter much if the students learn anything. Many teachers of general music would rather be directing high school groups, and they simply have not given general music classes much attention and thought. As a result, a number of junior high and middle schools have reduced or eliminated general music. From the early 1960s to the early 1970s, enrollments in general music fell by over 5 percent (Hoffer, 1980, p. 20). Although a few music educators have worked hard to make general music the heart of music education for students in junior high and middle schools, they have not been able to reverse the long-term downward trend nationally.

GENERAL MUSIC IN HIGH SCHOOLS

Until recently general music in grades 9–12 was only a small footnote on the page of statistical information about music education in American schools. That could change drastically in the next few years. Between 1979 and 1987 the number of states mandating some type of fine arts study for high school graduation jumped from two to twenty-six (Council of Chief State School Officers, 1985, p. 22). When states began improving their schools, nearly half of them wisely decided to add the fine arts to their graduation requirements.

These recently enacted fine arts requirements offer music educators an opportunity that comes along only rarely. Basically, music is an elective subject as of this writing. Only one student in three takes a music course during his or her four years of high school, and the proportion for any one year is only about one in seven (National Center for Educational Statistics, 1984, p. 63). Now many states are saying that every high school student must take a class in the fine arts in order to graduate. This means that about 1.5 million students who have not taken music during their high school years will enroll in music or another fine arts course. The opportunity to teach this many more students boggles the mind.

Opportunities have a way of being seized—or fumbled. How could music educators miss out on this opportunity to move into the mainstream of the high school curriculum? It is not difficult.

1. Fail to be interested in students other than those in performing groups. Generally speaking, the more musically motivated and able students are in performing groups, and teaching the less able students has not been seen as a way of achieving recognition in the profession. Classes for these students lack the visibility that performing groups enjoy, and no one ever wins a "first division" rating for doing a good job of teaching them. Music teachers are no different from other teachers: Given a choice, they would prefer to teach the better students and have the accompanying opportunities for recognition.

   The attitude of teachers is especially crucial because in the initial years at least the classes in general music at the high school level will need to be taught by choral and instrumental teachers as a part of their teaching load; there won't be enough classes to provide a full-time job for a specially trained teacher. The teachers' attitude will need to be one of achieving satisfaction through the growth of their students, a point mentioned in Chapter 2.

2. Fail to have a variety of content in the course. The world of music is wide and wonderful, and so should be the content of the course. It should not be confined to any one or two types of music. Rather, the course should include folk, popular, and art music, vocal and instrumental music, old and new music, and music from all parts of the world. Some of it should be familiar to the students, while other works and activities should be unfamiliar to them.

3. Fail to include a sizable amount of activity for the students. High school students, especially those who are not particularly motivated, will not be attracted to a course in which they only read about or listen to the teacher talk about music. There must also be plenty of opportunities for exploring and active learning.

4. Fail to achieve the appropriate level for the high school setting. The temptation for teachers will be to go one of two ways. One is to turn toward the approach found in the elementary and middle schools with its many brief encounters with musical topics. Not only is such an approach inadequate for a course that meets daily for academic credit and grades, it also has a negative effect on the attitude of the students, who think that the teacher is treating them as children.

   The other way is to turn toward the college-level music appreciation course with its more academic approach. It, too, is not suitable, because such an approach is too cerebral and too verbal for most high school students. It does not provide enough constructive activity to make the content come alive for them.

Because the possibilities for high school general music have developed so recently, almost no appropriate materials exist for use by music teachers. The MENC has published *Music in the High School: Current Approaches to Secondary*

School General Music, but more materials are needed from it and commercial publishers. And teachers need to be trained to teach high school music classes for students who are not in performing groups. In the meantime, the true character of the music education profession at the high school level will be tested to see if it really believes in "music for every child."

GOALS OF GENERAL MUSIC

General music classes operate under the same overall goals as the rest of the music program. The MENC publication *Music in General Education* presents a thoughtful attempt to establish a set of goals in terms of what general students (ones not in performing organizations) ought to know and be able to do by the end of their schooling. Although not a recent publication, it still presents the most carefully thought-out overall goals in terms of student outcomes. The goals can easily be grouped into the three domains presented in Chapter 5 and the three basic types of musical activities—performing, analyzing, and creating. The goals and the statements describing them are presented here in full for greater clarity and accuracy.

Skills

I. He will have skill in listening to music.
    The generally educated person listens with a purpose. He recognizes the broad melodic and rhythmic contours of musical compositions. He is familiar with the sounds of the instruments of the orchestra and the types of human voices. He can hear and identify more than one melody at a time. He can recognize patterns of melody and rhythm when repeated in identical or in altered form. He can concentrate on sounds and the relationships between sounds.

II. He will be able to sing.
    The generally educated person is articulate. He uses his voice confidently in speech and song. He sings in a way that is satisfying to himself. He can carry a part in group singing. His singing is expressive.

III. He will be able to express himself on a musical instrument.
    A generally educated person is curious. He is interested in how instrumental music is produced and willing to try his hand at making music, if only at an elementary level with a percussion instrument, a recorder, or a "social-type" instrument. He experiments with providing accompaniments for singing and rhythmic activities. He is familiar with the piano keyboard.

IV. He will be able to interpret musical notation.
    The generally educated person is literate. He understands arithmetical and musical symbols. He is able to respond to the musical notation of unison and simple part songs. He can follow the scores of instrumental compositions.

Understandings

V. He will understand the importance of design in music.

The generally educated person understands the structure of the various disciplines. He knows the component parts of music and the interrelationships that exist between melody, rhythm, harmony, and form. He is able to recognize design elements aurally, and he uses musical notation to confirm and reinforce this recognition. He realizes that the active listener can, in a sense, share in the composer's act of creation. By understanding how music communicates he has come to gain insight into what it communicates.

VI. He will relate music to man's historical development.

The generally educated person has historical perspective. He recognizes that music has long been an important part of man's life. He understands that its development in Western civilization is one of the unique elements of his own heritage. He is familiar with the major historical periods in that development and the styles of music which they produced. He has acquaintance with some of the musical masterpieces of the past and with the men who composed them. He relates this knowledge to his understanding of man's social and political development.

VII. He will understand the relationships existing between music and other areas of human endeavor.

The generally educated person integrates his knowledge. He has been helped to see that the arts have in common such concepts as design resulting from repetition and variation. Sociology and politics are recognized as pertinent to the development of art as well as to economics. He understands how literature and music enhance one another and together illuminate history. The mathematical and physical aspects of music are known to him through aural experiences as well as through intellectual inquiry.

VIII. He will understand the place of music in contemporary society.

The generally educated person is aware of his environment. He understands the function of music in the life of his community and he accepts some responsibility for exercising his critical judgment to improve the quality of music heard in church and on radio and television. He is aware of the position of the musician in today's social structure and understands the opportunities open to him to engage in musical endeavor both as a vocation and as an avocation.

Attitudes

IX. He will value music as a means of self-expression.

A generally educated person has developed outlets for his emotions. He recognizes music not only as a source of satisfaction because of its filling his desire for beauty, but also because of the unique way in which it expresses man's feelings. If he is not prepared to gain release by actually performing music, he has learned to experience this vicariously. He looks to music as a source of renewal of mind and body, as an evidence of beneficence in his life. He recognizes the importance of performers and composers and is grateful for the pleasure and inspiration which they give him.

X. He will desire to continue his musical experiences.
The generally educated person continues to grow. He seeks additional experiences in areas in which he has found satisfaction. He looks for community musical activities in which he can participate. He attends concerts and listens to music on radio, television, and recordings. He keeps informed concerning happenings in the world of music by reading newspapers and magazines.

XI. He will discriminate with respect to music.
The generally educated person has good taste. He has learned to make sensitive choices based on musical knowledge and skill in listening. He evaluates performances and exercises mature judgments in this area. He is not naive about the functional use of music for commercial purposes, nor to the commercial pressures which will be exerted to obtain what money he can spend for music (Ernst and Gary, 1965, pp. 4–8).

Where does the junior high and middle school general music course fit in in meeting these goals? It seeks to help adolescent students as much as possible in meeting these goals. It cannot do that by itself, of course. More time and instruction is needed for that to happen. Those goals, however, are the ones toward which the course is directed.

THE TEACHER AND GENERAL MUSIC

There is no area of music teaching to which the idea of a competent teacher, as presented in Chapter 2, applies more than to general music. The course demands ability, knowledge, and resourcefulness. Teachers of general music classes must accept and work with what one successful general music teacher calls, partly in jest and partly with respect, "the junior high mind." Teaching general music to adolescents is as much a matter of feeling and attitude as it is of knowledge and musicianship.

Teachers of general music need a well-developed sense of fairness in dealing with their students and an adequate supply of enthusiasm. However, once the students become enthusiastic, the trick is to keep it within bounds. There seems to be little middle ground between apathy and activity with young teenagers.

Teaching general music requires a broader knowledge of music than do most other areas of music teaching. Suppose the teacher is presenting a unit on religious music. Are there hymn tunes (with different words, of course) that are found in different faiths? What type of music is found in the services in Judaism? The *Shema* in Judaism and the *Credo* in Catholicism are each a basic statement of faith. Why are the two statements sung to such different music? These questions are only a sample of the kinds that can be raised by such a unit. And the teacher had better be prepared for such questions. The thirteen-year-old boy with a husky voice and a bad complexion and the twelve-year-old girl who giggles a lot can at times ask the most probing, serious, and difficult questions!

Teachers of general music should also possess at least rudimentary piano skills. While they do not need to be accomplished performers on the instrument, they must be able to play some accompaniments from the music series books. It also helps if the teacher can play the guitar. Again the teacher need not be a performer; simple accompaniment skills are what are needed.

The transition from child to adult that is so evident in junior high school students and its accompanying problems have perhaps been given more attention than they merit, as Chapter 15 points out. The new patterns of social behavior, the variety in physical and emotional maturation, the easily triggered emotions, and others are there, but many teachers (including the author) have found it not only possible but also enjoyable to teach students of this age in general music classes. These teachers have gone about their job of teaching without being conscious of the fact that these students and this course were supposed to be a "problem." There are difficulties that apply particularly to general music, but then there are difficulties in teaching music at any level or in any type of course. General music in the junior high and middle schools is not all that different.

Characteristics of Successful Teaching

Presents Definite Content.   Young teenagers need music instruction that is simple, unvarnished, and direct. They learn best from a straightforward approach and a clear understanding of what they are to do. They tend to take song texts literally, and they do not appreciate flowery or subtle messages in them. Some students at this age reject songs that they think are for elementary school students, whether their perception of what is used at that level is accurate or not. They like works like Aaron Copland's *Lincoln Portrait*. It is a work about a real person whom they admire; some of its music is derived from folk music sung and played by Americans around the time of the Civil War; its moods are easy to distinguish, plus the narrated lines make the meaning of the work very clear.

Many general music teachers have found that keeping notebooks and logs improves learning. The students keep an account of what the class has done— the songs sung, the records listened to, and the topics studied. In some cases, the students are encouraged to supplement the notebook with pictures and articles from newspapers and magazines, reports on reading or records listened to outside of school time, and a list of questions that come to mind as a topic is studied. Every so often the teacher calls for the notebooks and looks them over, possibly using them in helping to determine a student's grade. The notebook idea does have one drawback. Students who have verbal ability can handle such a project easily, but students who are weak in reading and writing find music another course in which success depends on those skills. Therefore, the notebook should never be the only factor by which grades are determined.

Other concrete evidence of learning in general music classes includes putting things on the chalkboard or charts. Some classes post a list of the songs they have learned. Even the criteria for deciding if a song is learned can be concrete. One set of criteria might be: (1) The song must be sung correctly. (2) Everyone in the class must join in singing the song. (3) One verse should be sung from memory. (4) The song should be sung with the right expression. Other ideas for charts include the singing ranges of the class members, the number of music events each class member has attended, and the like.

Achieves Results Quickly.   Early adolescents are an impatient lot. They want to see results—quickly. They do not enjoy working on something that might produce results a couple of weeks from now, unless they can see some progress in the meantime. Therefore, most of what is studied in general music classes should be completed (or a stage of it completed) within one or two classes. Leaving a point on Wednesday to be completed when the class meets again on Monday is not successful. By Monday the interest will have waned and some of what they learned on Wednesday may have been forgotten.

General music teachers need to develop "shortcuts" when teaching something so that results can be achieved quickly. For example, rather than teach the tonic and dominant chords in the common keys, name the notes in each chord, describe the tonal relationship between them, and explain how to derive the proper chord from the symbols I and V⁷ and F and C⁷, the teacher can say: "Here's the autoharp. When we sing 'The Cowboy's Lament,' Jason, play the F chord when I hold up one finger. Play it once on each heavy beat. When I hold up five fingers, push the C⁷ button, one chord to the measure. Just follow the number of fingers."

Shortcuts, which get quick results without an understanding of what is behind the action, may raise the question "When do the students finally gain an understanding of what they are doing?" The answer is that the points needed for an understanding will be taught in subsequent general music classes. The teacher might later ask: "How many white keys is it from F to C? . . . All right, suppose we wanted to start singing with the G chord instead of F. What chord would we substitute for the C⁷ chord?" Or the teacher might have pupils work at the piano to discover the notes in the F chord. Or in another meeting of the class they could sing simple harmonic progressions such as these:

The class can sing the chords on a neutral syllable. They can sing the appropriate chord as the teacher calls it out by name or number while the melody is played on the piano by a student or the teacher. Better yet, the teacher can hold up the right number of fingers for the chord number, so that there are no unneeded sounds intruding on the music. Different inversions of the chords can be tried, and the class can decide which they prefer. The class can be divided, with one section singing the melody to a song while the other half sings the chords.

The basic point here is that results be observed by the students rather promptly. Also, the experience with the chords was presented first, and then the class began to explore some of the aspects of harmony that contributed to what they had been performing. This learning sequence follows the suggestions presented in the preceding chapter.

Relates to Students.   Relating the subject of music to early adolescents is crucial. Sometimes teenagers feel that much of what they study in general music class is not immediate or vital, like songs about a girl in Italy or pretty flowers, or information about an inverted theme by a composer who lived nearly two hundred years ago. If they could see some connection between their lives and what they study, they would be more interested in the class and learn better.

The use of popular music comes first to mind when the topic of relating to students is raised. And there is much to commend using popular music in general music classes—within limits. However, no class should spend the majority of their time on any one type of music. That would be a serious violation of the criterion of balanced content discussed in Chapter 4. The overuse of popular music would also violate the criterion of teaching the students what they don't already know. As Bessom, Tatarunis, and Forcucci state:

> It is important to emphasize that the teacher who uses popular music should avoid adopting the "disc jockey approach," playing popular tunes one after another with little or no concern about how they relate to the lesson at hand. Such an approach uses popular music merely as entertainment, as a time filler, or as a reward when students have behaved well during the "teacher's portion" of the class. The purpose of general music class is to educate (1980, pp. 89–90).

Nor is popular music a cure-all for inadequate teaching.

What are the best uses of popular music in general music classes? One is as a "springboard" to certain topics. For example, the continuous bass line and beat in many popular works of music can be compared with the continuo idea in Baroque music. The same is true of the modal chord progressions of many popular songs today and the chord progressions in many folk songs. A second use is to attract student interest. Most of us, teenagers included, like hearing and studying some music that is familiar along with some music that is new to us; not everything need be new and different in music classes. Some music is just meant to be fun, and that certainly is a valid use of music. The fact that the class hears or sings some currently popular material also helps the teacher establish a better rapport with the class, and it helps break down the idea of two kinds of music, one for the students and another for teachers. The attitude should be one of interest in all types of music.

There are some problems for teachers in teaching popular music, however. Usually they are not as up to date on it as are their students, a point mentioned in Chapter 4. Also, the currently popular material has a short life, which makes it harder for the school to justify spending its funds for music and recordings of it. Finally, most popular music is not filled with musical subtleties and thematic development. One can quickly exhaust all that most of it has to offer.

There are other ways to make sure that what is studied in music class relates to the students:

1. The class can keep up to date on current musical events. Some teachers assign each student one week during which he or she is responsible for reporting music news to the class or preparing a bulletin board or chart. One class followed the writings of the music critic for the local newspaper, found them written in a language difficult to understand, and wrote a letter to the critic asking her why such language was necessary. Not only did the critic send the class a thoughtful and sensitive reply, she also published the students' letter and her reply in the paper. Alive and relating to students? Very much so!

2. The selection of music and activities also affects how well the instruction relates to the students. Gian-Carlo Menotti's *Amahl and the Night Visitors* is a serious opera, but its main character is a crippled twelve-year-old boy who stretches the truth, gets excited over things, and even is thoughtful of his mother some of the time. Early adolescents can relate to this opera, whereas many other operas would be of little interest to them.

3. A Student Talent Day can present performances by the students in the class who are studying or can perform on an instrument or can sing. Such a day can include not only piano and band and orchestral instruments but also such instruments as accordion and guitar and harmonica. And the music performed need not be long and complex; simple songs are fine.

Active Learning.   The point about involving the students, which was presented in Chapter 5, is especially important in general music classes. Several means for involving students are available, in addition to singing songs and other performing activities. Games and contests involve and motivate early adolescents. One technique is to have the class divide up into teams and then ask students for items of information about music. When a student misses a question, he or she has to remain standing and can't sit down until a question is answered correctly. (Unlike elementary school students, junior high school students are rewarded by sitting down, not standing up.) The questions can be about note names, musical symbols, themes, or songs. The teacher can play "stump the class," a game in which portions of musical works are played on the piano or tape recorder and the students attempt to identify the work. Scales, chords, and compositional devices such as canon can

also be included in this game. Students like friendly contests between themselves and the teacher.

The students should also be involved, as much as is reasonably possible, in making music, such as creating the second half of a phrase, determining the chords that best go with a melody, and deciding which instrument should accompany a song.

Builds on Student Maturity.   Most teenagers in middle school are anxious to leave childhood behind. Therefore, the general music class at this level should be different from the music classes the students had in elementary school, or at least they should appear to be different. Different songs should be sung and different musical works listened to, and a more mature approach is needed.

At this age, teenagers sometimes dislike and reject what they do not know or what differs from what they expect. The approach to this outlook might be something like the following one.

> *One thing that makes for the difference between an adult and a child is the attitude toward people and ideas that you don't know. Call it "fairness" or "tolerance" or whatever you want to, but a person who is growing up always gives a fair chance to something that he or she doesn't know. Now this piece of contemporary music may strike you as being pretty "far out." It has no regular beat, and it doesn't have a tune that we can sing, either. But give it a chance! Notice in what an interesting way the composer puts sounds together. Let's listen to it. Then while you are listening, think of one thing about it that you find interesting.*

Contains Variety.   Certainly the students in general music present an enormous variety of interest, abilities, and levels of musical experience. Attempting to meet the needs of all the students is a real challenge. Realistically speaking, it cannot be done all the time for all the students, but it certainly can be done some of the time for most of the class members. A variety of learning activities should be used in general music classes. One important way of meeting the variety of needs is through the individual or small-group learning activities mentioned next in this chapter. And there should be variety even in the activities the class works on together. The idea is similar to the reason for the multiple packages of cereal that one sees in the supermarket; at least one of the several kinds in the package will be liked. For example, many a boy who was self-conscious about his singing has succeeded in general music class by working with the sound-reproducing equipment. As a bonus, the assortment of activities guarantees that the class will be interesting for the teacher as well as the students.

Individual and Class Instruction

More than any other music course in the secondary schools, general music offers the most and best opportunities for having students do individual or small-group projects in addition to the usual group situation in which all class members do the same thing at the same time. In fact, a case can be made for including some activities that do not involve the whole class acting together. The diversity of student background and interests cannot be met by having the entire class always studying in unison. Some topics bore some students in a class because they already know the material, while other topics bewilder students with limited background in music. Some students are able to handle intellectual abstractions, although others can deal only with concrete information and experience.

Computed-assisted instruction is an excellent means of individual learning. Some uses are presented in Chapter 14.

Because the students usually come to a music room for general music, unlike the usual situation in elementary school in which the teacher goes to the classrooms, it is possible to have one set of equipment and materials serve many more students. The situation requires a smaller financial commitment. The music room should have equipment such as record or tape players with headphones and other equipment that permits independent study. Study carrels or small practice rooms are also very much needed for individual or small-group study.

The value of individual study in general music does *not* mean that the class should not also engage in some learning as a class. If the singing of songs is a part of the class activity, as it should be, that activity is hard to do on a small-group basis. There is a time and place for both small- and large-group instruction in general music classes.

ACTIVITIES AND MATERIALS

While hard and fast formulas for the content of general music classes should be avoided, teachers should usually plan for two or three different activities in each class period. One of these activities may be independent or small-group study projects. Most classes should include some singing, with the rest of the class time spent in listening and other types of music learning.

Singing

Singing in a choral group and singing in a general music class have different purposes and should therefore be approached differently. The singing of songs in general music class is less concerned with technique because the music is simpler and a polished performance is not necessary. Singing gives the students a personal experience with music, develops their most important means of making music, and contributes to their understanding of music.

How is singing best taught in general music classes? First, teachers should select songs carefully for range, number of parts, text, musical quality, variety, and application to other class activities. Then they should make themselves familiar with the song—accompaniment as well as voice lines—and think through the way to teach that particular song.

There are three possible approaches. One is to have the class hear the song without seeing the notation. This rote method is especially effective if the song has a mood that the class should grasp. The second method is to let the students hear the song as they follow the music in their books. This procedure is the one most frequently used by general music teachers and contains elements of both rote learning and reading. When a song is presented to the class by either of these methods, the teacher may sing it or play a recording of it. The teacher's singing is preferred, however, because a live presentation seems more immediate and effective. If the teacher is a skilled pianist, he or she can play the accompaniment while singing the song, but the piano should never substitute for the voice, because the piano's fading tones do not present a good model of singing style. In a third method of presentation, the teacher asks the students to attempt reading through the song at sight. This method should be employed occasionally because it develops skill in reading music. Whichever method is used to introduce the song, the teacher should be certain that the students know which part they are to sing and that they have the initial pitch clearly in mind. The teacher may indicate when the voice parts should enter by a nod of the head or by pointing.

The students' attention should be directed to the song's musical content. The song "Over the Sea to Skye" (on pp. 108–110) can serve as an example here. General questions can be asked first: "What's the mood of the song—happy, tender, athletic, dancelike, powerful?" For this song the class should be divided in half, probably according to changed and unchanged voices. If the students are experienced in sight reading, they can sing the melody when they have it. In most cases, however, they should hear the song through and then sing it themselves. The teacher can point out features of the song and ask such questions as "What phrases of the song are repeated?" "Are there some rhythm patterns that are repeated many times? Which ones?" "What is the form of the song?" "How do the two parts differ?" "Are there some places when the two voices sing the same music?"

At this point the teacher must decide what the class should do next with the song. Wrong notes may be the main flaw, or the students may indicate a lack of concept of the mood of the song by singing mechanically or in a style that doesn't suit the music. Perhaps a certain rhythmic pattern is being sung carelessly. Maybe the students are taking breaths in the wrong places or failing to make any dynamic changes. The class should work on trouble spots and then sing the entire song again.

Depending on how quickly and how well the class has learned the song so far, the teacher must decide whether to go on or to set it aside for the day. In any case, further study should ensure that the song remains technically correct and that the expressive qualities are kept intact. Each part may sing for the other and offer suggestions for improvement. A stanza may be read aloud and its mood, important words, and melody discussed.

So far the students have concentrated only on the melody of the song. As is true of other music of this type, the melody is the essential vehicle for musical content of the song, so the students should learn it thoroughly before going on to the harmony parts. Most general music classes are able to sing simple

Over the Sea to Skye*

Words by Robert Louis Stevenson
Old Highland rowing song arr. by M.J.

Music and You. Grade 8. Teacher's Edition. (New York: MacMillan, 1988).

†Tacet (ta′ set) means that Part II will not sing until indicated.

part-songs, so teaching the three parts in this song presents no unusual problem. If the class is composed largely of soprano voices, as sometimes happens in the seventh grade, all students should learn the lower parts as well as the melody. This activity stimulates interest and encourages flexibility in adapting to another part. The class can be divided arbitrarily, each section singing its part alone and then with the others. Later the parts may be reassigned if the range of music permits.

For boys with changed voices it may be necessary to choose songs having a bass clef part. However, when treble clef music is of sufficiently good quality, it would be too bad to withhold it from the class simply because there is an imbalance in voice distribution. These boys can sing one of the parts an octave lower, or the teacher can write out a simple part for them. Other techniques include clapping, tapping feet, other bodily movements, chants, rhythm or orchestral instruments, and dramatizations.

The textbooks themselves suggest good possibilities for song enrichment. Some songs contain a picturesque text or definite rhythmic patterns, and they appear to be the more likely candidates for additional elements. Other songs seem complete without added parts or are inappropriate for instrumental accompaniment. If a piano accompaniment is used, a student can be assigned to learn it. The accompaniment should be added only after the song is learned, and even then not with every singing of the song. The students can begin to rely on the piano, and also it tends to cover up small errors in singing.

Listening

The procedures for helping students to improve their listening skills are basically the same for a general music class as they are for other music classes. A number of specific techniques are described in Chapter 7 in conjunction with the teaching of music appreciation classes. A few thoughts are offered here that apply particularly to general music classes.

1. The students should always be encouraged to listen for something in the music; they need to have a reason for paying attention. Never, never should they be told, "Just sit and listen." Sometimes the reason for listening can be to decide if a song was sung well enough, while at other times it can be to discover how a theme is developed or to identify a rhythmic pattern or specific instrument.

2. Whenever possible the class should be actively involved while listening. The students can keep track of the number of times a theme or subject occurs; they can also tap beats and rhythmic figures, follow a listening chart or simple score, or sing along with a theme. The need for an active student response is one reason why some of the textbooks for use in general music classes have sections for student responses to works to which they are listening. If nothing else, such techniques help to keep the students' attention on the music, which is one large step forward in developing listening skill.

3. The students should learn to analyze what they hear. At a level appropriate to their knowledge of music, they should be able to answer the questions "What did the composer do and how did he do it?" This suggestion does not mean that seventh graders should make the detailed analyses expected of

college music majors. Rather, it means being able to tell if a theme is developed or varied, if an introduction is slow and soft, if a melody is songlike, or if the music works up to a mighty climax of sound. A student is on the right path with an answer such as "Well, the music started with a burst of sound, with lots of fast notes in the higher instruments, mainly the violins, I guess. Then this was followed by a smooth, slow, songlike melody that wasn't high or low; it was an oboe or some instrument like that. I think the composer wanted a lot of contrast, because the two sections of the music are so different."

4. Listening sessions should seldom exceed fifteen minutes (including discussion) on any one work, and not a lot longer if more than one work is being heard. Early adolescents generally have a low threshold of boredom. Besides, they need other musical activities in addition to listening. This time limit means that some works with long movements should probably not be used in general music classes.

Creative Activities

Creative efforts, whether in general music classes or elsewhere, operate under two broad principles. One is that creating is an individual matter; very few songs and no symphonies have been composed "by committee." Even when songs are written as collaborative efforts, one suspects that one person composed the basic song and then others came along and made revisions in the original effort.

The other principle guiding creative efforts is that the initial stages are most successful if the students are given a great deal of structure. It is easy to forget that the great J. S. Bach began his composing career as a boy by copying parts for his uncle, a task that can hardly be thought of as creative. As a person becomes more proficient and experienced at composing music, then the structure can be reduced or removed. Teachers should not tell students, especially the unselected and inexperienced students in general music classes, "Create some music." That is about as effective as telling a nonswimmer, "Swim."

Although providing a structure may seem to limit creativity, it is worth remembering that very little music is composed or improvised out of "thin air." Bach, Beethoven, Brahms, Bartok, and most other composers worked with existing styles, which they modified only slightly, if at all. When improvising—whether it be Hindu music or American jazz—the performer usually works within understood "rules of the game." To give a thirteen-year-old a definite mold within which to pour his or her ideas is not demeaning. Instead, it suggests what actually happens in composing or improvising music.

Here are some examples of how students in general music classes might be provided with structure for their creative efforts:

1. The students can record short examples of various sounds from virtually any source. The sounds can then be edited and arranged into a short "sound composition." The original sounds can even be gathered with a cassette re-

corder, but they will need to be transferred to a reel-to-reel recorder for splicing and rerecording.

2. Sounds may be manipulated on the tape recorder. Changing the speed of the tape is one way. Changes in speed can be achieved by switching the number of inches of tape the machine plays or by holding the hand against the side of one of the reels. One track at a time can be recorded by placing a piece of tape over one of the recording heads. Then the tape can be moved to the other recording head, the tape rewound, and a different set of sounds recorded on the tape. The result is a counterpoint of sounds. Taped sounds may also be rerecorded and arranged in patterns. Reverberation may be added on some tape recorders.

3. The students may try adding an accompanying part (not just chords) to a song they know. The part could be as simple as a rhythmic ostinato, and it certainly could be more complicated, such as a descant played on a glockenspiel or metallophone. An introduction and coda could be added.

4. Students could change one aspect of a song that they know. For example, a song could be rewritten in a new meter, or ornamental notes could be added to the melody. Such efforts can easily lead to more complex variations on a melody.

5. The students could be given a piece of music containing only the rhythmic values of the notes and measure bar lines. They could then individually add pitches.

6. The students could be given a line of pitches with no rhythmic values or bar lines. They would then individually add different rhythmic values.

7. The students can be given a stanza of poetry, as well as some suggestions for length and allocation of note values. Individually they could attempt writing a short song based on the message and mood of the text. This suggestion is somewhat more difficult than the other six ideas just offered. It seems more appropriate for the music theory class, which is discussed in Chapter 7. Other suggestions for creating music are presented in that chapter.

Often the words *improvisation* and *composition* are used as synonyms, which is not quite accurate. A composition is something that is planned and thought about over a period of time and then written down or recorded. When someone improvises, it is somewhat extemporaneous and done according to the guidelines for the type of music being performed. Although it may on the surface seem to be a contradiction in terms, people learn how to improvise, just as they learn how to do other things. In some situations, improvisation is learned by going over and over certain musical situations, and slowly the performer improves in his or her ability to make up music. Many students in America today are taught to improvise in more formal ways by using method books and applying a knowledge of chord structure. It is difficult to tell if the formal way is any better than the trial-and-error method. In either case, extensive efforts at improvisation are probably beyond the ability of most students in general music classes. They lack the time or the knowledge of music to learn to improvise at a complex level. Also, unless the improvisation is done with the voice, the technical problems involved with playing an instrument must be overcome before a person can improvise on the instrument.

PLANNING FOR GENERAL MUSIC CLASSES

Traditionally, planning for general music classes has been based on units, each involving songs, recordings, and other class activities centered on a unifying theme or topic. The unit idea adapts well in a course that tends to be more broad than intensive in its approach to the subject, because units allow for variety in a class while retaining a thread of continuity. It is not the only means of organizing lessons in general music classes, but it is particularly well suited to that type of class.

The number of units designed for use in junior high and middle school general music courses has increased significantly in recent years. Not only are many units found in the music series books, but some are available on a unit basis as well. Actually, the amount of teaching material available far exceeds the time available for teaching general music classes. While teachers can create their own units, they seldom have the time or the resources to do as well as the published materials.

The types of units available for general music classes can be grouped in a number of different categories:

Choral music: Several units provide music for choral singing.

Learning to play instruments: The guitar and recorder are especially favored.

Music of different cultures: Afro-American, Latin-American, Far Eastern, and other types of music are presented.

Music of different types: Jazz, rock, program music, and electronic music are available.

Music and the fine arts: Some units present music in conjunction with other arts.

Careers in music.

Fundamentals of music notation.

This list does not, of course, exhaust all the possible units that teachers could develop. One can easily imagine a good unit on how feelings and attitudes are expressed in folk songs, another on virtuoso music, another on simple conducting patterns, one on performers and composers of today, and one on musical comedy and opera.

Planning for a general music class differs little from the planning that should be done for any type of music instruction, which is discussed in Chapter 17. Preparation should take into account three of the main components of the teaching process mentioned in Chapter 1: What? How? With what result? The question of why music is being taught does not need to be thought about for every class, although it does affect what is taught. Certainly the matter of the content of the class and the amount of learning that takes place needs to be carefully planned for.

Earlier in this chapter it was pointed out that the general music class may represent the first instruction many students receive from a music specialist. Unfortunately, it may also be the last. During high school the majority of the students will not be in the performing groups. Their contact with music will largely be as listeners, with only occasional participation in making music. This fact places a special obligation on music teachers to provide all students with experiences and skills that will help them find music interesting and valuable for the rest of their lives. When considered in this way, general music classes become a very important portion of the school music program, one that is certainly equal to the performing organizations. General music classes deserve the best efforts of music educators.

Projects   1. Share with other class members some of your experiences as a student in junior high or middle school general music classes. Describe the organization of the class, the type of activity carried on, and the strong and weak points of the course.

2. Plan a unit of music study of your own choosing. If songs are included in the unit, indicate a source for each of them, listing the book and page number. Identify precisely any videotapes or filmstrips that might be used, and collect several pictures that are suitable for bulletin board display. Describe any field trip or other activities that will be involved.

3. Decide on two compositions or sections of compositions by each of the following twentieth-century composers—Béla Bartók, Igor Stravinsky, Aaron Copland, Paul Hindemith—that would be suitable for using in a general music class.

4. Examine three operas and evaluate them for their suitability for general music classes.

5. Study the list of objectives from *Music in General Education* (pp. 97). Think of one or two ways in which a music teacher can help the students achieve each of the goals.

6. Select two currently popular songs that you think would be appropriate for use in a general music class. Give reasons for your selections.

Suggested　Andrews, Frances M. *General Music Classes in the Junior High School.* Englewood Cliffs, N.J.:
Readings　　Prentice-Hall, 1971.

Metz, Donald. *Teaching General Music in Grades 6–9.* Columbus, Ohio: Charles E. Merrill, 1980.

Swanson, Frederick J. *Music Teaching in the Junior High and Middle School.* New York: Appleton-Century-Crofts, 1973.

Music in the High School: Current Approaches to Secondary School General Music. Reston, Va.: Music Educators National Conference, 1988.

References　Bessom, Malcolm E., Alphonse M. Tatarunis, and Samuel L. Forcucci. *Teaching Music in Today's Secondary Schools,* 2nd ed. New York: Holt, Rinehart & Winston, 1980.

Council of Chief State School Officers. *Arts Education and the States.* Washington, D.C., 1985.

Ernst, Karl D., and Charles L. Gary, eds. *Music in General Education.* Reston, Va.: Music Educators National Conference, 1965.

Hoffer, Charles R. "Enrollment Trends in Secondary School Music Courses," Bulletin of the Council for Research in Music Education, no. 63 (Summer 1980), p. 20.

National Center for Educational Statistics. *Course Offerings and Enrollments in the Arts and Humanities at the Secondary School Level.* Washington, D.C.: U.S. Government Printing Office, 1984.

CHAPTER 7

Teaching Music Appreciation, Fine Arts, and Theory Courses

Courses in music appreciation, the fine arts, and theory generally emphasize study-ing music rather than making music. Seldom do these classes present public programs. Many of the students who enroll are not members of a performing organization, a fact that is even true of some of the students in theory classes.

Courses in theory, appreciation, and fine arts are needed in the high school curriculum, even if teachers of performing groups decide to enrich their rehearsals and even if the general music course mentioned in Chapter 6 becomes much more of a reality. There are two reasons for this. First, even if teachers of a performing group are very interested in enriching rehearsals, they can never devote as much time to theory or literature as a specialized class can. Second, if well taught, these classes involve the specialized learning that justifies a place in the school day and granting credit.

Should all high school students be required to take at least one course in music or fine arts? As implied in Chapter 4, the answer is "definitely." Many students take their last music or art course in the seventh grade, and they probably won't take another unless it is required of them. Thus, twelve-year-olds are re-ceiving their last instruction in a broad and challenging area of their culture. Nearly all other curricular areas are required in high school: four years of English, two or more courses in science, mathematics, physical education, and social science. The omission of a requirement in the arts suggests that the arts are not important enough to merit study by the many students. Some music teachers shy away from requiring music because a few uninterested students will be in the class. However, if education is to provide students with understanding and appreciation they do not currently possess, then it is the uninterested teenagers who most of all should be enrolled.

TO COMBINE OR NOT TO COMBINE?

Can music appreciation and theory be combined into one course to reinforce the learnings of each? They probably cannot be combined in the high school, although taken at face value it appears to be a good idea. The general students in the music appreciation course usually are not interested in theory, nor can they profit much from studying it. Moreover, at the high school level the study in each area becomes too complex and specialized to allow for an easy combination of learnings. With an autoharp and vocal chording, a class can examine the harmonization of a folk melody, but the autoharp and voices are inadequate to study the harmonic intricacies of César Franck. Finally, although the integration of music theory and music literature has been explored by many colleges, it has been attempted only occasionally, with infrequent cases of lasting success.

What about the combined arts course? There is much to be said for it from both a theoretical and a practical point of view. A practical advantage is the fact that in a single course the students learn about several different arts. Because the high school day is crowded, the idea of bringing several subjects together in one course is a tempting one. Also, theoretically the arts reinforce one another. A student who gains a concept of Neoclassicism in painting will often more easily grasp the idea of Neoclassicism in music. The fine arts do have in common an aesthetic value, and a similar mental process is required to understand them.

Conditions to Overcome

As good as the idea of a combined arts course is, there are three practical pitfalls that must be avoided for such a course to be successful. One pitfall concerns time. A one-semester course meeting daily meets about ninety periods. If painting, sculpture, music, drama, literature, dance, and some philosophy are squeezed into ninety periods, one doesn't need to be much of a mathematician to figure out that no subject is going to be covered adequately. Perhaps a little study is better than none at all. But if the existence of the fine arts course lulls the school administration and community into a sense of complacency about its educational effort in the arts, then the limited understandings gained by the students may be too high a price to pay. The first pitfall can be avoided by allocating enough time for music, which is probably most easily accomplished by lengthening the course to one year, and by not permitting the fine arts course to substitute for other courses in the arts.

High school students, unlike college music majors, are usually not familiar with any of the arts. Some curriculum theorists maintain that a combination of intellectual disciplines should be attempted only after one of the areas to be combined is understood rather well. Otherwise, the students wind up with virtually no understanding; $0 + 0 = 0$. There is much logic in the advice to avoid combining bits of knowledge from several different areas. Adequate time must be allocated to each art presented in the course.

The second pitfall concerns finding faculty for such courses. Few teachers are competent enough in several arts to teach a combined course. It takes more than a couple of courses in music to teach the subject well, and it is the same with painting, dance, and the other arts. Team teaching is sometimes the answer, but it is not easy to create a compatible team of a musician, an artist, a dancer, and a drama teacher. And even if they work well together, team teaching is "teaching by committee." The committee must find plenty of time to meet. Actually, many team-teaching arrangements fall into a pattern of "let's each take a turn," in which the students receive several short courses instead of one integrated course. Either competent teachers must be employed, or a genuine team must be formed, with sufficient time for planning.

A third pitfall is the tendency to draw false relationships among the arts, to force parallels that simply do not exist. For example, you cannot hear the stained glass windows of a cathedral in a Bach organ work; the chords that accompany a melody do not support the melodic line as the pillars on a Greek temple support its roof; artists and musicians mean different things when they use the word *rhythm*. Now, the arts do have some points in common: similar reasons for being, similar value, and similar mental approach. However, direct parallels are as impossible and false as attempting to draw a picture of three minutes of time.

This discussion is not intended to imply that the combined arts approach should be avoided. Not at all. A combined arts course can be very good when handled properly, but it can also be quite bad when not taught well.

Infusion of Arts in Other Areas

An idea that was promoted actively at one time involved bringing the arts into the study of nonarts areas of the curriculum. The idea was to infuse or enrich the other areas with the arts. Most of the trials of "arts in education," as the idea was often called, were confined to the elementary and middle schools. The results at these levels were somewhat mixed, but in no case did the enrichment of the curriculum with the arts have a detrimental effect on the students' learning (Boyle and Lathrop, 1973, p. 42).

Music teachers should support the inclusion of materials on the arts in any type of class. If music and the other arts are a significant aspect of culture, then they have something to offer many other subjects. However, in no way can such infusion be a substitute for an organized music program. When music is presented as an adjunct to other subjects, it is not treated in a systematic way. The results are generally the enrichment of the other subject but only a tiny increase in musical skill or knowledge.

MUSIC APPRECIATION

Courses of this type appear under many different titles: Music Appreciation, Music Literature, Music Understanding, Introduction to Music, and so on. Course titles containing the words *history* or *literature* imply specialized courses that are more appropriate for music majors at the college level. The term *music appreciation* has been abused and misunderstood in recent years and now seems to connote superficial and unmusical lessons. The title *music understanding* is preferred because it connotes knowing, as well as enjoying and appreciating. This chapter will utilize the more common term *appreciation,* however.

Purpose and Problems

The music appreciation course has three goals. First, it should give the students some basic information about music. They should become familiar with the literature of music, its styles, forms, vocabulary, and other aspects that contribute to a basic knowledge of the art. Second, they should learn to listen to music more intelligently and sensitively so that they can hear what is happening in the music itself. Third, they should learn to like music. The struggle is lost if the course causes them to turn against music and to avoid it after the course is completed.

Each of these goals is vital. If attention is focused on only one aspect of the course, it will be only partially successful. Just as a violinist needs more than one string on a violin to perform the Beethoven Violin Concerto, student listeners need more than one aspect of a music course if they are going to listen intelligently to Beethoven's Violin Concerto.

Content

What constitutes "basic knowledge" in music? This is a difficult question on which no two people will agree completely. Each textbook written for the course provides a partial answer. Although teachers may disagree with some of the authors' judgments, the books do provide a starting place for decisions regarding content. Another practical way to answer the question is to ask, "What do students need to know in order to be intelligent listeners at performances of music?" This "rule of thumb" guideline can help teachers in making decisions about the music, terminology, and the like to teach in such courses.

Whether or not a book is used, the course content should follow the criteria recommended in Chapter 4 for all music courses: The material should be representative of the world of music, learnable by the students, up to date, and fundamental to the subject.

Should some popular music be included in high school music appreciation courses? Definitely, but such music should not be the main fare of the course. The use of currently popular music is a good way to lead students to more substantial works, as well as let the students know that all types of music are valued and interesting. Every piece of music includes aspects of melody, harmony, and rhythm that can be studied and compared with works of art music. Also, there are some popular versions of art works, and they are especially suitable for comparison with their original version. The reason why popular music should not predominate the course is that then the course would not offer the students enough music information that they do not already know, a point made in Chapter 4.

A persistent problem is organization of the content. Some teachers favor a chronological approach; others prefer to develop the course around mediums or compositional techniques; others like to start with popular or folk music. No plan is without its strengths and weaknesses. The chronological approach is a natural organization because it is the way music developed. Starting with familiar music—whether pop or folk or show tunes—also has merit because it begins where the students are. Therefore, some combination of a "familiar music" and a chronological approach seems best. After getting the students involved in the course, teachers can present music more or less as it developed.

Listening

Certainly listening is fundamental to the art of music. People cannot appreciate what they don't hear. But they must have more than aural skills. The sounds they hear are transmitted to the brain, which organizes, interprets, and (one hopes) appreciates them.

Suppose that an art appreciation course devotes its attention to developing visual perception skills. Through studying fragments of paintings and pieces of sculpture, the students are drilled in recognizing aerial and linear perspective, chiaroscuro, negative space, color value and hue, and axis. Assume further that most of the students actually do learn to see such aspects of artworks and that their interest in the course does not wane during the tedious visual drills. How valuable is it for them to recognize chiaroscuro if they have no clear idea how it fits into the world of painting, which painters use it, what its effect is, how it relates to other factors such as perspective, and, indeed, what the fine arts are all about? Art appreciation students should be able to observe all the aspects of a piece of art, but they also need the knowledge to make what they see meaningful to them.

Unfortunately, hearing all that happens in a piece of music is not as easy as seeing all that is present in visual works of art. The parallel between visual and aural study is not a perfect analogy. You can take your time to study perspective in a painting. But music moves; the motion of the harmony, the appearance of a countermelody, and the sound of a different timbre can occur almost simultaneously. So training in listening, *if handled in a meaningful way,* is a valuable part of a music appreciation course.

Methods of Teaching Listening

Teaching nonmusicians to listen carefully is no easy job.* The students must be sufficiently motivated to put forth an effort, and they must possess the intellectual capacity to retain and make sense of the musical ideas their ears transmit to their brains. Teachers should persistently encourage and prod students to listen selectively. Besides asking, "Did you hear that?" or directing, "Listen for the melody in the clarinet," they can ask the students to verbalize about a specific portion of the music.

As a beginning, students can be asked to render some judgments about aspects of the music they just heard. For example, was the tempo fast or slow? Was the melody in a high or a low range? Was there much dynamic change? Was the beat steady? At first the students may not be able to hear details, so the obvious characteristics of the music are especially suitable for consideration at this point. General observations can lead to more precise listening ability as their study progresses.

Early in the course students often grope for the right words in discussing music. Certainly it is important that they have the correct idea, even if they can't phrase it properly. Correct terminology should be encouraged, however, so that confusion is held to a minimum. Quick reminders are helpful: "What's the musical term? Not 'rate of the music,' but _____ ."

In discussing music, students should not be asked to tell how they feel about a piece. Their reactions are personal property. Besides, any discussion involving feelings soon reaches the dead end of opinion and personal reactions. Instead, insofar as words permit, the students should analyze what they hear in the selections, not their own feelings about the music.

There are a number of techniques or gimmicks teachers can use to aid students in listening:

1. Help them to recognize canonic treatment, for example, as in the introductory part of Berlioz's *Roman Carnival Overture*. Exactly when the imitation starts, the teacher can say to the class, "Now—what's happening in the music?" After the section is done and the record or tape stopped, the class can attempt to answer the question. Teachers should generally ask several students in the class before they indicate whether an answer is right or wrong. If only a few students get the right answer, the section should be played again, with the same procedure. A third playing may even be necessary.

---

*The author recalls that until it was necessary to listen carefully to pass dictation tests in freshman music theory, he had never really listened before.

2. Take a work such as the last movement of Brahms's Symphony No. 4, the movement containing the chaconne. After becoming familiar with the chaconne theme, the students listen to the first five or six variations, with the teacher indicating each new portion as it appears. The students are told to write in their own words what happens to the original melody in each section. They should put down specifically what they hear in each particular variation. An answer is not acceptable if it merely says that the violins are playing the fourth section; the description should be specific. Exactly what are the violins doing? Are they playing in a rough style? Are they playing the very high notes in legato style? Are they playing the variation on the melody, or a contrasting line? If two students disagree on what is happening in a particular portion, the matter should be settled by hearing that portion of the music again, not by the teacher telling the class.

3. Count the number of times a melody appears in a work such as a fugue. The class can be asked not only to keep track of the number of appearances but also to write down how the subject or melody is treated. Does it come back in a low voice or in a high part? Is it complete? Is it played in the same style as the first statement? Is the countersubject played with the subject?

4. Ask the students what happens in the development section of a symphony. Assuming that they have heard the themes often enough to remember them, they are asked to indicate which theme is featured in the development and what is done with it.

5. Have the students follow the theme in one movement. This practice works well with Mozart or Haydn, because they present themes in a straightforward manner with well-marked cadences and transitions, and most movements are not long. Students need not write anything in this case. The teacher merely stops the recording and asks what is being done with the theme and what this indicates about the form of the movement.

6. Give some simple ear training, but not necessarily of the type given to music majors in college. The teacher can play two brief patterns of pitches, chords, or rhythms, changing one note in the second version. The students are asked to tell whether the two examples were the same or different, and if different, to locate what was changed. The class can also sing back a short phrase. Music memory is developed in this way. So that both ear training and notation are involved, a simple example can be written on the chalkboard, overhead projector, or individual sheets. The instructor plays the example but includes one error for the students to locate.

7. Ask the students to make a "doodle map." The idea is for the students to listen to a section of a work and make their own personal "map" of what they hear. These maps can take many forms. One person may chart the dynamics and textural thickness, another the pitch level, a third person the instrumentation, and so on. Most students will come up with unique maps that validly portray something about the music. One example of what a map might look

like is this picture of the first portion of the third or "Chester" movement of William Schuman's *New England Triptych*:

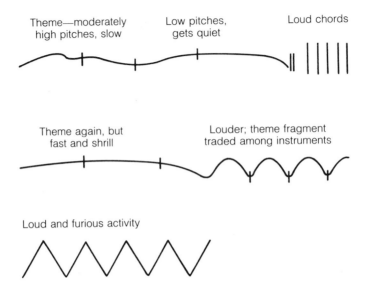

Theme—moderately   Low pitches,   Loud chords
high pitches, slow   gets quiet

Theme again, but   Louder; theme fragment
fast and shrill   traded among instruments

Loud and furious activity

The "doodling" aspect of the maps allows the students' minds to operate freely without the encumbrance imposed by words or standard notation. Many students find this freedom helpful.

8. Have the students follow notation. Most people can comprehend something from following notation, even if they can't read it. Themes can be placed on the chalkboard, projected, or followed in the textbook. A collection of simple line scores is helpful. Some line scores are included in the *Study Guide and Scores* that accompanies *The Understanding of Music.**

    A line score has several advantages: (1) It keeps the students' attention from wandering while they listen. (2) It helps them remember the music by providing visual support for their aural impressions. (3) It helps them learn instrumental timbres because the most prominent instrument at a given moment is indicated in the score. (4) The formal pattern is marked in the score so that nonmusicians can follow it.

9. Use a "call chart" or "blueprint." The teacher makes a chart listing the significant points in the music—changes of meter, instrumentation, tempo, texture, themes, and the like. The first important point is numbered 1, the second 2, and so on. Then as the work is played, the teacher can call or point out the numbers at the appropriate places in the music. If the students use the chart at times without the teacher present, the running time in seconds can be placed beside the call numbers. In this way the listeners know, for example,

*Wadsworth Publishing Company, Belmont, CA 94002.

that number 2 occurs 27 seconds after the music starts. All they need do is follow a clock or watch with a second hand. A blueprint is similar to the call chart but is a more graphic representation. A number of blueprints are available commercially.

10. Give listening assignments. For example, "Listen to the third and fourth movements of Tchaikovsky's Sixth Symphony and find out which movement has the faster tempo, which is generally louder, and which has the more clearly defined form." After a few weeks, rather than ask for a term paper, teachers can assign a listening project by suggesting a list of specific works to hear, or specific composers, or simply a certain number of major compositions from each stylistic period. The students listen to the music outside of class and prepare a report on it. In one way or another they must commit themselves on each piece heard by commenting on the form, style, unusual musical factors, or the expressive quality of the music. This eliminates the possibility of circumventing the assignment and encourages the students to listen carefully, rather than just put in time hearing some records.

11. Urge the students to listen to the same work several times. Only in this way will they become sufficiently familiar with it so that they can remember what they have heard. When one thinks how many times teenagers hear the latest pop tunes—pieces that are usually much shorter and less complex—it is easy to understand the need for repeated hearings of a piece of music. For this reason recordings of the music studied in this course should be easily accessible to the students.

    The role of memory in understanding is a vital one. When people hear music, they actually experience only an instant of sound at any given moment. This exact instant of sound can have meaning only if the hearers remember what they have heard prior to that instant and anticipate what they will hear in subsequent instants. Listening to music is like trying to view a picture that is entirely covered by a sheet of paper, with a small slit extending from the top to the bottom of the picture. The picture is seen only as the slit is moved across it. All that is in the picture on either side of the slit must exist in the viewer's mind in the form of memory or anticipation. In other words, the customary spatial comprehension of the picture is now changed to comprehension in time.

    Memory and anticipation also exist in relation to style. When trained musicians listen to a new work composed in a style familiar to them, they find it easier to remember what they have heard and to anticipate more fully what is about to occur. It is as though a slit were moved across pictures of similar subjects painted in a similar style.

12. Discourage using music as a springboard for personal fantasizing. Sometimes students enter a music appreciation class with the notion that they should visualize something concrete as they listen—ships sailing, sunsets, horses galloping. While some pieces are written to express feelings aroused by specific incidents, attention should be focused on what is happening musically. If

students need to be persuaded on the inability of music to express specific stories or pictures, the teacher can try one of two techniques. One is to make up a new and different story to fit a programmatic piece of music. Tell it to the class and ask them to judge as they listen to the record whether the story is the one the composer intended to describe. Play the record, and after hearing the students' opinions, tell the traditional story. The second method is to play, without mentioning its title, a short programmatic work, such as "The Great Gate of Kiev" from *Pictures at an Exhibition* or "Pines of the Appian Way" from *The Pines of Rome,* and ask the class to imagine a movie scene that would fit the music. Invite each student individually to describe the scene that the music suggests. Although the ideas usually bear some resemblance to one another, the details will vary sufficiently to impress the students with the fact that music cannot give accurate descriptions of pictorial or nonmusical ideas.

Aesthetic Sensitivity and Understanding

Besides gaining skill as listeners, students should understand the nature and value of the fine arts. Unless they sense their purpose—at least intuitively even if they can't verbalize it—they miss much of the reason for music as an art.

When students first enter a music appreciation course, they carry with them all their habits of thinking about subjects they study. They naturally expect music to be like the familiar academic disciplines, and they do not realize that if they are going to get the point, the *raison d'être* of listening to art music, they will have to reorient their manner of thinking. They should realize that the arts provide certain kinds of experiences, not "answers." They should learn to look for quality, not size or quantity, in a work of art. A student who claims that a certain pianist is best because he or she can play more notes per minute than anyone else is missing the point and applying a faulty, quantitative standard.

Teachers can encourage contemplation of musical sounds by playing a short example, sometimes only a few notes, from a recording or on the piano. A few seconds of silence should follow the example to allow the students to think about the musical excerpt. They should not be required to verbalize about each example they hear, however. If they are asked to express themselves about every musical fragment, they may spend the time thinking up what they will say if called on rather than contemplating the sound itself.

To stimulate the students to think about qualities in music and the arts, teachers can ask them to pair off paintings and musical compositions on the basis of mood, not subject matter. Sometimes students should be asked to explain their pairings. Another technique is to discuss or debate such questions as these: "Is photography an art?" "Does a ballet have more artistic quality than a square dance? Why or why not?" "Are both knowledge and intelligence necessary to appreciate works of art?"

Most students bring to the course mental habits that must be overcome if they are to gain an understanding of music as an art. One condition is the "pro-tective coating" most of us acquire to protect ourselves from the sounds that are around us every day. We learn *not* to notice sounds—traffic noise, background music, airplanes, talking that doesn't include us, and so on. This lifelong habit of not noticing needs to be reversed if listening to subtle and complex music is to be appreciated.

A second predisposition is the time sense that students have about music. In popular music nearly all the musical ideas are presented in the first thirty or forty measures; subsequent music is a reworking of the opening material. Art music involves the manipulation of musical ideas over much longer time periods. So when listening to art music, teenagers must greatly expand their comprehension of musical time.

A third condition involves dynamic levels. After hearing popular tunes booming in their ears at loud dynamic levels, adolescents are likely to find the gentle sounds of Debussy or Palestrina pale and ineffective. So another readjustment is called for, one in the appreciation of sounds that are not loud.

A fourth outlook is the students' attitude toward the manipulation of sounds. Few popular works contain much thematic development or large formal schemes. Sometimes teenagers become impatient when listening to a portion of a symphony or a concerto in which the melody is not present. The composer's skillful manipulation of musical ideas seems to them to be "busy work."

Correcting each of these conditions involves careful, persistent effort by the teachers.

Recognition of Styles

Sometimes students are asked to memorize a list of characteristics of a musical style before hearing the music or without ever hearing the piece at all. Such a procedure is like taking an art course and being required to memorize phrases, such as "form through color," "distortion of depth dimension," and "informal design," without seeing paintings that represent those terms. A much better approach is to see the painting or hear the music and then deduce what its features are. This procedure conforms to the guidelines for teaching music suggested in Chapter 5.

In most cases it is better for teachers to do a thorough job on a limited number of musical works than to scatter the emphasis. They should use a "posthole" approach by which they help the students remember a particular work and composer. Between the postholes they will need to "string lines," so that one area of concentrated attention can be logically connected to the next. This approach means leaving out some good composers and music, but it is better to do this than to inundate the students in a flood of information and music.

The students should gain an understanding of musical styles. A study of styles places the emphasis on musical qualities and adapts well to the posthole approach. The stylistic periods represent a solid element of musical experience and knowledge for the students to hang on to—an element to which other aspects of music and other fine arts can be related. Although the classification of periods is by no means parallel or perfect, there is a Romantic movement in painting, sculpture, and literature, as well as in music, and the students' understanding of one will contribute to their understanding of the others.

The study of musical style helps them approach works that are unfamiliar to them. When they say they do not like this or that music, often the problem is that they are missing something that is there, or they are looking for something that is not there. A course in understanding music should lead students to look at a musical work through the proper pair of glasses, so to speak. They should not expect to be overwhelmed in a bath of sound when hearing Mozart, for example.

Introducing a New Work

New works of music should not always be presented in the same way. There are times when a record may be played with no preparation by teachers. Then they can ask the class to describe the features of the music. They may simply wish to set a mood. For example, during the playing of a Grieg number, the class might be shown color slides of fjords and other Norwegian scenery. Sometimes certain portions of the music can be played as "teasers" for the entire work. On other occasions the class can learn the theme and sing it before hearing it in context. The learning of themes is especially helpful in enabling the students to follow forms. Sometimes the themes can be placed on the board or on large pieces of paper on the walls of the room, and the teacher can point to them when they occur in the music. Before an opera is presented, the libretto might be presented as a play, with acting. This device works well with Menotti's *Telephone,* for example. Perhaps the class can sing the first sixteen or so measures of three or four of the solos. In any case, the methods of presentation should be as imaginative and varied as the works of music. Teachers should do more than announce the next selection to be played.

Testing

In addition to the traditional cognitive tests, which are discussed in Chapter 17, students in a music appreciation course should also be evaluated on their skill in listening to music. Some teachers allot up to half of the examination score to listening items. In view of the importance of listening, such a proportion does not seem excessive.

Because the students are usually nonmusicians, general questions are preferable to exacting, specific items. For example, a minute or two of an unfamiliar work can be played, and the students can be asked to classify it according to style period. Other general listening questions about a selection might be these: "Listen to this concerto. Is it of the solo type, or is it a concerto grosso? Is there a cadenza? Is the form *A B A* or theme and variations? What instrument or type of voice is featured?"

In preparing the listening section of a test, teachers should select works that are typical of the period they are intended to represent. Also, if teachers stress the organ only during the presentation of Baroque music, they will have to prepare the class especially for Romantic organ music if they expect the students to identify correctly the period of a César Franck organ work.

At some point in a formal pattern the recording can be stopped and the students asked to identify where the music stopped in the form. Or after the exposition of a fugue, the class can respond by telling how many voices the fugue has.

Listening questions adapt easily to a multiple-choice format. For example:

The music will stop during the performance of a movement in sonata form. Where did the music stop?

(a) introduction
(b) first theme of exposition
(c) second theme of exposition
(d) development
(e) beginning of recapitulation

Usually about two minutes of a selection is sufficient. If a student wants to hear an example again, and if time permits, it should be repeated before going on to the next item. Jumping back and forth between items can be confusing to the students. Listening examples can be dubbed on tape prior to the examination to ensure against incorrect needle placement and related problems.

Textbooks

Most music appreciation textbooks are written for college, rather than high school, students. There are of course wide differences among such classes, so an able class of high school juniors and seniors can benefit from a book written for college freshmen. The following books are generally appropriate for high school classes:

Hoffer, Charles R. *A Concise Introduction to Music Listening.* 4th ed. Belmont, Calif.: Wadsworth, 1988.

————. *The Understanding of Music.* 6th ed. Belmont, Calif.: Wadsworth, 1989.

Machlis, Joseph, and Kristine Forney. *The Enjoyment of Music.* 6th ed. New York: W. W. Norton, 1990.

FINE ARTS AND HUMANITIES

There are nearly as many types of arts courses as there are schools offering them. Basically the courses can be divided into two categories. One category emphasizes the role of the arts in human thought. Often they carry the title *humanities*. The other category is more confined to the arts as disciplines in themselves (painting, music, dance, and so on). Such courses are known as "fine arts," "allied arts," and "related arts."

Because lack of time is a problem in combined art courses, the fewer areas the course attempts to cover, the better it will be able to educate students in those areas. For this reason, humanities courses are usually more difficult to teach well. When philosophy and social ideas are included, music almost gets squeezed out. For example, one state humanities guide once suggested that the instructor "play a Beethoven symphony here." This was the extent of its treatment of music in one of its chapters!

In the interest of a balanced overall program for high school students, music teachers should promote the idea of omitting English and American literature from the combined course. All students take English classes, so literature is better covered there. Duplication is avoided, and more time is left for art and music, which students do not cover in other classes.

As in the case of music appreciation, there are several approaches to course content, and each has advantages and disadvantages. The chronological plan shows the development of the arts and emphasizes styles, but it starts in ancient Egypt and Greece, not where the students' interests are, and it may unduly emphasize historical relationships. The aesthetic principles approach focuses on the basic characteristics of the arts, but it tends to overlook the influence of time and place and is inclined to make sweeping generalizations. The theme approach (for example, "Humanity and Nature" or "Society and the Artist") coordinates well with the experiences of the students, but there is a temptation to bend the subject to fit the chosen theme. The conceptual approach (line, texture, rhythm, and so on) is appropriate for dealing directly with art media because it aids perception, but it encourages false analogies among the arts and may neglect style. Some teachers of humanities courses have moved from an interest in subject matter content to activities that they believe will create better human beings out of their students. In most cases, the "humanistic" goals of these teachers have been quite vague, and the classes end up being largely a waste of time.

Teaching music in a combined arts course is much like teaching it in a music appreciation course, except for the limitation of time. Both situations can answer the need for basic information, for development of listening skills, and for building positive attitudes. In addition, the aesthetic aspects may receive greater emphasis in the arts course. Basic concepts such as tension and release, repetition, and variation become even more important.

Many fine arts teachers believe that no textbook should be used for such a course. Also, because of the wide diversity in the organization and content of the courses, only a few textbooks have been published. Included among them are the following:

Cross, Neal M., Robert C. Lamm, and Rudy H. Turk. *The Search for Personal Freedom*, brief edition. Dubuque, Iowa: William C. Brown, 1989.

Wold, Milo, and Edmund Cykler. *An Introduction to Art and Music in the Western World,* ninth ed. Dubuque, Iowa: William C. Brown, 1990.

MUSIC THEORY

Music theory, like music appreciation, enjoys a variety of names such as "basic music" or "fundamental musicianship." As with music appreciation, it is difficult for high school students to work a full-year theory course into their schedules. Many schools must settle for a one-semester course, while others can offer the class only in alternate years.

At this point the similarity between theory and appreciation (or fine arts) ends. The theory course is not for the general student; it is for the person with at least a minimal musical background.

Except in a few specialized high schools, there is insufficient enrollment to permit courses in several areas of theory. As a practical measure, the high school theory course must integrate aural and analytical skills, or else significant topics will be left out. Besides, the combined approach to theory is more musically and educationally valid. For both practical and pedagogical reasons, then, most high school theory courses should be integrated.

Teaching theory in the secondary schools differs in three respects from teaching it at the college level. First, high school classes are usually limited in time, often being only one semester long. Second, the students are not as facile in music notation, so they require more time to write out music. Third, the students in high school classes are not as highly selected and able as their college counterparts. For these reasons, efficiency in the use of time is very important in teaching secondary school theory classes.

The high school theory course should be both functional and versatile. The approach to harmony, for example, should be sufficiently broad to include traditional music and some aspects of jazz and other styles. A class should not become so involved with a certain style or approach to music that its members never learn about other styles and approaches. Nor should it confine its study to highly specialized techniques and problems that pertain to only a small portion of the world of music. Sometimes attention has focused on intricate rules. Not only does this teaching procedure violate the students' need to experiment with actual music, but many of the rules themselves are more complex than they need be, and some of them are only partly true.

Theory instruction should be functional, enabling students to write and arrange simple music for their school jazz bands and student musicals. Writing or arranging is both motivating and educational for students, and it makes the class more relevant.

Two criticisms have sometimes been leveled against theory courses as they have been taught in many high schools. One is that they deal mostly with the traditional style of the common practice period. While the course should not be confined to only such music, the critics might be reminded that even today most music—popular songs, Broadway musicals, hymns, film scores, and much art music—still contains tonality and tertian chords. Serialism, quartal and secundal harmonies, pandiatonicism, and the like may be studied, but the basis for the theory course should be the past three centuries of music.

The other criticism contains much truth: The theory course has often been unmusical. Students have learned to spell scales and chords, name intervals, avoid parallel fifths and octaves, and figure out correct meter signatures, but they had little idea of what these intellectual tasks mean in relation to musical sounds. The content of such a course is oriented toward the "head" rather than the "ear." Keyboard work, singing, ear training, and composing have sometimes largely been ignored.

Content

Even though a minimum musical knowledge is a prerequisite for the course, the first efforts should concentrate on fundamentals of musical nomenclature. Although some members of the class may be good performers, their knowledge of theory may be spotty and not cohesive. Few students are at ease with double-dotted notes, the 12/8 meter signature, or the forms of the minor scale. The work on fundamentals in the high school class should proceed rapidly, consuming not more than about eight weeks of daily class meetings to cover the following content:

note names, both treble and bass clefs

rhythm: note and rest values, meter signatures, borrowed units

major scales: constructed by interval and key signature

minor scales: constructed by key signature; natural, harmonic, and melodic forms

intervals, including inversions

chord types, including inversions: major, minor, augmented, diminished, seventh

chord functions, identified by name and roman numeral

Henry Lasker, who for years taught theory at Newton High School near Boston, offers this listing of content for a one-semester theory course:

> In Theory I, all the major and minor scales and the modes are taught with a great deal of emphasis on the singing experience, with or without the syllable methods, as well as the application of scales and modes to the piano keyboard. . . . The primary chords—tonic, dominant, dominant 7th, and subdominant—in root position and inversions, form the vocabulary in Theory I. Here again, the singing experience is constantly used. The chords are sung in arpeggio form in unison and then concerted with the class divided into the necessary parts.
>
> Knowledge of the ranges of soprano, alto, tenor, and bass is required for the voicing

of these chords in four parts in open and closed positions. This is followed by the progressions of the chords in cadences according to accepted procedures. All progressions are sung and played at the piano.

As the students do their work, they are urged to do it independently of the piano at first, in order to help them develop a sense of hearing mentally before they perform their work. "See with your ears; hear with your eyes." . . .

With all the above as a foundation, the students proceed to the harmonization of 4- and 8-measure sopranos to be sung and played with an understanding of the following functions: section; phrase; sentence; half- and authentic cadences; harmonic rhythm; use of inversions and root positions, with the economy of the primary chord vocabulary to create bass line interest; proper doubling, spacing, and voice leading, employing principles of stagnation and activity in relation to tempos; the three principal motions; and avoidance of the traditional errors of cross parts, tritones, consecutive fifths and eighths.

Analysis of intervals and construction of intervals above and below a given note, significance of consonance and dissonance in relation to intervals, and chord construction are gradually taught. Ear training, melodic, rhythmic, and harmonic dictation are an important part of the course too. Figured bass in relation to the primary chords is presented, as well as elementary analysis of materials within the vocabulary (1971, pp. 50, 52).

Keyboard Experience

Limited work at the keyboard should accompany the study of fundamentals. The word *keyboard* as used here does not encompass the complex activities sometimes required of college music majors. In the early stages, keyboard experience in the high school class involves simply playing the right notes on the piano. This is a necessary preliminary step because some students entering the course have no experience with the piano.

As major and minor scales are studied, they should be played at the keyboard, and the same is true for intervals and chords. Then as students progress into creative work, they will be more free and musical in their approach to the piano, especially in writing and playing simple accompaniments.

Ear Training

One of the most important and continuing phases of the theory class is ear training. Although the ability to listen carefully and selectively is not easily taught, a "good ear" is a necessity for any musical effort, be it composing, teaching, or performing. Music is an aural art, and never should this fact be forgotten, least of all in the theory class.

One technique for furthering aural skill is the taking of melodic dictation. The use of numbers instead of notation in teaching dictation can save class time. By writing scale step numbers without a staff, the students gain the essential experience of writing down what they hear without spending time putting it into musical notation. The number system is of course limited to tonal music and phrases that do not modulate. The technique is this: The teacher simply tells the class the number of the starting note. (Later, when the class is able to isolate a particular note in a chord, the teacher can play the tonic triad and let the students find the first number from it.) For example, the teacher plays the figure below twice, and the students write or sing back 1–3–4–2–7–1 from memory.

As the phrases become longer, the numbers will need to be written down. So that the students see the relationship between numbers and musical notation, a melody that has been taken down correctly with numbers should every so often be transcribed into musical notation.

Another practical way to relate musical sound with notation is for the students to recall a familiar melody, perhaps a popular song, and write it on the staff. This exercise saves the time normally spent in dictating the melody.

Whether the response involves numbers or notes, all melodic dictation should follow essentially the same procedure. First, the students should be told the starting pitch or should be given a clue about how to find it. Then the teacher should play the phrase *twice*. Long melodies should be dictated phrase by phrase. During the first two hearings the class should *not* attempt to write anything; they should just listen. The no-writing policy trains the students to listen more closely and develops their musical memory. Besides, trying to write while listening can seldom be done fast enough to keep up with what is being sounded. After the second hearing the class can sing back the melody to gain a concrete experience with it. Then and only then should they attempt to write down the melody. The teacher should play the melody two more times, pausing after each playing to allow for checking of work.

Another type of melodic aural training that is even more practical than dictation is to have the students follow notation as the line is played and to locate the places where what is seen differs from what is heard. To do this, the teacher performs music unfamiliar to the students on any instrument and inserts mistakes while they follow the notation.

Occasionally the students should hear some dictation on an instrument other than piano and once in a while something sung. Also, every so often dictation should be in a range other than around middle C. Sometimes students become so accustomed to hearing melodies in that register that they have trouble hearing accurately patterns that are in other registers.

Rhythmic dictation is helpful, especially early in the course, if melodic dictation is confined to numbers instead of the complete notation with its rhythmic symbols. The procedure for rhythmic dictation is similar to melodic dictation in that the students should listen carefully to the pattern the first two times it is tapped or played on the piano. As the use of notation is increased, rhythmic dictation becomes less necessary because rhythm is present in melodic dictation.

In addition to melodic and rhythmic dictation, the students should learn how to identify aurally the soprano and bass members of a chord. Before actual identification is attempted, the class must have experience in singing major triads with numbers. The first singing should be from the root; later the starting tone can be the third or fifth. As soon as the triad pattern is established in the students' ears, the following steps are recommended:

1. Play a triad in root position, or inversion, with one note doubled. Arrange the pitches so that the bass note is a distance of a fifth or more from the others, and play it more loudly. Hold the triad until the sound fades away. After a short pause, ask the class to sing back the bass note.

2. Play the chord once more, and again sustain it. Ask the class to experiment by assuming that the note sung is 1 and singing 1–3–5–3–1. If the starting pitch was not 1, this will be obvious to the class. Proceed then to 3, and to 5 if necessary.

3. When the class becomes proficient at singing patterns starting from the bass member of the chord, drop the singing and have the students merely identify the pitch as 1, 3, or 5.

4. When the bass can be heard fairly well, follow the same procedure to find the soprano member of the triad.

A fourth phase of ear training in the secondary-school theory class is identifying chord types. The initial attempt should be confined to a choice between major or minor chords in root position. Then the work can progress to inverted positions as well. This is followed by the introduction of the diminished triad and finally the augmented triad. For the first several weeks, practice in chord identification should involve hearing only two of the four types during one session. This restriction avoids overwhelming the uninitiated ears of the students with too many types at once.

Ear training can be promoted with especially designed tapes and computer disks. They provide exercises that have been carefully developed and graded. The teacher may play them for the class to vary his or her performance at the piano, or the students can listen on their own in study carrels in a language laboratory or at listening tables in the library. Some of the ear-training programs available are cited in Chapter 14.

Singing

In his theory course outline Lasker rightly emphasizes the importance of singing. Because singing seems to be the surest way to develop tonal imagery—the ability to hear tones "in the mind's ear"—it should be a component of other class activities. For example, scales and chords should be sung as well as written. Melodic dictation should be sung back, and sight singing should be undertaken. A variety of material is available for this work: folk songs, octavo music, and books especially written for sight singing.

Creative Work

Creative exercises are valuable because they (1) stimulate students to think musically, (2) motivate them to feel a personal involvement with what they have written, and (3) encourage them as creators of music. Even if not particularly successful, those students who have attempted to write some music will have a greater understanding and appreciation of the process of creating music.

The term *creative work* may bring to mind original musical compositions of some magnitude. In the high school theory class, however, the time available and the abilities of the students seldom permit efforts at major compositions. At this level creativity is best nurtured through short creative exercises, often not more than sixteen or thirty-two measures in length. Also important is the degree to which teachers structure the assignments. Never should students be told, "Go home and write a song." Although it may appear to be an inconsistency, creative work for most high school students is better fostered at first if they are given a set of specifications for their work. What they need at first are ideas of how to go about writing music and a successful experience in doing so.

There are several ways to approach creative exercises. The more successful ones are usually based on song style. A jingle or couplet with a definite meter is selected for the students to set to music. Even the familiar "Roses are red" is a possibility. The advantage of a jingle is its definite meter, which makes it easier for the students to come up with a logical rhythmic structure. After the words are metered out with accents and bar lines, the note values can be written in. Next come the pitches. For early creative efforts teachers should restrict their use by suggesting a particular key and a range, perhaps one octave. Students should be encouraged to give their melody as much coherence and logic as they can while at the same time maintaining some novelty and interest.

Another approach is to select a stanza of poetry with a definite mood. In this approach the students attempt to capture in the music the mood that prevails in the poem. Depending on the ability and experience of the class, the teacher may wish to suggest note values for the composition.

There are other ways for teachers to introduce creative activities. They can create a tone row for the students to manipulate or list the serial techniques to be followed after writing their own rows. They can offer a rhythmic pattern—either an overall plan like the jingle or an ostinato figure. They can suggest a harmonic pattern from which the students can derive a melody, which is an approach similar to conventional jazz, except that the result is composed rather than improvised.

At first, students should be instructed to write only the melody. At the next class session the teacher plays the melodies and discusses with the students how well they meet the criteria of unity, variety, and appropriateness with the text (if one was given). If the melody is satisfactory, the student can add a simple block-chord accompaniment. If the melody is not so good, another try is called for. At this point in the course, writing a good melody and proper chords is a sufficiently ambitious undertaking. One or two more melodies can be attempted, with the teacher withdrawing some of the specifications each time. How long the structuring of assignment is continued depends on the success the students achieve with their compositions.

After several block-chord accompaniments have been written, the class should be shown how to embellish the chords and make them more interesting. Pianists find this rather easy, but nonpianists usually need help. The class should hear many song accompaniments. This experience makes them aware of the countless ways of sounding the essential harmonic structure without resorting to thumping out block chords.

Before the end of the course the students should have an opportunity to write a melody for one instrument to be accompanied by two or three others. Whenever possible, teachers should specify that compositions be written for the instruments played by class members so that there can be live performances of the music. Composing for instruments will probably entail teaching transposition. Because of the limited amount of time available, the problem of range and orchestration is best handled by the teacher specifying the easy and practical ranges of the instruments for which students plan to write.

Some teenagers who enroll in the theory course may be interested almost exclusively in electronic or computer music. Should they be allowed to pursue only their limited area of interest? Probably not. Young composers ought to become acquainted with a broad spectrum of music and should learn how to compose in conventional media as well. As soon as they have acquired some skill at handling compositional problems, they can specialize in the manipulation of computer and synthesizer.

Theory classes should be musical-learning laboratories in which works are presented for examination and evaluation. A most desirable outcome of these classes, and one that does much to stimulate interest in music theory and composition, is performance of students' works by one of the school's performing organizations. Possibly the best student composition in each theory class can be arranged with the help of the teacher for performance. The composition need not be pretentious. A march, a simply arranged melody, or a song is adequate to impress the student body and to provide educational benefits for the student composer.

Given time and student ability, there is no limit to the possibilities for work in theory classes. Whatever the extent of its content, the theory course should be functional, versatile, creative, and, above all, musical.

Questions 1. Suppose the high school principal asks the music teacher: "Why is a music appreciation course so important for the high school students who aren't in band or chorus? After all, they had music all through school up to the seventh grade. Why do they need more? If they were really interested in music, they'd be in band or chorus." How would you answer?

2. What are the advantages and disadvantages to beginning the music appreciation course with folk music? With Gregorian chant? With a Broadway musical? With a standard, easily accepted symphonic work? What could be the procedures for beginning with each?

3. Why is a music theory course not appropriate for general students? Could some of its value be given to general students in some other way? If so, how?

4. What are the advantages of the combined arts course? What are some of the practical problems associated with such a course?

Projects

1. Look over textbooks in music appreciation and evaluate their appropriateness for a high school class. Consider the writing style, amount of material covered, degree of emphasis on musical qualities, and presentation of material that is significant for the listener who is not a musician.

2. Examine the textbooks or computer materials in music theory, and then evaluate them for use in a high school class. Consider to what degree each presents the learnings functionally, encourages creativity, and is versatile. Consider also whether the book or other material would be appropriate in an integrated theory course.

3. Listen to these recordings and decide what features of the music could be suggested as a focus for the students' listening. Mention any particular teaching procedure that would contribute to the value of the listening experience.
    Aaron Copland, *A Lincoln Portrait*
    César Franck, Violin Sonata, fourth movement
    J. S. Bach, Brandenburg Concerto No. 5, first movement

4. Select a musical work and develop a "call chart" or "blueprint" for it.

5. Develop a short test to give students in a music appreciation course. Make about half the test consist of listening questions.

6. Prepare a set of directions and specifications to give the students in a theory class for their first attempt at composing.

Suggested Readings

Instructor's manuals for the Hoffer and Machlis music appreciation textbooks cited on page 129.

Lasker, Henry. *Teaching Creative Music in Secondary Schools.* Boston: Allyn & Bacon, 1971.

References

Boyle, J. David, and Robert L. Lathrop. "The IMPACT Experience: An Evaluation." *Music Educators Journal,* 59, no. 5 (January 1973).

Lasker, Henry. *Teaching Creative Music in Secondary Schools.* Boston: Allyn & Bacon, 1971.

CHAPTER 8

Teaching Performing Groups

It is a bright, warm day in early September. Joe Fontana, just graduated from college and on his first day at his new job, steps before the Crestville Middle School band. Before the students is a piece of music, which he promptly has them try to play. Cacophony results! These students can't read the music as the bands he was in back at college did, or even the high school band that he played in. A feeling on the order of panic strikes him. What should he do now? What exactly can he do to teach this or any other piece of music?

BEING PREPARED

As for Joe Fontana's state of panic, it should not have happened. He should have thought about such a possibility before the class period began. Sometimes future music teachers have the wrong impression about planning. At college and other places they have worked under master teacher-conductors, and these teachers usually don't give any evidence of a lesson plan or other specific preparation. To all appearances, a conductor just improvises, relying on good musicianship and quick wits. In a few cases this is true. Usually, however, much thought has gone into preparing for what appears to be made up on the spot, even though the planning may not be written down in a formal lesson plan. Also, the fact that a college or professional conductor may have rehearsed a work many times during his or her career is one reason why he or she is well prepared.

What should Joe Fontana do about his first rehearsal? If the students' folders contain less difficult pieces, he should try a simpler number—one so easy that it is certain to be performed with some degree of success. This technique will salvage some order from a potentially chaotic situation. However, teaching is not just leading groups through music simple enough to be performed at sight. For the next meeting of the group Joe Fontana should be prepared to teach the students something about music. Here are some ideas of how to go about teaching groups to play or sing works of music.

BRINGING OUT MUSICAL QUALITIES

At the same time a new piece of music is being presented, teachers should begin working on getting both the right notes and rhythms and the proper interpretation. As soon as possible, students need to think of the work as a piece of music, not just a technical challenge.

There are many ways to give the students an idea of the work. It may be read at sight, especially if it is quite easy, even though it is far from a perfect rendition. Then with the whole piece in mind, the group can begin working on particular problems. For an emphasis on the mood in vocal music, the work can be sung the first time on a bright or dark vowel sound, whichever is appropriate. The text of the music can be read aloud in unison wth expression, or the accompanist can play the voice parts while the students follow the music. A representative section can be played or sung to give the students a clear and immediate idea of how the piece sounds, if they can't sight-read it. A recording of the work can be played. In a fugal work the teacher can take a thematic phrase and have each part perform it as it appears. This theme can be learned first, the countermelody second, and the free material left until later. If the melody does not appear until a third of the way along in a work, the first reading can start with the appearance of the melody. If the emphasis is to be rhythmic, the words or rhythms may be chanted, clapped, or played in unison. In some cases a technical or rhythmic problem can be studied just prior to learning the new piece. To give the students a better idea of the music, teachers can tell them something about the history or the style of the work.

Whatever the introductory procedure, it should move quickly. The students want to sing or play; they do not want to be told about problems they *might* have.

TEACHING INSTRUMENTAL MUSIC

The logical groupings of instrumental parts vary with each piece of music and from place to place in the music. For example, the traditional march of Sousa has about five groupings. The excerpt from "Semper Fidelis" (p. 142) contains these groupings: (1) a melody, mainly for cornets and trumpets; (2) a bass line; (3) a decorative part in the piccolos and clarinets; (4) a harmony part for horns, trombones, and baritones; and (5) a percussion part (often not indicated in a condensed score). For teaching of this section of the march, the following steps are suggested:

1. Start by giving the students an idea of the entire march by using one of the techniques just suggested.

2. Work on the melody, because it carries the main burden of the music at this point. Briefly help the players learn the correct notes, rhythms, and expression. Before leaving them to work with another grouping, make sure the essential music expression has not been lost while working out the technical problems.

3. Work with the bass instruments. In this case, considering the ability of many high school tuba players and the difficulty of this passage, it might be wise to suggest that they practice the music individually outside of class. Better yet, say, "I'll help you with this again during your free period or just after school today." In any event, avoid holding a bass section rehearsal during the rehearsal of the full band. As soon as they can play the part reasonably well, combine it with the melody.

4. Listen to the high woodwind part. Rhythmic precision is important here. When sufficient clarity is evident, combine it with the other two parts just rehearsed.

5. Work with the horns and the low clarinets. This simple part should require little assistance.

6. Help the percussion as much as necessary, recognizing the need to fit their part into the total ensemble.

7. Have the entire band play the section, with special attention to style and balance.

To assist or help means to do whatever is necessary to get the music performed correctly. In the melody parts it may call for making sure that the students play the line in bugling fashion with the first and third valves for all notes. It may mean achieving rhythmic accuracy by holding the dotted half note over into the first eighth note of the next measure. It may involve singing to the players the style in which the notes should be tongued. It may require checking the players' fingerings on the high woodwind line to see that they use the easiest and best-sounding combination on their particular instrument. And so it goes through each line— counting rhythms, demonstrating style, checking fingerings, adjusting dynamics, bringing out accented notes, and pointing out other parts to listen for—until everyone's playing fits into the mosaic of sound that is this portion of "Semper Fidelis."

Teachers must exercise good judgment in allotting attention to the various sections. For example, if a harmony part has many afterbeats, it is fruitless to spend much time on the part alone because it makes sense only in conjunction with other parts. Discretion is needed in the amount of time given a part and the degree of accuracy expected in the first few tries through a passage. A teacher might spend fifty minutes with the woodwinds and might even get their parts just right. But what about the rest of the band during those fifty minutes? Their interest has hardly been stimulated, and they have not learned much either. Probably the

Semper Fidelis

John Philip Sousa (1854–1932)

woodwinds will have slipped a bit when the passage is rehearsed again a few days later. Teachers should content themselves with correcting as many errors as possible in about three or four playings of a passage. Further improvement should be left to another day—a teaching procedure that is consistent with the idea of distributed practice mentioned in Chapter 5.

TEACHING CHORAL MUSIC

Teachers of choral groups should follow a sequence of instruction similar to that recommended for instrumental teachers. After giving the singers a sense of the entire piece of music (always a necessary first step), they may have them sing the entire number together, if this was not done initially. They must make a judgment at this point based on how well the students succeeded in their attempt to sing the work the first time through it. More often than not, each part needs some specific help. It may be that the tenors and basses need only sing their parts again with the accompaniment. Perhaps the altos need to sing a passage while the other parts are hummed.

The procedures suggested here are on the "bedrock" order; that is, they assume that the singers need the maximum amount of help. Actually, the amount of assistance required will vary from one day to the next, from one piece to the next, and from one passage to another within a piece of music.

The usual method for helping singers to learn their parts is hardly imaginative. It consists of playing or singing a part for a section and then having them sing it back. The procedure is slow, but choral music can be learned by this rote approach. The problem is that musical qualities of the music are often lost in the process, something that should definitely be avoided. Teachers can do much to retain the quality of music by working in musically logical segments and by pointing out and performing the similar phrases of music that appear throughout a piece. Students are sometimes surprised and pleased to realize that by learning one phrase they have mastered others that are nearly identical. Above all, interpretation and notes should be learned together, a point that is stressed and explained more in Chapter 9.

When the students have an idea of the musical qualities of a work, choral teachers can follow these steps to teach the parts:

1. Select a phrase of from two to eight measures. If the music is a typical homophonic SATB* work with the melody in the soprano part, ask the ac-

---

*A mixed chorus consisting of sopranos, altos, tenors, and basses sings music arranged for SATB, the acronym made up of the first letter of each part. A similar scheme is carried out for girls' glee clubs, which sing SA or SSA music, the two S's standing for first and second soprano. Music written for boys' glee clubs is arranged in two parts for tenor and bass (TB); in three parts for tenor, baritone, and bass (TBB); in four parts for first tenor, second tenor, baritone, and bass (TTBB).

companist to play the bass line. (A male teacher may want to sing it.) Then have the basses sing their part back in full voice. Ask the tenors, altos, and sopranos to sight-sing the bass part *softly* with the basses. Singing along with other parts strengthens the singers' ability to read music in both clefs and contributes to their understanding of the music and its harmony. Naturally the girls will sing the bass part an octave higher than written. Repeat this unison singing a time or two more if necessary. Then ask the bass section to sing the passage alone, unaccompanied by the piano or other singers. Another way to check the learning of the section is to select one or two individuals at random to sing it. At this point whatever is not learned adequately will have to be left until the next rehearsal.

2. Cover the tenor part in much the same manner. The girls can sing the tenor line with the boys. When the tenors have learned their own part, direct them to sing it with the bass part, while the accompanist plays the two lines on the piano and the girls drop out. The use of accompaniment depends largely on the difficulty of the vocal line. Piano support can be omitted entirely, or the written piano accompaniment can be played, or the accompanist may play all four voice parts.

3. Repeat this procedure for the altos. The sopranos may join softly on the alto line. One singing of the phrase may be enough. The altos, tenors, and basses should then combine their respective parts for the phrase.

4. Approach the soprano part last because it is frequently the simplest and most easily learned; often it is the melody. The entire group then performs the phrase or passage.

In this procedure a passage of music is built up layer by layer with everyone singing during much of the process. There are several reasons for rehearsing the bass and tenor parts first in a mixed group. (With all male or female groups the lowest part should also be learned first.) Inexperienced basses and tenors find it tempting to sing the melody an octave lower rather than to put forth the effort to learn a different part. This is especially true if the boys know the melody before they learn the bass or tenor part. Because the bass part is sometimes the most difficult, the boys need the practice of singing in several combinations. Boys at this age are usually less sure of themselves vocally than girls, and so they need more guidance. Also, more girls than boys audition and enroll in choral music, so they are more highly selected than boys.

Some teachers prefer to have the other parts remain silent while one section is receiving special help. They object to asking girls to sing along on the boys' parts for two reasons: A few of the notes are out of range, and singing four different lines may be confusing for the sopranos. Some of the notes in the soprano part are usually out of range of some of the sopranos, and the same is true of every section. As for confusion, it is likely to happen only if the practice is continued after the initial work on the piece.

The basic teaching steps are the same whether or not the girls sing with the basses and tenors. Although having the higher parts sing with the lower parts is not essential, it does give all the singers something do to. Because singers do not have the concrete experience of fingering an instrument, telling them to follow their part silently is not as successful as it is with instrumentalists.

While soft singing with other parts is suggested, humming is not. Too many wrong notes and careless vocal habits can be covered up by humming.

REHEARSING SCHOOL GROUPS

Directors of school music groups can be more effective if they are efficient in rehearsing the music and are able to have each student involved in learning. The following sections offer a number of ideas for achieving greater efficiency and student effort.

Using Verbal Commentary

It is often more efficient and effective to communicate with the performer *while* the music is being rehearsed—but not during a performance, of course. A good teacher is one who foresees a point on which a quick reminder will save a minute of class time. Noticing the pattern below in the trombone part, the instrumental teacher can call out to the trombones, "Sixth position on that F," just before the

figure is to be played. It is not necessary to stop the band and say, "Trombones, in the third measure after letter G, play the F in the sixth position." Not only is time lost by stopping the group, giving instructions, and starting again, but the musical flow is interrupted as well. The successful music teacher calls out, "Smooth, smooth," at the approach of a legato passage. When the students are slow to cut off a tone before a rest, teachers should snap out a distinct "Off!" just at the beginning of the rest. The rest may also be conducted by holding the hands still to indicate the cessation of sound. The verbal command serves the additional purpose of calling attention to the conducting.

Commentary from the teacher is a vivid, live way to bring about a good performance of a live art. Its main rehearsal limitation happens when the music is too loud for the teacher to be heard. Verbal commands should never be thought of as replacing conducting motions, nor should they ever be used in a performance.

Indicating Musical Entrances

A problem for some inexperienced teachers is how to indicate attacks and entrances. Many school students are not able to watch the conductor and follow their music at the same time. In fact, some of them can scarcely keep from getting lost even when their entire attention is on the music. So in the initial stages of learning a work, some way must be found to supplement the conducting motions. Teachers can mark time by clapping their hands or tapping on a hard surface. Or they can provide verbal commands. After the starting place has been indicated, and in vocal music the opening pitches given either by voice or piano, the teacher says, *in the tempo of the music,* "Ready, go," or "Ready, begin." After the first few times, verbal commands should be dropped completely so that the students do not become dependent on them.

In choral music it is sometimes necessary for the teacher to sing with a section the first time or two. It may be especially useful for a man to sing with the boys, because they may lack the confidence and zeal to get started on the right note at the right time. A teacher may occasionally have the unsettling experience of giving a start and having no one come in. The teacher should check to make sure the students understand what is wanted and try again. When students do not come in on an entrance, it is usually due to inattentiveness, lack of understanding, or lack of confidence, rather than to contrariness on their part.

Isolating Trouble Spots

One of the keys to more efficient and effective music teaching is the teacher's ability to determine the exact point on which the students are having trouble. Sometimes one note in a phrase is the cause for incorrect performance. It is not necessary, or even wise, to practice all the notes in a phrase again and again just to get a certain note right. For example, the basses in the chorus are learning this phrase from the "Hallelujah Chorus" from Handel's *Messiah:*

And He shall reign for ev - er and ev - er

The basses may falter on the F sharp, B, and D, missing the B and losing their accuracy. It is useless to sing the entire phrase over and over, mistakes and all. The pianist should play the pitches while the basses listen to the pattern. Then they can sing the notes with the piano. When they sing it correctly, they should go over the spot about three times. Between each repetition the teacher need only say, "Again" or "Once more," in the tempo of the piece. The whole process would be as follows: "*shall reign for*,"—"Once more"—"*shall reign for*"—"Sing the whole phrase"—"*And He shall reign for ever and ever.*" Sometimes it helps to tape-record the correct piano or teacher version and then the incorrect version so that the students can hear their mistakes more clearly.

Some teachers make a list of such trouble spots and use them for "spot practice" in rehearsal. This technique provides a quick review of the troublesome passages without performing the entire work, which speeds up the learning process and makes it more thorough and accurate. To keep the group alert and to check on the learning of a passage, the teacher can say without warning, "We're having trouble with the F sharp, B, and D above the words 'shall reign for.' Demond, let's hear you sing the passage," and have Demond sing it. Then, "Stan, let's hear you sing it," followed by one or two other basses in the same way.

Prior to working on a trouble spot in the music, the students should be acquainted with the entire phrase or piece so that they understand as fully as possible its rhythmic, harmonic, and melodic characteristics.

Students should be encouraged to inform the teacher of passages that they find difficult to perform correctly. They know, better than any listener, the passages on which they are insecure. This technique is more useful for high school groups, because they usually don't need to go over music so often to learn it, and they have a better sense of their capabilities.

Keeping All Students Occupied

A rehearsal of a professional group is marked by long periods of inactivity for some players, but in the schools a music class should be a learning situation for all students. They should be involved in the class work as much as possible during the entire time. Long waits encourage discipline problems and boredom and waste time for many of the students. What's more, long waits are usually unnecessary.

The problem can be alleviated by efficient teaching techniques. When an instrumental group is in the early stages of work on a piece, the students can be told to finger silently through their music while another section rehearses. (Silent fingering is a good pedagogical practice.) The teacher does not ask students to practice fingering on a piece that they have been playing for some time. By then, the work with individual sections should be mostly over.

Many a baritone player is not interested in listening to the clarinet parts, even though the second and third clarinets may be playing the same musical line that appears in the baritone part. The same is true of singers in choral groups. Student musicians seldom realize that there is much they can learn by following what goes on in rehearsal, even though it may appear not to pertain to them. The teacher should not hesitate to ask questions of unoccupied students: "Altos, at what place are the tenors missing the rhythm?" "Mary, why should the second and third trumpets play the accompaniment figure staccato?" Drawing attention to other sections is especially important in instrumental music because each player sees only his or her own part.

Reviewing Learned Music

After the students have grasped the basic style of a piece and are able to execute the correct pitches and rhythms, they should review the work to retain what they have learned. The amount of forgetting that is characteristic of the human mind, as was pointed out in Chapter 5, means that review is certainly a part of every teacher's job. Not only will some of the learning be forgotten by the next time the class meets, but a few students may be absent and miss the initial presentation entirely. Teachers need not go back to the first step of the learning process. Instead, they might have a small group or section perform its part alone. In choral music, for example, the piano can play the accompaniment with the singers. If the results are satisfactory, then two sections can perform their parts together. The parts can be hummed while the section in need of help sings the words. Essentially what the vocal or instrumental teacher does is move *quickly* through some of the previous teaching procedures.

Another helpful device in reviewing music is to have a section stand while performing its part (cellos excepted). This procedure provides a change of position and allows the standing students to be heard more easily. It also strengthens the confidence and independence of a section and encourages alertness and better posture.

Critical Listening by Students

To allow for critical listening, teachers can set up "teams" consisting of from four to eight students. They should be drawn from a cross section of instrumental or voice parts to avoid depleting a section. They can be called on to hear the rest of the class perform or possibly to perform themselves. The team listening should be invited to stand near the teacher to hear better.

After listening to the group perform, the team members can offer comments. Sometimes the listeners will accuse the group of making an error that it did not make, or they will fail to notice a glaring mistake, especially when first given the chance to listen. The teacher should not be discouraged when this happens. As long as the students are learning what to listen for in music, and are improving in sensitivity and in the accuracy of their evaluations, the procedure is achieving its goal. The teacher needs to guide the students in this evaluative listening process. Here is an example of what might take place after a team has just listened to the rest of the choir:

MS. GORDON: Now, what was the biggest error in the singing?

PAUL: The alto part was too weak, I think.

MS. GORDON: Well, that's partly true. But that isn't what I noticed.

DIANNE: I think the tenors let their tone sag as they went for the high note.

MS. GORDON: Yes, a little, but still that's not what I noticed most. What was the main fault in the singing?

RAMON: They didn't put the "d" on the word "heard."

MS. GORDON: Yes, but we're still missing a lot of final d's. But what I heard was the harsh tone quality. It's entirely out of place in this piece. (*To the singers*) Let's sing at letter E exactly as you did it the last time.

Group sings the phrase.

MS. GORDON: (*To the singers*) Now let's do the same thing again; only this time, sing it very gently and warmly. Imagine you're saying goodnight after a big date.

Group sings the phrase again.

MS. GORDON: (*To the listening team*) Now, can't you hear the difference? The first version sounded very much like our school fight song, while the second had a more tender, serious sound—just what this piece needs.

Admittedly this process is more time-consuming than telling the group what to do. But the educational values make it well worthwhile. A student whose opinion is considered is less likely to feel lost in the large group, and students will pay more attention to details when they know they must understand them to form an evaluation, a fact indicated by the cognitive taxonomy on page 80. Also, this type of listening adds interest and variety to the class. In fact, often the students are so eager to listen that the teacher finds it necessary to keep a record of the number of times each team is asked to listen to the group.

Another benefit of this technique is the clarification it gives the words of the teacher. Such problems as balance among sections, precision, phrasing, accents, tone quality, and intonation become more understandable to the students after they have heard them in live performance.

Students should also learn to tell when they have an important part in the music and when they don't. Every so often when a group is performing homophonic music, the teacher should stop the group and ask, "Who has the melody here?"

Sensitive musicianship is also required for performing parts other than the melody. When performing an accompanying part, if the student cannot hear the melody, either he or she or the other members of the section are too loud. Not only should they allow the melody to be heard, they should also vary the dynamic shadings, phrasing, and tone quality to correspond to the melodic line.

Objective Listening by the Teacher

Teachers need to listen objectively to the classes they are teaching. In one large high school the teachers periodically trade groups. While one director rehearses the students, the regular teacher sits in the back of the room and listens much more objectively than is possible when on the podium. In a smaller school the choral teacher might exchange classes with the instrumental teacher, or student conductors can be trained. If these procedures are not feasible, the teacher can start the group on a familiar number and then back away from the group as far as possible. Holds, rubato passages, and the like can be conducted with oversized motions from the place where the teacher is standing.

The objective quality in such listening needs to be emphasized. After the arduous labor required to prepare a performing organization, objectivity does not come easily, but it is necessary if the teacher is to evaluate the group accurately. Teachers should occasionally imagine that they are an adjudicator at a contest. What criticisms would be made? What suggestions could be offered?

As an aid to objective listening, good recordings of the organization are useful. They give everyone a chance to listen, and the teacher can take them home to listen to a passage as often as desired. They can be saved as a record of progress throughout the year and from one year to the next. One recording can be compared with another so that the students can be instructed by hearing changes in the performance.

A word of caution: Making tape recordings correctly is time-consuming. More than one teacher has realized on Friday that a whole week has been spent preparing a few tapes. For conservation of time only a few of the tapes need to be played back to the group. Everyone involved should realize that the tapes are not enhanced or "cleaned up" by a recording technician, as is done for most commercial recordings.

If the teacher can hear objectively what the group is singing or playing, a second question must be faced: How good should the execution of the music be? Should teachers adhere to the standards of a professional group, or should they accept almost anything short of cacophony? A school group should *execute the notes and rhythms of the music with a pleasing tone quality and with the essential musical expression of the work*. If the students cannot perform the music to this degree, it should not be performed for the public, regardless of the age of the students or the amount of progress they have made. No teacher should be lulled into thinking, "Well, they're just kids," and accept sloppy, unmusical performance. Failure to meet this standard indicates the work is too difficult or requires additional rehearsal, or both. The words *with essential musical expression* are especially important. It is far better to perform a simple work musically than to perform a more difficult work unmusically.

Providing for Individual Attention

Because performing groups are usually larger than other classes, there is a tendency for the student to feel as unimportant as a little stick in a large woodpile. And teachers sometimes tend to think in group terms. As a result, a student may not feel sufficiently responsible for his or her own work. One way to overcome the problem is to offer short individual assistance sessions.

> *Bill is an average student and an average clarinet player. Just as the band period ends, the director, Tom Witkiewicz, asks him to remain for a moment. Bill isn't upset, because Mr. Witkiewicz usually has someone stay for a moment after class.*
> *"Okay, Bill," he says, "let's hear the third clarinet part at letter C in the* Water Music.*"*
> *Bill plays it in a satisfactory way.*
> *"That's fine, Bill! You know some of the clarinets were having trouble with that place,*

and I wanted to make sure that you could play it. You'd better get to your next class now. Keep up the good work."

This technique helps to keep students "on their toes," because they realize that anyone can be called at any time. In addition, it lets them know that the teacher is observing their progress and is interested in each person.

Another way to hear students individually is to have them go to another room and tape-record a specified portion of the music, a procedure suggested in Chapter 17 for grading purposes. In this instance the students would receive only comments, not grades.

Practicing Outside of Rehearsal

There are several ways to arrange for additional practice for members of performing groups. In one situation the middle school vocal music teacher is able to attend two practices of the high school choir each week. Simultaneous sectional rehearsals are then held for the boys and for the girls by moving one group to another room. In another school, the teacher has the choir meet three days a week, with another day set aside for work with the boys and another for work with the girls. Some teachers have students practice in a supervised fashion during their free time. The attempt to find a way to work with small portions of an entire group is a matter on which the music teacher will need to advise the school administration. It can significantly affect what the teacher is able to accomplish.

Teachers of performing organizations should not overlook the benefits of homework for the students. Besides practicing parts at home, students can keep a music notebook that includes information on the music studied, facts about composers, musical styles, technical problems encountered, and other material.

Saving Time

Class time in performing organizations can be saved if the teacher takes these practical actions:

1. Write the titles of the music, in order, on the chalkboard so that the students can locate it in their folders and put it in order before class begins.
2. Ask the librarians to service the folders by passing out or collecting music during study period or after school rather than during class time.
3. Appoint student assistants to take attendance. One person can be responsible for checking each section in a choral group or large family in instrumental groups. Pupil absences should be indicated on a card for each student or on some kind of class roll, not in the teacher's grade book.
4. Provide an electronic tuning device or several tuning bars so that instrumentalists may tune their instruments themselves before class.

Pacing in Rehearsals

In a rehearsal, where time is at a premium, a teacher must be both efficient and pleasant. The following example of how *not* to operate a class will indicate some errors to avoid.

Choir is stopped by Mr. King.

MR. KING: Well . . . (*pause*) . . . Why don't we start at letter A and sing it over again. . . . (*pause*) . . . ah . . . Piano, give us the notes after letter A.

Three things wrong here:
1. The teacher should know what he is going to say before he stops the group; there should be no delay.

ACCOMPANIST: Do you want to start with the pickup?

2. There should be a reason given for going over the music again.

MR. KING: Yes, I guess so. . . . (*pause*) . . . Anyway, give us the notes.

3. The exact starting place was not made clear.

Notes are played. Choir starts singing but is soon stopped by Mr. King.

MR. KING: I think you should put a crescendo on the words "o'er all the earth" so that "earth" is louder than the three words preceding it. . . . Uh . . . I guess we'll start at letter A again.

Good suggestion.

More delay. The students can't help wondering if the man knows what he wants.

Choir sings phrase exactly as before with no crescendo; sings to end of piece.

MR. KING: (*pause; stands looking down at the music*) . . . That was a pretty good job, I guess. . . .

What about the crescendo? He guesses it was good. Doesn't he know? He still is working much too slowly.

Well, let's get out "The Heavens Declare the Glory of God"—the Beethoven.

Good number; the students like it.

You know, I ordered this music from Smith's Music House, and they sent me the music all right, but it was in a book with about ten other pieces. So I sent it back to them and told them about the mistake they had made in sending me the right music but in the wrong book, you know. Well, you know what they did? They sent me the right music after a couple weeks of delay, but they billed me for the postage *both ways* on the books *they* had sent me by mistake. Was I ever disgusted! So when I sent the money to them for this music, I didn't send the money for postage and told them why. They sent me a letter apologizing for their error. Guess you have to be firm sometimes.

Be sure the story will be interesting to the group before you tell it. This one might be—it depends.

Just like the time I got a parking ticket because the parking meter was broken. (*Mr. King goes on in detail about how he refused to pay the fine and was finally vindicated.*)

Oh yes, we were going to sing "The Heavens Declare." (*He smiles at students . . . pause*) . . .

Now, at the beginning you should sing with a full, round sound. Basses, do the best you can on that low note. The music is in unison so you shouldn't have any trouble with that part. . . . Ah . . . Now along about the middle we have a modulation. Does anyone know what a modulation is? John?

JOHN: It's when the music goes into a different key.

MR. KING: Right! You'll have a good chance to hear this modulation because the piano plays it for several counts before you come in. . . . (*pause*) . . . When you have the same note repeated, remember to make a crescendo up to the eighth chord. That word "heavens" should go HEAvens. . . . Ah . . . Also you . . . ah . . . um . . . notice that the first melody comes back here near the end.

Any questions? . . . (*pause*) . . . Gary?

GARY: Here (*points to the music*) the basses have some little notes written in above the larger notes. What do we do about them?

(*Mr. King walks over and looks at Gary's music.*)

MR. KING: Oh yes! I nearly forgot. Well . . . ah . . . let's just omit them. I think that those notes are there in case you can't get the low ones. You won't have any trouble with those low ones, will you?

Any other questions? . . . (*pause*)

OK. Let's get going!

Choir begins singing.

What, another? When does the group get to sing? What happened to Beethoven?

At last!

Oh, oh, another delay. He'll be lucky if he doesn't have some behavior problems before the period is over.

How helpful to the students are these comments?

A question—good.

Delay again.

Hesitating manner and further delays.

Good for Gary! Mr. King should have mentioned this.

He did forget. His lack of preparation on this music is showing.

This technique of openly inviting questions is all right once in a while, but it can turn into a great time-waster if used often.

Finally! How many minutes have been lost?

This rehearsal excerpt represents only a few minutes out of a single class. Mr. King's slow pace, personal revelations, indefiniteness, and piling up of suggestions could be tolerated for a while. But imagine what it would be like to sit through this sort of thing one hour a day, five days a week, for an entire semester or school year! It would take a very patient person, or one who simply had become insensitive to conditions around him or her, to be interested and educated by the experience.

Mr. King had no discipline problems in the excerpt, even though this type of teaching encourages misbehavior. Neither did he say things that were obviously foolish or unmusical. He appears to be a sincere and devoted teacher with an adequate musical background. He did, however, make a number of errors in handling the rehearsal.

One error was his slow pace. To the students, music is only as alive as the teacher makes it. If the learning experience does not move, the students either become mentally numb or attempt to create excitement themselves. *A quick-moving class is a must.* One of the more frequently observed differences between student teachers and experienced teachers is the fact that experienced teachers can teach the same amount of material in much less time.

Another foible of Mr. King was his indecisive manner. A lack of self-confidence is shown by tone of voice, omission of eye contact, and general attitude of the individual.

A third error was that Mr. King talked too much. This is not to say that teachers should never talk about personal matters in front of the group. However, a beginning teacher should generally avoid this habit until he or she has had some teaching experience and is better able to judge what would be useful and interesting to the students. Conversational ramblings should be indulged in sparingly, if ever, because they don't contribute to learning.

There are two ways for teachers to check themselves in being overtalkative. They can make an audio or video tape recording of an entire class period and then play it back at a later time. Or they can place a reliable student in the back of the room with paper, pencil, and a watch that indicates seconds. The student then lists every activity and the amount of time it consumed. For example, a portion of the time sheet might look like this:

	Minutes	Seconds
Band played first phrase		8
Teacher talked		10
Played first phrase		8
Teacher talked		12
Played to end of piece	3	47
Changed to "Noël Français"	1	2
Teacher talked		48

The amount of time spent in various activities can then be totaled.

Closely related to the problem of overtalking is that of unclear explanations and directions. Mr. King has trouble with this problem. Directions must be complete and exact. If the group starts at a letter where there is a pickup note, they must be told whether the pickup is included.

DEVELOPING MUSIC READING

Up to this point, little has been said about music reading. In fact, the steps outlined for choral teaching are basically rote procedures in which the students hear their part performed and then repeat it. This type of learning is slow, and because it involves small segments of music, it is difficult to keep musical. The best solution is to teach the students to comprehend more fully the musical notation seen on the page.

Teach music reading? Wasn't that done in elementary school? Some students can and do sight-read well, but most teenagers cannot read even simple music. The National Assessment of Education reports that only between 8 and 15 percent of all thirteen-year-olds and 10 and 18 percent of all seventeen-year-olds could individually sight-read a very simple phrase of music without words (*First National Assessment of Music Performance,* 1974, pp. 15–20). These results are seldom the fault of the elementary music specialists. At best, they can spend about fifty or sixty minutes each week with a class, which is not enough time to develop a complex skill like reading music. Often they don't have that much time. Sometimes elementary school children are taught to read music, but not music as complex as a four-part choral work. Sometimes the students have lost the skill they had if they did not participate in music for a couple of years. This result should not be surprising to music educators, who, when they were in college (and had some time to practice), could tell the difference when they failed to practice for two or three days.

The ability to read music is a continuum, not an either-or proposition. Very few people (even trained music teachers!) can individually and unaided sight-read perfectly every piece of music. On the other hand, most persons can ascertain something about the music from looking at it. The elementary school teachers are doing what they can under the circumstances, but the secondary school level requires more reading skill. The groups are divided into a greater number of parts, there are changed voices, and the works of music are longer and more complex.

Fortunately, the reading ability of a group is always better than the individual abilities of its members, the manner in which the National Assessment tested students. If one person misses a note, others in the group can often get it. In addition, students are more confident and have less fear of mistakes when doing something as a group.

Although reading procedures are nearly identical for vocal and instrumental music, a few differences should be mentioned. The main reading problem in vocal music is to maintain pitch. Once a singer loses the proper pitch, he or she must depend on experience and ability to find it again. Not so in instrumental music. On a clarinet, if a certain arrangement of holes and keys is covered, the player can be sure (barring a squeak) that the right pitch will result. If a note is missed, the next one can be easily found. The singers can be told, "When the notes go up, move the voice up; when they go down, move the voice down, and when they remain the same, do not change." The teacher can then explain that the staff is a graph of musical pitch. Even this simple and limited approach can produce marked improvement in the singers' abilities to comprehend the printed page.

Another reading problem in vocal music is the presence of two lines for each part: one of music and one of words. Not only do the eyes of the singers move from left to right, they must also move up and down to take in the words. To complicate matters, the position of the words below the notes, used throughout elementary school, is now reversed for the boys whenever the tenor and bass parts share a single staff below the text. Because of the more complex eye movements required, the students should sing many pieces through the first time on a neutral syllable such as *loo* or *lah*.

The reading problem in instrumental music arises from the greater number of parts (in some cases there is only one player on a part) and the need for keeping in mind the key signature and correct fingerings. The reading ability of an instrumentalist is determined largely by the speed and accuracy of the player's reaction to the visual stimuli of notation. A particular F is fingered a certain way, and the wind or brass player reacts to the symbol with a certain combination of fingers and feeling in the lips and mouth.

The way to learn how to read music is to read music. There are no secret systems, tricks, or easy formulas. The author has observed teachers successfully employing a number of different systems for teaching reading. One method is to teach interval recognition by associating each interval with a known song; the perfect fourth is associated with Wagner's "Wedding March," for example, or "I've Been Working on the Railroad." Another reading method is the fixed *do* or solfège, complete with extensive use of chromatic syllables. Another is the movable *do* system used in Hungary, England, and America. Other systems stress tonal patterns. Some teachers ask the students to read letter names or numbers.

The fact that such different approaches have been made to work indicates that success lies not in a particular method but rather in persistent practice at reading. Notes and rhythmic patterns must be experienced so often that they can be recalled quickly and easily. Reading is not taking one minute of time to figure out a rhythmic pattern; reading is recognizing the pattern and executing it almost instantaneously.

To give students experience in reading, teachers should have them read a piece of music at most of the class meetings. The music should be simpler than the numbers normally performed. When students try to sight-read material that is too difficult for them, they become frustrated because they leave the piece without performing it satisfactorily. Some states, such as New York, have music graded by difficulty for use at contests. If a group is performing grade 5 music, then its sight-reading training pieces should be grade 3 or 4, with an occasional grade 5. As the group progresses, more difficult music can be tried.

In every sight-reading effort, the performers should keep going unless there is complete chaos. It is hard for a conscientious teacher with sensitive students to continue when the music doesn't sound good. The temptation is to stop and give some help to make the music sound right. The teacher can call out rehearsal or page numbers, letters, or other assistance, but the music must be kept moving if at all possible.

Functional Music Reading

Sight-reading technique can be developed on an informal, functional basis. Various patterns in the music can be pointed out so that the students gain a concept that is transferable from one piece to another. When the problems are derived from actual music, the training seems logical and necessary to the students, and they are far more likely to remember what they have learned. This procedure is better than devising a scheme that covers every pattern and then telling the students, "You learn this because you might need it some day."

Drawing examples from works of music for sight reading will include almost all the problems found in the repertoire of the group. The more complex patterns probably will have to be taught by rote when they are encountered anyway. They are few in number, however, and do not appear to be a serious drawback.

The functional approach has another feature to its credit: It fulfills the whole-part guideline discussed in Chapter 5. Students should learn to read rhythm and pitch together, because that is the way music is. Teachers may temporarily isolate a rhythmic problem so that it can be studied, but the occasions during which rhythm and pitch are separated should be short.

Even the functional, informal approach requires teaching such basic music knowledge as common note and rest values, meter signatures, accidentals, interpretive signs, and note names. This much knowledge is necessary so that the students will have a basis for their concepts. Although much of this information may have been learned in elementary school, review of it is often necessary.

As for the teaching of rhythm, it is important to stress the 2:1 ratio, which is the basis of rhythmic notation, and to clarify the role of the beat in determining the duration of notes. In this way the students are not so disturbed when, after being told that a quarter note lasts for one beat, they encounter music in 3/2 meter. Dotted notes can be explained as additions to the note. Actually, some students just have to learn that a dotted half note usually receives three beats and a dotted quarter note one and a half beats.

Counting Systems

To help the students read rhythm, teachers should teach a system for counting it. Several methods of counting rhythm are available. The beats are almost universally counted off "one," "two," "three," and so on. Eighth notes in duple time are usually counted by adding "an" or "and." Sixteenth notes are easily counted by "one-ee-an-da" or "one-a-an-da," and triplets by "one-tee-toe," "trip-o-let," or "one-la-lee." Unless one syllable such as *ta* is used for every note, the counting system should avoid using the same word symbol for different rhythmic figures:

A trained musician can count these patterns correctly, but a beginning student is more confused than helped by them.

Occasionally words can be associated with rhythmic figures, such as

Am - ster - dam.

The following rhythmic pattern is seen often:

It can be remembered as the "here-comes-the-bride" phrase because of its prominence in Wagner's well-known "Wedding March" from *Lohengrin*.

It is important in teaching rhythmic understanding to separate the beat from the execution of a rhythmic pattern. Many students are not clear on this point. They are inclined to think that music with a pounding, obvious beat has lots of "rhythm." To keep the distinction as clear as possible, teachers can have the students tap the beat with one foot and continue the execution of the notes in either the mouth or the hands. However, inexperienced students find it difficult to produce even a rudimentary rhythmic pattern while simultaneously maintaining a steady beat.

A concept of rhythm can be promoted through warm-up routines without notation. In this routine the teacher calls out the type of note just before the beginning of a measure:

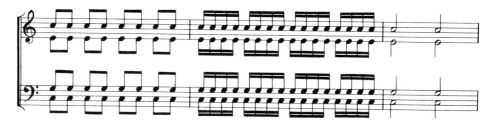

Singers can also perform with neutral syllables if desired: "may," "me," "mo," and so on. Instrumentalists play the note values as written.

The exercise offers practice in counting and thinking ahead, both of which are necessary for accurate reading of rhythm. It can be varied by moving the pitch up a semitone on each measure and then returning by half steps to the original pitch. Triplets may be added later.

The best method for presenting 6/8 or compound meters has long been debated by music educators. What is sometimes forgotten is that since they first learned "Pop Goes the Weasel," students have been singing and hearing music in compound meter. So they know about it through experience, even if they don't recognize it in notation. The most practical approach to 6/8 meter is to consider it as six beats in a measure, with a strong emphasis on one and four sometimes stressed by tapping the foot. In this way counting is maintained, regardless of whether the tempo is fast or slow.

With a little practice the students can read 6/8 or 9/8 as easily as any other meter.

Reading Patterns

Psychologists have known for over seventy years that when a person reads, the eyes do not move letter by letter or word by word but rather by group of words (Schmidt, 1917). The better the reader, the larger the groups of words encompassed in a single fixation of the eyes. The same principle applies to music reading. Musicians are taught at first to react to each note, but eventually, by drawing on previous experience with music, they learn to group notes together and perform them as a single entity. So when competent clarinetists or flutists see

they can grasp the eight notes at once and react with the proper kinesthetic movements in the fingers and embouchure.

The perception of interval patterns is especially valuable to vocal students because they do not read by a set reaction of fingers but rather by a sense of relative pitch, which utilizes mental imagery of the tone and a memory of the physical sensation involved in singing it. The pitch B just above the bass clef feels one way for the male singer, and B on the second line feels another way. Through experience in associating notes and their sounds, singers develop a sense of pattern that helps them read. Although successful reading does not usually consist of an "interval plus interval" approach, the teacher should point out common intervals and patterns as they occur in pieces of music. For instance, when the basses begin to see and hear the similarity between

and

they are learning to read music. The same is true for reading rhythmic patterns. The more the students see a particular pattern in different settings, the more quickly they can understand and read it.

Vocal teachers can offer some direct reading practice by writing a major scale on the chalkboard in any key that is comfortable to sing. Under the note can be written sol-fa syllables or the numbers 1 2 3 4 5 6 7 1̄ (a dash above or below a number indicates a pitch in an upper or lower octave). Sol-fa syllables are satisfactory if the students are familiar with them; otherwise they should be avoided, because the students feel that they are too mature to spend the time that is required to make the syllables meaningful. They are more suitable vocally because their pure vowels are without diphthongs and there are no two-syllable words such as *seven*. On the other hand, numbers are in the same language in which the students sing most of their music, and a number series by its nature implies a relationship between the numbers. When used to define the distances between scale steps, a number system helps clarify the understanding of intervals.

The teacher can start by asking the singers to sing a major scale with the numbers. This procedure establishes a feeling of key center. Once the tonic feeling is established, the students will have some basis for relating intervals to one another. By pointing to notes on the board, the teacher can direct the class to sing simple three- or four-note groups that begin and end on the tonic: 1 3 1, 1 3 5 1, 1 2 3 1, 1 2 3 4 5 1. Later, longer and more difficult patterns can be sung at sight: 1 2 4 5 7̱ 1, 1 3 4 5 6 1, and so on.

After some practice with scales written on the board, simple tonal patterns in various keys can replace the scales. These patterns should not be haphazard groups of notes but short combinations similar to those found in the music the group is singing. When the patterns are sung in unison, the bass clef may be used occasionally in place of the treble clef, because it will do no harm to have the girls become familiar with the bass clef, too.

Because of transposition and greater variety of clefs, instrumental teachers find it harder to use the chalkboard for simple reading work. Fortunately, many supplementary books have been published. Some of these stress technique, while others emphasize rhythm, style, scales, or chords. These materials are written at varying levels of difficulty.

Sight-reading practice should not become separated from the main thrust of the classroom effort, which is fostering skills and understanding. Exercises in reading are valuable only to the extent that they teach something better than it can be taught through reading actual music. Reading will help students reach that goal but will not replace it.

TEACHING MUSICAL UNDERSTANDINGS

So far this chapter has discussed techniques for teaching students to perform music. Performing, however, is not all there is to music, and it should not be the only aspect of the subject that is taught in secondary-school performing groups. Just as one should eat more than one type of food, students should be taught more than one aspect of music. The plea here is not to do away with the performing of music or to be satisfied with carelessness and minimal skills. Rather, the hope is for some enrichment of what has been the traditional skill-development experiences of students in a band, orchestra, or choral group.

Most college music majors—after years of experience in performing organizations—have some notion of how to rehearse a group. Not so with the idea of bringing cognitive or analytical learning into a rehearsal situation. Because only a few directors have made an organized effort to incorporate the learning of useful musical information in the rehearsal, both prospective and experienced teachers have had little chance to observe and evaluate how such information is taught.

Here are some guidelines for teaching more than performance skills in the rehearsals of school groups:

1. As much as is reasonably possible, integrate learning aspects of theory and literature with the pieces of music being rehearsed. One director, who believes that his band members should know the fundamentals of notation, sets aside two rehearsal periods following each big concert. The students are told to leave their instruments in the lockers on those days, which are then spent learning to write scales and figure out meter signatures. Although he should be commended for realizing that the students need to do more than play their instruments, his method leaves something to be desired. First of all, the

students are tacitly led to believe that theory consists only of scales and meter signatures. A more basic flaw, however, is that looking at a suspension or a rondo *apart from works of music* is not successful with most teenagers. Trained musicians find segmented learning useful because they can relate it to music they know. Most secondary school students cannot do this because they don't have enough background in music.

2. Organize active learning. The director mentioned earlier was content with a passive and unrelated study of theory, which does little to interest the average student. If the learning revolves around the music being rehearsed, the material comes alive through playing or singing. One of the advantages of a performing group is its potential to perform *and* study a piece of music. The sum of these two aspects of music is educationally greater than either activity alone, and students do learn more in this way. Sometimes it is impossible for a group to perform a particular work. Perhaps it is too difficult, or it is written for another medium. In such cases a recording should be listened to.

3. Plan the content for such learning according to a definite scope and sequence. Tossing out tidbits of information won't "add up" for most students, again because they don't have the background to assimilate bits and pieces. Also, the "tidbit" approach often results in gaps and repetition in coverage. Long-range planning is necessary.

4. Include both the student's performing skill and nonperformance knowledge in deciding his or her grade. This practice makes clear the importance of learning information such as the difference between polyphony and homophony, the tertian pattern of chords, and the characteristics of a concerto grosso or cantata.

Thomas Morley's late Renaissance madrigal "April Is in My Mistress' Face" (pp. 163–165) illustrates how basic learnings can be related to the performing of music. The exact information that students learn along with and by means of this piece of music will vary according to what they have learned previously and will learn in the future, and the results are further affected by all the other variables among schools and students. In addition to performance skills, some of the information that can be learned through the use of this madrigal is the following:

1. Notation, including key signatures.

2. Polyphonic style, especially the imitative entrances that are clearly present in measures 23–35.

3. Intervals and minor chords. Especially noticeable are the intervals prevalent in counterpoint (measures 1–2, for example). The students can learn to identify basic intervals such as thirds and fourths with specifying whether they are major, minor, perfect, and so on.

4. The madrigal as a type of music literature: its text, the number of singers originally involved, the typical performance setting, a few composers of madrigals, and similar information.

5. Characteristics of Renaissance music and other fine arts. In Morley's madrigal students can see the partially systematic harmony, the lack of a stable tonality (measures 9–11), a restrained style, and suspensions (measures 29 and 37). The characteristics of the Renaissance period can be presented, and the rehearsal room can be given some interest by hanging a few Renaissance prints on the walls.

6. Aesthetic aspects of the music: the effect of the falling lines in measure 21, the overlapping entrances in measures 23–24, the suspensions, the missing

April Is in My Mistress' Face

Thomas Morley (1557–1603)

third in some chords, the ascending bass line in measure 11, and the change to major on the final chord. In the case of aesthetic qualities, it isn't so much that the students need to know these qualities so that they can answer questions about them but rather that they notice and be sensitive to these qualities in the music.

Instrumental music teachers may wonder how studying a madrigal applies to them. First of all, "April Is in My Mistress' Face" has been transcribed for band (*Two Madrigals* arranged by McLin, published by Pro Art). Transcriptions of Renaissance music for band or orchestra are rare, which is unfortunate. Although transcriptions are not as appropriate as original music for a particular medium, they are better than nothing. If instrumental teachers choose not to perform a madrigal transcription, at least once in two years the students should hear a madrigal from a recording so that they learn a little bit about this type of music. For study purposes an instrumental teacher can show the choral version on an overhead projector, make copies, or borrow copies from the school choral library. The student instrumentalists should figure out which part of the choral version they are playing and then look over the text carefully for clues to the appropriate style. In fact, it is a good idea for band and orchestra members to sing through the madrigal. They will be better musicians for doing so.

Flexibility and imagination are necessary in deciding when to include non-performance learnings. Many teachers find that devoting half a period twice a week is most successful. Others prefer to spend five or ten minutes during each rehearsal period. Teachers find that even a few minutes of such study can add welcome variety to rehearsals. During the week or so prior to an important performance, the study of theory and literature may not be undertaken at all, but during other weeks the teacher may give it substantial attention. Sometimes the students become so interested in what is being discussed that it is difficult to stop after a short time. When this happens, a good portion of the class period can profitably be spent on the material.

For "April Is in My Mistress' Face," two short sessions of about ten minutes each might be spent helping the students hear and understand its polyphony. Other sessions can be devoted to (1) recognizing that the most frequent intervals are thirds and sixths, (2) determining the pattern of the minor triad, and (3) learning about Morley and the Elizabethan madrigal. Of course, this list could be expanded or contracted.

It's a simple proposition, but one that sometimes gets lost in the rush to get ready for the next concert: A school performing organization exists for educational purposes. More important than high ratings at a state contest or hearty applause from an audience is the learning that takes place in the students' day-to-day encounter with music. Because most performers seldom take other music classes during the years they are in these groups, their education should include broad and basic information about music. Acquiring only technical performing skills is simply not a well-rounded education in music.

SELECTING MUSIC FOR A PARTICULAR GROUP

General Considerations

A music teacher should select music for its usefulness in furthering the music education of the students. Two requirements must be met for a work of music to contribute to the students' musical education: (1) The music must be of a good quality (a topic discussed in Chapter 4), and (2) it must be suitable to the musical understanding and technical ability of the group. No music teacher should choose a number that sounds best with a hundred musicians and attempt to perform it with thirty. Neither should a teacher pick music that is far beyond the ability of the students. Some points for teachers to consider applying to selecting both vocal and instrumental music are given next.

Repetition. If sections of a work are repeated, this repetition reduces the amount of time required to learn it—and also to memorize it, in the case of choral music.

Length. All other things being equal, the longer the work, the longer it will take to learn it. In addition, there is a certain amount of fatigue and loss of interest in learning a work that requires a lot of time and effort.

Rhythm. Adolescents are attracted to music that has rhythmic interest. They are able to perform difficult patterns, if these occur in almost all parts simultaneously and if they contain much repetition. Problems can appear when greater independence is required of the performers.

Musicianship of Students. There is an essential quality in music that is more than pitches and their durations. The work "How Lovely Is Thy Dwelling Place" from Brahms's *Requiem* requires a mature concept of tone quality and feeling in order to perform it well. The notes in the work can be sung by a good high school choir, but the proper expression is not easy to attain. If such a number is tried, it will need to be worked on intermittently over a period of time so that it has time to "settle" in the students' minds.

A work that is soft, slow, sustained, and subtle demands much musicianship and control. This is not to say that teenagers should not perform anything that is mature, but there is a limit to which adolescents can be pushed in subtleties or symbolism.

Quality of Music. Some works of music are so logically written, and so clear in their musical intent, that many of the technical barriers are overcome. This situation may happen because the performers work with added zest on the music. Secondary school groups often require quite a bit of work to prepare a piece, so the music should have a lasting quality about it.

Vocal Considerations

Text. Teenagers are more discerning about good and bad poetry than adults sometimes give them credit for. They may not be able to say why one poem is better than another, but they can sense the difference. Unfortunately, at this age students tend to be critical of any text that is abstract or symbolic. "Lo, How a Rose E'er Blooming" is a fine text, but its symbolism must be carefully explained to the singers to avoid a halfhearted effort on the song. In schools with little choral tradition, it is wise to select music with rather specific messages that the students can easily understand. A distinction should be made between texts that are abstract and those that are serious. Teenagers usually undertake willingly a serious text that they can understand.

Some works of music have texts written in dialect. Too often these attempts at writing in the vernacular are grossly inaccurate, because most dialects contain tonal characteristics that are impossible to indicate fully on the printed page. Furthermore, adolescents can seldom phonate them accurately, even though they may spend some time in practicing the new pronunciations. Sometimes attempts at dialects convey an unintended sense of comedy and ridicule of the ethnic group that is associated with the song.

Range. The ranges of the various adolescent voices are discussed in Chapter 11. Generally the problem is not so much with those few notes that lie at the extremes of the range but rather with a tessitura that is consistently too high or too low. Therefore, the tessitura of the parts must be carefully checked, especially when changing voices are involved.

Tenor Part. The tenor part is very important in SATB music, but few teenage boys have the experience and vocal development to sing it well. Tenor sections in school choral groups vary in their strengths and weaknesses, so each teacher has to know the characteristics of the section. If it is made up largely of boys whose voices are still changing, then high notes may present no problem. In other tenor sections, high notes are out of the question. One of the problems is that composers and arrangers have never quite agreed on what a tenor voice is. Some tenor music demands a light quality, some a dark and dramatic quality; some parts go to a sixth above middle C, others go to an octave below middle C. Adolescent tenors usually sing best around B flat or A below middle C, and they cannot be relied on for much volume.

Accompaniment. Choral groups that are not musically advanced usually sound better on a work that is accompanied. The piano gives them a feeling of confidence and supports their sometimes shaky pitch. There are two conditions under which an accompaniment might hinder rather than help a choral group. One is when the accompaniment is considerably different from the singers' parts, especially when it plays pitches that are dissonant with what the singers have. The other occurs when the piano part is too difficult for an accompanist to play well, a not unknown situation in secondary schools.

Dissonant Intervals.   The singing of dissonant intervals sometimes presents difficulties for teenage singers. The trouble lies not so much in the actual intervals themselves as in the way they are approached. The minor second in the following example can usually be sung accurately:

But when the approach differs, the same harmonic interval may become very difficult to perform well:

The character of the lines also affects the difficulty of the interval. For instance, if the singers are divided into two groups, and one group sings "Three Blind Mice" in G while the other sings "America" in F, they could probably sing the dissonances without too much difficulty. However, if the same dissonances occur between two lines that are unfamiliar or have little melodic character, most students find them almost impossible to sing accurately.

Number of Parts.   In general, the more voice parts a piece contains, the more difficult it will be. A TTBB work for boys' glee club is definitely a more difficult arrangement than a TB work. This is true for several reasons. The number of singers on each part is cut in half, which requires more independence from each singer. The length of time required to learn the notes may be longer because there are twice as many parts. Also, the highest and lowest parts are likely to be harder because the notes must be closer to the extremes of the voice ranges. With each additional part there is also a greater chance of error in singing the notes of the part. For inexperienced glee clubs, then, two-part music is much more suitable. The change from SA to SSA or from TB to TBB can be made without extensive reorganization of the group. In a girls' glee club some sopranos and altos are able to sing second soprano on three-part numbers. The same is true of the boys in changing from TB to TBB music.

Tenor voices are usually in short supply in secondary school choral groups. Some mixed choruses, especially in smaller schools, have a hard time finding enough tenors to make up a section. Arrangers have attempted to overcome this problem by providng SAB (soprano, alto, baritone) arrangements in which boys with changed voices sing the baritone part and boys with unchanged voices sing the alto or sometimes the soprano part. Although these arrangements are not completely satisfactory in harmonic structure, they do provide acceptable music for such groups.

The change from SAB to SATB is not made as easily as the change of voice groupings within a boys' or girls' glee club. There is usually a greater difference between the SATB tenor part and SAB baritone part than there is between the first and second tenor parts in glee club music. The change can be made easier if the teacher emphasizes to the prospective tenors that the B in SAB stands for baritone, not bass. However, it is no easy matter to create a tenor section out of a group of boys who are used to singing baritone. For this reason, SAB arrangements should not be used to the exclusion of all SATB arrangements, unless the prospects for a tenor section are nil.

Musical Arrangement.   Arrangements that teenagers sing best are solid, "clean," and uncluttered with close harmony or excess parts. Members of school choral groups are not always talented, well-trained singers, so the presence of complicated effects and extra parts can make the music sound worse, not better. There is nothing wrong with many of the complex arrangements except that they are not suitable for most secondary school groups. Even if achieved, there is always the question "Is the complicated effect worth the time and effort required to learn it properly?" In most instances the answer is no.

Instrumental Considerations

Key.   The easiest key for a band is B flat, while G and D are easiest for strings. The next easiest keys move toward more flats for the band and more sharps for the strings. In both cases the construction of the instruments and the traditional keys used in teaching encourage this difference.

Scalewise Runs.   Sometimes the assumption is made that if the page contains many sixteenth notes, it is automatically difficult. Although this is sometimes true, it makes a difference whether the notes jump around without much pattern or move scalewise. Almost all students have at least minimum experience in playing scales, so they know scales better than any other musical pattern. If the passage is in an easy range and key, the demand for speed in playing does not present a huge problem.

Range.   On woodwinds and strings, range affects the timbre and quality of intonation and involves certain technical problems of fingering. On brasses, range is very important. Tones that are too high for the brass players may be missed or played with strain and poor intonation. A high tessitura in a brass part is exhausting for the less mature player.

Length of Difficult Passages. The length of technically difficult passages should be considered. For example, the clarinets might rather easily play

but have trouble playing sixteenths of similar difficulty if they appear on four or eight consecutive beats. The longer runs require that much more skill and experience.

Musical Arrangement. As with choral music, the easier, and often better, arrangements for teenage instrumentalists contain clear, basic outlines without unneeded decoration. There is, of course, considerable variation between music that is suitable for players with only a year or two of experience and music that is possible for select players at the high school level. The simpler music requires fewer different parts and less independence of each part. The reduced number of independent parts may not be readily apparent in the score; even though the same number of instruments may be mentioned, many of the parts are doubled. With less experienced players, doubling is desirable because of the additional support it provides. But when the players are more advanced, it steals color and interest from the group's performance. An overuse of doubling tends to make the group sound the same no matter what it is playing.

Another difficulty in judging an instrumental arrangement is the disparity in the number of instruments on a part and in their amount of sound. On the score the first trumpet, oboe, and flute each occupy a line and appear to be equal. The flute, however, is not as strong as the oboe, which in turn is not nearly as strong as the trumpet. Neither can the E-flat alto clarinet play a concert B flat below middle C as fully as can six soprano clarinets. Teachers should understand instruments well enough to evaluate an arrangement for its potential in permitting the important parts to be heard. The recordings of works supplied by most publishers can be of help in this evaluation.

The main problem orchestra teachers face is quite different from that of band directors: having enough strings to balance the wind and percussion sections. Therefore when looking over music, orchestra teachers need to check that the strings are given a chance to be heard. Some of the earlier arrangements for school orchestras seemed most concerned with making the music complete, no matter how many strings might be lacking. The result was a "band with string" effect that does not do justice to the orchestra.

A final word about orchestra arrangements. The piano appears infrequently in the symphony orchestra, and it should be just as scarce in the school orchestra, except for groups that have studied only a year or two. The only justifications for using a piano in a school orchestra, beyond those valid for the professional orchestra, are for limited assistance to the strings in learning the music and for strengthening a particular part that lacks adequate instrumentation.

Program Requirements

Almost all music should be selected for secondary school bands, orchestras, and choral groups on the basis of its educational value to the students. Only occasionally should a number be programmed just to please the audience; a little of this can go a long way. Much of the problem of selecting an interesting program is solved if teachers choose music of different types, which they should do anyway. Also, each year the format for programs can be varied. One year a choral group might sing a cantata, another year a program of folk music and dancing, and another year a musical. The instrumental groups might present a program featuring three or four outstanding students playing solos with the group, and another year they might present the more usual program of concert music.

The musical interests of the community should be considered in selecting music for programs. Teachers should present the most worthwhile music they can without losing the students and audience. A little give and take is needed. It is a rare community that appreciates an all-art music program. On the other hand, there is no community in which some art music cannot be presented.

It is difficult for listeners to sit through entire programs of unfamiliar music. At Christmas they want to hear a few familiar carols, and they find "The Battle Hymn of the Republic" a stirring piece of music (in most parts of the United States, at least) because they know and like the song. The average adult listener would rather hear the familiar, established "old favorites" than the current "top forty."

Finding Appropriate Music

Where do teachers locate music for their groups? First, many pieces of music are presented in methods classes. Future music teachers should start then to build up a music list or a professional library of musical works that appear to be good possibilities for secondary school students.

Second, there are several graded listings of music appropriate for school groups, including the lists of contest music published by a number of states. Band directors can use the *Band Music Guide,* ninth edition (Northfield, Ill.: The Instrumentalist, 1989).

A third practical step is a "program exchange" idea. Some teachers have standing agreements with other teachers to exchange concert programs. A few music stores also publish programs that have been sent to them.

A fourth source for music is the catalogs that publishers make available. These pieces may be ordered directly from the publisher or through a music store. For many large-ensemble works the publisher supplies an audition recording. Copies of music can be ordered on an examination basis, and teachers can study them at their leisure. Works that are not wanted can then be returned.

Copyright Law

A major revision of the United States copyright law became effective on January 1, 1978. This law gives the owners of a copyright the rights of reproducing,

distributing, performing, and displaying books, poems, and music (including recorded sounds). The term of a copyright is the author's life plus fifty years or, in
the case of "work made for hire" (which includes most textbooks), seventy-five
years after publication. The law also granted an increased term for works copyrighted before 1978 by increasing the old fifty-six-year limit to seventy-five years.
The year of copyright is printed on the book or music, along with the symbol ©.
These changes put the United States law in closer agreement with the international
copyright law.

The new law gives a general legal status to "fair use" by teachers and libraries,
something that had already been recognized by the courts and had become somewhat established in legal precedents. The general guideline for teachers is that
they are restrained "where the unauthorized copying displaces what realistically
might have been a sale, no matter how small the amount of money involved."
More specific fair-use guidelines have been developed by representatives of educators and publishers. These guidelines allow for unauthorized copying (by hand
or photocopy, it doesn't matter) of single copies for purposes of the teacher's
research or preparation for class of up to one chapter of a book and a percentage
of other short works such as poems and pictures. A single recording is permitted,
and a lost part may be copied in an emergency if it is replaced by a purchased
copy in due time.

Multiple copies for classroom use, not to exceed one copy per student, must
meet the tests of brevity, spontaneity, and cumulative effect. Brevity allows for
500 words of prose or 10 percent of the work, whichever is greater, or one picture
and the like. No work may be reproduced in its entirety. Spontaneity requires that
copies be made only on the request of the teacher and that at a time when the
teaching effectiveness would suffer by the delay of seeking permission from the
copyright owner. The cumulative effect requirement sets limits on the number of
times a short work by the same author may be used (two) and the total number
of multiple copyings in a single course (nine). Penalties for infringement range
from $250 up to $50,000 for "willful" violations. Teachers who were "not aware"
that they had committed an infringement may have the fine reduced to $100.*

If teachers wish to photocopy in excess of the fair-use guidelines, they must
secure written permission from the copyright owner. Music publishers have a
spotty record in replying to such requests; some are very prompt, while others
simply never respond. In some cases a publisher has recently bought a list from
another publisher and does not know every work in that catalog. In other cases
such requests are shunted off to law firms, which have little interest in or knowledge
about educational matters. Usually permission to make changes in a musical work
will be granted if the work is not available in a form that the teacher needs and
if the teacher has purchased the existing arrangement.

A distinction needs to be made between original music that is copyrighted
and arrangements of songs that are copyrighted. The original tunes to songs such
as "Home on the Range" and "Yankee Doodle" are not copyrighted and therefore

---

*No court has yet decided if reading this page deprives one of the "unawareness" defense!

are in the public domain. However, arrangements of them can be copyrighted. Another arrangement can be made of the melody, but the copyrighted arrangement cannot be photocopied without permission beyond the limits of fair use.

Most publishers of educational materials try to be fair with teachers. They are often reluctant to pursue their rights in court because of the legal costs and damage to their public relations. They do, however, want the copyright law observed. As one publisher states:

> *Copyright was provided for in the Constitution to encourage talented people to create more books and music and other works of art and to share them with the public. Unauthorized exploitation of a work which exceeds the boundaries of fair use, therefore, not only violates the creative rights of the author and publisher, it also jeopardizes society's right to an environment that is conducive to the dissemination of new ideas* (The New Copyright Law, 1979).

Adapting Music

There are several ways in which teachers can simplify music without infringing on a copyright. Because the range of the voice parts in vocal music is sometimes a problem, it can help if the accompanist transposes the entire work. Intonation can often be improved by moving the key up a half step.

A second way to simplify and often improve a work is to cut the number of parts or reduce the number of performers in a section of the music. In both instrumental and vocal music the amount of doubling can often be reduced. In choral music the singers can be told to sing other parts, while in instrumental music the player will have to rest unless a new part is written for him or her.

Two other simplifications are possible in choral music. If a group is not very advanced, a section of a song can be sung in unison by one part or by a combination of parts. The amount of time required to learn the full arrangement may not be justifiable.

In some choral numbers the harmony parts are changed when the melody is repeated. The music can be simplified by merely instructing the singers to repeat the harmony parts as they were first learned—sometimes with different words. A good example for this technique is the Christmas carol "The Twelve Days of Christmas." The song can be easy or difficult, depending on the presence of repeated harmony parts.

Music teachers should not be hesitant about trying changes in the music. Perhaps a soloist can perform one portion, or the teacher can compose a descant, a countermelody, or simple harmony parts. The need for teacher-arranged music is greatest at the middle school and junior high level. The changing voices, with their range limitations and the unique nature of each group, make it desirable for teachers to try their hand at arranging. Instrumental teachers may also find it advantageous to do some arranging, especially if the group is of unusual size and instrumentation.

Questions   1.   In the early stages of work on a piece, why is it suggested that a particular section be worked on only a limited number of times? What guidelines for teaching pertain to this suggestion?

2.   What guidelines of music teaching are involved when trouble spots are isolated?

3.   In practicing music reading by pointing to a scale on the chalkboard, why is the major scale recommended first? Is a teaching principle behind the suggestion?

4.   When one is teaching parts to an instrumental group, it is suggested that the melody be rehearsed first, while a choral group should learn the lowest part first. What are the differences between vocal and instrumental music that would account for this difference in approach?

5.   When one is teaching students to play or sing accompanying parts, should these parts be studied and learned by themselves or in conjunction with the melodic lines? Why?

Projects   1.   Select a choral or instrumental work. Decide what information you can teach the students with that particular piece of music.

2.   Study the score to a march and a choral work. Mark out the important lines and other parts as if you were going to teach it to a school group. Mark also the places at which the students might encounter problems of rhythm, pitch, and so on.

3.   Select three easy pieces (one each for band, orchestra, and choral group) that would be appropriate for a first rehearsal of the group.

4.   Using the same three numbers, decide how you might present each work so that the students gain an idea of the whole work.

5.   Observe a teacher rehearsing a school performing group. Notice the kind of procedures that are used, both the effective and efficient ones and those that aren't. Observe the amount of time it takes to change from one work of music to another, and notice whether the students waste time in getting started or in talking.

6.   Visit two secondary school choral teachers and two instrumental teachers. Find out the following:

(a)   What arrangements, if any, are made for sectional rehearsals

(b)   What work, if any, is expected of the students outside of the rehearsals

(c)   What procedures, if any, are used to enable themselves to listen to their own groups objectively

Suggested Readings   Bessom, Malcolm E., Alphonse M. Tatarunis, and Samuel L. Forcucci. *Teaching Music in Today's Secondary Schools.* 2nd ed. New York: Holt, Rinehart & Winston, 1980. Chapter 12.

Boyd, Jack. *Rehearsal Guide for the Choral Director*. West Nyack, N.Y.: Parker, 1970. Chapters 6, 9, and 10.

Colwell, Richard J. *The Teaching of Instrumental Music*. New York: Appleton-Century-Crofts, 1969. Chapter 6.

Gattiker, Irvin. *Complete Book of Rehearsing Techniques for the High School Orchestra*. West Nyack, N.Y.: Parker, 1977. Chapter 7.

Harmon, Russell A. *Pragmatic Choral Procedures*. Metuchen, N.J.: The Scarecrow Press, 1984.

Hefferman, Charles W. *Choral Music: Technique and Artistry*. Englewood Cliffs, N.J.: Prentice-Hall, 1982.

Kohut, Daniel. *Instrumental Music Pedagogy*. Englewood Cliffs, N.J.: Prentice-Hall, 1973. Chapter 8.

Labuta, Joseph A. *Teaching Musicianship in the High School Band*. West Nyack, N.Y.: Parker, 1972.

Otto, Richard A. *Effective Methods for Building the High School Band*. West Nyack, N.Y.: Parker, 1971. Chapter 8.

Pizer, Russell A. *How to Improve the High School Band Sound*. West Nyack, N.Y.: Parker, 1976. Chapter 3.

Robinson, William C., and James A. Middleton. *The Complete School Band Program*. West Nyack, N.Y.: Parker, 1972. Chapter 7.

Roe, Paul F. *Choral Music Education*. Englewood Cliffs, N.J.: Prentice-Hall, 1970. Chapters 6 and 9.

Whitrock, Ruth. *Choral Insights* (Baroque Edition). San Diego: Neil A. Kjos, 1985.

References   *First National Assessment of Music Performance,* Report No. 03-MU-01. Denver: National Assessment of Educational Progress, 1974.

The New Copyright Law. Chicago: Scott, Foresman, 1979.

Schmidt, William A. *An Experimental Study in the Psychology of Reading*. Chicago: University of Chicago Press, 1917.

CHAPTER 9

Teaching Musical Expression

Music, dance, and drama depend on someone's ability to re-create them, to bring them to life. The exclusively visual arts need no mediator between the creator and the observer. But in music (except for recorded or electronic works), the performer is the intermediary between the composer's directions and what the listener hears. The performers' interpretive skill—their treatment of the music's expressive qualities—can make the difference between a rewarding musical experience and one that is not.

Although music has a notational system, it is incomplete. It indicates pitch level and duration rather accurately, but directions about dynamic level and style are broad and subject to personal judgment. Music notation is like the script of a drama. The words are there on the page, along with a few general directions about stage action and the way in which a line should be delivered, but the actors are responsible for bringing the words to life. In the same way, the performers' interpretations are a necessary part of music.

What does this mean for school music teachers? First, it means that they must make the interpretive decisions, just as professional conductors or solo performers must. Second, they must teach their students to perform the music with correct interpretation and to make some valid judgments on their own. Let's begin by examining the decision-making process.

DECIDING ON INTERPRETATION

Where do school music teachers get their ideas about how a piece of music should be interpreted? They get them from the existing body of information about how the work should be performed and from their own musical knowledge. Both sources have merit. However, when the school group is performing a work in the traditional repertoire, school music teachers should consider how persons in recognized positions of musical leadership have treated the work.

Performance Practices

The largest source for interpretive ideas is recordings. There are regular commercial releases on familiar labels and "service" recordings provided by publishers. They can be listened to for ideas on tempo and style.

A second source is the written body of knowledge about performance practices. Conductors of major professional ensembles who make commercial recordings are well aware of the writings and traditions about performance styles in music, so what is heard on the recording is partially a manifestation of that knowledge. Books such as Donald Grout's *A History of Western Music* (New York: W. W. Norton, 1980) and the musical styles series published by W. W. Norton, Prentice-Hall, and others provide information about performance practice. In addition, there are specialized and authoritative books on performance practices. Some of them are as follows:

Crocker, Richard L. *A History of Music Style.* New York: McGraw-Hill, 1966.

Dart, Thurston. *The Interpretation of Music.* New York: Harper Colophon Books, 1954.

Donington, Robert. *The Interpretation of Early Music.* London: Faber & Faber, 1963.

Dorian, Frederick. *The History of Music in Performance.* New York: W. W. Norton, 1942.

Authenticity

How carefully can or should performers adhere to the sound the composer had in mind? There are strong arguments for authenticity. A Baroque concerto grosso played in a passionate romantic style is hardly genuine—it's like illuminating a great Rembrandt painting with blinking, colored neon lights. And it does seem that the judgments of the composer or ethnic group should be respected. After all, they created the music in the first place, and if it is worth performing, it should be done competently and honestly. A black spiritual should not be sung like an English folk song, and a Bach organ fugue transcribed for band should not be souped up with snare drum and cymbal.

There are some counterarguments, however. Maybe Bach would have written for snare drum and cymbal had he been able to work them in. Such a question can never be answered, of course. More important is the fact that fully authentic performances of early works can never be achieved. In some cases modern instruments such as clarinets and trumpets are clearly superior to original models and different both acoustically and technically. Furthermore, it is impossible to know exactly how music was performed two hundred years ago. Musicologists can make only educated guesses about the presence and style of vibrato, the execution of certain rhythmic figures and embellishments, and tempos.

Practically speaking, about all that school music teachers can do is be as authentic as reasonably possible. They certainly should avoid gross errors in interpretation and style, but they must accept the fact that teenage voices cannot render authentically all types of music from Irish folk songs to early Renaissance masses. Similar limitations exist for the instrumental teacher.

Even though there are limitations on the degree of authenticity student groups can attain, the young people should at least know what type of sounds they are trying to achieve, even if they can't execute them fully.

Personal Judgment

Teachers should neither overinterpret nor underinterpret the music. Both extremes are equally undesirable. Teachers who abuse their license add many "personal touches" to the music: extreme tempos, additional sforzandos, sustained *m*'s, *n*'s, and *-ing*'s in choral music, excessive rubato, exaggerated dynamic changes, and so on. The opposite type of director seems to think that as long as "the letter of the law" is fulfilled—all the notes sounded in tune and on time—that is sufficient. Their conducting beat is the same size and style whether the music is loud or soft, staccato or legato, fast or slow. They have a mechanical view of music.

Both of these poles in interpreting music indicate a lack of understanding about music. Conductors should use, not abuse, their license to interpret. Knowing accepted interpretations of the style in general and the work in particular, they should exercise discretion, judgment, and good taste. *Some* latitude is available in tempo, dynamics, articulation, and the like, but radical departures from the norm merely detract from the music.

TECHNIQUES OF TEACHING INTERPRETATION

When a teacher has decided on the best interpretation, the more difficult task of teaching it begins. Most teachers face several problems at this point. One is the mistaken belief that interpretation is something to be reserved primarily for advanced students. This notion is based on the assumption that skills must be perfected *before* musical expression is considered. An extreme example of a belief in technique before interpretation is the case of a principal viola player in a major symphony, a graduate of a fine European conservatory, who assigns his private students only scales and exercises for at least the first two years; no pieces of music are studied during that time. Some teachers speak of first giving their students the necessary "equipment" to perform musically. Such thinking is probably better suited to setting up a factory or buying a baseball team bats and gloves. It does not apply very well to human beings; people learn playing techniques and interpretation at about the same time. If learning expression must be temporarily postponed, it should be only a brief lag, certainly not two years!

Technical skill and musical expression complement each other, because each provides a sense of purpose for studying the other. Clearly teachers should not ask students to do something they are unable to do; they cannot play something in a lyrical style if they can't play the notes. But as much as possible, teachers should teach a sense of phrasing, style, and expression. Even the simple songs in beginning instrument method books can be played musically instead of the "duh, duh, duh, duh, duh" so often heard.

A second problem is teenagers' apparent lack of interest in subtlety. There are several probable causes. Adolescent behavior is characterized by enthusiasm, impatience, and straightforwardness. And many young people have a limited musical background and they simply do not know that there are different styles in performing music. Furthermore, conditions in some students' environment encourage them not to notice subtleties. Students who live in a home with a blaring television set or radio and people yelling at each other soon learn not to listen.

A third problem in getting teenagers to interpret music is that they are taught one aspect of expression at one time and another at another time, with no attempt to pull them together. They may practice making crescendos and decrescendos in warm-up, but when they turn to a piece of music they are rehearsing, nothing more is said about dynamic changes. The students should be aware of the overall effect of a musical work, a point that was stressed in Chapter 8.

Contest adjudication sheets divide the total performance of a group into various elements so that adjudicators can discuss them specifically. However, at the top of the sheet adjudicators give the group one final rating, which represents a summation of all the factors considered. Music teachers should treat the area of interpretation in the same manner by considering the parts that go into it but then making sure that the whole does in fact become greater than the sum of its parts.

Integrating particular aspects can be aided by the right kind of work on aspects of interpreting. For example, a choral director may devise some experiences in which the attention of the group is devoted almost entirely to dynamics. The members gain further understanding of the concept of dynamics, experience the actions necessary to sing softly and loudly, and become more sensitive and proficient in their responses to dynamic markings. If the practice on dynamics is related to the music the group is singing, the members will realize more fully how the dynamic contrasts affect the music.

Sensitivity to expression can be fostered by focusing attention on the dynamic levels as the music is being learned and by providing structured experiences that make the students aware of each element. Both techniques are necessary for successful teaching to take place. This chapter presents some specific structured experiences for making students more sensitive to expression and style.

Rhythm

Rhythm is essentially a physical phenomenon, not an intellectual one. Groups that are not musically advanced need many physical experiences with rhythm—tapping feet, chanting words, counting patterns. The rhythmic reading methods suggested on page 158–159 involve this type of response. There is a need to feel the rhythm, especially the sensation of the beat.

When problems are encountered in performing a rhythmic figure, the pattern should be isolated temporarily and then returned to its proper musical context as soon as possible. Here are two examples of this technique, the first one from Wagner's *Die Meistersinger von Nürnberg* and the second from "Mary Had a Baby."*

Count with syllables, then play:

Then practice with the tie:

Count with syllables, then sing on *tah*:

Some specific rhythmic problems can be taught by rote. The teacher demonstrates the proper execution of the figure and the students imitate what they heard. In this way, the students get a feeling for style and correct rhythm at the same time. Most rhythmic teaching should be done in a singsong voice. Suppose that a group of singers is experiencing trouble with the following phrase:

*SSA, arr. Theron W. Kirk (Westbury, N.Y.: Pro Art Publications, 1959). Used by permission.

We'll RIDE   the   SIX - four - teen

The teacher can start by asking the singers to repeat exactly what he or she says, regardless of rhythm or words. Many times a wrong pattern must be broken down before the correct one can be established. So it is best to start with a simple rhythm entirely different from the problem phrase. A quarter note phrase is simple and enables the students to imitate the teacher and feel the beat (see below).

The procedure illustrated can be lengthened or shortened according to the needs of the group and the difficulty of the music. The instrumental teacher can use the same technique. The students say the syllable *ta,* then play a unison tone, and then proceed to the particular phrase of music.

Some teachers, rather than have the students singsong the words or repeat a neutral syllable, have them clap out rhythms. This is a good technique, but clapping is not as fast or precise as the articulating action of the tongue.

A rhythmically dynamic work should occasionally be rehearsed without stops so that the momentum of the rhythm is not impeded.

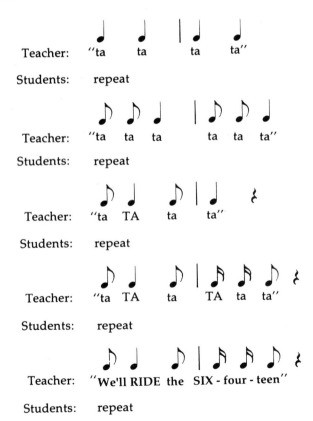

Teacher: "ta   ta   ta   ta"

Students: repeat

Teacher: "ta   ta   ta   ta   ta   ta"

Students: repeat

Teacher: "ta   TA   ta   ta"

Students: repeat

Teacher: "ta   TA   ta   TA   ta   ta"

Students: repeat

Teacher: "We'll RIDE the SIX - four - teen"

Students: repeat

Teacher: "We'll RIDE the SIX - four - teen"

Students: repeat

Teacher: *(Talking)* "Now let's keep the same
                rhythm, but this time sing the notes."

Students: sing the phrase

Minor errors on such occasions should wait for correction until the piece is done. Rhythm in such a work should be alive, exciting, and pulsating.

Blend

Although *balance* and *blend* are used interchangeably by some music teachers, the two words do not mean exactly the same thing. *Blend* refers to the homogeneity of sound, usually with a section, although the term can apply to the uniformity of timbre between sections. *Balance* refers to the distribution of loudness and emphasis among the various sections. Thus, Allan's voice may not blend with José's (if it is a different quality), or the cornets may overbalance (be too loud for) the clarinets.

Teachers should not assume that a blending of tone quality is always desirable or necessary. In choral music, some teachers exaggerate the importance of blend, and they try to bleed the color and character from the voices of the singers. The most suitable degree of blend is determined largely by the type of music being performed. A reverent, chordal piece requires far better blending of sound than does an exciting, barbaric selection. Good musical judgment must be the guide.

If more blend is needed, the first step is to make the students conscious of what it is. Teachers should remind them that it is not necessarily the best musician who performs loudest and has the most "piercing" quality. The comparison with a speaker (the best speaker is not always the one who talks loudest) can be made. The importance of unity must be emphasized again and again. Each section should sound like one performer and not like five or ten soloists crowding into the same part. The idea of each performer fitting his or her sound into the whole group must be carefully nurtured.

In many respects, secondary school choral teachers do not find the problem of blend as serious as does the collegiate director (or the church choir director!). The lack of mature voices may hinder school directors in many respects, but blend is one area in which an immature voice has an advantage. Few teenage singers have an inordinate amount of vibrato or highly individualistic voices.

Chapter 11 presents some basic singing techniques for choral groups. A good technique encourages uniformity of tone production, and this in turn contributes much to the blending of voices, as does a uniform vowel sound. With advanced groups, teachers may instruct the singers to form a somewhat rounded *oh* position of the lips on vowels such as *ee* and *ih*.

The proper method of tone production improves the blend in instrumental music, too. Unusual embouchures with pinched lips and squeezed tones do not contribute to uniformity. Instruments and mouthpieces should be as similar as possible. With strings a healthy tone and a consistently produced vibrato improve blend.

Several specific techniques will increase the students' consciousness of blend.

1. Choose two singers with the same range, or two players on the same instrument, who do *not* blend with one another. Have them play or sing a phrase in unison. Then select another performer who blends well with one of the original two, and have the new pair perform together. In this way the students can hear blend, or the lack of it, for themselves. One variation of this procedure is for the teacher to sing or play with a student. The teacher can first use a timbre that does not blend and then one that does blend with the student.

2. Start with one voice or instrument and then add another. When the two sounds are blending well, add a third, and so on. This technique is generally more successful with college students than with secondary school students, perhaps because it is time-consuming, and to younger musicians it seems far removed from the actual performance of music.

3. Organize student listening groups, as was suggested in Chapter 8.

4. Make tape recordings of the rehearsal. When students hear music played back with individual sounds popping out all over, they are more likely to appreciate the problem. Be sure that the recordings are representative of the sound of the group. It would be unfair to leave a microphone too close to one individual or section.

5. Work on good unison singing or playing. Outlining triads is excellent for developing accuracy in pitch and blend; singers may try various vowel sounds in so doing. Unison songs are good for choral groups because the same words will be sung by all voices at the same time, and this frequently does not occur in part-music. During unison playing or singing, the students can strive for a more homogeneous tone. In band the cornets can be told to sound more like the French horns, and vice versa; in chorus the tenors can work toward a quality that blends better with the basses.

6. Develop the group's ability to play or sing softly.

7. Remind individual students whose tone stands out in a section. If handled tactfully, students do not mind being asked to hold back, especially if a compliment can be paid them for their above-average work.

8. Encourage the more timid students to sing or play with more confidence.

9. Work with individual problems in extra, private sessions. In singing, unusual quality can be caused by tension in the throat or overarching of the tongue. An instrumentalist may possess an unusual embouchure or an improper sense

of tone production. No amount of class work on blend is likely to remedy these problems. Individual instruction is the most successful solution.

10. Perform at moderate dynamic levels. Loud playing or singing encourages individual voices or instruments to stand out.

Finally, poor blend is sometimes a symptom of more basic problems, such as poor intonation, bad ensemble, or faulty tone production. In such cases teachers must work on the cause, not the symptom.

Balance

School music teachers face a problem that the professional conductor is spared: unbalanced sections. Except for select school groups, teachers must work out the best balance among the singers or players they have available.

Achieving correct balance is largely the job of teachers, because they are the only ones who can listen to the entire ensemble, and it is their judgment that will determine what the correct balance should be. Good music education requires that the students learn what balance is and that they understand why one part should be stressed at a particular moment in a piece of music. But they can't hear the performance the way a listener hears it.

Teachers generally control balance by indicating either verbally or through conducting gestures that one part should be louder and another softer. There are several ways to fortify a part that needs emphasis. Instrumental teachers can rewrite parts into a better range, assign two players to a solo passage, or ask an instrument to play a cued-in part. Choral teachers can assign a few students to be "travelers." These singers sit near the boundaries of sections and move from tenor to bass, or from a first to a second part, as necessary. Such changes may slightly alter the timbre of the line. This technique may or may not be acceptable, depending on the particular passage in the music.

Good balance does not necessarily mean a uniformity of parts. In almost all works there is an interplay between parts, as one section is more prominent and then recedes to allow another section to bring out its more important line. This interplay exists also in homophonic music when all parts are marked at the same dynamic level.

Balance is often better achieved by reducing the volume of the less important lines rather than by encouraging the performers of the more important lines to come out more loudly.

Dynamics

Good control of dynamics depends on two things: a consciousness of dynamics on the part of the students and the ability to make dynamic changes. It may be desirable to offer specific training in performing at six dynamic levels (*pp, p, mp, mf, f, ff*) and in making crescendos and decrescendos, accents and sforzandos.

Many students are hazy about such matters when they first enroll in music. Choral teachers can make up any combination of dynamic markings to serve as exercises and write them on the board or call them out. An especially good exercise combines arpeggios with crescendos and decrescendos:

There are several other routines that stress dynamics. One is to hold a long tone or chord for twenty slow counts. The dynamic markings can also be reversed in this exercise. In either case the training develops the ability to spread out a crescendo or decrescendo and to sustain long tones.

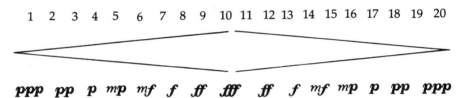

Another exercise is to take a technically simple figure and have the students perform it in whatever manner the conductor indicates by conducting gestures. This exercise makes the students conscious of both dynamic level and conducting motions.

Fine as such exercises are, they are not part of a musical context. A group may master an exercise designed to gain dynamic control and yet not play or sing expressively when performing a work of music. Good teaching demands that work on various elements of music be made functional by centering on the context of the music being studied.

In the initial stages of learning a work it is often necessary to exaggerate the dynamic levels. The students need to realize that there is a big "fall off" between what the performers think they are doing and what listeners actually hear. What seems to the performers to be a noticeable crescendo may seem to be almost no crescendo at all to the listeners. The students need to be encouraged to exaggerate dynamic levels by such statements as "Make twice as much crescendo as you think you should." A tape recorder may be valuable here. Tape recorders often do not produce the changes of dynamics as fully as what is actually present. As a result, the dynamic levels must be exaggerated to be noticeable in the recording, and an exaggerated performance is good training for the students.

Probably the most important factor in achieving variation in dynamic level is the use of proper methods of tone production. Although it may seem illogical, a good tone is more easily produced on winds or in singing at forte than at piano.

As described in Chapter 11, when singing with a full round tone, the chest seems to stay up more easily, the throat is relaxed, and the tone seems to roll out. In soft singing the chest wants to cave in, the throat muscles become tight and lack responsiveness, and the tone can be squeezed out. The result is a flatting of the pitch and tight little tones that do not project. The singers should be reminded repeatedly that in singing softly *nothing changes except the amount of air that is released*. The rib cage remains expanded, the lungs are filled with air, and the throat remains at ease. What is changed? The muscles of the abdominal wall hold the air back, the mouth is open, and the throat muscles are relaxed. Enough breath escapes to support a soft tone. It is tiring to maintain an expanded rib cage and open throat without the aid of a full stream of air flowing by. For this reason, time and conditioning are required for good soft singing.

To help the students sing softly and yet maintain intensity in the tone quality (some teachers call this "spinning" the tone), ask the group to sing a chord or a tone *ff*. Then ask them to repeat the chord *pp* but maintain the identical body feeling, except for the holding back of air that accompanied the singing of the *ff* chord. Another way to maintain intensity in singing *pp* is to start by humming the passage. Then sing it, keeping as much of the humming style as possible—a somewhat closed mouth, minimum jaw movement, and a continuous feeling of hum and resonance.

With wind instruments the technique for soft playing is almost identical to that required for soft singing. The correct method of tone production demands adequate breath support and attention to the basic steps outlined in Chapter 12. The throat is not pinched, squeezing the air out and distorting the tone. As in singing, the air is held back by the muscles of the abdomen and the diaphragm.

On string instruments there are three variables: (1) the pressure of the bow on the strings, which is regulated by the forefinger of the right hand; (2) the speed with which the bow is drawn across the string; and (3) the position of the bow in relation to the bridge and fingerboard. String instruments are designed to produce their biggest tone with the bow drawn quite near the bridge. The farther the bow is from the bridge, the softer the tone becomes.

Unless the adolescent possesses above-average voice development or tone production technique, his or her dynamic range is narrow. There is only so much forte. Any attempt with singers to go beyond their limits results in a frenzied, distorted tone. An effective pianissimo can be aided by reducing the number of performers on a part, a technique not unknown to professional music organizations.

Levels of loudness are relative. Driving 100 miles per hour may seem fast in an automobile, but for a jet plane this speed is slow. Similarly, a forte in the music does not mean the same thing to all pieces of music. The basic element in dynamics is the principle of contrast. If performers want climactic passages in the music, they must save some volume for them. The accented note is a good example of this. If all the notes in this measure are performed *ff*, it will be impossible to make

a noticeable accent on the notes so indicated. However, if the unaccented notes are executed piano, the accented notes will be more prominent. A good way to practice music that contains many accents is to go through it performing only the accented notes. The rest of the notes are heard in the "mind's ear" of the students. Most of the effort should be directed toward keeping the unaccented notes soft, while the accented notes are allowed to spring out.

Use of Amplification

Microphones and amplified performances of music have become more and more a part of the school music scene, especially in the case of jazz bands and swing choirs. In fact, amplification is almost an integral part of the style for those groups, and so teachers can use sound equipment when available for such performances. However, in the case of the concert band, orchestras, and choirs, amplification is not in character and should be avoided. Even the best equipment changes or "colors" the true sound of voices and instruments. Furthermore, the placement of microphones and the balancing of sound among them requires the work of an expert technician, and even then it is not always successful.

Some leaders of jazz bands and swing choirs have attempted to overwhelm their audiences with music presented at a high decibel level. It is easily achieved by simply turning up the knob on the control panel. However, a great majority of the audience would prefer to hear *quality* rather than *quantity* of sound, and certainly better music education happens when the students learn how to perform the music well and do not rely on blasting the audience into submission. Like so many other things in music education, amplifying equipment should be used with discretion and good judgment.

Sustained Tones

At times it is more difficult to interpret long, sustained tones in the melodic line than short ones, perhaps because the greater movement of short tones hides a lack of expression by the performer. Sustained tones must somehow convey a feeling of progress; something must always be happening with a sustained tone.

Two types of sustained tones should be cited here. One is the final chord of a piece, and the other is the long tone that leads toward some climactic point. The latter is well illustrated by Handel's "Thanks Be to Thee":

The long A progresses toward the apex of the phrase on the word "be." It is logical that the sound should increase in dynamic level and intensity as it is held. A feeling of "holding back" at the beginning of such crescendos, and a faster rate of increasing loudness at the end, will make sustained tones more effective.

A final chord can increase or decrease in loudness, depending on the character of the piece. If the work ends in a triumphant manner, the last tone, if it is long, will probably sound better with a slight crescendo. For some reason a tone that is held at one dynamic level seems to decrease slightly, so a slight crescendo gives the impression of a steady dynamic level. On the other hand, if the composition ends in a subdued and pensive vein, the last chord can diminish in dynamic level. A conductor can achieve a dramatic effect by slowly letting the closing tone fade into silence. Even after no more sound is audible, everyone remains motionless for several seconds.

Staccato

One of the more difficult aspects of interpretation is to execute separate, detached notes. The song style, which is basic to music and is the type of sound youngsters first learn, is flowing, not abrupt. Staccato is a more advanced and intellectual phenomenon. In addition, it is hard for teenagers to grasp the idea that there is more than one style of detached notes. The length of note, the separation between notes, and the crispness of attack vary with each musical work and often within the piece itself. Composers and arrangers have not been consistent in their use of staccato markings. Sometimes students are told, "Staccato means to cut the value of the note in half, so that the latter half of its value is silence." While the statement is true of some phrases, it is not true of others, and it is not helpful if it discourages consideration of the musical intent of a particular phrase.

To teach the proper degree and style of detachment, teachers must rely largely on demonstration. The correct rendition may be played or sung by the teacher or by an advanced student who has prepared the passage. Verbal directions help to some extent, but "short" does not mean the same thing to everyone. The phrase "play it shorter than you did last time" is more precise, but it still may not convey the idea of the style adequately.

On string instruments short notes are regulated by the style of bowing—staccato, spiccato, ricochet, détaché, martelé. Teachers who want to help their string players with various styles of bowing should examine one of the books on the subject.

Achieving staccato style and properly detached notes on wind instruments is discussed in detail in Chapter 12. Along with intellectual understanding, wind instrument players need good tonguing, proper breath support, and coordination between breath, tongue, and fingers. With them, the act of tonguing is more than an interpretive device; it is a necessity for good playing.

Staccato singing is difficult and should not be attempted until a group has mastered the proper method of tone production. The difficulty seems to be that singers want to pronounce the words as slowly as they do in legato singing. The vowels must be executed very rapidly in staccato. Some distortion may result when certain vowels and diphthongs are sung short, but because of their brief duration this distortion is not serious.

In contrast to wind instrument tonguing, singing requires a short pushing action of the diaphragm to produce the abrupt start that is necessary for each staccato note. This diaphragmatic action is similar to that required for the accent and sforzando. The latter require a greater push of the diaphragm and a heavier initial sound.

Tones ending in consonants (except -m, -n, and -ng) are concluded automatically by the formation of the consonant. If the final syllable ends in a vowel, students are likely to stop the tone by closing their mouths or by tensing their throat muscles as they clamp down to shut off the flow of air. A more effective way, however, is to keep an open, relaxed throat and to stop the flow of air by a holding-back action of the diaphragm. This method is more consistent with proper tone production.

Adolescent singers are prone to go flat on short notes. This loss of pitch can be caused by the practice of "scooping" tones, by failing to make the notes lean toward the logical culmination of the phrase, or by allowing the throat setup to collapse to some degree when starting and stopping the tones. Another cause for inaccurate pitch in singing short notes is the inability to think the correct pitch in the "mind's ear." Many young singers find the proper pitch only by "tuning up" the note as they sing it. If the notes are short, there is no time in which to do so, and the result in extreme cases sounds more like talking than singing. Experience with correct tone-production methods is the best remedy for pitch problems in staccato singing. It is helpful from the standpoint of intonation to sing a staccato passage occasionally in legato style.

Legato

Music teachers spend a lot of time teaching the *beginnings* of notes. The system of counting beats decrees precisely where a note starts, and students learn the system. The conclusions of notes are another matter. Many students think that a note that is three counts long stops just after the beginning of the third beat. At best they are hazy on this point. Therefore, both vocal and instrumental teachers have to counteract the students' tendency to rob some of the value from the ends of notes. Gaps caused by incomplete durations, of course, diminish the legato effect.

Instrumentalists, with the exception of trombonists, usually do not have any particular difficulty in slurring and achieving a good legato. For inexperienced singers, however, it is harder to master a good legato style. Much vocal control is needed to sing with a flow of tone that seems to permeate through each word and between words.

The best way to teach legato to teenagers is to stress again the idea of continuity of tone. Such expressions as "Sing through the words," "Keep pulling the tone," and "Don't drop you words" can establish the concept. Singers can imagine that the notes are glued together, their flow interrupted slightly only at phrase endings.

The concept of "pulling the tone" can be taught by singing the phrase on a neutral syllable and then adding the words while maintaining the same smoothness of sound. Another technique may be used occasionally during practice. The teacher may insert holds at different places in the music, particularly on the last note to the piece, to impress on the singers the idea of sustained sound.

Phrasing

A machine makes identical sounds, but human beings seldom do when speaking or making music. Human beings put sounds together into phrases so that they have meaning and logic. Phrasing is the process of dividing the music into logical units and then relating the notes within the units according to their importance and purpose. Phrasing is not just a question of where to breathe or when to change bows.

A discussion of phrasing is limitless, because in music there are infinite numbers of phrases, each requiring a different treatment according to its unique construction. Proper phrasing depends on the musical judgment and sensibility of the teacher. The most effective way to begin teaching correct phrasing is by rote. Words are inadequate for describing how to execute a phrase, how to make an appropriate tenuto, and how to integrate a decrescendo into the musical line. As in teaching staccato style, teachers should sing the phrase first. Instrumental teachers may prefer to demonstrate on an instrument. Initially the students should be told, "This is how it should be done." After a while, when they have absorbed many phrases, they can begin to figure out phrasing for themselves. Both the running commentary suggested in Chapter 8 and musical conducting will help establish good phrasing. But much of the instruction must be by teacher demonstration.

There is another technique to make students more conscious of phrasing and interpretation. After they have gained an idea of how a phrase should sound, they can be asked to sing or play it with the dynamics and style markings reversed. The deliberately wrong rendition draws attention to the interpretation of the passage. A variation of the procedure is to offer two or three different ways of interpreting the same phrase. For example, the following examples can be drawn on the board and the class invited to perform both. Then the teacher can ask which is more suitable in the particular phrase of music.

By penciling a circle around a phrase unit, the students can indicate the notes that are combined into meaningful phrases. For instance, a figure may be written but it should be thought out in this way:

A series of repeated notes can sound monotonous unless handled in a musical manner. The students may circle

to remind themselves about the need for the three notes to "lean" or be pulled toward the half note. String instrument bowings, which are very much involved with phrasing, should definitely be marked in the music, as should breath marks in wind music.

In instrumental music in march style, the longer notes, *up to one beat in length,* frequently receive greater emphasis. For example, in a syncopated figure such as

the eighth notes are generally only half as loud as the quarter. In most cases, a slight separation between the first two notes improves the musical effect:

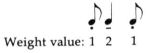

Weight value: 1 2   1

The same general idea applies to many other rhythmic figures, such as

and the combinations of

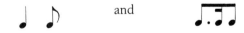

in 6/8 meter. To convey the idea of loudness or weight, teachers might refer to weight values as "pounds"—one pound for a quarter note, a half pound for an eighth note, or some such allocation. Middle school students may find it helpful to write weight values in pencil on several pieces of music.

The beat on which the note occurs likewise affects the amount of stress it receives. Usually the first beat of a measure receives slightly more emphasis, and the last beat, the least.

INTERPRETING VOCAL MUSIC

Unlike instrumentalists, singers pronounce words as they sing and use their voices to create certain musical effects such as humming. These actions require special consideration.

There is no fixed relationship between the relative importance of the text as compared with the music. The proper balance can range all the way from Gregorian chant, in which the text dominates the melodic line, to a work such as Randall Thompson's "Alleluia," in which the one word "Alleluia" is the text and the music is the essence of the work. Teachers must judge the proper relationship between the two when deciding on the interpretation.

In speaking, certain words are stressed more than others. The same is true of syllables within a word. Vocal music teachers should read through the text of a particular work, judging which words are more important and trying to make themselves sensitive to the sounds, colors, and poetry of the words.

Sometimes the phrasing of text and music do not jibe. If no compromise can be worked out, the logic of the musical phrase should take precedence.

Tone Color

Because the tone color or timbre of the human voice shows a person's feelings so readily, and because a song is a musical setting of specific feelings, the tone quality of a choral group is important in interpretation. Different emotions projected in a song require different timbres. It comes as a surprise to some students that there is no single, best singing tone.

When teachers begin to stress to their students that different songs require different tone qualities, it is wise to work on the two poles of tone color: the light and the dark. When the tonal extremities are mastered, other timbres can be approached in relation to them.

Change in timbre is brought about partially by specific physical action. The dark tone color is nearer the basic tone quality, which will be described in Chapter 11. Adolescents usually find this dark quality more difficult to produce, because their voices tend to be light. The physical setup for the dark tone is a wide-open, relaxed throat, with the tongue relaxed and low. The position of the mouth and lips is similar to the one used for producing the sound *oh*. In fact, the *oh* vowel should be used to practice a dark tone quality.

The light, bright tone quality is produced by raising the jaw slightly from the *oh* position and narrowing the opening of the mouth, as for the vowel *ee*, by bringing the tongue up somewhat. Sometimes the simplest way for teenagers to think of the difference between the dark and light timbres is to think of the dark as being vertical and full and the bright as being horizontal and flat-surfaced. The bright tone should not be squeezed out so that it sounds pinched and strained, however. In such a case the result would not be a bright tone but merely a poor tone quality.

To achieve a change of timbre, students need not only a knowledge of physical procedures but also a feeling for the music. The teacher or an able student may demonstrate or play a recording of the tone wanted and in effect say to the singers, "This is the tone color we want. Go ahead and try to get it." This technique resembles an imitative rote procedure, but it encourages the students to base their responses on feeling for the music rather than on conscious physical actions. When the voice is filled with anger, grief, or other emotion, people are not aware that they are tightening a certain muscle, closing or opening the back of the throat, tensing or relaxing the tongue. It all happens as the result of a certain feeling. Therefore, the efforts of teachers to promote an understanding of the piece—its text, historical setting, and musical qualities—are helpful in getting the right tone quality. A song should be felt emotionally as it is being sung, and this feeling will affect the timbre of the voice.

Humming

Many teachers question the value of having choral groups hum. Like several other musical effects that have been mentioned, humming should be used sparingly and with discretion.

Students should be taught how to hum properly. Too often the hum is produced by squeezing the throat muscles. The result is a sound that does not project. To produce a resonant hum, students should sing the basic *ah* vowel and then close their lips. They should not close their teeth! The *ah* vowel can be varied at times with other vowel positions to give the humming tone a slightly different color.

Accurate pitch is hard to achieve when teenagers hum. Basically the problem is one of attitude. The singers seem to think that sloppy pitch won't be noticed during humming. In a musically less developed group, it is hard enough to make the singers aware of pitch when they sing, so the task is even harder when they hum.

Slurring

The singing of more than one note for a syllable of a word can encourage sloppiness. One way to achieve accuracy in such passages is to have the singers place a small "bump" or "pulse" at the beginning of each note, much as they were encouraged to do in staccato singing, except in this case to a lesser degree. The phrase

A - men

would then be thought of as

A(a) (a) (a)men

with the *u* over the notes indicating the little diaphragmatic bump at the beginning of each note. Some teachers tell their singers to put a small *h* in front of each note. This technique is all right as long as it is made clear to the singers that they should not stop or break the airstream before each note. The bump or the slight *h* sound will eliminate the siren effect that singers sometimes get on such passages. If the technique is exaggerated, it can ruin the musical effect when only one person is singing. But when used with moderation by an entire group, it helps make the pitches clearer. Two more elements are needed to make a run sound clean: accurate pitch and accurate rhythm.

Pronunciation of Foreign Languages

When songs are sung in languages other than English, the words should be pronounced as correctly as possible. The most authoritative book on the pronunciation of ecclesiastical Latin is *The Correct Pronunciation of Latin According to Roman Usage.** This book is especially useful in giving the correct pronunciation to such often mispronounced words as *excelsis, coeli,* and *nostrae.*

For modern languages such as French, Italian, Spanish, and German, several textbooks and dictionaries are available. Many schools own sets of language disks or tapes that can be studied. In addition, language teachers will probably be glad to assist if they can. If no teacher in the school is competent in the particular language being sung, someone in the community might be located who knows that language well. Accurate pronunciation helps to produce the correct timbre and unique tonal characteristics that add to the effectiveness of a work in a foreign language.

MUSICAL FEELING AND TECHNIQUE

In their eagerness for a good performance, teachers should never become so preoccupied with such technical considerations as blend, balance, and rhythm that they lose the spirit of the music. It is better to let some technical aspect go unperfected than to destroy the heart of the work.

Both technique and musical feeling are necessary, and this fact presents a problem to which there is no easy solution. Constant and unhurried effort is

*St. Gregory Guild, 1705 Rittenhouse Square, Philadelphia, PA 19103.

required to bring each of the two elements into proper perspective. First, technical work should be integrated as much as possible with the pieces of music currently being studied. Functional learning, not isolated drill, is most effective.

Second, teachers should help the students recognize the relationship between technique and musical feeling. Musicians have much in common with actors in this respect. Until the end of the nineteenth century acting consisted of artificial, pompous, formal motions. Techniques were the basis of acting. Then Constantine Stanislavsky, in his books and in the Moscow Art Theatre, began a revolution toward a combination of feeling and natural technique. According to Stanislavsky, the actor must project himself as deeply as possible into the character he is to portray, but at the same time he must never lose sight of the fact that he is acting and that a certain amount of objective technique is necessary to project the part successfully.

When a group sings "By the rivers of Babylon, there we sat down, yea, we wept, when we remembered Zion," they must feel the anxiety and privation of the captive Israelites. But more than that they must know the technique required to project the correct feeling through the music to an audience. The students should know in objective terms how to achieve a warm tone or a decrescendo, and at the same time they should understand and feel what the music is trying to convey. When objective technique and subjective feeling are united, a vehicle of artistic expression has been created.

Questions   1.   Is tapping the foot while playing or singing a good practice for the secondary school student? Why or why not?

2.   Does achieving good blend mean giving up individual quality for the performer in a group? Is this a good educational practice?

3.   What can a choral teacher do to achieve good balance in a group with forty girls and twenty boys? What can a band teacher do to balance eight clarinets against nine trumpets? What can the orchestra director do to balance a complete wind section with eleven violins, two violas, one cello, and two bass viols?

4.   Is it desirable to have each performer learn an exact degree of loudness for each of the six dynamic levels (*pp, p, mp, mf, f, ff*)? Why or why not?

5.   Suppose that the group you are conducting shows no flexibility and does not follow the tempo changes as you conduct them. What teaching device might you use to get them to be more responsive to tempo changes?

6.   Examine the adjudication forms used for the music contests in your state. Do these forms give proper emphasis to pertinent musical factors? Are they too much centered on the technical phases of music and too little concerned with the overall effect? Why or why not? What suggestions, if any, could you make to improve the forms?

7. Page 182 contained the example of a teacher using rote methods to teach the singers the syncopated phrase "We'll ride the six-fourteen." Would it have been better to have made the students use a system of counting and figure it out for themselves? Which method, rote or reading, is more effective musically in this instance? Which will the students remember longer? Which is more efficient in its use of class time?

Projects

1. There are several recordings available of the "Hallelujah Chorus" from Handel's *Messiah* and the *Firebird Suite* by Igor Stravinsky. Listen to two records of each work. Compare and contrast the tempo, dynamic levels, tone color, style or articulation, and other interpretive factors at selected places in each work. Decide which is preferable and be able to state why.

2. Listen again to the middle of the "Hallelujah Chorus." Note the smooth quality of the words "The kingdom of this world," as contrasted with the more martial quality of "and He shall reign forever and ever." Plan how you would work with a teenage choral group to achieve this difference in the style of singing.

3. Devise some simple unison exercises to be sung or played to give teenage students a clearer idea of the exact ending of dotted quarter notes, half notes, dotted half notes, and whole notes. Decide on the verbal explanation that should accompany the presentation of the exercises to the group.

4. Look through copies of choral and instrumental music for works, such as Handel's "Thanks Be to Thee," that are especially suitable for developing an awareness of dynamics and a technique for producing the proper dynamics.

5. Listen to commercial records of recognized choral groups singing (a) a cowboy folk song, (b) a chorus from an oratorio, (c) an old English folk song, (d) Stravinsky's *Symphony of Psalms,* and (e) Brahms's *Ein Deutches Requiem (A German Requiem)*. Note the different choral tone used for each work. Decide how you would work with a high school choral group to achieve the proper timbre for each type of music.

6. Select a phrase of choral music requiring some flexibility and imagination in phrasing. Take it to your class and insist that they phrase it in the way you suggest.

Suggested
Readings

Bollinger, Donald E. *Band Director's Complete Handbook.* West Nyack, N.Y.: Parker, 1979. Chapter 6.

Kohut, Daniel L. *Instrumental Music Pedagogy.* Englewood Cliffs, N.J.: Prentice-Hall, 1973. Chapter 5.

————. *Musical Performance: Learning Theory and Pedagogy.* Englewood Cliffs, N.J.: Prentice-Hall, 1985.

CHAPTER 10

Achieving Accurate Intonation

"Tune it up, altos!" the conductor urges a section of the choir. A good direction, no doubt about it. Trained musicians know what the conductor means. They respond by careful listening and the slight adjustment of fingers or voice necessary to "tune it up." But what about the thirteen-year-old violist now in the third year of study, all of it in group situations? What about the junior bass who is back in choral music for the first time since seventh grade? How much does he know about intonation? School music teachers face a real challenge. Not only do they encounter the usual vicissitudes of intonation—acoustical problems of instruments, difficult places in the music, and fluctuations due to heat and cold—they also face the job of teaching students what it is to be in tune and what they must do to achieve accurate intonation.

A few music teachers seem to accept poor intonation as a fact of school music life. Perhaps they assume that teenagers can't perform in tune, or maybe they don't know how to teach them to do so. Possibly they just don't listen carefully themselves. In any case, it is a mistake to regard poor intonation as inevitable. Skill and persistence on the part of teachers are required to keep teenagers performing in tune, however,

INTONATION ILLUSIONS

There are many reasons, some musical and some physical, for problems with intonation. In addition, however, there are two factors that give the *illusion* of faulty intonation. One is simply the presence of wrong notes. As an experienced band director once observed, "You know, when everyone's playing the right notes, it's remarkable how much better the intonation is."

A second illusion regarding intonation involves the relationship between timbre and pitch. Two tones may be sounding at the same pitch level but seem to be out of tune because of their differing qualities. This is one reason for urging work on uniform vowels in a choral group. Oddly, a poorer, less distinguished tone quality can more easily conceal its pitch. A fine, alive tone with a solid "center" cannot do so. The phenomenon is best illustrated by a good trombone player. If he or she blows a firm, well-rounded tone, any movement of the slide is noticeable to the ear. But if a sickly sound is emitted, the slide can be moved an inch or more without much effect on the pitch level.

Good intonation has another illusion that should be mentioned. Because of the effort involved in getting students to perform in tune, teachers sometimes lose their objectivity in judging pitch as the days go by. Mentally they begin to correct out-of-tune notes or to let them pass because they are an improvement over earlier efforts.

MUSICAL INEXPERIENCE

The musical inexperience of many teenagers, an important cause of poor intonation, makes itself evident in three ways: poor listening habits, lack of coordination, and a limited concept of pitch.

Poor Listening Habits

People have music sounding so much—in their cars, in restaurants and stores—that they psychologically "tune out" much of what they hear; they no longer notice the clock ticking, the refrigerator turning on and off, or the noise of cars going by on the street outside. Unfortunately, they develop the habit of not listening. Such a habit makes it more difficult to teach students to listen carefully so that they can perform in tune.

To compound the problem, most teenagers have had even less experience in careful listening to parts or themes or to accuracy of pitch. Their situation can be appreciated by many a music major who discovered this fact when he or she first started taking dictation in college theory class.

Lack of Coordination

The second manifestation of inexperience is inability to coordinate the directions of the mind and ear with the voice and fingers. Adolescent violinists may falter when shifting to a new position, not because they can't hear it and don't know better, but because their muscle movement is too inconsistent to enable them to find the same place twice. The same is true of adolescent singers, especially teenage boys. Teachers must remember that the first efforts in any endeavor are often inaccurate. Control in making musical responses only comes with practice.

Lack of a Concept of Pitch

The lack of a concept of intonation is also evidence of musical inexperience. It is not enough to tell students that intonation is "the quality of in-tuneness" or that being in tune is "the accurate reproduction of pitch." These are mere words, and no one can learn about intonation by definitions alone. Words can only help.

Several analogies are useful in establishing the idea of accurate intonation. One analogy is that of hitting the center of a target. Musicians should aim at a target with each note they perform, but the target in this case exists in sound, with the center determined by physical laws of sound.

Teachers may also suggest the analogy of tuning in a station on a radio. Or achieving good intonation can be compared to focusing a camera so that the picture is not blurred or fuzzy.

To provide a more concrete experience with pitch, the science teacher might be invited to give the class a short, simple demonstration of the physical properties of sound. Few students fail to be interested in a well-planned demonstration of acoustics. It is especially valuable for them to hear the simultaneous sounding of tuning forks that are two or three vibrations apart. The "beats" created by this phenomenon are a revelation to the students.

POOR METHODS OF TONE PRODUCTION

Poor methods of producing the sound have a detrimental effect on a group's ability to perform with accurate pitch. On wind instruments it is more a matter of consistency than of general pitch level, which is partly regulated by the tuning. There are few things as frustrating for a teacher as the presence of brass players with unstable embouchures. Each time they play a tone with a different lip formation, they produce a slightly different pitch. It is impossible to tune such players. Some reed players tend to bite down on the reed when under tension, and a sharpness in pitch is the result. Some brass players when tense press the mouthpiece back hard against the lips, and this action causes pinching and sharping, plus other complications.

Correction involves working not on intonation directly, because in this case it is a symptom, but rather on the fundamentals of playing the instrument. The cure for this type of intonation problem requires attention to points inadequately covered in the students' previous instruction.

In singing, pitch is likewise affected when the sounds are strained or inconsistently produced. If the proper singing routine has not been established, the pitch of a tone is subject to every psychological and physiological vagary.

The practice of "scooping" or "shoveling" is harmful to accurate pitch. Although some popular solo singers use the device almost constantly, teenage students should be told of the damage this practice inflicts on a group. Frequently the cause of scooped notes is a lack of mental and physical preparation on the part of the singer.

Vowels that are not uniform are detrimental to intonation. This result is primarily due to the different timbres present when the vowels are not produced in a similar manner by all the singers. Uniform vowel production is more easily achieved when the singers retain an open throat position and confine the changes for different sounds to the front of the mouth and lips.

PSYCHOLOGICAL FACTORS

Because music is so involved with emotion and feeling, it is not surprising that pitch is affected by psychological factors. As already mentioned, the best remedy for faulty intonation is alertness and understanding on the part of the students. Anything that dulls their acuity will impair intonation. Some teachers have spent an entire class period on a single piece of music. Any teacher, vocal or instrumental, who does so should expect attention to wane.

Singing is especially susceptible to the psychological condition of the singers. They can become tired of singing in a particular key. Choral groups do perceive a difference when a piece is transposed a half step up or down. Some songs are rarely sung in tune when performed in the original key. An example of this situation is the familiar "Silent Night," which is usually sung with better intonation when transposed up a half step from the original key of C major. Attention should be given to the range when transposing keys. If the top tones become too high, then perhaps transposing down is more practical. However, the basses should not be asked to sing so low that they either rumble or stop singing.

Sometimes students sing the wrong pitch because they are inattentive or indifferent. One individual picks up the pitch from his neighbor, who in turn may be doing the same thing from someone else. If many singers do this, the right pitch can get lost.

Singers are often affected emotionally and mentally by changes in the dynamic level of the music, and their reactions, in turn, affect the pitch level. This situation sometimes occurs after they have sung continuously at a forte dynamic level. When they attempt to sing a soft section, they frequently go flat. Their attention decreases and psychological relaxation sets in, resulting in a feeble, unsupported tone. Singers should be made aware of these tendencies to relax or to overexert themselves as they vary the dynamic level. To overcome such reactions by singers, teachers can provide simple scale or chord exercises, with slow changes in dynamics, followed by rapid changes of forte to piano and back to forte.

The solution to psychologically caused intonation problems in both vocal and instrumental groups is to reexamine the fundamentals of music teaching discussed in Chapter 5. Especially significant is pacing the work on a piece of music and distributing the effort. Some psychological causes, such as nervousness in public appearances, are overcome only through experience.

Closely related to students' alertness is their physical condition on a particular day. Colds sometimes affect the ability to hear and cause general sluggishness. The voice is especially susceptible to the physical condition of the body. Sometimes it is said of a person, "His voice sounds tired," and it is true. When the energies of many students in a group are consumed in an event such as a basketball tournament or a school play, this is apparent in the tired sound and the increased amount of out-of-tuneness. If students leave home at 5 A.M. and ride a bumpy school bus fifty or more miles to perform in a contest, intonation problems are almost inevitable because of fatigue.

ENVIRONMENTAL FACTORS

Atmospheric conditions can play havoc with intonation. Not only does hot, humid weather deplete the musicians, causing singers to flat, but it also affects the quality of tone from reeds. They sound soggy, flat, and listless. Other instruments are affected as well. Strings tend to lower in pitch, and the brasses and winds tend to rise. Probably the most critical problem exists at the outdoor concert on a cool night. The end of the horn nearest the player's mouth is kept warm with breath, while the far end is cool. Each time a player rests for a few moments, the instrument cools and becomes flatter.

Sometimes faulty intonation can be traced to environmental factors in the classroom. Chairs of the wrong type are a hindrance to proper posture. Poor ventilation and overcrowding have an adverse effect on the physical well-being of the students. Overcrowding has an adverse effect on the group. If string players are so confined that they have hardly enough room for a full bow stroke, their physical discomfort will usually be apparent in the sound. Such a situation encourages intonation problems.

Acoustical conditions vary from room to room. If the students are accustomed to rehearsing in a "live" room and are confronted with an auditorium that is acoustically dead, they will tend to overextend in their effort to combat these altered conditions, or they will become frightened and emit only tense little sounds of uncertain pitch.

INSTRUMENTAL INTONATION

Instrumental music teachers have an additional responsibility. They must cope with mechanical frailties and strive to overcome them, as well as develop a sense of proper pitch within their students.

Wind Instrument Intonation

Errors of pitch are inherent in all wind instruments. The first step is to convince wind instrument players that they do indeed have to be concerned with intonation. It is obvious to string players and singers that they control their own pitches, but the same responsibility is not as apparent to students who get a note by pushing valves or keys. As one student told his teacher, "But I know my clarinet is in tune. The man at the store who sold it to my dad said so." The techniques suggested on page 205 will help to drive home the need for attention to intonation. Teachers can say, "When you push down the right fingers, you're only in the neighborhood of the note, not exactly on it. Getting exactly in tune is your job."

Students should be shown what tones are chronically out of tune on their instruments. Some of these are predictable, such as the 1–2–3 valve combination on brasses and the throat-tone B flat on clarinets, but others depend on the unique qualities of the instrument and the manner of playing it. These troublesome pitches become evident through the efforts of the group to achieve good intonation. It is the successful teacher who says to his or her first flutist, "Latosha, you know that D flat is sharp on your instrument, so humor it down as much as you can."

The teacher's directive to "humor" the pitch down raises the simple question: How? There are both technical and psychological approaches to doing this. Wood-wind fingerings can be varied to change the pitch slightly. On the clarinet, covering the holes with the second and third fingers of the left hand when playing throat-tone B flat and using the little finger of the right hand on the E-flat key on certain high notes are examples of ways to adjust pitch. Alternative fingerings are available on brasses, especially on the French horn, which can also vary pitch by the degree to which the tone is stopped by the right hand in the bell. Flutes may tip just a bit to alter the angle between the blowhole and the lips, tipping away to sharpen and turning in to flatten. When flutists do this, they should think of moving their head slightly, not the flute. The tension or "squeeze" of the lips and jaw on the reed affects the pitch of other instruments. Advanced players are very precise in manipulating this technique, and secondary school players can master it if they have a well-established embouchure. Brass players also make slight adjustments by regulating the amount of tension in the lips.

Although it is hard for instrumentalists to realize, just thinking about sounding a pitch sharper or flatter causes some changes of throat and tongue tension, intensity of the airstream, openness of the throat, and adjustment of embouchure that affect a pitch change. So when the first flutist Latosha is told to lower her D flat, she is conscious of making certain responses to accomplish this, and she can also "think" of playing the pitch flatter.

Woodwind instruments with chronic intonation problems can sometimes be improved by a skillful repairperson. There is hardly a professional clarinetist or bassoonist who has not had pads raised or lowered or a hole made slightly smaller to flatten it or larger to sharpen it.

Sometimes instruments can be adjusted at points other than the usual tuning place. For example, if a clarinet is sharp on its usual tuning note of C but in tune on throat tones, it can be "pulled" somewhat at the center joint. On brasses the entire relationship between fingered notes is altered when the main tuning slide is changed very much. The procedure for getting the individual valve slides in tune is as follows:

1. Play the second open tone (G on trumpet, F on bass clef baritone, and so on).
2. Play the same tone with the first and third valves. Frequently this tone is sharp to the open tone.
3. Pull out the first-valve tuning slide slightly and the third-valve slide twice as much.
4. Experiment until the pitches of the fingered and open note match exactly.
5. Play one whole step higher (A on trumpet, and so on) with the first and second valves.
6. Compare it with the same note played with the third valve only. If the first- and second-valve pitch is higher than the third-valve pitch, the third-valve slide has been pulled too far and the first-valve slide has not been pulled far enough.
7. Experiment until the pitch of the two fingerings is exactly the same.
8. Check the open-tone G against the first- and third-valve G.
9. If this is not in tune, repeat the procedure until the fullest possible pitch agreement has been attained.

The second valve is so short that its adjustment has little effect. It can be checked on the trumpet by comparing B played with the second valve against B played with the first and third valves.

The quality of the instrument has much to do with the quality of its intonation. Possibly the most noticeable difference between an economical and a quality instrument is in their tuning properties. Teachers should try to convince parents that a quality instrument, not necessarily a luxury instrument, is well worth the additional cost because of the satisfaction their child can get from it, to say nothing of the additional resale value.

A special problem with wind instruments is the influence of dynamic level on pitch. Clarinets tend to lower in pitch as they get louder, brasses tend to sharpen. Players must be taught to compensate for this difference, to avoid pitch discrepancy at the extremes of dynamic range.

String Intonation

When instruction is first offered on strings, only students with a good sense of pitch should be encouraged to start. A string student who cannot hear pitch accurately will find the experience a frustrating one. For a check of pitch sense, a Seashore or Gordon test may be administered. Oddly, a lack of ability to sing in tune does not always indicate a poor sense of pitch.

String teachers should stress slow and careful work. A primary cause of bad pitch on strings lies in asking the students to play something too difficult for them—something for which they have not yet developed adequate neuromuscular control. When string players are pushed into higher positions before they are ready, intonation suffers. Sometimes intonation improves when the teacher can ask the group to play the music at half speed. This gives the players additional time to think, move fingers, and listen, and the result is better pitch.

Faulty intonation on strings is often caused by a poor left-hand position. On violin and viola young players sometimes display three habits that result in a lack of consistency in the placement of the fingers on the strings: (1) Players allow the wrist to bend or become unstable. (2) They turn the fingers far from the strings, which causes the player to be less efficient in finding the proper pitch at the proper moment. (3) They allow the neck of the instrument to rest on the joint connecting the index finger and palm. This causes tension and cramping in the hand, which reduces the accuracy and facility of the fingers, particularly on the highest string. This habit can be observed best by viewing the player from the scroll end of the instrument.

Inaccurate pitch also results when string players do not think of the pitch they are trying to get. They must hear the pitch in their mind and associate it with the kinesthetic feel of the correctly placed hand and finger. Slow and careful practice helps to establish this association.

The effect of vibrato on string intonation is an interesting topic, but it has little practical application for school music teachers. Vibrato greatly improves the tone of the player, and it may, because of its pitch fluctuations, make the intonation appear to be better, although not all string teachers agree on this point. At least, vibrato will not harm pitch if the players are ready for it—that is, if they can place their fingers consistently and accurately on the proper notes.

Procedures for Instrumental Music Class

1. Teach the students to tune their instruments. As elementary as this step may appear to be, it is surprising how many teenage musicians cannot do this. Allow sufficient time for the development of such a skill; it cannot be taught in one fifteen-minute lesson. Furthermore, the student himself or herself must be given a chance to judge the tuning. The temptation is to say, "Dave, pull the slide out just a little," without giving Dave the opportunity to find out for himself. Call attention to the "beating" of out-of-tune notes and the tonal characteristics that identify one tone as being sharper or flatter than another. Strings, of course, must learn to tune fifths (or fourths on bass) or match a pitch played on the piano. Not only is accurate tuning necessary for good intonation, but the process gives students good experience in learning what is meant by being "in tune."

2. Tune wind instruments to pitches other than the usual concert B flat. Because of the construction of many instruments in B flat, this particular pitch may sound good when played on several instruments, while a concert G or F sharp may be quite out of tune. Tuning on more than one pitch will give a more valid means of setting the overall pitch of the instrument.

3. Take two identical instruments, perhaps clarinets. Have them tune perfectly on the usual third-space C. As they sound the C in unison and in tune, have one player transfer to the C an octave higher. Nine times out of ten this note is sharp on a clarinet, and the students can hear the "beating" caused by the out-of-tuneness. This technique works to some extent on wind instruments on almost all pitches one octave apart.

4. Instruct two players to take the major third C–E and tune it up to everyone's satisfaction. Then have each player move up a semitone to C sharp–E sharp, or a whole step to D–F sharp. The new third will usually be out of tune and require adjustment. The players can progress to other thirds with similar results.

5. Have the group slowly and carefully play Bach chorales, unison scales and arpeggios, and chord studies.

6. During practice on the regular repertoire, work out passages in which the intonation is faulty. Learning to play in tune should not be isolated from learning music.

7. Use the tape recorder to analyze intonation. Individual performers, recorded one at a time, can hear themselves more clearly and objectively than is possible when the whole group plays together. Also, two performances of the same passage can be compared.

CHORAL INTONATION

Because of the characteristics of the human voice, and because singers do not have the benefit of preestablished pitches, certain factors of intonation relate primarily to choral groups.

Range and Tessitura

The intonation of singers is affected by the range of the music and by the tessitura—the average or median pitch of the vocal line. Whether strain is caused by attempting to sing a note in an extreme range or by singing too long in an uncomfortable tessitura, the effort encourages out-of-tune singing. When this occurs, it is not so much the fault of the singers as it is of the teacher, who selected music too difficult for their voices. Occasionally one or two notes, which might throw an entire phrase off pitch, can be altered or given to another part. For instance, a few tenors might help the basses with some high notes, or a few altos might help the tenors. This assistance gives the line more support and helps retain pitch while increasing the singers' confidence on the difficult passage.

Tempo

A piece of music in a slow tempo is often more difficult to sing in tune than one in a rapid tempo. This statement does not mean that if a work such as Palestrina's "Adoramus Te, Christe" cannot be sung in a slow tempo, then the tempo should be increased until the piece is in tune. The quality of the music should never be sacrificed for the sake of a technical element such as intonation. It may help the singers if they think of continuous forward motion or of tonal energy moving ahead. The notes are not static like big stagnant pools. On the first long tones in "Adoramus Te, Christe," for example, the singers should mentally lean toward the next syllable of the word. This technique will help them maintain their pitch without destroying the intent of the music.

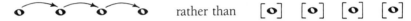

Modulations

While modulations to a closely related key seldom cause a problem, unusual modulations can present difficulties. Teachers must carefully accustom the students' ears to the musical logic of the harmonies. As the sounds become familiar, they can suggest ways to find the new notes. The best procedure is to rehearse the spot with the modulation several times. In doing so, the singers can find the tonal relationship between the two keys or chords.

Intervals

When singers perform a series of ascending chromatics, their tendency is to miss just slightly getting all notes up to pitch. With descending chromatic passages the inclination is to overshoot and end below pitch. There is often a tendency to undershoot ascending wide intervals. The appearance of the interval—the way it is written enharmonically—can also affect the accuracy of its performance. Although the good aural judgment of the students should prevail, with groups that are not particularly experienced it is advisable to say, "Lean a bit on the sharp side as you go up for that top note."

The other notes in the chord likewise affect intonation. For example, it is much more difficult to sing an accurate B natural against a C than against a D. One of the most taxing chores for secondary school choral teachers is to teach a group to perform dissonant pitches in tune. A healthy dissonance sometimes becomes unpleasant because of poor intonation. A dissonant work demands slow, careful practice and thorough orientation to the new sounds.

Lack of Ensemble

A final reason for intonation problems is what might be termed "lack of ensemble." Sometimes, especially in choral groups, individuals feel like they are out in the middle of the ocean trying to keep their head above water. The group plays or sings along and the student can scarcely hear himself or herself, least of all hear what the other sections are doing.

There are many reasons for this inability to hear other parts. The individual, or the people around him or her, may be too loud, and the other sections may be too weak or located so that they are difficult to hear. It is important, however, that students develop mental control of their music making.

If a choral group has been singing in a raucous, out-of-tune manner, a calming effect can be produced by directing the students to place their hands or fingers over one of their ears when singing. This technique seems to center attention on the mental control of singing and permits the individual to hear himself or herself. As students become aware of what to listen for in music, learn to fit their voices into the group, and stay on the alert for sagging pitch and other errors in singing, much of the "lost in the ocean" feeling will disappear.

Another cause of lack of ensemble in choral music is inability to hear the piano. If this situation occurs during public performance, the singers are at a distinct disadvantage. The audience is likely to hear both piano and singers and is thereby provided with a constant pitch comparison. The problem can usually be remedied if the position of the piano is changed or its lid opened. The group can sing more softly and the accompanist can play more loudly. As the group advances, less and less dependence should be placed on the piano. When the pianist gives the pitches for a cappella singing, the notes should be struck with sufficient power to be heard by all the singers. Even if the audience hears the pitches, this is preferable to the hesitant, out-of-tune start that results when singers can't find their starting notes.

Procedures for Vocal Music

Here are some procedures to help develop the students' listening ability in vocal music:

1. Play a tone on the piano and ask someone to match it, singing a neutral syllable. When that person has attempted to sing the pitch, ask someone else if the rendition was flat, sharp, or exactly on pitch.

2. Encourage careful singing of major scales and chords. At first the students should sing each note simultaneously with the piano or immediately after the piano has sounded the pitch. When they can sing accurately in this manner, play the entire chord or scale and let them repeat it unaccompanied. After several days give them a pitch and tell them to sing a chord or scale from it.

Initial work should be confined to major scales and chords. If minor is in-

troduced before major is learned thoroughly, the result will be a hybrid of major and minor. This does not preclude singing songs in minor, however. If singing in major is accurate, the minor seems to take care of itself when it appears in a song. Accuracy must be emphasized to the students during such exercises. Triads should be sung from the root, third, and fifth. Unless the students are used to the solfa syllables, it is best to use numbers or a neutral syllable for these drills. A section or an individual should sing these patterns alone once in a while.

3. Assign a chord and let the singers trade parts. For example, the first time the basses can take the root or 1, tenors and altos 3, and sopranos 5. The next time the basses take 5, tenors 1, altos 5, and sopranos 3.

4. Play a chord on the piano, call out "one," "three," or "five," and ask someone to sing back the proper chord member. This procedure can be made more elaborate by calling out a complete chord with correct doubling, so that there is one chord member for each section. The use of chord imagery not only makes the students more conscious of pitch but also gives them a technique for finding the correct notes at the beginning of a phrase, a valuable skill in choral music.

5. Lead the group in a familiar melody, unaccompanied and on a neutral syllable. Start the singers with a conductor's beat, and at some point indicate by a prearranged signal that they are to stop singing aloud. They continue singing silently in their "mind's ear," following the conductor's beat, until they see the signal to resume singing aloud again. This exercise gives them practice in thinking pitches.

6. Encourage the singers to try some harmonizing by ear outside the regular class. Such practice makes them conscious of tuning their voices with others. Harmonizing by ear is not recommended on regular four-part music, of course, but there are many familiar melodies that are well adapted to impromptu harmonizing.

7. When the group is singing a work of music, stop on any chord that is being sung out of tune and rebuild it with the help of the piano. Don't let the singers become accustomed to poor intonation.

8. Make use of the tape recorder. Students can be more objective about their ability to sing in tune when they hear a recording of their singing.

Questions   1.   What justification might a vocal music teacher give for having a group sing a piece with the piano in order to stay on pitch rather than sing unaccompanied with poor intonation?

2.   Which aspect of unaccompanied singing should the teacher emphasize: staying in tune within the group itself, or being able to finish the song exactly on the properly notated pitch?

3.   What is wrong with each of these examples of teaching correct intonation?
   (a)   With a pained expression on his face, Ray Jones complains to his group, "You're out of tune! *Out of tune!* OUT OF TUNE!"
   (b)   Sherri Knapp says to her girls' glee club, "Now sopranos, we're going over this piece until you can sing it in tune."
   (c)   Sally Wong tells her string players, "Just play everything a little higher than you think you should. That will keep us from going flat."
   (d)   On a warm May afternoon Teresa Russo has had her singers sitting for over half an hour. As they finish a song out of tune, she whines, "Now, there you are, flat again!"

Projects   1.   Think of two analogies in addition to those mentioned on page 200 that a teacher can use to describe proper intonation.

2.   Listen to a trumpet, cornet, French horn, trombone, and tuba each play middle C. Have the players tune to this pitch until the intonation satisfies you. Notice how the timbre of each sound affects the impression you get of the pitch of the instrument.

3.   Talk to a specialist on a wind instrument that is comparatively unfamiliar to you. Ask him or her which notes on the instrument are most difficult to play in tune and what is done to compensate for these notes. Ask how the dynamic level of the music and the weather affect the pitch of the instrument. Request that he or she play the same pitch several times using a slightly different embouchure each time. As this is done, notice the effect on the pitch.

4.   If you are a wind instrument player, take a trumpet and pull the tuning slide out at least two inches. Then tune the individual valve slides. (If you are not a wind player, observe someone do this.)

5.   Have two classmates who play the same wind instrument bring their instruments to class. Listen to them as they tune notes an octave apart. Also, listen to them tune major thirds as they raise the pitch level by a semitone.

6.   Have the class sing without accompaniment two stanzas of "Silent Night" in C major, carefully checking the pitch with the piano at the end. Then have them sing it in C-sharp major, again checking the pitch at the end. Notice which is easier to sing in tune.

7.   Have the class sing in tempo a well-known song such as "Dixie," checking the pitch carefully at the end. Then request that they sing through the song

at a much slower tempo, and again check the pitch at the end. Compare the accuracy of pitch of the two singings.

Suggested
Readings

Colwell, Richard J. *The Teaching of Instrumental Music*. New York: Appleton-Century-Crofts, 1969.

Kohut, Daniel L. *Instrumental Music Pedagogy*. Englewood Cliffs, N.J.: Prentice-Hall, 1973. Chapter 3.

————. *Musical Performance: Learning Theory and Pedagogy*. Englewood Cliffs, N.J.: Prentice-Hall, 1985.

Pizer, Russell A. *How to Improve the High School Band Sound*. West Nyack, N.Y.: Parker, 1976. Chapter 6.

Stauffer, Donald W. *Intonation Deficiencies of Wind Instruments in Ensemble*. Washington, D.C.: Catholic University of America Press, 1954. Chapters 3 and 7.

CHAPTER 11

Teaching Teenage Singers

Most teenagers have only a vague idea of the correct methods of singing. In fact, many are not aware that there are correct methods or that methods make a difference in the musical results. These students think that singers just open their mouths and whatever sound comes out is the way it is, be it good or bad.

Choral music teachers face conditions that differ from those prevailing in instrumental music. Students in vocal classes are sometimes less selected than instrumentalists, who usually have survived the attrition of several years of study. Some students enter vocal classes after having had almost no contact with music making for a year or more, but this almost never happens in instrumental music. Teenagers know that techniques are required to play an instrument; but singing, which has been spontaneous since childhood, does not appear to demand a learned technique. Most singers of popular music—the only ones many students know about—are untrained, and their singing earns them a sizable income.

Vocal proficiency may not be required for the singer of folk songs or the recording star whose singing is manipulated by electronic amplification, reverberation, and spliced tape. But at the secondary school level, singing technique must be taught for students to sing well. In art music, singers need an appropriate aural image to work toward and a firm technical foundation. They cannot sustain tones and phrases, reach high pitches, or attain good tone quality without instruction in how to sing.

Because singing methods in a choral music class must usually be taught in a group situation, with a variety of student abilities and interests, and in a limited amount of time, teachers should use methods that meet the following criteria:

1. Be usable in a group situation. There is little time for individual instruction, and few students have the time, money, opportunity, or inclination for private voice lessons outside of school hours.

2. Be simple, direct, and as natural as possible. Few teenage choral groups can

learn much from a voice lesson as it is generally taught in the private studio. Private instruction is often too advanced for them, and it requires for its success much personalized attention from a teacher.

3. Be applicable to the music the group is singing. Young people need to see improvement in their singing of the repertoire more than in their performance of isolated drills.

4. Be based on the fundamentals of good singing technique.

WHAT IS CORRECT SINGING?

There is little consensus among singers on proper methods for correct singing. Voice teachers differ on matters of tone, diction, boys' voice change, and range; they disagree further on whether or not the sinus cavities help resonate the tone, whether air is released or "blown out" while singing, what muscles should be used to produce the proper tone quality, and whether or not physical actions for correct singing should be taught. The differences of opinion cause confusion for school choral directors, who conscientiously want to teach their students how to sing.

The lack of consensus derives partly from the differing views on what artistic singing should do. Some singers strive for brilliance and power in singing, others for expressiveness, and still others for a kind of prettiness. The position singers take on this matter naturally affects their tone, loudness, and diction, and determines to some extent the methods they advocate for singing. What is a "big tone" to one singer is "forcing" to another, and what is proper breath support to one voice teacher is muscular tension to another. A further reason for disagreement is the highly individualistic nature of singing. Two excellent singers may have been taught to sing in ways that are the antithesis of each other. Or the opposite may be true: Two singers of apparently equal interest and ability are taught by the same teacher, one turning out to be an excellent singer and the other mediocre.

Although the differences of opinion leave school music teachers in an uncomfortable position, because almost anything they tell their students can be disputed by some specialist, they cannot stand helplessly by while their students flounder through the music. They must act. Therefore, this chapter will present suggestions for giving teenage singers a proper vocal foundation. The suggestions are a synthesis of the different views on singing techniques that have proved to be workable and practical in secondary school choral classes. This synthesis is *one* method for helping teenagers to sing; it is not the *only* method. It represents one attempt to meet the criteria previously mentioned for successful class instruction.

Two approaches should be undertaken simultaneously. One is developing physical actions that result in proper singing. The other is that of "mind over matter"—instilling the right aural concepts and psychological attitudes in students so that they can sing well.

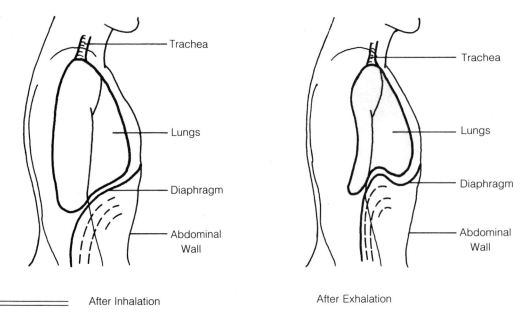

After Inhalation   After Exhalation

Figure 11.1   *Position of lungs, diaphragm, and abdominal wall after inhalation and exhalation.*

PHYSICAL ACTIONS FOR CORRECT SINGING

The simplified drawings in Figure 11.1 show the position of the lungs, diaphragm, and abdominal wall after inhalation and exhalation (Westerman, 1955, p. 14). Below the lungs is the muscular floor called the diaphragm, which is lowered when taking a breath, allowing air to enter and fill the lungs. The abdominal wall moves out somewhat to make room for this action. As breath is released, the diaphragm moves up and the abdominal wall moves in. The chest and shoulders do *not* move. Although some room for breath can be made by sharply expanding the rib cage (thorax) with each inhalation, it is difficult to control this breath, and not as much air can be inhaled as when deeper breathing is employed. Deep, abdominal breathing is necessary for breath support.

Because the vocal cords remain silent until activated by breath, control of the breath becomes all-important. The diaphragm is responsible for this control and requires the singer's attention to the abdominal area. The vocal cords, on which inexperienced singers are so prone to center their attention, are merely a passage through which air moves. By slight and almost effortless adjustment, the vocal cords regulate pitch. Because they sound best when vibrating freely, any tension in the throat is detrimental to both intonation and tone quality. The only place where muscular tension should be present is in the large muscles associated with the diaphragm and abdominal area. The cavities of the sinuses, nose, and eyes serve as resonators.

This brief description of the physical processes involved in singing covers the essential points basic to a good singing technique. How can these physical actions be organized so that students in a class can master them? They can be organized by formulating a simple routine, which, if followed strictly, will establish the correct physical actions for singing. The following four steps have proved successful with teenage singing groups.

1. Without taking a breath, straighten the spine, relax the shoulders, and hold the chest comfortably high.
2. Inhale a full breath, as if the air is going directly into the abdomen.
3. Keep an open and relaxed throat.
4. Sing a full sound that "floats" out.

Correct Position

When introduced to the first step, the students should realize that to make room for the needed air, the bottom of the lungs and the diaphragm cannot be squeezed or cramped in any way. This is why they are instructed not to take a breath for the first step. Room should be made for the breath rather than the breath having to make space for itself. The students also should know that lifting the shoulders is just that—lifting the shoulders—and it has little to do with expansion of the lungs. To help keep the chest up, the students can think of the top of the rib cage as the top of a barrel with a very light lid that is trying to float away.

Initially the students should stand when working on the correct singing routine. The position should not be like a soldier standing at attention, stiff as a ramrod. Rather, it is a natural but alert bodily attitude. Many voice teachers suggest leaning slightly forward so that the weight of the body is on the balls of the feet. If the singers are sitting, they should be instructed to sit straight with their back two inches away from the back of the chair. Good sitting posture is aided when the feet are placed slightly back under the seat of the chair. It is much more difficult to slouch in such a position. Holding music in the palm of the left hand also encourages a good position, because if slouching occurs, the music will drop.

Teachers should walk among the students from time to time to remind individuals who are not assuming good posture. Maintaining the right position is necessary because if the physical setup for singing collapses, so does the tone quality. Maintaining proper singing posture has another function: It gives students something on which to concentrate while singing. If they focus attention on the wrong muscles or on their feelings of inadequacy, tension will result and will hurt the sound. The more they concentrate on establishing the proper position, the more they transfer their attention from places that cause tension to areas that can absorb concentration and improve singing at the same time.

Deep Breath

For the second step, inhaling a deep breath, the students should place one hand lightly against their abdominal wall. Later they can place both hands, thumbs forward and fingers to the back, on each side of the waistline and feel expansion under the hands at those points. If they take a deep breath properly, the wall will expand somewhat around the belt line. The lungs are larger at the bottom than at the top, so most of the expansion and control comes from the muscles in and around the abdomen. The expansion should occur not only in front but also at the sides. The students should learn that during inhalation the abdominal wall moves *out,* and during singing and expending air the wall moves *in.* To get the feel of this action, they should try a simple experiment at home: Lie on the back with arms relaxed at the sides. Keeping the chest motionless, take a deep breath and notice the expansion of the abdomen. Release the breath slowly and there will be a gradual contraction. If one hand is rested lightly on the abdomen, the out-and-in motion becomes more apparent. The exercise is recommended because in a supine position the deep breathing necessary for singing is natural and practically unavoidable. It then becomes relatively simple to duplicate the action while standing.

You cannot control your diaphragm directly; the abdominal muscles do that (Appelman, 1967, p. 33). The results of its action can be felt, particularly when clearing your throat. Control of the diaphragm in singing depends on the correct action of muscles around the abdomen.

To convey the correct muscular tension in the abdominal muscles, a teacher may describe the process as follows:

> *Take in a full breath and hold it, using the* abdominal muscles only. *They should be just tense enough to hold back the breath. The sensation should be one of firm but flexible muscles, something like a light steel spring being gently pulled. . . . Exhale.*
>
> *Now this time when we repeat the deep breath, make sure there's no tension anywhere else—don't squeeze the throat shut or get a tight feeling in the chest. Just let the abdominal muscles do the work of holding back the air. Everything else is relaxed. Try it. . . . Exhale.*
>
> *Now let's see what happens when you sing and use up air. As the abdominal wall moves in, you'll feel an increasing amount of muscle tension there. If you sing to the point where you have no breath left, the muscles begin to feel as though they're in a knot. Let's try it. Here's a D major chord. . . . Sing your pitch as long as possible, and then notice how your abdomen feels.*

A teacher's words should suggest a balance between effortlessness (which is impossible to achieve) and tremendous tension (which inhibits action and causes tension at other places, such as the throat and neck). A teacher can say:

> *Look, when you walk, your leg muscles can't be completely relaxed because you would just drop to the floor. They can't be too tense, either, because then you would look like a stiff-legged clown. The same is true in singing—some tension is needed, but not too much. Pretend that you're going to blow the seeds off a dandelion, but stop just before blowing out*

any air. The amount of tension in your abdominal wall is the amount you should have when you sing.

Relaxed Throat

The third step, maintaining an open throat, is necessary for a full, pleasant, and freely produced tone. The correct throat position is similar to a yawn. In fact, some teachers refer to the tone produced as "yawny." The tongue is low and relaxed, and the back of the mouth where one swallows is open and round. It may be helpful to vocalize on the sound "awe," which requires openness in the back of the throat. This sensation should be maintained even when the lips are closed.

The students should be told that the throat is a passageway, and once it is set up, it should not be disturbed. In singing, the throat should be the sphere of calm through which the tone must be allowed to flow freely. Singers should sing *through* the throat and not *with* it. It should not produce the sensation of shifting, even for very high or very low notes. If the position of the throat changes, the swallowing muscles take over and upset the structure, which should remain stationary. Evidence of muscular interference is not hard to see when it happens. A high larynx is one symptom of tension, as are raised eyebrows and sluggish articulation. The most common indication, especially among boys, is the protruding, raised jaw, accompanied by a straining of the muscles under the chin. For some reason, boys will try sticking out their chins to sing what seem to be high pitches. It never helps, but they do it anyway. The jaw should be relaxed and loose, as if it were suspended by rubber bands.

Action of Breath in Singing

The fourth step emphasizes the term *float* in connection with tone production to indicate that the air is not rammed through the vocal cords but rather rises slowly through the throat. Students should learn that singing does not require large amounts of air. As Paul Roe writes: "Ask a good singer who smokes (there are a few) to inhale and then sing a tune. It will be noticeable that no smoke will appear until the smoker stops singing; then smoke will come in a gush. In other words, there is so little air used in good singing that no smoke is visible during the act of singing" (1970, p. 80). When singers push the tone or expel air carelessly, they achieve a forced, fuzzy quality that lacks resonance, intensity, and solidity. It has no "center."

To be efficient, singers must achieve a maximum amount of vocal cord vibration with a minimum amount of air. Teachers can say, "The breath coming out as you sing should move as slowly as if you were warming your hands with it." Another way to achieve intensity is to imagine that the air is "spiraling" or "spinning" as it comes from the back of the throat and moves out of the mouth. Most students know that a football must be spiraled for a good pass. This analogy is often helpful in gaining a concept of a good singing tone.

An excellent exercise that combines the four actions required for good singing is to have the singers practice long hisses. The hiss requires little air and no effort in the throat. The extended hiss—at first twenty seconds, but working over a period of time up to forty or more seconds—calls for correct breath action, smooth and sustained, as in singing. After the students have learned the correct routine, the hiss can be alternated with singing on a vowel: "Hissss–Aaaah–Hissss–Aaaah," executed without a break.

Resonance

If the students are progressing well in their comprehension of correct tone production, teachers should start to develop resonance in the voices. Although advanced work is best undertaken in private lessons, school music teachers can begin the initial steps. First, the singers should be shown what resonance is. They can experience it by feeling vibration in the head. To do so, they should place the fingers of one hand lightly on the nose and sing "ping." After experimenting to discover the tone placement that encourages the greatest vibration and resonance, they should work to achieve the same vibrant sensation on sounds other than *ng*. The object is to encourage resonation by sending the tone through the head and face.

Teaching the Correct Physical Actions

Whether the procedures for good singing should be taught together or independently is a matter of judgment. One step makes sense only as it is related to the others, and yet some attention needs to be given each step by itself, so a process of alternation between whole and parts is called for. The teacher should consider the level of development of the singers. A musically immature group may not be ready to tackle these techniques for some time. *Interest and motivation also must be present to some degree before the steps will bring forth positive musical results.*

By way of further preparation, the students should have memorized some songs that can be sung while learning the correct physical actions. Memorization lets the students concentrate their attention on the actions. To be meaningful to the singers, the actions for correct singing should always be presented in association with actual music. As soon as possible, they should be applied, even though imperfectly, to the students' current repertoire.

Teachers must be persistent in presenting these singing steps. The steps involve a complex of skills that cannot be mastered in a few rehearsals. They need to be worked on day after day in many ways, especially through imaginative warm-up and careful attention to the music. Singers should know the reasons for building good habits and letting proper actions become so ingrained that they won't be forgotten during a performance.

AURAL-PSYCHOLOGICAL APPROACH

Since the advent of the phonograph, there have been several cases of young singers who, without any private instruction, have demonstrated rare ability, to the astonishment of auditioning committees from conservatories and opera companies. How is it possible for a totally untrained person to sing a difficult Verdi or Puccini aria so well? By listening to a recording of a renowned artist.* These cases illustrate again the shaping power of a singer's concept of singing. It is no accident that Italian operatic tenors have a similar sound, as do Irish tenors, to say nothing of Wagnerian sopranos and French chanteuses. They sound alike because they have similar concepts of singing.

Because singing involves so many muscles and bodily parts, which makes it impossible for a teacher to describe adequately all the muscular sensations, no physical routine in itself is sufficient to teach correct singing actions. Physical steps are needed to get the student started in the right direction and to avoid developing habits that hinder singing. But along with those efforts teachers should teach an aural concept of singing and then have the students strive for that vocal quality. The human voice is so involved with feeling and thought that what singers think in their mind is certain to affect how they sound. In a very real sense it is the mind that controls the throat position, the action of the diaphragm, and the amount of tension in the tongue. At times, vocal teachers feel as much like psychologists as they do music teachers, and perhaps this is as it should be.

Style and Tone

As a first step toward developing a concept of good singing, teachers need to get students to give up the notion that currently popular styles in singing represent the acme of vocal performance. Popular song style is fine for popular music, but for art music it won't be good enough. When students realize that there are distinct styles of singing, they can begin to develop a concept of a legitimate art style. Basically they learn good singing by hearing it, be it from other students, recordings, or teachers.

Students learn more from one another than teachers like to admit. One good bass or alto can do much without realizing it to teach the other singers in the section. If the members of a section, say the tenors, get the idea that a certain tenor is a good singer, they will imitate him.

When selecting recordings for models of tone, teachers should be particular about the choice of singer. A mature performer may have a highly developed tone that no teenager can or should emulate. Recordings of good collegiate singers are often more suitable.

A choral music teacher who is himself a good singer has an advantage. Pianists

---

*In fairness, it should be pointed out that no doubt some very promising young singers have ruined their voices trying, without proper singing technique, to imitate recordings of great artists. These young singers are never heard from again.

and other instrumental majors should take heart and notice that the word *singer,* not *soloist,* is used. A highly trained voice is fine, but it is not necessary. What is needed is a voice with pleasing quality and sufficient flexibility to illustrate various aspects of phrasing, style, and tone. To make their illustrations as effective as possible, some teachers practice singing with a breathy tone, pointed chin, constricted throat, or other handicap. Then they can say to the class, "Look, here's what you're doing—notice what it does to the tone. Now I'll do it right. . . . See what a difference it makes?"

Teachers can strengthen the concept of correct singing by word as well as by example. "Hey, that's too rough and blatant. Smooth it up. Be gentler." "Men, that sounds sick. Come on, let's hear some muscle in your tone." Or with word and example together: "Now the rest of you girls listen to the altos at letter G. This is what I mean by a beautiful tone. Notice that it's warm and flowing, with body to it."

One style, encountered often among boys, especially in middle school, is what might be called "pianolike" singing. The boys do not sing through their tones, and the result is a combination of speaking and singing. Each note is a short spurt of sound, usually with a pushed tone of debatable pitch, folowed by a rest. Probably this style is caused by a lack of self-confidence in singing. The cure may involve singing the songs on a neutral syllable, allowing breaks in sound only at breathing points. Other suggestions for legato singing were offered in Chapter 9.

Range

The ease with which singers adapt to range is affected by their mental outlook. For instance, if you were asked to walk along a line on the floor, you would have no trouble doing so. But if that line were along the roof edge of a ten-story building, you would find this feat nearly impossible. The way in which a singer thinks about a tone, especially a pitch at the top of the range, will determine in most cases whether or not he or she can sing it. Some teachers with the best intentions talk this way: "Now I know that high A is a difficult note to reach. Why, even professional singers have trouble with it! I hope you can get it, or else we'll have to move it down an octave." The result is, of course, that the students are talked out of singing the note. The teacher should say, "Space suits on. Let's get that A, with a good tone. Sing the line by using the technique we worked on—deep breath, open throat." The students should be encouraged to try, but they should not be "whipped" into further effort: "Listen, we're going to get that high A or else!"

Girls will gain more freedom in the top part of their range by vocalizing on patterns such as these:

Ah _____

Ooh hoo_____
Ah hah_____
Ooh-ah-ooh

Ah_____

With each singing the pitch should be raised a half step. Altos may sing, as long as they are able, in unison with the sopranos. Perhaps the girls can be held on the high pitch, then cut off and told, "You know, that note is a whole step higher than the highest note in the 'Hallelujah Chorus,' which we're singing." In this way the exercises are made functional. The vocalization should be continued on a somewhat regular basis until the "high-note phobia" has been overcome. The ranges of boys' voices are discussed later in this chapter.

DICTION

Singing has been defined as sustained speech. Making the words intelligible is one of the singers' more significant responsibilities. Unless the words are understandable, listeners are receiving only half of what the composer intended. Furthermore, singers should produce the words understandably without allowing them to detract from the tone quality and musical effect. Some singers vocalize beautifully, but when they add words, the singing loses quality. The words have interfered with the singing.

To make words understandable, singers should be made conscious of the need to pronounce words clearly as they sing. In speaking, sloppy pronunciation is more easily covered up because the sounds are relatively short, but in the sustained tones of singing such concealment is hardly possible. To some degree, pronunciation should even be exaggerated during singing. One simple device that helps diction is to whisper the words, because whispering requires much clarity to be intelligible.

A common fault in singing is negligence regarding final consonants, especially *d* and *t*, before a rest or breath. The students may be careless, or they may be uncertain about when the tone should end. If this is the case, the teacher when conducting can close the thumb and second finger of the right hand precisely at the end of a word, and this device will help the singers to execute the final consonant together.

A difficult task for inexperienced singers is to keep the proper throat and mouth position while forming words. There must be freedom from tension in the jaw, tongue, and lips, and consistent application of good methods of singing. Both conditions are helped if jaw movement is kept to a minimum. As Walter Ehret states, "In *legato* singing, particular attention must be paid to the jaw, which should move very *little* if a legato flow is to be preserved. Actually the jaw has to move only for six letters (B, F, M, P, V, and W), and even in these instances the motions are small" (1959, p. 36). Excessive jaw movement creates tension and often leads to less accurate pronunciation. To correct this fault, the students can practice singing while touching their fingers lightly on their chins. They will be surprised to discover that they can sing and enunciate just as clearly with more economy of movement.

Some teachers and singers want the different vowels to be sung with almost no change of mouth and throat, but others feel that such rigidity drains the singing of color and variety. In either case the students should put first things first. They should concentrate on the proper method of tone production and especially on the open throat, so that changes from one vowel to another cause as little disruption as possible.

Because vowels are the vehicles for sustained sound, which is the essence of singing, they deserve attention. When singers sing the same vowel but do not all sing it alike, they create an illusion of faulty intonation and blur the words. People who speak the same language in generally the same way are sometimes inconsistent when singing it; they speak a word one way and sing it another. So the terms "cleaning up vowels" or "working on vowels" are frequently heard in discussions of choral music.

In some cases good intentions have led teachers into long and complex discussions of palate position, nasalization, and diacritical marks, accompanied by tedious sessions on how to sing the thirty-plus vowel sounds of the English language in conjunction with a labial, aspirate, or lingual-palatal consonant. This approach bewilders the students, because for years they have been saying words without being conscious of shaping their palate or moving their uvula. Also, such manipulative efforts sidetrack their attention into areas far removed from the qualities of the music itself.

One remedy for the varied phonation of a vowel is to practice singing it uniformly from a model sound in a familiar word. Traditionally voice teachers have confined their efforts to the five Italian vowels *i, e, a, o, u,* (ē, ā, ä, ō, o͞o). English is not Italian, however, and these vowels account for only 12 percent of the sounds on a written page of English (Westerman, 1955, p. 61). Just the English short ĭ as in *sit* accounts for over 12 percent. Kenneth Westerman in his book *Emergent Voice* lists fifteen vowel sounds, which he claims represent more than 90 percent of the sounds and 95 percent of the muscular movements involved in singing English:

vē as in *veal*	nō as in *note*
sĭ as in *sit*	pû as in *push*
tā as in *take*	r͞oo as in *room*
thĕ as in *them*	mī as in *might*
shă as in *shall*	bou as in *bounce*

lä as in *large*   few as in *few*

gô as in *gone*   coi as in *coin**

dŭ as in *dust*

A chart of vowel sounds can be posted on the wall of the classroom. If a word in a song is not being sung consistently, the teacher can point out the sound for the students to practice.

Some vowel sounds are diphthongs, or compound sounds. Perhaps the most common is the pronoun *I*. When singers "chew" its execution as shown here,

Ah - a - ay - ee,

the effect is unpleasant and unclear. For a more satisfying result the singers should hold the initial vowel sound and then at the last moment move to the second or "vanish" sound. Thus, *I* is sung as follows:

Ah - - - - ee.

Some choral directors feel it is their "deeyoooty" to teach a special verison of the English language for singing—a version that is aesthetically superior to spoken English. The value of such a project is questionable. The English language needs little enhancement to be an artistic means of communication.

Because singing exaggerates the unpleasant as well as pleasant sounds of the language, music teachers might spend a few moments (but no more) to make the undesirable sounds less conspicuous. One is the sibilant *s*, which if sustained produces a hissing effect. The singers should execute it together and should never prolong it. Conductors can help by closing their fingers to indicate the end of the sound. Another troublesome consonant is the *r*. Instead of singing the word *father* as *fahtherrr,* the singers should sustain *uh* and add the *r* at the very end: *fah-thuh-r.* To soften a vowel so that it will not be harsh, the singers should open the back of the throat and round the lips slightly.

Whether or not the last consonant of one word should be attached to the first of the next word in legato singing depends on the word and on the musical phrase. For example, the words *lost in the night* can be sung *law-sti-nthuh nah-it.* In this case, clarity is improved. However, Mendelssohn's lovely "He Watching over Israel" becomes comic if this technique is stressed for the words *slumbers not.*

*Westerman, 1955, p. 63. Used by permission.

GIRLS' VOICES

The voice quality most often encountered among teenage girls, especially in the middle and junior high school, is breathy, thin, or fluty. It is typical of many young girls in the process of physical and vocal growth, and it is a result of many factors—muscular immaturity, lack of control and coordination of the breathing muscles, and insufficient voice development. Precise and concentrated effort applied to the steps involved in proper singing will help to develop a more vibrant singing tone.

In the high school there are few true altos with a rich quality in the low range around A and G below middle C, and there are almost none in middle school. Most teenage altos sound like second sopranos singing low. A word of warning is appropriate here for those teachers who assign a few altos to sing tenor in a mixed four-part chorus. If this practice is followed extensively for any one alto, it will tend to strengthen and overuse the tones in her middle and lower range. In addition, she may develop a lack of confidence for singing high notes. Therefore, transferring an alto permanently to the tenor part should be avoided.

High school sopranos should not sing much higher than top-space G, or perhaps an occasional A. Younger sopranos should stay about one step lower. The range used depends largely on the experience of the singers.

BOYS' VOICES

Boys' voices are usually less breathy than girls'. In the untrained high school boy singer there is often a decided difference between the quality of the low range and the quality of the high. As long as the bass voice does not develop signs of a raucous, hard tone quality, the teacher can be assured that there will be no strain if the basses are encouraged to sing (not shout) out in the low part of their range. In baritones and tenors the quality will often be light and almost colorless in the upper range.

One cannot arbitrarily set up a neat chart of voice ranges, although many writers attempt to do so. The top usable note of the average high school tenor may be either F or F sharp, and that of a baritone either D or E flat.

High Notes for Boys

The topic of extending the upper range for boys leads into a matter about which there is some confusion: the falsetto voice, variously referred to as the "head voice" or "half voice." Music teachers have never been sure about whether the falsetto voice is desirable or usable. There is no doubt that boys can extend their upper singing range by the use of falsetto. True, the tone lacks power and healthy

masculine sound, and for that reason boys are not eager to try it. However, as Harry Wilson points out, "It is the normal production for changed male voices to use on high tones. It is both easy and natural" (1959, p. 206).

For years fine professional tenors have been mixing falsetto with the full voice without anyone's being quite sure which voice was being used. These singers have demonstrated the closeness of the two voices. With adolescent boys, teachers can say, "Use falsetto to reach tones you can't get with your regular voice." But they should add, and this is very important, "After you've learned the part, try to sing those tones as much as you can with your regular voice. Approach the high tones easily and freely if you're going to sing them falsetto, and in time you can probably sing them with regular voice." If a few weeks most boys will be able to sing the high pitches in regular voice, because their doubts about singing higher pitches have been eliminated. Falsetto is a good model for singing higher pitches because it is unstrained and free.

Special attention to developing the falsetto will facilitate its use. The object is to effect a smooth transition from one voice to the other. The first step is for each boy to find his falsetto voice by singing with an *oo* sound on D, E flat, or E above middle C. After the voice has been found, he can then slur down an octave. Wilson suggests moving from the light quality *down* into the regular voice (1959, p. 207). The boys should not be taken beyond this point for a few days, although the slur can be slowed down with practice. The next step is to sing a descending scale, making the transfer from falsetto to regular voice as smooth and inconspicuous as possible. Finally, after some experience with the scale on the *oo* sound, other vowels may be tried. Until the boys are proficient in the use of falsetto, they should start the tone on an *oo* sound and then change to the desired vowel as they sustain the pitch. Gradually the starting note of this pattern can move chromatically from D above middle C up to A. Basses should be included with the tenors in this work, because occasionally they also have problems with high pitches.

Procedures for achieving falsetto must be presented with caution. Teachers cannot walk into class the first day and ask healthy teenage boys who are proud of their newfound manhood to sing a tone that sounds like an owl hooting. Teachers should bide their time until the boys encounter difficulty with a particular note. Then they can say, "Here's a way for you to get that note." Another condition should be met: The boys must have confidence in the teacher. They need to feel that his or her directions can be trusted to help them sing better. Finally, the beginning work on falsetto should not be done in the presence of girls. The boys will be sensitive at best, so even if it means putting the girls in another room to study, it is advisable to separate the two groups. Let the girls hear the results of the work as the music is sung; they need not observe the process.

Voice Change

Most boys at some time or another during the period of voice change are involved in music, sometimes while they are in general music classes. What happens to them during the voice change not only shapes their current attitude toward music but also influences what they will do with singing during the rest of their lives. For these reasons the topic of the changing voice should not be treated as a passing curiosity.

There is almost no subject in the field of music education that is more fascinating, frustrating, and fraught with differences of opinion than what happens to a boy's voice at puberty and what should be done about it. To begin with, there is the question of whether or not the boy should sing during the period of change. The first published work on the topic appeared in England in 1885 under the title *The Child's Voice: Its Treatment with Regards to After-Development*. It concluded that singing during voice change was injurious and ruinous. This theory found little acceptance in America, nor is it held in England today (McKenzie, 1956, pp. 11, 14).

The significant questions for music teachers are these: What pitches should boys with changing voices sing, and how can teachers best help them in learning how to handle their new voices? Over the years these questions have been answered in a variety of ways, but today there is more agreement than there was previously. Both Duncan McKenzie and Frederick Swanson point out that there are basses among boys at the most frequent ages for voice change, which is around fourteen years of age (Swanson, 1973, pp. 184–89). And both agree that there are tenors, or "alto-tenors," as McKenzie refers to them.

These two authorities disagree somewhat on whether the change is gradual or erratic and sudden. It appears that no two boys change in the same way or at the same rate. Because McKenzie believes change is gradual, he advocates following a "comfortable range" policy in which the boy is transferred to the next lower classification as soon as he begins to have difficulty with the highest notes of the part he is now singing (1956, p. 34). In his research Swanson found that a number of boys could continue to sing in the treble range, even after the bass notes emerged (1961, p. 63). Some boys had "areas of silence" between treble and bass notes. These upper notes slowly disappear, especially if the boy no longer uses them.

Swanson urges, and followed this practice in the Moline, Illinois, schools when he was in charge of the music program there, that the boys be segregated from the girls for a portion of the year during the eighth grade. Boys are sensitive and uncertain about what is happening to their bodies during these years, and the presence of girls in a class that is working on singing at this time inhibits their learning. Swanson sees the purpose of such segregated instruction as the "opening of doors":

1.   Open the psychological door so that finding this new singing-speaking voice is a challenging adventure.

2.   Open the door that reveals methods for getting control of this new voice.

3.   Open the door that leads to a repertoire of songs that can be sung with correctness and pleasure (1973, pp. 191–94).

The content of Swanson's classes consisted largely of finding the notes that each boy had and then getting them to apply those notes in singing simple songs, including such songs as "Take Me Out to the Ball Game." He also advocates the teaching of singing in falsetto to help them reach notes that they can't sing with their regular voices.

John Paul Johnson (1983, pp. 18–20) suggests the following stages for the male changing voice:

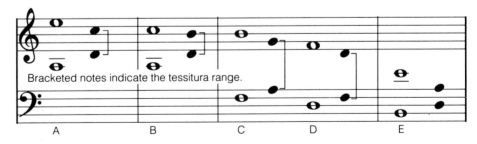

Bracketed notes indicate the tessitura range.

A. STAGE 1: Premutational   B. STAGE 2: Early Mutational
C. STAGE 3: High Mutation   D. STAGE 3: High Mutation
E. STAGE 4: Post Mutation

Stage 1 is the unchanged voice, which is very similar to the girls' voices of the same age. Stage 2 is not easily detected. Signs of it are a tightening of jaw and a more husky tone. Pitch problems are more common at this stage. Stage 3 is the voice in the throes of change, which is usually accompanied by increased height and weight and the development of the larynx. The stage usually lasts from three to twelve months (Cooksey, 1977, pp. 5–17). Stage 3A is marked by the appearance of facial hair and a more narrow and lower tessitura. Stage 4, or the "new baritone" stage, is one in which the voice begins to "settle"; this happens around the end of the eighth grade. The range and tessitura are still limited, but both will gradually increase as the male matures.

Here are some other general suggestions that should guide teachers in working with boys with changing voices:

1. Take a positive approach to boys with changing voices. Help them understand what is happening to their voices. More important, let them know that this change can add new pitches and color to the music sung. Talk of progress: "Doug, let's see, according to my records you could sing from C up to G two weeks ago. Today you got up to A, and with good quality, too, so you're improving. Keep it up."

2. *Never* allow a class to ridicule or laugh at the singing efforts of a boy in the throes of change. Although they may pretend to be unconcerned, boys at this age are very sensitive about the status of their masculinity, and one bad experience can cause permanent withdrawal from further efforts at singing. More positively, an effort should be made to build a feeling of mutual assistance, understanding, and encouragement in the class. This point is directly related to the first, because to some extent the students reflect the teacher's attitude.

3. Check the range and quality of the boys' voices at least three or four times each year during the period of change. Encourage each boy to ask for an immediate voice check when he feels his range has changed to the point that he is having trouble reaching the notes of his part. The rate and extent of change are highly individual matters, and there is as much variation in voice development as there is in any area of physical maturation. Nor is change consistent within the individual. There may be plateaus, sudden changes, and inexplicable regressions.

    By checking and observing the development of each boy's voice, an inexperienced teacher can learn firsthand what voice change sounds like and how it progresses. With experience it is possible to judge range by the boy's speaking voice and physical appearance. A short conversation with the boy will indicate the general pitch level of his voice. Heavier facial features, stature, and enlarged larynx usually indicate a maturing voice.

4. Attempt to meet boys' vocal needs in general music classes. Too often teachers in a general music class of thirty teach as if the three boys with changing

voices weren't there. Begin by seating them together in the front row near the piano. Add to the section as other boys' voices change. Then on easy unison songs help the boys with changing voices sing an octave lower by playing their pitches on the piano, especially the starting pitch. If the teacher is a male, he should sing some of the time with these boys. Select songs with parts for the changing voices, especially lines that are *easy*. When none is included with a song, try writing a simple part—perhaps the chord roots to a song such as "Down in the Valley" or a short ostinato figure. True, it is hard to do much for the first boy whose voice changes, unless he is a capable musician who can hold a part on his own. But what happens to a boy's voice during the change is so important that special efforts should be made to ease the transition.

5. Be especially careful in selecting music. Vocal numbers should not consistently violate the pitch limits revealed through checking the boys' voices. Again choose simple music, at least until the voices are stabilized. If a number doesn't fit the needs of the group, don't use it.

6. Stress correct singing, with proper breathing and freedom from tension. Voices are not helped by forcing or straining to reach certain tones or by singing with a blatant quality in an attempt to sound like a male ten years older. Occasionally a boy may be asked not to sing certain notes because of range, but as a regular practice this hurts interest and should be avoided.

CLASSIFYING VOICES IN HIGH SCHOOL

Testing voices has two purposes: to serve as a means of selecting singers and to place the singer in the right part. Initially teachers should screen would-be members of a performing group to see that they possess the minimum requirements to profit from choral experience. After hearing the voice, teachers must judge whether or not the rewards of study *for the student* justify the student's expenditure of time and interest.

The best time for auditions is in the spring, so the class can start right to work in the fall, without delays to wait for testing voices. Otherwise the first weeks of school will have to do.

Voices are generally grouped according to two criteria: range and quality. In high school, the customary ranges for the various classifications are as follows:

Soprano   Alto   Tenor   Bass

Many students cannot sing all the notes in any one classification. Such singers are assigned to the sections that most nearly represent their ranges.

Although prospective teachers may be familiar with the timbre of the various voice classifications of professional or collegiate singers, the quality of adolescent voices is noticeably less mature. The quality of a typical adolescent bass or alto can be recognized only after experience in working with teenage singers. There are a few good recordings of high school choirs, and they can be studied with profit.

For several reasons it is almost impossible to classify adolescent voices with certainty:

1. Adolescent voices, especially boys' voices, have not settled.

2. Psychological factors enter into a student's performance. Under one set of conditions he or she may capably sing passages that under other circumstances can't even be approximated. Usually the conditions in an audition are about as unfavorable for adolescents as they can be.

3. Many students who audition at the beginning of the year do not know how to sing correctly. Developing correct singing habits can make quite a difference in a student's range and tone quality.

4. The voices of teenagers, especially girls in early adolescence, are rather homogeneous. What is frequently encountered is an SATB chorus largely composed of second sopranos and baritones with a limited range.

Balance within the group should be considered in classifying voices. If a girls' glee club consists of one hundred voices, clearly there cannot be fifty second sopranos and only fifteen altos. Some adjustments must be made. This does not mean that teachers can or should get an additional alto merely by moving a soprano into the alto section. But classifications within the group should be considered to maintain a reasonable balance of parts. To an extent, teachers have to do the best they can with the available apportionment of voices.

For these reasons an extensive discussion of the "break," color in the voices, and elaborate tonal patterns to aid in classifying does not seem warranted for school vocal teachers. Some voice teachers even reject the idea of registers in the voice, because they feel the voice is derived from one pair of vocal cords and should have a continuous compass.

Because some classification is necessary for part singing, however, teachers must make judgments on range and quality, imperfect as these judgments may be. If possible, students should be heard privately.

Place singers where they cannot see the keyboard, because some students with musical training may have preconceived ideas about the notes they can sing. Then have them sing a five-note ascending and descending scale pattern:

Begin girls on middle C and boys an octave lower, and move up stepwise until the top notes of the pattern show strain. Then shift to this pattern, starting at what appears to be the student's middle range and moving down:

Ah_____

Next, have each student sing a familiar song such as "America." Transpose the song into three different keys about a fourth apart, possibly into C for a low range, F for a middle range, and A or B flat for a high range. Listen for intonation as well as for range and quality. Other simple testing procedures may be included if time permits. The range, general tone quality, and other pertinent facts about each voice should be written down, dated, and filed for future reference.

Occasionally teachers want to identify the better students for a select choir or ensemble. In such a case, the procedures can be expanded as follows:

1. Check the student's ability to match pitch quickly and accurately. Play a series of three or four pitches in the singer's range on the piano and see how rapidly and accurately they are sung back.

2. Listen for a highly individualistic tone quality that may not blend well with other voices.

3. Present the singer with a line of music to sing at sight.

If individual auditions are not possible, group methods will have to be used. The patterns recommended for individual testing can also be used for group testing. Work the boys up to D above middle C. Then arbitrarily place in the tenor section all boys who can sing the D comfortably; the remainder of the boys will make up the bass section. The same technique can be followed with the girls—all who can sing F on the top line comfortably are placed in the soprano section. An individual audition should follow as soon as possible.

ORGANIZING FOR CHORAL MUSIC TEACHING

Choral music teachers have to consider several matters that can affect how well a group sings. These matters include what the group and sections within a group are called, the size and seating arrangement, and the quality and use of piano accompaniment.

What's in a Name?

Students at the junior high and middle school level are sometimes concerned about the name of the part they sing. Boys are sensitive about being called "soprano" or "alto," names associated with girls. To eliminate any problem here, some teachers call boy sopranos "first tenors."

Caution must be exercised in designating certain parts as *first* and *second*. No one wants to be second in anything in present-day America, so the term *high* can identify the girls' or treble part, and the term *low* the boys' or bass clef part. Because girls' voices are so much alike in early adolescence, some teachers regularly have girls trade parts, one section learning the high part for one song and the low part for another.

Whether an organization is called choir, chorus, glee club, troubadors, sextet, or ensemble is not a serious matter to the teacher. As long as the terms are used conventionally—a sextet contains six singers, and so on—almost any name is acceptable. However, students, especially in early adolescent years, place considerable importance on the name of a group. In some schools "choir" is for the talented and "chorus" is for anyone else. Teachers should discuss with the group the possibility of another name. In some schools it has been the making of a new attitude, and the students can contribute ideas on the subject.

Group Size and Seating

Teenagers, whose voices are usually not yet fully developed, need the support of a number of singers on their part. This support gives them confidence and makes their efforts more satisfying. Happily, a group of average voices can, when put together properly, sound quite beautiful. The individual voice timbres appparently combine to make a rich tone, and minor pitch deviations are hardly noticeable. If two performers are five vibrations apart, the "beats" are easily heard. But when other voices are added, some of them being one, two, or three vibrations apart, the "beats" seem to disappear. A tone with such pitch variation may lack clarity, but it can still be pleasing.

Optimum group size depends on the ability and age of the singers, the demands of the music, and the acoustics of the place of performance, so no ideal size can be recommended. Probably student choral groups sound best with forty to eighty voices; beyond this number the size becomes unwieldy for a teacher to handle in the regular manner. Nor can the proper distribution of singers on each part be stated with much certainty. Because the lower pitches of a singer's vocal range do not have the carrying power of high pitches, and because the lower parts in a choral group are more easily overbalanced, the low voice parts generally need more singers.

In the assignment of seats in a section, two strong singers should be placed side by side so that they can support each other. Then less mature singers can be placed on either side of the more able students. In this way, the weaker singers can learn from the better ones. The seating should be changed from time to time so that the singers learn to sing with different persons and have a chance to hear the group from other locations.

Selecting an Accompanist

A poor accompanist can seriously hinder a choral group by slowing the rehearsal pace or confusing the singers by playing the music incorrectly. Teachers should select the accompanists carefully and then train them to follow and even anticipate the conductor's directions.

If possible, several accompanists should be selected for the group. One can substitute for another, and an entire rehearsal will not be disrupted because an accompanist is absent. Most teachers choose their accompanists from within the choral group. In such situations the rotation of several accompanists gives more students the experience of accompanying and also gives them a chance to sing.

Unfortunately, a distinction often must be made between accompanists and pianists. It is possible for a player to perform a few etudes well and still not be able to read simple music. These pianists usually make poor accompanists because they have to memorize almost every piece they play, and sometimes there isn't time to memorize the accompaniment. This type of pianist also tends to be inflexible in following a conductor.

To select accompanists, teachers can give three simple tests:

1. Have the applicants sight-read the accompaniment to a piece of octavo music that is not very difficult. Rate them on their ability to keep going without stopping and, of course, on their general accuracy in playing the music.

2. Have the applicants sight-read only the voice parts of a choral number. Do not select a contrapuntal work for this purpose, because music of this type is too difficult for most high school students to read at sight. Some applicants will have trouble reading the voice parts in SATB music.

3. Choose a simple octavo selection, and have the applicants learn the accompaniment before the audition. At the tryout have each pianist play the piece while you conduct. To see how well the student can follow, go through the piece and alter the tempo several times. Then ask him or her to play a certain passage—for example, the tenor part of page 4, second score, fourth bar. This exercise will reveal alertness in following verbal directions. If the accompanist can transpose and modulate, this is an added benefit.

Few teachers are fortunate enough to have accompanists who can play fluently through the three tests just mentioned, so some training is in order. Learning to play the notes on the page and to read the voice parts is simply a matter of individual practice. If an accompanist studies privately, the private teacher is often willing to cover the music in lessons. At the beginning of the year it is wise to hear the accompanists play their music privately *before* the piece is practiced with the singers. The most common cause of trouble for inexperienced accompanists is the clef sign used for the tenor part. It is usually necessary to explain this phenomenon to pianists. When used on a tenor part, any of the first four clefs shown below indicate that the notes do not sound as written but rather sound one octave lower. The fifth sign is the tenor clef, on which the pitches sound as written, with middle C on the fourth line.

The important task in training accompanists is to teach them to anticipate tempos and verbal instructions. The development of this ability will be hastened if teachers are consistent in their approach to the music. Accompanists should also learn to think by phrases and sections rather than note by note. This technique helps them to play more musically and to anticipate possible starting and stopping places.

Use of the Piano

The piano is of limited help in teaching vocal music. Aside from the initial playing of parts on the rote-learning process, the piano should be avoided for demonstration purposes because its sounds are unlike singing.

Beginning choral teachers who were not voice majors in college may be self-conscious about singing in front of a large group of students, and consequently they may be tempted to rely on the piano for all demonstrations. To correct this habit, they should at first sing short and easy passages for the group to gain confidence in their ability to demonstrate musical ideas.

The proper amount of accompaniment depends on the ability of the singers. Musically advanced groups can and should sing frequently without the piano, even on works that will be accompanied in performance. Inexperienced musicians, too, should do some singing without the piano in almost every rehearsal. Care must be taken so that the piano does not cover up faults in the singing. Also, the singers should develop a degree of independence from the piano, because in the unfamiliar circumstances of a performance they may find it more difficult to hear the accompaniment.

MEMORIZING MUSIC

Choral groups almost always memorize the music that they perform before an audience, while instrumental groups never do, except for one or two standard numbers played while marching. There are good reasons for choral groups to memorize:

1. There are no distractions caused by holding music or turning pages. All of a singer's attention can be centered on singing and watching the conductor.

2. The appearance of the group is improved because there is no chance for singers to bury their heads in the music.

3. Many annoyances are eliminated—loose pages fluttering to the floor and music brushing the back of a singer's neck.

4. Memorized pieces are usually thoroughly learned.

Memorization is aided by applying the psychological principles described in Chapter 5. The principle of distributed effort means that memorization is most easily and thoroughly accomplished in many short periods rather than in one or two long ones. Recognizing patterns and relationships in music is also directly applicable to memorization, because most works of music have an overall pattern or form. The music can be scanned for accents, holds, solos, and tempo changes, because these features often show a pattern in themselves. Noting the phrase endings that rhyme is helpful in recalling both words and music.

There are several teaching devices to help students memorize. They can be asked to write the words to the songs as a test that will affect their grades. A group memorization technique can be operated in this manner. Select a logical section of from two to four lines, and let each student study it for about twenty to thirty seconds. Then ask the entire group to recite the words together without music. If this recitation goes well, call on two or three individuals to recite the phrases. Move on to another portion of the text, and after it has been memorized, ask the group to recite both segments. Move the process along as quickly a possible, and do not keep it up very long at one time.

As a variation of the procedure, words can be passed back and forth between teacher and singers. For example, "Now let EVERY TONGUE ADORE THEE," or "now LET every TONGUE adore THEE." Another variation is to recite a line and ask for the first word of the next line. Chorus: "Now let every tongue adore thee." Teacher: "George?" George: "Let." Chorus: "Let men with," and so on.

Teachers can facilitate memorization by asking the students to sing the piece from memory at an early stage of preparation. Singers can become so accustomed to the "crutch" of looking at music that it is difficult for them to break away from it. Memorization should not be urged too soon, however, because it may encourage faking.

Teachers should impress on the singers the necessity of thinking ahead when singing. Foresight is necessary to prevent such serious mishaps as singing through a break or starting out on the wrong section of the music. Lines are less likely to be forgotten when the singers think ahead.

Breakdowns can also be averted by good spot practice. In a piece of music there are frequently a few crucial places at which the music is most likely to break down—change of section, change of key, and so on. The singers should be made to feel especially confident at these points.

Some teachers, in an effort to build the confidence of their singers, unconsciously develop habits that increase the students' dependence. One of these is the habit of singing along with the group. Generally this should be done only in rehearsal to help a part that is weak or to encourage the singers in a strategic place such as the beginning of a new section. The danger is that the singers begin to rely on the help teachers give. Because teachers cannot sing along in a concert, the students should learn to do well without such support. Another disadvantage is that singing by teachers tends to make the music sound better to them than it actually is. They should be listening carefully to the group, not to their own voice—even though the latter may sound better.

Teachers should also avoid mouthing the words. This technique is of only limited help to the singers. If all the parts do not have the same words at the same time, the help is negligible; and even if the words are synchronized, it is doubtful whether the singers are able to lip-read. They should have the words learned well enough to get along without this assistance.

All music memorized by the singers should also be memorized by the teacher. Teachers make a poor impression when they conduct from the printed page while their singers perform from memory. Teachers should maintain eye contact with the singers at all times during performance, and this precludes looking at the music.

Questions   1.   How would you explain to a choral class of high school freshmen and sophomores why it is important for them to learn how to sing correctly?

2.   How would you explain to a ninth grader that the style of singing used by the latest popular recording group is not appropriate for art music?

3.   Should choral teachers attempt to develop an adultlike singing tone in a high school choir? In a junior high school choir? Why or why not?

4.   What analogies can be used to give the students the idea of the open throat?

Projects   1.   Find three choral pieces that contain long tones suitable for work on proper breathing. They should be simple, yet musically worthy of study. Handel's "Thanks Be to Thee" is an example.

2.   Review three part-songs for boys' changing voices. Note the range and tessitura of the parts in each of three.

3.   Listen to recordings of solos by sopranos, altos, tenors, and basses. Select one of each voice type that is suitable as a model for teenage singers to emulate.

4.   With your college music-methods class, work out a consistent vowel pronunciation on the following phrases: "I'm going away," "Still are your thoughts." Then practice singing these words together:

chance

o - ver

Suggested Readings

Appelman, D. Ralph. *The Science of Vocal Pedagogy*. Bloomington: Indiana University Press, 1967.

Baker, George. *The Common Sense of Singing*. New York: Macmillan, 1963.

Cooper, Irvin, and Karl O. Kuersteiner. *Teaching Junior High School Music*. 2nd ed. Boston: Allyn & Bacon, 1970. Chapter 3.

Garretson, Robert L. *Conducting Choral Music*. 3rd ed. Boston: Allyn & Bacon, 1970.

Jipson, Wayne R. *The High School Vocal Music Program*. West Nyack, N.Y.: Parker, 1972.

McKenzie, Duncan. *Training the Boy's Changing Voice*. New Brunswick, N.J.: Rutgers University Press, 1956.

Miller, Richard. *The Structure of Singing*. New York: Schirmer Books, 1986.

Roma, Lisa. *The Science and Art of Singing*. New York: G. Schirmer, 1956.

Rosewall, Richard B. *Handbook of Singing*. Evanston, Ill.: Summy-Birchard, 1961.

Vernard, William. *Singing: The Mechanism and the Technic*. New York: Carl Fischer, 1987.

Westerman, Kenneth N. *Emergent Voice*. 2nd ed. Ann Arbor, Mich.: Westerman, 1955.

Wilson, Harry R. *Artistic Choral Singing*. New York: G. Schirmer, 1959.

References

Appelman, D. Ralph. *The Science of Vocal Pedagogy*. Bloomington: Indiana University Press, 1967.

Cooksey, J. M. "The Development of a Contemporary Eclectic Theory for the Training and Cultivation of the Junior High School Male Voice." *Choral Journal,* 18, nos. 3 and 4 (November and December 1977).

Ehret, Walter. *The Choral Conductor's Handbook*. New York: Edward B. Marks Music, 1959.

Johnson, John Paul. "Aural/Visual Identification of the Male Changing Voice." *PMEA News,* 47, no. 2 (January 1983).

McKenzie, Duncan. *Training the Boy's Changing Voice*. New Brunswick, N.J.: Rutgers University Press, 1956.

Roe, Paul R. *Choral Music Education*. Englewood Cliffs, N.J.: Prentice-Hall, 1970.

Swanson, Frederick J. *Music Teaching in the Junior High and Middle School*. New York: Appleton-Century-Crofts, 1973.

Swanson, Frederick J. "The Proper Care and Feeding of Changing Voices," *Music Educators Journal,* 58, no. 2 (November–December 1981).

Westerman, Kenneth N. *Emergent Voice*. 2nd ed. Ann Arbor, Mich.: Westerman, 1955.

Wilson, Harry R. *Artistic Choral Singing*. New York: G. Schirmer, 1959.

CHAPTER 12

Teaching Instrumental Music

Instrumental teachers face conditions different from those encountered by choral music teachers. Instrumental music involves a conglomeration of fingerings, embouchures, bowings, and other specialized techniques and knowledge. Scraping a bassoon reed, stopping notes on the French horn, spiccato bowing on the violin, the several fingerings for high G on the clarinet—these are all highly technical bits of skill and learning.* Teachers of choral music face many challenges, but at least all human voices produce sound in the same way.

BEGINNING INSTRUMENT INSTRUCTION

In most school systems, instrumental music is begun around the fifth grade. But in some districts such instruction is not offered until middle or junior high school. Even in systems that begin instruction in the elementary grades, beginning classes should be offered in middle and junior high school for students who are new in the district or who are just now becoming interested in music study. This situation makes some beginning instrument teaching a distinct possibility for instrumental music teachers at the secondary school level.

Using Pre-Band Instruments

In some instrumental music programs much emphasis is placed on pre-band instrument classes. These inexpensive and easy-to-play instruments are like mod-

*An aid to the teacher in recalling instrumental fingerings, trills, positions, and transpositions is *Fingering Charts for Instrumentalists,* by Clarence V. Hendrickson (New York: Carl Fischer, 1957). The book is a convenient pocket size.

ern-day recorders, although they lack the range and gentle tone of the recorder. They are included in the instrumental program to weed out the less talented and less interested students and to provide training in reading notation.

The involvement of instrumental teachers with special classes of pre-band instruments is questionable on several counts. First, it is a pre-*band* program. What is being done to encourage and train string players during this experience? Second, these simple instruments have little carry-over to real band instruments. There is no transfer of embouchure and very little of fingering. Third, the validity of pre-band instruments as predictors of success in instrumental music has not been established. Finally, if training in music reading is valuable, it should be carried on as a part of the regular elementary basic music program so that the benefits will accrue to all students.

In the elementary music program, work with keyboard and recorders, or an exploratory program including strings, is a more valid way to encourage children's continuing participation in music. Teaching legitimate instruments is a surer way to build a successful instrumental music program.

Guiding Pupils

Because the instrumental program is part of the music curriculum, its goals and practices should be consistent with those of music education in general. Instrumental music sometimes deviates from other music courses in its selection of students. Because the school music program exists to educate all students as fully as their interest and ability allow, the idea of selecting only those young people who are most likely to succeed is objectionable. As in learning any valid skill, all except the clearly incapable should be allowed a fair trial. If, after a year, Carlos decides the trumpet is not for him, at least he has had that educational experience and, it is hoped, has learned from it. It would have been fine if he had shown the interest and ability to continue the trumpet or attempt another instrument, but no one has suffered because he was offered the experience. Furthermore, no one could really have predetermined whether or not Carlos would be a success in instrumental music. Sometimes a student who shows little promise or motivation turns out to be a fine instrumentalist a few years later.

Furthermore, through rental instrument plans with music merchants, the rental of school-owned instruments, and the cooperation of an informed board of education, all but the most financially depressed districts can now make it possible for sincerely interested students to try instrumental music.

Only general guides can be offered regarding what instruments should be assigned to individual students. If a youngster faces a lengthy session with braces on his or her teeth or has an underbite (lower teeth in front of upper) or crooked teeth, the student should be guided away from brasses. Generally, small students should not try large instruments. Boys who have thick fingers should be encouraged to try instruments other than violin, because notes in the higher positions are too close together to allow for thick fingers without some kind of compensatory movement, which is difficult. Students whose pitch sense is below average should especially avoid strings, French horn, and trombone.

The most important point to consider in assigning an instrument is the student's desire. Teenagers can accomplish wonders—when they want to. They can become proficient on an instrument while appearing to defy all the physical qualifications. Teachers should guide students in instrument selection but should not require that a student take a particular instrument or none at all. There is a higher-than-expected incidence of dropping out among students who begin on an instrument other than their first choice.

Although instrumental music is offered for the values that accrue to the students, teachers should attempt to maintain some balance in instrumentation, for playing music both in the near future and in high school. To achieve this balance, they have to exercise tact and judgment in guiding students in their selection of instruments. Even then there is no guarantee that three years hence they will not have a half-dozen drummers and no baritones. The number of students encouraged to begin on each instrument should be in proportion to instrumentation needs listed on page 256, with consideration given to the fact that a few clarinet players, for instance, will transfer to oboe and bassoon. It is helpful if the school owns the instruments so that the inventory available to beginners is balanced.

Many schools own instruments that are rented to beginning students for a nominal charge, but many school systems do not provide instruments. In these districts the students rent from merchants. Some school systems closely integrate their activities with a certain merchant, in which case ethics must be closely observed as to bids and equal opportunity for all merchants. If at all possible, students should not be required to purchase an instrument before study is undertaken, because this entails a sizable financial risk for the parents. Instruments that are relatively expensive, uncommon, or difficult to play (oboe, viola, tuba, bass clarinet) should not be offered beginners, if for no other reason than to cut down on the variety of instruments in the class. Generally, beginning instruction is offered on the following instruments: flute, clarinet, trumpet, horn, trombone, baritone, percussion, violin, and cello.

Organizing the Beginning Class

Class lessons are necessary in school, because few schools can support the high cost of individual instruction. Besides, in many communities competent private teachers are not available on all instruments. Class lessons, then, are an expedient, but they are a good expedient in several ways. There is a unity in what is taught and in the rate of progress, so that within a year or two the students can be combined to form a band or orchestra. There is also motivation when students work together and learn that other people do have difficulty in playing their instruments, too. Finally, as teachers become experienced in class techniques, they find that they can accomplish during the first year or two of the students' study almost as much as they could in private lessons. Naturally, as the students advance and playing problems become more individualized, private lessons become more valuable.

Beginning classes should meet a minimum of two times a week for thirty to forty-five minutes, and each group should not exceed fifteen members. If class sizes are consistently too large, the teacher should work to secure additional teaching help. With strings, for instance, it takes some time just to tune fifteen instruments, and the larger the number, the less time there is in which to teach and give attention to each student.

The class should be as homogeneous as possible, although this feature will depend primarily on the schedule of the school and the teacher. Mixing strings and winds should be avoided. Sharp keys are better for strings and flat keys for winds, and the two do not mix well until the intermediate level. Even families of instruments in the same class present problems to teachers. Just as they get ready to call out a note to the clarinets, they remember that the note will be different for the flute; when they mention one fingering to the violins, they must be ready to suggest another to the cellos. Range problems occur when the instruments are mixed. Concert F is easy for the trumpet but either somewhat high or low for a young French horn player depending on the octave attempted.

Beginning Instruction Books

Several publishing companies offer instruction books for beginning instrumentalists. The books often contain simple pieces that can be played by a complete ensemble at an early stage of development. Many of them reveal a similar outlook. There seems to be an attempt in thirty-two pages to give the young players all the signs and notes that might appear on the printed page. Fortunately, there has been a trend toward more interesting music in these books. Some questions for teachers to consider in selecting an instruction book might include the following:

Are there instructions on the care and use of the instrument?

Are there accurate illustrations of posture, position, and embouchure?

Is there a readable fingering chart?

Is the music interesting and worthwhile?

Are the technical problems presented logically?

Are the directions clear and simple?

Is some ensemble music included?

Are recordings of some of the music available on tapes or records?

Are suggestions on embouchure, breath support, counting, and the like made in the book?

Are a score and a teacher's manual available?

The question about the availability of tapes or records is certainly one for teachers to consider. Several publishers make available tapes or records for individual practice. The success of students on violin and other instruments taught by the Suzuki method has demonstrated the power of presenting students with a good aural model to emulate. If one picture is worth a thousand words in the visual world, perhaps one well-played phrase or piece is worth a thousand words in teaching music.

Teaching the Beginning Class

The teaching principles presented in Chapter 5 are of course applicable to teaching beginning instrumental music. The most challenging problem for teachers is to clarify the complex nature of playing an instrument, as was illustrated on page 90 in the multiplicity of instructions given the young violinist. Beginners can't do everything at once. Therefore, teachers must settle for concentrating on one thing at a time, and by alternate emphasis on wholes and parts, they can slowly build the complex actions involved in playing an instrument.

Because kinesthetic learning is so basic to instrumental playing, teachers' efforts should also be directed toward building good habit patterns. For example, developing an embouchure is largely a matter of muscle movement and strength. Teachers cannot hope to establish proper embouchure if they present it once and then proceed to other activities. Embouchure must be reinforced over a long period of time, through a variety of approaches and frequent short reminders.

Mastery of an instrument is a complex amalgamation of many simple habits. Teachers must carefully combine different phases of learning to play. They might ask the clarinet players to play long tones on open G, checking with their left hand to see that they are "keeping their chins down" as they play. When the students are successful at this technique, teachers can point to a line of music that has been studied previously and say, "Now that you have the position of your lower lip and chin right, let's see if you can play this line *and at the same time* keep your good lip and chin position." If the students have worked enough on developing their embouchures and notes and rhythms, they will be able to put together these two aspects of correct playing. If they fail, they should again concentrate on one thing.

Two procedures are helpful in the beginning class. One is to have the students sing the line of music *in rhythm* at proper concert pitch, singing the note names while fingering the notes on their instruments. Sharps, flats, and naturals can also be sung, using only the note names while the students think and finger the accidentals. Teachers should draw the students' attention to the key signature and accidentals before going through the line. A variation is to have the students sing "tah" or "lah" for each note. Singing while fingering is especially helpful in the first semester of study. A second practical step is silent fingering. There is no need for players to sit idly by in an instrumental music class. While one section is playing, the others can be fingering a new line or one on which they need practice.

Using Rote Procedures

Rote teaching is useful in the early stages of study, because beginning students find it difficult to coordinate the mechanics of instrument playing with reading notation. Rote procedures allow the proper mechanics of playing to be assimilated without the distraction of notes. When there are no music stands, teachers can move about freely to help with fingering or playing positions. There is no reason for them to remain in front of the group, because formal conducting is not meaningful to students at this stage. The class is started by verbal cues instead of hand motions. Usually teachers should count out a complete measure, inserting "Ready, begin" or "Ready, play" in tempo on the final two counts.

Sometimes difficult problems, such as crossing the break between registers on the clarinet, are best introduced by rote. A portion of "Three Blind Mice" (B–A–G, B–A–G) can help the players get across more easily, and it makes the relationship between the two registers more clear to them. "Three Blind Mice" is also a helpful pattern for trumpeters who cannot get low C easily (E–D–C, E–D–C) and for trombonists who need to practice slide positions (D–C–B flat, D–C–B flat, or A–G–F, A–G–F). On violin it provides practice in crossing strings (B–A–G, B–A–G).

Rote procedures are especially valuable in string classes because all string instruments are in concert pitch, all produce tone in the same manner (whether plucked or bowed), and all have most of their open strings in common. The teacher can say, "Pluck the notes D and E; open D then first finger. Let's play it this fast (*said in tempo, using quarter notes*): D–E–D–E–rest–rest, D–E–D–E–rest–rest. Instruments in position … (*in tempo*), ready, play." The class plays the pitches and says the notes and rests aloud. Many variations are possible to enliven the class. For one, the teacher may turn his or her back to the students, pick up a violin and play a simple pattern (D–E–F sharp–E–D) and ask, "I started on D. What other notes did I play?" If the students are quick to tell the proper note names, this step can be tried: "I started on D. Don't tell me what I played. Just play it back to me … (*in tempo*), ready, begin."

On another occasion the teacher may show the students the notation for the patterns presented in the rote experience. Three approaches can be used. In one, for the five-note pattern D–E–F sharp–E–D, the teacher can write the notes on the board and say, "Here's a picture of the notes we played. This is what they look like when they're written down." Another approach is for the teacher to write the pattern on the board before the rote instruction and have the students read it, which is of course the normal reading process. A variation of this is for the teacher to say, "Follow the notes on the board. I may or may not play what's there. Check me to see if I do." The third approach, and in some ways the most educational, is to ask the students to think up five-note patterns and sing them to the class, being sure to get an accurate starting pitch. Then the teacher can play them on an instrument and write them on the board. The singing is more likely to be an accurate representation of the pattern the student thought up, so it serves as a check on the accuracy of writing and playing.

Rhythm and bowing on string instruments are closely integrated. Rote work is excellent for getting the bow arm to move properly in rhythm, and such training should be introduced early in the study of the instrument. "Now we've played on the four open strings G, D, A, and E. Let's play one note down bow and one up bow, rest two counts, then go to the next string. Do G first, then D, A, and E. After that, we'll come back down E, A, D, and G." The students then play the pattern below:

Other patterns can be approached in the same manner so that the players simultaneously gain freedom of bow movement and comprehension of rhythm.

Because time is at a premium in every beginning class, instruction should be as efficient as possible. One way to hear individual students quickly and still keep everyone learning is for the class to play a line together. Then, in rhythm, the teacher calls out, "Ralph, play," and Ralph plays the line alone as the rest of the students finger along. Then the teacher calls for the entire group again or for another student. In this way there is no break in the music until the teacher requests it. Another way to save class time is to hear individual students play their assigned lesson on an informal rotation basis. Only two or three students selected at random need play a line of music alone. In this way all students prepare the lesson because they may be called on.

Stressing the Musical Qualities

Teachers of beginning instrumental classes should make a special effort to keep the activities musical. Because so much attention must be placed on moving a finger and counting a note, musical expression often seems to get lost. After all, when the students know only three or four notes, and whole notes at that, it is difficult to perform with much expression. A certain amount of technical facility must precede making music on an instrument. But teachers should not give up making music. Again, rote learning and memorization are real aids in making music. Because of the effort required to learn a piece from the written page, many students will have nearly memorized the piece anyway, so not much additional effort is required to have the class play it from memory. When the distractions of reading music are eliminated, it is easier to introduce the concepts of musicianship.

When the class learns its first melody, the teacher should work further to bring out its musical qualities. What is the high point of the melody? What groups of notes belong together? Should the piece be smooth or choppy? Books of simply arranged solos and duets are available to supplement most of the available method books. Whatever the materials selected, beginning instrumental classes should make music.

Teaching Rhythm

An instrumentalist who gets lost and cannot perform the notes with the rest of the players is a hindrance to any group effort. One of the first requirements of music instruction is that it teach the execution of rhythm. Beginning students can be permitted to tap the foot lightly on each beat. Unless they have quite a bit of previous musical experience, the students during the first year may continue to maintain the beat with the foot.

If students have trouble performing a rhythm correctly, they can set aside their instruments and clap out the pattern. If they have trouble maintaining a steady beat, they should practice standing up, marking time, and playing the music as they march in place. A frequent problem among young students is lack of distinction between the beat they tap and the rhythmic figure they play. Many times they will do this:

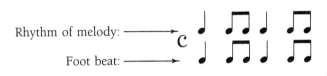

Marching helps to correct this tendency.

In addition to feeling a steady beat, students must know a system of counting. Suggestions for rhythmic syllables were given in Chapter 8. Students should count out lines of music in vigorous singsong fashion before playing them. Singsong counting accentuates the rhythmic swing or pulse and helps prevent a dry, mechanical recitation of beats.

Practicing

Strange as it may seem, teachers need to teach their instrumental students how to practice. Telling young students "Practice thirty minutes every day" is comparable to the physical education instructor saying, "Spend thirty minutes a day building up your muscles." How? Doing what? A portion of each lesson must be devoted to giving specific directions on what is to be done outside of class. Beginning students need to know how fast to play the line of music, and they should know how to check their embouchure or position. Above all, they should realize that practicing is not a matter of "putting in time." The emphasis should be on practicing *correctly*. Short practice periods with a high level of concentration are more productive for the beginning instrumentalist.

If possible, students should establish a daily practice time that is respected by their family and friends. Some teachers ask each student to fill in a card that parents initial to indicate the amount of time spent practicing. Such efforts are fine, as long as they do not stress time rather than results. It helps if the parents know what their child should be practicing.

NEED FOR TEACHING FUNDAMENTAL SKILLS

Teaching fundamental techniques should not end when the students have completed a year or two of study. Teachers cannot assume that such fundamentals as breath support and tonguing have been learned adequately in one year of class lessons. If only it were that easy! Fundamentals must be taught over a span of time, from beginning classes into the bands and orchestras of the secondary schools. Fortunately, as in the case of singing, if students grasp the fundamentals of producing the sound properly, they have come a long way in their study of music.

Almost all prospective instrumental music teachers are required in college to take instruction on instruments other than their major instrument. These "skills" classes provide future teachers with a basic knowledge of tone production, fingerings, playing position, and the like. Because the presentation of the first lessons is usually covered in such classes, this chapter will stress the basic points that need to be taught in some degree to most secondary school students.

The preceding chapter devoted considerable attention to the topic of a correct method of singing. The concern was, as it is in this chapter, for techniques that can be taught successfully in a group situation. This book does not cover all the worthwhile points that singers or instrumentalists should learn. Indeed, entire books have been written on just the techniques of playing the clarinet or violin. So the information here is merely introductory.

Through reading, conversation, and firsthand experimentation, instrumental teachers should gain as much specialized information as they can about instruments other than their own. It will all be useful in their work.

FUNDAMENTALS OF WIND INSTRUMENT PERFORMANCE

All wind players should learn (1) to play with adequate breath support, (2) to form the correct embouchure, and (3) to start and stop tones with the tongue. Each of these three basic skills can be advanced in a group situation.

Breath Support

Rafael Mendez considers breath support alone to be 40 percent of playing a brass instrument (1961, p. 10), and most wind players agree with his sentiment, if not with his precise percentage. Instrumental breath support is similar to the breath support required for singing. The same organs and muscles are used, and their function is the same. The differences are in the degree of abdominal muscle action demanded and in the natural resistance offered the airstream by reeds and brass mouthpieces.

Students should first place their free hand lightly on their abdominal wall to see that the wall moves out as they inhale and moves slowly and steadily in as the tone is played. In instrumental playing, the *depth* of breath should be emphasized. Mendez says to his students, "Think DOWN ... DOWN ... DOWN ... against the belt. Now fill the middle part of the lungs. Think ... OUT ... side-to-side ... front-to-back (1961, p. 12). Keith Stein tells his students to imagine, if they can, filling only the top half of a pitcher, the point being that the deep part of the lungs must fill first (1958, p. 18). Students should try this exercise:

> *Stand. Place a hand against the abdominal wall. Inhale, filling the lungs deeply. Then with the teacher or students timing the action, blow out the smallest possible stream of air between the lips, and note the slow inward movement of the abdominal wall. If a span of ten seconds is achieved, repeat the exercise, increasing the time to fifteen seconds, then to twenty, and so on over a period of days until a span of at least sixty or even ninety seconds is reached.*

For a strengthening of muscles for breath support, both Stein and Mendez suggest this simple exercise, which can be done at home (Stein, 1958, p. 20):

> *Lying on the back, feet together, toes pointed away from the body,* slowly *raise stiffened legs to a 90-degree angle with the body, then* slowly *lower again.*

Two home exercises are as follows:

1. Inhale a deep breath, hold it *with the throat open,* and place a mirror close to the open mouth. The mirror will get cloudy if breath escapes.
2. Inhale, counting to four, then exhale while slowly counting to eight, again keeping the throat open.

As in singing, playing a good tone requires a relaxed and open throat and a slow, controlled airstream. Tension should be maintained in the abdominal muscles as the sound is produced. Advanced players may not require a great amount of abdominal muscle tension because they know precisely which muscles to use and how much to use them. But for almost all wind players in secondary school, the abdominal wall should be kept as firm as possible at all times when playing.

It is more difficult to maintain breath support when the player's attention is diverted to fingerings or rhythmic figures. Breath support, therefore, must become a habit. When students forget about breath support because their attention is on getting the correct notes, the teacher can refer to the passage and say, "Now, the last time at letter L you got the right notes, but the tone was weak. Do it again, and this time *no matter what happens* keep up your support, even if it means a wrong note." Strangely, instead of bringing forth many wrong notes, such a direction usually leads to better playing from the standpoint of both tone and technique.

To convince students of the need to support tones, teachers can demonstrate if they are brass or woodwind players. They can play an unsupported and then a supported tone, so the students hear the difference. They can also demonstrate the effect of proper control when playing at the extremes of the range of dynamics. The upper range on brasses demands much support, unless these notes are obtained by pinched lips, which produce undesirable sounds, or by mouthpieces with shallow cups and narrow bores.

Basic Embouchure

The subtleties of embouchure are best taught in private lessons, but by close observation and reminders teachers in a group situation can prevent many bad embouchures from developing.

Single-Reed Instruments.   The embouchure for both clarinet and saxophone is set in this way: Without pulling the corners of the mouth back, tighten the muscles in the corners of the mouth. Then with the lips just barely touching, try vigorously to pull them apart in an up-down separation. This exercise will stretch out or thin out the muscleless areas around the mouth, especially just below the center of the lower lip. The result should be a "pointed" chin. The reason for the pointed chin may be explained to the students in this manner: "A car can't go far on a flat tire; the wheel on the road needs to be firm. The lower lip needs to be firm, too, so that the reed can vibrate without being soaked up in a flabby lip." The lower lip in single-reed playing should be the consistency of a pencil eraser. Teachers should be on the lookout for lower lips incorrectly "rolled up" underneath reeds. Correct embouchure is needed at all times, particularly on high notes. When playing correctly, most students will show muscle action along a line running 2 inches down from each corner of the mouth. Clarinet and saxophone embouchures differ in the amount of lip tension or "grip"; the saxophone requires less.

The clarinet should form a 45-degree angle with the chin and teeth. Some students hold it straight out like a cigar and then try to achieve the proper appearance by tipping the head down until the chin is almost to the collarbone. A 45-degree angle means that the upper teeth touch the mouthpiece at a point about an eighth of an inch from the tip of the mouthpiece, while the lower lip touches the reed halfway up the vamp or cut of the reed. The lower lip should rest on top of the lower teeth, with half remaining in front. Unless a student has thin lips, some of the lower lip should show while playing. One suggestion that usually helps single-reed embouchure is for players to stick out their chin a little, just enough so that the front teeth would meet if the mouth were closed.

The correct embouchure for clarinet is shown in the figure on page 249.

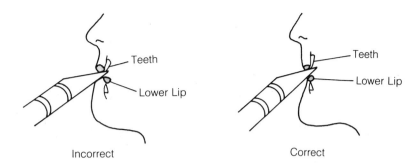

Incorrect   Correct

Double-Reed Instruments. The embouchure for oboe and bassoon is similar to that used for clarinet. The upper lip is brought more into play because, like the lower lip, it goes between the reed and the teeth. A little more side-to-side stretch between the corners of the mouth may be required so that there is a pulling away of the broad outer circle of muscles below the eyes, in the cheeks, and on the chin, and a squeezing in of the inner circle of muscles around the lips.

Much of a player's success on a double-reed instrument depends on the quality of his or her reed. Commercial reeds are made to one major specification: They must produce a tone easily, even for the immature player. As a result, they are usually too soft, with the raspy sound characteristic of a soft reed. Good players make their own reeds, but it is an unusual secondary school student who has learned to do this. So teachers should try to make arrangements with a professional double-reed player, who can then make suitable reeds for the students. By the way, when a willing professional is found, he or she should be treated with deference. It takes time to make reeds, and seldom is the effort financially profitable for the maker.

Flute. The aspect of flute embouchure to watch is the angle between flute and lips and the degree of tilt at the blowhole. The flute should be held parallel to the lip line, with the edge of the blowhole at the lower edge of the lower lip. The flute should tip neither high nor low on the right side of the mouth. The blowhole should tilt just slightly toward the player's lips. The precise angle can be determined only after carefully listening to the tone quality.

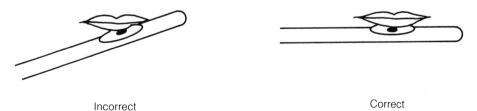

Incorrect   Correct

The flute achieves its change of register by the speed and angle of air going into the blowhole. Many students attempt to play high notes not by making the

opening in their lips smaller and by pushing the chin slightly forward, but by blasting out more air (which can make the player dizzy). The result is a breathy tone and frequent inability to reach high pitches, to say nothing of the unnecessary effort expended by the player. For high notes the opening of the lips should be made "as small as the eye of a needle." This technique results in a smaller but faster airstream.

Brass Instruments.   The basic formation for the vibration or buzzing of the lips is the same for all brass instruments. The corners of the mouth should be tightened, and the center of the lips slightly puckered, as for a kiss. The mouthpiece is set lightly, *not pressed,* on the lips in the center of the mouth, with an equal portion of the mouthpiece on each lip (French horn excepted). Slight variations or off-center positions caused by individual differences in facial and dental structure are no problem as long as the tone is free and clear. French horn players should be taught to rest the rim of the mouthpiece on the rim of the lower lip, thus placing one-third of the mouthpiece over the lower lip and two-thirds over the upper. The adaptation of the embouchure required for trombone, baritone, and bass depends mainly on lip tension and the degree to which the lips are pursed out.

Pushing the mouthpiece against the lips is a poor technique that is too often used as an emergency measure. It achieves temporary improvement, especially in reaching high notes. But the sacrifices are great: Feeling is lost in the lips, notes crack or fail to speak, the low register is weak, intonation suffers, slurring is uneven, and permanent damage can be done to the lips (Mendez, 1961, pp. 22–24). This quick solution is to be avoided. Players should pretend that the instrument is suspended from the ceiling on strings and that without touching it with the hands they can move up to it and play it. Some teachers hold the instrument lightly for students so that they can experience the sensation of playing without pressure. The muscles in the corners of the mouth, plus support from the diaphragm and abdomen, should do the work in reaching correct pitches. For this reason, teachers should select music that does not move brass players into high notes before sufficient facial muscles or "lip" have developed. One practical remedy to too much pressure on the lip on trumpet or cornet is to encourage players to try a hand vibrato in private practice. To achieve a vibrato, players must withdraw pressure, and the process helps wean them away from a dependence on pressure (Weast, 1961, p. 34).

Brass players should not be seduced into quick and easy playing of high notes by relying on shallow mouthpieces. For whatever is gained in the one phase of playing, something is lost in tone quality. Mouthpieces with medium cups, rims, and bores are best for middle and high school players.

Tonguing

A third fundamental of wind instrument playing that can be taught in the group situation is correct tongue action. Tonguing is more than merely a technique for executing staccato runs in eighths and sixteenths. It is a fundamental action necessary to articulate any note regardless of speed or rhythmic pattern. To play "America the Beautiful" requires the same basic tongue action as a difficult solo.

In a way, *tonguing* is the wrong word, because making a tone depends on air and a vibrating mechanism. So the first requirement for proper articulation on wind instruments is breath support. Students sometimes complain that they cannot get their tongues to work properly, when the real problem is a lack of breath support.

Instruction in tonguing should start as soon as the students have learned breath support. It might be better for them to wait a year, but this is not a realistic expectation. They see music that calls for tonguing, and even slurred phrases need to have the initial note articulated. Besides, students experiment with tonguing whether teachers like it or not.

Tonguing is based on the *release* of air, not the *pushing out* of air, as uninitiated students often think. First, the tongue acts as a dam to hold back the air. Air pressure resulting from continuing breath support builds up behind it. Then the tongue is quickly pulled away from the reed or teeth. At that exact moment the sound starts distinctly. This action is referred to as the *attack* (in many ways a misleading word for the tongue-breath action it describes). The process is like turning on a garden hose at low pressure and attempting to hold back the water with the thumb. When the thumb is removed from the opening, the initial forceful squirt is comparable to the "spring" or "kick" of a good attack on a wind instrument. With the hose it does no good to turn the water on harder after the flow starts, because the initial spurt is unaffected by later increases in pressure. The same is true of the tongued attack. Once the air has started, additional air will merely give a pushing effect that is musically undesirable. Because of this fact, the attention in tonguing is on the *beginning* of the note. In fact, when tonguing rapidly, players can think only about the start of each tone.

Unnecessary movement complicates the tonguing process. Too often students move the jaw, lips, and throat in an attempt to improve on an action that should involve only continued breath and coordination of the tongue. Because it is difficult for players to work at just holding still, they can be directed to concentrate their attention on breath support and the quick action of the tongue in pulling away to start the tone. They should work harder on active breath support when no sound is heard than when it is, illogical as that may seem. To emphasize the buildup of pressure before the note is sounded, the students can be told to feel a "ping-pong ball" of air pressure between the tongue and the roof of the mouth just before the tone starts.

As Chapter 9 pointed out in discussing interpretation, the style of attack differs with the demands of the music. The difference in attack is determined by the amount of air pressure built up (with greater pressure bringing a harder attack) and by the speed with which the tongue is pulled away (the faster movement causing a more distinct start).

On brasses and flute the tip of the tongue is placed behind the upper teeth at or near the point where the gum meets the teeth. On lower brasses some fine players tongue at the edge of the teeth with no audible difference in the quality of tonguing. On reeds the tip of the tongue is placed lightly (not pressed) against the tip of the reed (the lower reed on oboe and bassoon). Clarity is improved if the tip of the tongue is made firm and pointed. On all winds the movement of the tongue to start the tone is mainly down, not backward, and only the tip of the tongue moves. The tongue is rather large, and if all of it moves, speed and clarity are impossible.

Students who have trouble feeling the tongue movement might try this: Rough the tip of the tongue on the edge of the teeth by rubbing it back and forth. Then practice flicking the tip against the edge of the teeth.

On brasses the best syllable for tonguing is determined by the pitch level of the note. *Tah* is good for the middle range, *toh* for low notes, and *tee* for high notes. *Tah* is used on woodwinds.

Closing off a staccato tone is too often hindered by unnecessary effort. On a reed instrument it is not easily noticeable if the tone is stopped with the tongue, but on a brass instrument this action causes an undesirable *ut* sound at the end of the tone. Players need to focus their attention on the start of tones of moderate or long duration and avoid using the tongue to end them. The closing operation will then be taken over by a holding-back action of the abdominal muscles.

FUNDAMENTALS OF STRING INSTRUMENT PERFORMANCE

In a majority of schools the strings work by themselves several times a week, while the winds are brought in for only one or two periods to form a complete orchestra. Because string instruments are difficult to play well, and string parts are often more demanding than wind parts, the extra time is needed to learn the music. Furthermore, string players who are not advanced benefit from the additional work on basic skills.

Bowing

Young string players tend to place their entire attention on the left hand when playing. Advanced players know that the skill of the bow arm is at least as important as the dexterity of the left hand. Because the right arm is generally neglected, special work on bowing is urged.

Students should understand the factors that affect bowing: pressure on the bow, length of bow stroke, and speed of bow stroke. Each one affects the quality and volume of sound. A slow bow with much pressure produces one timbre, while a fast bow with light pressure produces another. Several books on bowing are available, or teachers may create their own bowing routines.

Common bow patterns should be learned so well that they become second nature. The first patterns should be very simple so that the players' attention can be centered on drawing the bow properly, and they should be patterns that are common in the repertoire of the group, such as the following:

WB UH UH WB LH LH   WB UH UH WB LH LH

WB   UH UH WB

(WB indicates whole bow, UH upper half, and LH lower half)

Slurred notes of equal value should receive nearly equal portions of the bow so that none of the tones sounds cramped or squeezed:

L⅓ Mid⅓ U⅓   U⅓ Mid⅓ L⅓   L½ UM¼ U¼ WB

Dotted figures in one bow are more difficult, especially if a change of bow occurs immediately after a short, detached note. In such a situation beginners are likely to become confused over bow direction. Slow and rhythmic practice will establish the feeling of the proper bow motion.

Many styles of bowing are best taught in the private lesson, but even in a group situation the students can work on two of the most common styles. *Legato* bowing requires smooth change of bow direction and a generally consistent bow speed. Beginning students should strive first of all to develop a fine legato style, like the singing tone of the human voice. This style is the essence of string performance. A second style of string playing often encountered in orchestral literature is the *détaché,* or full, detached stroke. The secret of détaché is the "catch" at the start of the tone, indicating an abrupt, precise beginning. A slight bit of extra weight on the bow, plus a sudden and fast initial movement, produces this effect. It is imperative that students be able to draw a straight bow parallel to the bridge. Any lack of bow control will show up when détaché is attempted, because the bow will either skid out of control or move at an incorrect angle.

No orchestral string part contains complete bow markings, so the students have an opportunity to figure out bowings in an actual work of music. Teachers can give the players an unmarked page of photocopied music and request that they mark in bowings as homework. These can be examined in class, compared, and discussed. The string players should be asked questions such as "Why did you start with another down bow? What's the musical effect of this bowing? What style of bowing does the music suggest here? Should it be bowed another way?" These questions help the players to understand the mechanical and musical factors involved in bowing a string part.

Left-Hand Techniques

Intermediate string methods move the left hand into higher positions, and this entails work on shifting. For a few moments the attention of the players should be concentrated on the two pitches involved in the shift. At first the players can practice the shift silently, using a light pizzicato occasionally to check the accuracy of pitch. The quickness and precision of the left hand should be emphasized. Then the two notes involved in the shift can be played, followed by a playing of the entire phrase.

The real beauty of string tone is brought to life with vibrato. Without it the quality remains thin and colorless, especially when the players are performing on instruments that are not of good quality. Some successful string teachers begin vibrato in the second year of study, although others prefer to wait a little longer. In any event it is started when the teacher feels that the basic playing fundamentals are well established.

Some teachers feel that it is best not to become too technical with the students, preferring the original advice of Monteverdi to "shake" the hand. Too much technical talk, they feel, may inhibit the proper muscle action. At any rate, teaching vibrato requires persistence, because the process may take up to two years with some pupils. The goal should be to increase the speed and narrow the amplitude of the vibrato to the extent that the change of pitch is not perceived as such by the ear. It is important that the students have a chance to see and hear good vibrato, from either the teacher or an advanced student.

PERCUSSION

Percussion playing requires a variety of techniques. Many teenage drummers do well on the stroke-bounce technique for the roll; the trouble is they cannot put it in the right place in the music. There are occasions—in jazz bands and marching bands—when drummers have little need for reading music. It is sometimes hard for percussionists to integrate the part they play with the group in phrasing, dynamics, and style. The problem is not usually one of technique but rather of musicianship. By asking the right question at the right time, teachers can encourage percussionists to think more musically. "Which snare should you use at letter A, the five-inch or the six-and-a-half-inch? Why? Which stick are you going to use on the timpani at letter G? How important to the music is the roll at the repeat of the melody?"

INSTRUMENTATION

Any suggestions for instrumentation must be considered in light of the quality of the players. One alto saxophone is sufficient for a band of fifty players, if he or she is a creditable performer; if a weak player, an additional alto saxophone is needed. Teachers have differing tastes, some wanting more mellowness, others more bass sound, and others more brilliance, all of which require somewhat different instrumentations. Although orchestral instrumentation has been fairly well standardized over the past 150 years, band instrumentation has changed frequently and is still in the process of being modified, often on the specifications of the composer or arranger.

In an orchestra the difference between a large or small group is mainly accounted for in the strings, because in the winds only one player is normally used on a part. Therefore, teachers of small orchestras find it more difficult to achieve proper balance. Table 12.1 gives suggested numbers of players for three sizes of orchestra.

Table 12.2 represents one concept of balanced band instrumentation. Unless players of much ability are available, instruments such as bass saxophone and E-flat soprano clarinet should be avoided, because they can do more harm than good.* If these instruments are vital to a particular piece, it is best to have a good clarinetist double on the E-flat clarinet for that number. The numerical balance of first, second, and third parts in the clarinets, and the proportion of trumpets or cornets, can be determined only by the sound of the particular group. Because low notes apparently do not "carry" as well as higher pitches, and because less advanced students usually play the lower parts, these parts may require a greater number of players for a balanced sound. The choice between trumpets and cornets is a matter of taste for each band director. Double B-flat upright tubas are suggested in a ratio of three to one over E-flat tubas (if the latter are used at all), because

Table 12.1   *Instrumentations for Orchestras*

Instrument	Small	Full	Complete Symphonic
Flute and piccolo	2	2	3
Oboe and English horn	1	2	3
Clarinet	2	3	3
Bassoon	1	2	3
French horn	2	4	6
Trumpet	3	3	3
Trombone	3	3	3
Tuba	1	1	1
Percussion and piano	2	3	4
Harp	0	0	1
Violin	12	24	30
Viola	4	7	10
Violoncello	4	7	10
Bass viol	3	4	6
	40	65	86

*John Philip Sousa reportedly said that the E-flat soprano clarinet should be used only on February 29, and then played very softly.

Table 12.2   *Instrumentations for Bands*

Instrument	Small	Average	Large
Flute and piccolo	2	5	7
Oboe	1	2	3
B-flat clarinet	12	20	25
Alto clarinet	1	2	4
Bass clarinet	1	2	4
Bassoon	1	2	4
Alto saxophone	1	2	2
Tenor saxophone	1	1	2
Baritone saxophone	0	1	1
Cornet and trumpet	6	9	12
French horn	3	4	8
Baritone	2	3	4
Trombone	3	4	6
Tuba	2	3	6
Bass viol	1	1	2
Percussion	3	4	5
	40	65	95

of their bigger tone quality, stronger low notes, and better intonation. Generally the E-flat tuba doubles the BB-flat tube one octave higher, but because these notes are well within the range of trombones and baritones, this function of the E-flat tuba is of limited value.

Seating

Traditionally players in a section have been seated in order of ability. If all players are highly competent, as in a professional symphony orchestra, this system works well. In a school group where the level of capability may vary greatly from first to last in a section, it is better to assign places by putting the best player in first chair, the next best at the second stand (or at the first stand of the second section), and so on. This arrangement puts stronger players on all parts and stands, not just the first. In the violin sections it puts the better players on the outside, where they are most easily heard and seen and where they can keep playing when a page of music is turned. A minor variation of this plan is to place the best three or four players in the first chairs and then seat players according to ability, moving back a stand or part with each one. These seating systems help to remove the stigma of playing a part other than the first.

In instrumental music, especially band, some teachers encourage competition for the best chairs. While this motivates some students, it should not be the primary spur to improvement. The work in band and orchestra should be sufficiently interesting and pleasurable to motivate the players without teachers hanging the carrot of a better chair in front of them. Students can study and learn no matter what chair they are sitting in, and a sour note detracts from the group's performance regardless of its source in the section, so the chair in which a person sits should not be an important matter.

The most educationally valid method of seating is for teachers to rotate either students or music so that all members of a section get to play first, second, or third parts. Rotation gives the students a greater knowledge of all the parts and more experience in reading music, besides diminishing the emphasis on seating. For performance, teachers without much ado should seat players according to ability and seniority. If and when chair tryouts are held, they might have another music teacher in the system hear them also so that they cannot be accused of personal bias. So that musical ability is not confounded with personal popularity, students should not be involved in evaluating other students.

Transferring Students to Other Instruments

Students in elementary school are seldom started on several of the instruments needed for band and orchestra. Either the instruments are too large, too delicate, or too difficult for beginners. For this reason, middle and junior high school teachers should be prepared to transfer some students from one instrument to another. Transfers should be planned well ahead of the time they are made, and they should take into full consideration the student's desires, parents' wishes, and the student's musical potential. Sometimes a student begins clarinet with the intention of switching to oboe after a year or two of study. The clarinet training provides a good musical foundation and contributes to success as an oboist, while starting on oboe might have ended in frustration. Some changes will seem advisable after study is begun, as in the case of a trumpeter who lacks sufficient lip strength and is therefore transferred to tuba. The following list suggests the more logical transfers.

- B-flat clarinet to saxophone: The upper octave of the clarinet is almost identical to the saxophone; the player must learn to relax embouchure for low notes.

- B-flat clarinet to oboe: The upper octave of the clarinet is similar to the oboe; the player will require a little time to get used to the smaller reed and use of both lips in playing.

- B-flat clarinet to bassoon: Fingering of open holes is similar, but the keys are different; the reed change is not as difficult as with the oboe; the player must learn bass clef.

- B-flat clarinet to alto or bass clarinet: Fingerings are identical; the player needs only a short time to become accustomed to the larger reed, mouthpiece, and instrument.

- Flute to saxophone: Fingerings are similar. Tone production is quite different, however.

- Saxophone to other sizes of saxophones: Fingerings and notes are identical; a very short time is needed to get used to the new size of reed, mouthpiece, and instrument.

- Trumpet to low brasses: Basic fingerings are identical; time is needed to learn bass clef and become accustomed to the larger instrument. The change to trombone is more difficult, although the slide positions are related to valve combinations.

- Trumpet to French horn: Fingerings present only a minor problem; the main difference is in the concept of tone. A change of embouchure is necessary, which requires careful attention.

- Low brass to trumpet: Treble clef must be learned; fingerings present no problem, but the change from an instrument requiring less embouchure tension to one requiring more is difficult.

- Violin to viola: Time is needed to learn alto clef. Some authorities believe that all advanced violinists should have at least some experience on viola.

- Piano to bass viol: Pianists know the bass clef and have an understanding of how a bass part is organized in music.

- Piano to percussion instruments with definite pitch: Pianists read music and know the keyboard.

Students who transfer to other instruments will need special help at first, the amount depending on the difficulty of the change and the talent and diligence of the student. It is helpful if such students can have access to a practice room during study period, with the teacher stopping by occasionally. The teacher can also work with them after school. Progress will be most rapid, however, if they can study privately with a specialist teacher. As soon as they can play the parts on the new instrument, they should be moved back into the band or orchestra.

A special word should be said about the French horn. Because the horn uses primarily the partials in the harmonic series that are one octave higher than partials on other brass instruments, the pitches are much closer together in the harmonic series and are more difficult to play accurately. For this reason there has been a persistent problem about how best to start young players. At one time the E-flat mellophone was thought to be the answer, but it doesn't sound like a French horn. The argument then centered on the virtues of the F and B-flat horns, with the former having the proper timbre and the latter being easier to play. Double horns are ideal, but few school systems can afford to provide them for beginners. More and more horn teachers now advocate starting the students on a single B-flat horn. (They read F horn music but are taught B-flat fingerings.) After about three years they are transferred to double horn and taught to use the F horn for the lower pitches, gradually increasing its use for notes in other ranges.

Substituting Instruments

Sometimes an instrument called for in the score is not available. Rather than deny the rest of the players a chance to play the music, as an expedient teachers can assign another instrument to substitute. Although there are no "good" substitutions, some are more satisfying than others. Following is a list of common and passingly successful substitutions. An asterisk indicates that transposition is required in making the substitution. The E-flat instruments indicated by the double asterisks may read bass clef by adding three sharps to the signature and reading the notes as if they were in the treble clef.

oboe: muted trumpet,* viola

English horn: alto saxophone,* oboe*

E-flat clarinet: flute*

alto clarinet: alto saxophone

bass clarinet: tenor saxophone

bassoon: tenor saxophone,* bass clarinet,* cello

tenor saxophone: bass clarinet

baritone saxophone: bass clarinet*

French horn: alto saxophone,* clarinet,* cello*

fluegelhorn: cornet

baritone: trombone

tuba: bass viol, baritone saxophone**

viola: violin (Many publishers sell a violin III part, which is the viola part put in treble clef with the lower notes moved up an octave.)

cello: tenor saxophone,* alto saxophone**

bass viol: tuba, piano

harp: piano

EQUIPMENT AND SUPPLIES

The physical needs of the instrumental music program are clearly more extensive than in other phases of the music curriculum. Instrumental teachers must deal with unique matters of equipment and supply.

Supplies—items such as reeds, strings, rosin, valve and slide oil—can be sold at cost through a student supply store operated by the school or the music department. Some dealers will provide and stock a reed vending machine that eliminates the need for handling. When the school makes supplies available, the students don't lose time waiting to get to the music store for a reed or string.

Repair on privately owned instruments is facilitated if they are sent in with school-owned instruments to the repairperson. The school pays the repairperson for all work done, the teacher keeps a record of the cost of repair on the privately owned instrument, and the student reimburses the school. The instrument is returned to the student upon payment of the bill.

In the purchase of school-owned instruments, teachers should inform the administration of the need for two grades of instruments. One is the rugged, adequate instrument for beginners. The other is the good instrument (not an artist model) for high school players. Because most schools limit the amount of time during which one student has an instrument as a beginner, well-built plastic clarinets and similar "student line" instruments are appropriate. But for advanced work in the high school band and orchestra, better instruments are needed. A cheap instrument at this level is poor economy. Many secondary schools provide these instruments for competent players: alto and bass clarinet, piccolo, oboe, bassoon, baritone saxophone, French horn, baritone, tuba and sousaphone, harp, cello, bass viol, and percussion equipment.

Some specifications for particular instruments can be suggested. The mouth-piece and reed have much to do with clarinet tone. A good medium to medium-wide lay mouthpiece and a reed not softer than 2½ in strength work best for most high school players. All hard rubber mouthpieces warp over a period of two or three years. Refacing is not expensive and often improves the mouthpiece. Quality clarinets should be wood, as should the piccolo, which should be pitched in C, not D flat. Oboes and bassoons should be checked by a specialist on the instrument before a purchase is made. The good French horns should be double horns. If the school can afford both sousaphones and tubas, upright-bell BB-flat tubas are favored, with either a fourth valve or a compensating mechanism to improve the intonation.

Cases and stands or chairs are needed for tubas or sousaphones. Percussion equipment of good quality gives a noticeably better sound. There is something musically disappointing about hearing a group build to a beautiful climax followed by a cymbal crash on a cheap, small pair of cymbals with handles. The advice of a professional symphony percussion player can be valuable when deciding on brands and equipment. A movable cabinet helps to preserve the percussion equipment and prevent the loss of small items such as maracas, triangle beaters, and brushes. The cabinet should have a lock to prevent unauthorized use of equipment. It is desirable to have fine tuners on the two highest strings of violins, violas, and cellos.

When the time comes for students to purchase a trumpet or clarinet, some parents hurry off to the nearest discount house. Often the "buy" they get is a cheap instrument that is out of tune and carelessly made. To combat this situation, teachers should try to establish the point in a letter or other communication with the parents that a cheap instrument may be a poor buy. Next, they should urge parents to have a performer or teacher who plays the instrument inspect the instrument they plan to purchase, and teachers should announce their availability to consult with parents about instruments. They should recommend all music merchants in the area who sell quality instruments and follow ethical business practices. They might also list good used instruments that families in the area have told them they would like to sell. Not only does this make it possible for prospective purchasers to buy a good instrument at less cost, it also lets them know that a share of their investment in an instrument is redeemable. In listing used instruments, teachers make no contacts and suggest no price. The listing is only a service to interested parties.

Other specifications for equipment are contained in the MENC publication *The School Music Program: Description and Standards,* Second Edition.

PREPARATION ON THE SCORE

Instrumental music teachers should understand the transpositions and technical problems in a score containing as many as twenty lines occurring simultaneously. In addition, they must decide on the correct tempos, phrasing, and methods for teaching the music to the students.

More often than not, secondary school conductors face an additional obstacle: the condensed score. Because complete scores are expensive to publish, and many school music teachers do not buy them even when they are available, music publishers are reluctant to prepare complete scores. So instrumental teachers must learn to do the best they can with the condensed score. When the music is simple, like a chorale, a condensed score is usually sufficient. The more complex the music, the more inadequate a condensation becomes. Its most limiting feature is that it does not indicate exactly what each part is playing, and some parts, such as the E-flat alto clarinet, are ignored. The condensed score is similar to a piano reduction of an orchestral score and is in concert pitch. In fact, not too many years ago the part for the conductor was called "Piano-Conductor," probably as an outgrowth of the performance custom of the theater pit orchestra of the nineteenth century.

Before directing from a condensed score, teachers should compare it with the instrument parts. Pencil in hand, they should look through the condensed score and stop at the first place where the instrumentation is not clearly indicated. Then they can examine the parts at that point, writing in the score more indications of what is happening. For marches written on the small march-size sheet, teachers can take one first clarinet, first cornet, baritone, French horn, trombone, and percussion part, tape them together to form one large sheet, and make a score of sorts.

A rehearsal can deteriorate rapidly when a teacher is not thoroughly familiar with the disposition of notes.

Bill Morgan stops the band and says to the second alto saxophone, "Mary Ann, we missed your F sharp in the first chord at letter H."
"I don't have F sharp there," Mary Ann answers. "I have a D."

"Well, who has a concert A besides the second flutes? . . ."
(No answer.)
"Good grief! Tenor sax, what do you have?"
"D natural," comes the reply.
"Bass clarinet, according to my score somebody has a concert A. Do you?"
"No, I have a D."
"Are you sure? Well, let's begin at letter G again and see if we can figure it out this time."

STAGE OR JAZZ BAND

In many secondary schools a jazz or stage band is a valuable component of the music program. The group expands the variety of music available to the students and is, therefore, an enriching experience for the students.

The jazz band's strength is also its weakness: The music it performs is confined to only a small portion of the world of music. For this reason instrumental music teachers should select the members of the jazz band from the ranks of the concert band, with the possible exception of upperclassmen who have previously spent several years in concert band and instruments such as piano and electric guitar. Most fifteen-year-old students need a broad musical experience; specialization can come later.

Music teachers should educate their school administrators and communities to (and keep in mind themselves) the fact that the jazz band is only one part of the total music program in the secondary schools. Because the group can often achieve a big sound (often aided by the use of microphones), nonmusicians are easily impressed with the group. For this reason it is tempting for teachers to devote an excessive amount of attention to the jazz band. As is true of several other music organizations in the secondary schools, the importance of jazz bands has been promoted through the many contests that are available for such groups. Some of these contests have a variety of classifications, as well as individual honors for players, so that nearly every group receives some sort of favorable recognition. For the sake of music education, teachers must resist the temptation of giving the jazz band more than its fair share of attention.

If members of the concert band comprise the majority of the membership of the jazz band, then it is difficult to have the jazz band meet during the school day. Few students have time for two music courses in their schedules. Because the group is smaller than the concert band and somewhat more selected, a successful jazz band can function quite well with a couple of rehearsals a week before school or in the evening.

Currently the repertoire of jazz bands is more or less in the "big band" style, and a number of compositions are now being written for it. Such music is not the type of music used at school dances, so the band seldom plays jobs; it's largely a musical endeavor. Over the past couple of decades publishers have brought out many jazz band charts written specifically for school players. In general the music is well arranged, without technical demands and extensive ad-lib solos.

Although jazz is written down with conventional notation, it has its own special stylistic characteristics. The subtleties of the style are too numerous to explore here. Actually, a firsthand acquaintance with the music is the best preparation for teaching it. Some publishers provide recordings of their arrangements, and these performances are good examples of the style needed.

A sizable amount of material for school jazz bands is available, and more is being published each year. Most of the new publications are reviewed in the *Jazz Educators Journal*. Some of the jazz materials are concerned with learning to improvise on particular instruments. Several series of books are designed for use with school musicians. Among these publications are many books by Jamey Aebersold, David N. Baker (who also has many publications, including the *Modern Jazz Series*), and Dominic Spera (who has authored the *Learning Unlimited Jazz Improvisation Series,* a series that includes instructional tapes).

MARCHING BAND TECHNIQUES

The training and administration of a marching band is a specialized area of music education. Several books are available on the subject, and the person who desires information on marching bands should consult one of these sources:

Binion, W. T., Jr. *The High School Marching Band*. West Nyack, N.Y.: Parker, 1973.

Foster, Robert E. *Multiple-Option Marching Band Techniques,* 2nd ed. Sherman Oaks, Calif.: Alfred, 1978.

Hopper, Dale F. *Corps Style Marching*. Oskaloosa, Iowa: C. L. Barnhouse, 1977.

Spohn, Charles R., and Richard W. Heine. *The Marching Band*. Boston: Allyn & Bacon, 1969.

In addition, several computer programs for developing marching band shows are available. These are cited in Chapter 14.

MUSICAL INSTRUMENT REPAIR

A second specialized topic beyond the scope of this book is the repair of musical instruments. A reader who is interested in the subject may refer to the following books:

Mayer, R. F. *The Band Director's Guide to Instrumental Repair*. Port Washington, N.Y.: Alfred, 1973.

Springer, George H. *Maintenance and Repair of Wind and Percussion Instruments*. Boston: Allyn & Bacon, 1970.

Tiede, Clayton H. *Practical Band Instrument Repair Manual*. 3rd ed. Dubuque, Iowa: William C. Brown, 1970.

Questions

1. Suppose Ahmed has his heart set on playing the trumpet. The teacher already has more trumpets than can be used in a balanced group. Should the boy be allowed to start on trumpet, or should he be told to take something else or not be in instrumental music? Why or why not?

2. Suppose Sandy is studying violin privately with a teacher who suggests that she withdraw from school instrumental music organizations "so that she won't get any bad habits." What arguments could you offer to persuade Sandy and her parents that she should also participate in the school group?

3. On page 242 the combination of singing-fingering is suggested. Why should the singing be done on the correct pitch level? From what was said in Chapter 6, why is it logical that this teaching technique is a good one?

4. Why is it a good practice from the standpoint of music education to utilize the procedure suggested on page 243, in which the student thinks of a note pattern, sings it, and then writes it down or plays it?

Projects

1. Using the criteria for evaluating beginning instrumental instruction books mentioned on page 241, make a study of all such books that you can secure for examination. Report your findings to the class. Compare evaluations with other class members.

2. Study the beginning instrumental program in a school system near your college. Find out at what grade level instruction is first offered, whether it is offered in subsequent years, how large the classes are, how homogeneous they are, whether the instruments are rented through the school or a dealer, what instruction books are used, how much time is devoted to class sessions, and what instruments are offered beginners. Report to your class. Compare reports with other class members.

3. Study the complete instrumental music program in a secondary school near your college. Find out how much variety if offers, whether there are "second" groups for the less talented students, whether there is an orchestra, what credit is given for private instruction, whether technical instruction is included in group rehearsals, and whether there are small ensembles. Report your findings to the class. Compare evaluations with other class members.

4. Take a simple melody, such as "Twinkle, Twinkle, Little Star," from an elementary instrumental instruction book. Look it over and decide, seriously,

what you could teach the students about its *musical* qualities—important notes, phrasing, style of articulation, and repeated melodic patterns.

5. Practice the breathing exercises described on page 247 to see if they seem applicable to the wind instrument you may be studying privately or in class.

6. Think of analogies other than the one mentioned on pages 251–152 that might be useful in helping teenage students understand the proper action of tongue and breath in starting a tone on a wind instrument.

7. Study the embouchures of fine wind players. On single reeds notice the appearance of the muscles of the chin, the appearance of the lower lip, and the angle of the instrument in the mouth. On brasses notice the placement of the mouthpiece, and ask the player to pull the mouthpiece away while playing a tone so that the position of the lips can be observed. Watch the embouchure of a flutist while slurring up an octave and of a brass player while slurring to a higher tone with the same fingering.

8. Take a simple community type of song, such as "America the Beautiful," and mark in all the bowings a violinist might use in playing it. Compare your bowings with those of others in your class.

9. From a condensed score, select eight consecutive measures that are fairly complex. Then refer to the individual parts, find the same eight measures, and copy the parts in full score on manuscript paper. Compare and contrast the two scores, and evaluate the adequacy of the condensed score in giving an accurate picture of what the instruments are to play.

10. Visit several instrument dealers and look over the "student" quality instruments. If you are an instrumentalist, check your major instrument for intonation and tone quality, quality of construction, and case. Compare them with instruments of the next higher level in quality and cost. Report your findings to the class.

11. Prepare a letter for parents regarding the purchase of an instrument for their son or daughter. Explain the need for buying a quality instrument and offer your services in making a selection.

Suggested Readings

American School Band Directors Association. *ASBDA Curriculum Guide*. Philadelphia: Volkwein Brothers, 1973.

Baker, David N. *Jazz Pedagogy*. Chicago: Maher Publications, 1979.

Bollinger, Donald E. *Band Director's Complete Handbook*. West Nyack, N.Y.: Parker, 1979.

Colwell, Richard J. *The Teaching of Instrumental Music*. New York: Appleton-Century-Crofts, 1969.

Gattiker, Irvin. *Complete Book of Rehearsal Techniques for the High School Orchestra*. West Nyack, N.Y.: Parker, 1977.

Kuhn, Wolfgang. *Instrumental Music: Principles and Methods of Instruction*. 2nd ed. Boston: Allyn & Bacon, 1970.

Otto, Richard A. *Effective Methods for Building the High School Band*. West Nyack, N.Y.: Parker, 1977.

Pizer, Russell A. *How to Improve the High School Band Sound*. West Nyack, N.Y.: Parker, 1976.

Robinson, William C., and James A. Middleton. *The Complete School Band Program*. West Nyack, N.Y.: Parker, 1975.

Rothrock, Carson. *Training the High School Orchestra*. West Nyack, N.Y.: Parker, 1971.

Taylor, George. *The High School Stage Band*. New York: Richards, Rosen, 1978.

The School Music Program: Description and Standards. 2nd ed. Reston, Va: Music Educators National Conference, 1986.

References   Mendez, Rafael. *Prelude to Brass Playing*. New York: Carl Fischer, 1961.

Stein, Keith. *The Art of Clarinet Playing*. Evanston, Ill.: Summy-Birchard, 1958.

Weast, Robert D. *Brass Performance*. New York: McGinnis & Marx, 1961.

CHAPTER 13

School Music Performances

Helga Geiger has just started her new job teaching music at Westport High School. As she goes to her mailbox in the office, the principal says to her, "Oh, Helga, better get your concert dates set on the school calendar by next week, because we want to get the thing run off by then." Helga checks last year's school calendar and sets dates for programs at approximately the same times for the coming school year. As she plans for her next day's classes, she wonders, "Just how will the music I'm teaching now be related to the concert I've set in May—or in December, for that matter. I haven't even decided what to do—I've merely set a date for a program." After another moment she wonders, "Really, why am I having public performances in the first place? Why particularly in December and May? Should I have more or none at all? What kind of programs should I present?"

REASONS FOR PERFORMANCES

To begin to answer Helga Geiger's questions, one must return to the issues raised in Chapter 3. The goals of music education are crucial in deciding why there are performances and what they should be like. Certainly they should not be the "be-all and end-all" of school music, although they have sometimes been so regarded by teachers. Performances do contribute to the music education of students, but teachers should keep their priorities straight. Students in school music groups give performances because they have learned; they should not learn *only* to give performances.

Some teachers think of school programs as being much the same as professional concerts or recitals. Such thinking is not logical. Professional musicians perform because that is their chosen work and because they get paid to do so. Any educational or psychological values accruing to them are largely irrelevant. It is the

268

opposite with school students. The educational benefits are paramount. Both school and professional musicians wish to give musically creditable performances, of course. This goal is the main objective of professional musicians, but it is only one of several desirable outcomes for school groups.

A distinction is being drawn in this discussion between the performing of music, such as singing songs or playing works on the piano. The making of music is vital to the art of music, because music is inert dots and marks on paper until someone brings it to life through performing it. Performances for an audience are a somewhat different matter. *If done properly,* they are definitely of value to school groups.

Performances can benefit school musicians in a number of ways:

1. They provide a definite goal toward which to work. Learning is satisfying for most students, but they are more strongly motivated when they have something concrete to work for.

2. Student motivation is helped by the presence of definite goals. It is only human to work harder at something you know will be observed.

3. Performances can educate the audience about music and the school curriculum. The performance is in a sense a report about what is going on in the music class.

4. Social and psychological values accrue to the students from participating in performances. Teenagers achieve recognition for their accomplishments as performers, and they gain poise and self-confidence from appearing before an audience.

5. Group consciousness is aided by performance.

6. Performances benefit the school and community. The pep rally is peppier when a band is present, and the civic ceremony is more impressive when young people contribute music to it.

GUIDELINES FOR PERFORMANCES

A careless or poorly managed performance can reduce the benefits just mentioned. What can be done to achieve quality performances, without detracting from the music education of the students?

1. *Performances should be an outgrowth of actual school work.* Education should not be interrupted to prepare a work for a performance.

2. *Performances should present music of the best quality appropriate for the occasion.* The marching band and concert choir perform under very different circumstances. The type of music suitable for one is not necessarily suitable for the

other. Each, however, should present music of quality that is suitable for the occasion.

3. *Performances should receive proper preparation.* It is impossible to spell out specifically how much time is required to prepare a program. There are too many variables—the ability of the group, the length of the program, the difficulty and newness of the music, and the efficiency and standards of the teacher. Fortunately, if the performance is an outgrowth of class activity, time for preparation and time for learning the subject are no longer distinct and separate. For this reason, except when special circumstances prevail, all preparation should take place in the regular class periods for curricular groups. Such preparation also includes routine matters such as publicity, tickets, and equipment.

4. *Performances by any one group should not be so numerous that they interfere with the total education of the students.* The precise number cannot be indicated for the reasons discussed under preparation time. However, when the curriculum of a choral or instrumental group becomes merely preparation for one performance after another, the number is excessive. Time should be allowed to study music, as well as to perform it. Without such learning a band or choral group ceases to be an educational organization and has gone into the entertainment business.

    The MENC publication *Guidelines for Performances of School Music Groups* contains a summary table of the recommended number of performances per school year. It is reproduced in Table 13.1.

5. *Performances should adhere to acceptable moral and ethical standards.* The vast amount of music available makes it easy for school music teachers to avoid musical productions that cast students in morally undesirable roles or in situations that are inappropriate to their age and experience. As an influential social institution, the school should promote the best aspects of civilization and personal conduct. With so much to teach and so little time to teach it, the schools cannot afford to do less.

6. *Performances should include all students who study music in performing classes.* The temptation, of course, is to concentrate on the most talented students, because they present a more favorable picture of what is being done in music. This situation occurs when a chorus of seventy-five presents a musical built around two or three principals and five or six minor roles. The other sixty-five students sing a few simple chorus parts, make scenery, assist with makeup, and pull the curtain. The principal performers sometimes get an inflated opinion of their abilities and contributions. This is not to say that talented students should not be given additional opportunities, but they should not be given special attention to the detriment of the others. For example, teaching a solo number should take place in private sessions, not during class while the rest of the students sit watching.

Table 13.1   *Recommended number of student performances per year*

	Elementary School	Middle School/ Junior High School	High School
	General music		
Performance events	1–2	1–2	—
	Choral groups		
Concerts	2–3	2–3	2–3
Musicals	0–1	0–1	0–1
Other performance events	—	0–2	6–13[a]
Evaluation festivals	—	1	1–2
Solo/ensemble festivals	—	1	1–2
Vocal jazz competition festivals	—	—	0–2
	Orchestra		
Concerts	2–3	2–3	2–3
Musicals	—	—	0–1
Other performance events	—	2–3	4–5[a]
Evaluation festivals	—	1	1–2
Solo/ensemble festivals	—	1	1–2
	Band		
Concerts	2–3	2–3	2–3
Musicals	—	—	0–1
Parades	—	0–2	0–3
Other performance events	—	2–3	4–8[a]
Evaluation festivals	—	1	1–2
Solo/ensemble festivals	—	1	1–2
Jazz festivals	—	—	0–2
Marching band competitions	—	—	0–2
Athletic contests	—	—	12
Postseason championship games	—	—	0–4
Pep assemblies	—	—	0–6

[a]including adjunct groups

7. *Performances should be planned to receive optimum responses from the audience.* Unless the audience generally feels good about the program they have heard, the social or psychological values will be reduced for the student musicians. The success of the performance affects future students as well as present members of the group. When the performance is well received, not only are more students motivated to enroll in music courses, which in turn increases

the effectiveness of performing classes, but there is also better support and understanding on the part of the school administration and public.

8. *Performances should be viewed in proper perspective by students and teacher.* If a concert is an outgrowth of class work, then it should be treated as such. Some teachers believe that by whipping up fervor for a performance, they will achieve the optimum effort from the students. Unfortunately, they usually achieve the optimum effort plus tension and anxiety. Certainly this is a misuse of performance. A month's work is not ruined because of a missed entrance in a concert; a month's work can only be lost in the classroom. Teachers should not get the cart before the horse here. Their primary concern should be the musical education of students, not the presentation of flawless performances.

PLANNING FOR SUCCESSFUL PERFORMANCES

The education of the students and the interest of the audience are not necessarily contradictory propositions. In fact, imaginative teachers can combine the two. Less successful teachers see good music education and a high degree of audience enjoyment as irreconcilable, and they proceed either to ignore the listeners or to forget about music education for the sake of audience amusement.

If performances by school groups are to achieve their goal of being both educationally valid and successful in the eyes of the audience, then teachers should keep in mind two points. One is the need for informality. Secondary school students are not collegiate or professional musicians, and music teachers need not present concerts that pretend they are. Teenagers have personality, imagination, and genuine audience appeal, if these attributes are not snuffed out in a stiff atmosphere. There is no reason why students cannot offer a few comments about the music during the program, no reason why there cannot be informative notes in the printed program, and no reason why a class activity other than performance cannot be shown to the audience. Music teachers sometimes overlook the fact that people are curious about simple things: how a French horn player who has been resting for several measures knows when to come in, how the singers find which pitch in a chord to start on, and what a conductor does to indicate loud and soft.

The second point is the age of the students. Younger students should be presented with greater informality. A seventh grade class can present a number or two using water glasses it has tuned to study the intervals of the scale and tuning, or it may sing a simple unison folk song with Autoharp accompaniment. A senior high school group, however, should present more polished performances and more sophisticated music, simply because that is the level at which it studies music.

School Assemblies

With the exception of the marching and pep bands, school groups perform mostly for school assemblies and public programs at school. In a number of schools, however, assemblies have been largely abandoned because the auditorium holds only half of the student body at a time or because student behavior has become too unruly.

In secondary schools that still present assemblies or convocations, music teachers are presented with both an opportunity and a challenge. The opportunity is the chance to show the students what the group has accomplished and in the process to encourage interest in the group. Such performances can greatly influence student opinions about music and may determine whether or not some of them will enroll in a music course in the future. The challenge comes from the fact that the audience at an assembly is volatile and responsive. Therefore, the type of music presented and the way it is presented must be carefully thought out ahead of the performance. The program should inform the students about music and give something to listen for in each work, and yet it should also give them something to applaud. One teacher planned one number each year that was designed to appeal to students in the assembly situation. The assembly program must "move"; "dead spots" in it are deadly.

Informal Programs

So far the discussion of music presentations has centered on the band, orchestra, or choral organization, each of which is a performance-oriented class. These are not the only groups, however, that appear before the public. General music classes, frequently in combination with other sections of the same course, may perform once or twice a year. In addition, performing organizations make informal appearances, such as a Parents' Night. On these occasions audience interest is achieved by showing the learning activities of the class. Students can play portions of recordings they have studied and offer explanatory comments; they can display the music notebooks they have compiled; they can describe current class projects. The Autoharp can be used to accompany songs, and part singing can demonstrate the use of changing voices.

With performances of this type, attempts at a formal presentation are out of character. The appeal to the audience lies in the personalities of the students and their responses to the music. Instead of entitling a performance "Spring Concert by West Middle School," teachers might call it "Music at West" or "Invitation to Music at West Middle School." People appreciate an unassuming program appropriate to the age and nature of the students.

Programs Outside of School

School groups are often invited to perform for community organizations. It may become necessary for the teacher to apportion the number of such appearances so that the educational purpose of the music group does not suffer. If refusals for performances around the community are necessary, they are usually best handled through a policy statement on out-of-school appearances drawn up by the music teachers, student officers, and school administration. In this way the onus does not fall on an individual teacher, and the matter receives the attention of more than one person.

Two special considerations should be given to performances away from school. First, they must not infringe on areas that properly belong to professional musicians. The Code of Ethics, reprinted in the appendix, states that school music groups may perform at educational, nonprofit, noncommercial functions, as well as at benefit performances for charitable organizations, nonprofit educational broadcasts and telecasts, and civic events that do not usurp the rights and privileges of local professional musicians. Performances by school groups at other civic programs are permissible only if they are mutually agreed on by the school authorities and official representatives of the local musicians' union. Professional musicians have in their province such events as community concerts and community-centered activities and other nonschool activities, and functions furthering private or public enterprise, partisan or fraternal organizations. The Code says further:

> Statements that funds are not available for the employment of professional musicians, or that if the talents of the amateur musical organizations cannot be had, other musicians cannot or will not be employed, or that the amateur musicians are to play without remuneration of any kind, are all immaterial.

The second consideration is the place of performance. If it is impossible for the group to practice in the new location, the teacher should at least see the surroundings beforehand. Some teachers have had the unfortunate experience of agreeing to sing for the Rotary Club only to find that the Rotary meets in a room that is too small to hold both the singers and the Rotarians. If a piano is needed, the position and quality should be determined ahead of time.

Adjusting to Performance Conditions

There are several ways teachers can facilitate the adjustment of the performers to the place of performance and expedite the mechanics of presentation. If at all possible, the group should practice at least once in the place of performance. The shift from rehearsal room to stage can be unsettling to the student musicians. A new location sometimes gives the performers the uneasy feeling that each of them is performing alone. The seating or standing arrangement will probably be different, at least to the extent that the distances are altered among musicians and between the conductor and musicians.

During the practice, teachers should check to see whether the students can hear one another and whether the choral groups can hear the piano. Then they should check the sound from the back of the room. If there are hearing or balance problems, some adjustment of the stage arrangement may be called for. Draperies around the back and sides of a stage can be drawn together or apart. The piano can be moved, and its top raised or lowered. In instrumental groups, instruments with less volume can be moved forward, and louder instruments can be moved to the back of the stage, where more of the sound is absorbed in the curtains and lost in the gaping ceiling. If seated instrumental risers are available, their use can improve balance and ensemble. The performers should also be forewarned about the effect the audience will have on the acoustics of the room; the sound may be noticeably more "dead."

When a stage absorbs too much sound, making the tone appear weak to the audience, the possibility of a shell should be investigated. Manufacturing concerns produce shells that are quite adaptable, and some of them are portable. If a commercial shell is too expensive, stage flats can be made and painted with several coats to give them a hard surface. Most important are the overhead panels that keep sound from rising up between the lights and becoming lost. If no other means of support are available, the panels can be suspended.

Choral teachers often find it feasible to have two seating plans, one for the rehearsal room and one for performance. The rows on the risers may be a different length from the rows of chairs in the rehearsal room. Furthermore, in performance the students are arranged somewhat according to height to prevent unevenness in the appearance of rows and to prevent tall singers from blocking out the shorter people standing behind them. When a mixed chorus is arranged by height, the boys, who are generally taller than the girls, are often placed in the back and center of the group.

Although a few outstanding collegiate and professional choirs scatter the sections, this technique is too difficult for most school groups. Inexperienced singers need the confidence and help derived from others on their part who are located near them.

The exact arrangement of the vocal or instrumental group is not a vital matter. Traditional seating patterns and placement of sections are based as much on appearance as they are on musical results. Generally the larger and louder instruments are put in the back rows. However, many unique and valid placement patterns are observed in both choral and instrumental organizations. Teachers should feel free to vary the arrangement according to their personal desires, the size and instrumentation of the group, and the characteristics of the stage, so that the arrangement will produce the optimum in appearance and musical results.

The movements of a group must be carefully planned. Time and energy can be conserved by having the performers in place when the curtain is opened. Watching one person after another walk onto the stage is not very interesting. The footsteps make a distracting noise, and some members of the group are obviously ill at ease. A row of singers may overshoot its place on the risers and someone from the wings has to signal them all to move back a bit. Why not save valuable class and concert time? Get in place, open the curtain, and start making music.

Occasionally the group may perform where there is no curtain, and the musicians will have to get in place in full view of the audience. With choral groups the simplest way to handle this situation is to have the front row come out first, then the other rows, starting with the last and working down to the second row. In this way the first row can somewhat shield the others as they line up. Military marching maneuvers, including the about-face used by some music groups, seem out of character. If the students walk in a dignified manner, nothing further is needed to improve their entrance.

If soloists are to step forward from their place in the group, a way must be cleared for them. If a music stand is to be moved into position, someone should be assigned this chore. Soloists should know how to acknowledge applause. If they perform from their places in the group, they should be invited to step forward or to stand afterward to receive recognition for their efforts.

Teachers, too, should plan to acknowledge applause of the audience graciously, with dignity and humility. By stepping to one side of stage center and making a modest bow, they acknowledge the fact that the applause is for the students as well as for themselves.

Proper deportment before an audience is such an obvious necessity that teachers may forget to mention it, only to look up at the concert and see a singer chewing gum or a violinist chatting with another player. Students should be impressed with the fact that their total attention must be on their performance and that their eyes should be fixed on the conductor. The students should be strongly warned about behavior in the event of a mistake. They should not look around, giggle, look startled, or in any other manner show knowledge of an error. Such behavior makes the group look disorganized and childish. They need to be reminded that *someone* in the audience will be looking at each one of them every moment they are on stage.

A problem faced by choral teachers, especially at the middle school level, is singers fainting. As little as possible should be said about this matter, because partly it is psychological. The more the students think about fainting, the more they faint! However, they need to be instructed to sit down on the risers if they begin to feel faint or to assist a neighbor if they suspect he or she is becoming wobbly. If someone sits down because of feeling ill or faint, the group should finish the number they are singing and then help the person off the stage.

When students wear robes, uniforms, or similar dress, they should not wear any article of clothing that focuses attention on an individual. Conspicuous appearance, like poor deportment, is distracting to an audience and therefore inappropriate, especially when singing sacred music.

Planning the Program

In selecting music and deciding on the manner of presentation, teachers should keep these points in mind:

Select an opening number that will give the students a good start. Choose something that is not difficult, with a solid beginning and no undue demands for subtleties of intonation or phrasing. The opening number should set a mood of confidence for the performers.

Arrange the numbers in meaningful sequence. Some teachers like to put the heavy, serious numbers at the beginning or end of the concert, the light numbers first or last, and so on. Some go so far as to talk about building up a concert like a crescendo; others mention musical climaxes. Such considerations seem unrealistic, because what is a high point for one listener may be a low point for another. The only aspect on which there seems to be general agreement is this: Works should not be arranged helter-skelter, so that Palestrina winds up next to "De Camptown Races." It is more cohesive for the audience and students if the numbers are grouped into logical units, such as religious, Baroque, or American music.

Limit the overall length of the program. Young teachers in their eagerness often give concerts that are too long. Professional concerts may last for two or more hours, but the patrons of school music programs differ considerably in their musical interests from the patrons of opera or symphony. Furthermore, few school groups are of professional caliber. If any misjudgment of time is to be made, err on the side of having the concert too short. It has been said a thousand times: "It's better to have the audience leave wishing to hear more than it is to have them leave with a sense of relief that their ordeal is over at last." *One hour and fifteen minutes is plenty of time for most school programs,* and that amount of time includes time for changing the stage, moving pianos and stands, tuning, and (one hopes) some applause.

To estimate the length of a program, compute the duration of the music, the time for applause between numbers, and the time needed to get groups on and off the stage and to move music stands, chairs, and pianos. If an intermission is scheduled, add that time, although an intermission is unnecessary when the length of the program is kept within bounds.

Plan to keep the program from dragging. Let other teachers or student officers help manage the groups so that when one is through performing, the next is lined up ready to go on stage. Get the performers on and off the stage as quickly as possible. Assign separate rooms to each group so that the students have a place to leave their coats and cases, do a little warming up, and generally get organized. If the stage has a halfway curtain, small ensembles or soloists can perform from the front half of the stage while another group is *quietly* getting into place in the back half. If many organizations are participating, it is not necessary to have all groups appear on the stage. A choral group may sing from the balcony of the auditorium, while the band and orchestra remain on stage. In many auditoriums, the best place acoustically is immediately in front of the stage in the pit or on the floor. This area can be used just as effectively as the stage. In any case, plan carefully to keep the program moving.

WAYS TO ENHANCE THE PROGRAM

How can teenage musicians capture the interest of an audience? What, if anything, is needed beyond the creditable performance of music? One way to add interest is to tie the performance together through the use of a narrator, who may or may not be the teacher. Not only does the narrator integrate the program, he or she also eliminates "dead spots" between works of music and changes of groups. Another method is to feature several groups—ensembles, glee clubs, soloists, stage band, and others. In some cases, ensembles can be included from both middle and senior high schools in the performance.

Methods for enhancing the appeal of performances must differ between instrumental and vocal music, for several reasons. The stage setup for a choral performance can be altered quickly, because it involves only risers and piano, but changes in an instrumental setup require moving stands, chairs, podium, music folders, and instruments. Vocal music with its words can suggest specific actions or props, while even programmatic instrumental music can seldom be treated so exactly. There are differences in length of pieces, with instrumental works usually being longer. Finally, vocal music seems generally a more personal, direct experience between performer and listener than instrumental music.

Staging Vocal Music Programs

The day is past when a school group could just stand on the risers, sing its program, and thrill the audience. Only musicians of exceptional performing ability are able to do this. Motion pictures, television, marching band shows—all have contributed to the fact that audiences now want programs with some visual as well as aural appeal.

In many schools, the concerts have been lifted out of the doldrums by "staging" some numbers. Staging includes props, backdrops, and dress, as well as activities such as dancing and pantomime. In one school, for example, a choir prepared three religious songs. To create the proper atmosphere, the students built a white altar rail to stand in front of the singers and two artificial stained-glass windows. At another concert the singers presented a group of folk songs, with a few students performing an appropriate folk dance to two of the numbers.

Through such techniques the audience can be educated and entertained at the same time. It is easy to forget that many listeners cannot fully appreciate what the group is doing. Their attention can be stimulated by a little action or a simple prop. It need not be much, as long as it helps break the spell of watching the students perform from one unvarying position.

The impression should not be given that every number should be staged. Probably one in four is sufficient.

Does staging reflect good music education? Yes, it does, if the visual elements are not emphasized to such an extent that they detract from the music. Staging is essentially a means of expanding a song from an auditory experience into a visual one as well. The music maintains its proper position as the primary ingredient of the concert.

Staging is good music education because it involves all the students in the group, not just the most talented. It presents music in an appealing way without spending time on the spoken lines and complex stage movements of a complete show. Most important, it allows teachers to choose the music they want rather than accept some less interesting pieces because they are part of a musical.

Good staging has some of the advantages of a musical without the cost. Musicals call for a large expenditure of time and money. Time is required to memorize spoken lines, stage directions, and dance steps—activities that are only peripheral to music. Money is required for royalties, costume rental, and scenery; staging concerts eliminates these problems almost entirely.

There are many ways to develop ideas for visual effects in choral music. Student committees can be formed for each song or group of songs to be staged. The categories might include religious music, songs from other countries, or excerpts from Broadway musicals. The committees then meet to draw up plans, with the teacher meeting with each committee at least once to exchange ideas with them. After each committee, with the teacher's help, comes to an agreement on an idea or two, the thoughts are presented briefly to the whole group and further refinements are sought.

Next comes implementation of the idea, and another student committee is formed to do this. Membership on these committees is determined by the type of work involved. If a prop is to be built, students enrolled in shop courses can do the job. If painting is required, students taking art courses can demonstrate their talents. Those who have a common free period can work together on a project, and no one will have to be removed from class—always a delicate operation in maintaining a friendly atmosphere in the school. The result is that students do most of the planning, purchasing, and actual work. Their increased sense of responsibility is a desirable outgrowth of this experience.

Three precautions should be mentioned. First, teachers should not attempt extensive staging without the assistance of the students. A prop may not sound like much work, but when it has to be built and painted, in addition to a teaching load, it can be a burden.

Second, teachers must *not* assume that they can turn the staging over to the students and go on about their other business. Teenagers need guidance and assistance in such an undertaking. Teachers will often have to tell the students where to find what they need, what to buy, when to work, and how to do the job.

Finally, no group should attempt too many projects, especially the first year. Until the students have had experience in working at such things, they are slow and require much assistance. In addition, the last weeks before a concert are busy enough without the burden of extra projects. Some props can be saved for another year, and this makes staging subsequent concerts easier.

Types of Staging Activities

Dancing. Because the whole group cannot sing and dance at the same time, a few individuals are selected to do the dancing. Folk and square dances are effective, as are other types of dances, if good dancers are available. Physical education instructors can be helpful in teaching dance steps to the students. In addition, one or two couples can be selected to perform the latest teenage dance. This feature usually draws a favorable response from a high school audience.

It is better to use dancers who are members of the choral organization. This may create a vacancy in the ranks for some numbers, but the gain in singer interest makes this procedure well worthwhile.

Change of Dress. Variety can be achieved by simple changes of clothing. Because robes hide nearly everything worn underneath them, the singers can have one change of dress by simply removing the robe. Many choral teachers feel that it is inappropriate to sing secular and semipopular songs in robes, so dual costuming is advisable for presenting a mixed repertoire.

The teacher must allow enough time for a change of dress, designate a place to change clothes, and provide a room in which to keep the robes or clothing.

Lighting. Lights can change the entire atmosphere of a scene. Campfire settings and night scenes with carolers can be suggested with appropriate lights. Sometimes the mood of a song will suggest a predominant color, and some song titles mention colors. If the stage has a rheostat, infinite variations of dim and bright light are possible. Lighting mixtures should be planned by the teacher with the help of someone knowledgeable about lighting rather than by a nonmusician alone. While the lighting should fit the mood of the music, it should never be obtrusive.

Props and Scenery. Props and scenery should be more suggestive than literal. If the action takes place on a Pacific island, one palm tree is enough to lend atmosphere. If the boys are supposed to be sailors, sailor hats will convey this idea, along with a mop or two for scrubbing the deck and a few naval flags strung on a rope.

Props and scenery should be kept simple; no waterwheels with real water running over them, please. The school may have pieces of scenery that the drama or art teachers have used, and these articles may be well suited to the purposes of the music department.

Music teachers should supervise scenery building themselves rather than turn it over to the art, shop, or drama teachers. It is unfair to burden other teachers with the hard work required by such building projects when the program is not their responsibility. Also, an embarrassing situation can result if a colleague is not clear on what is wanted and the finished product may not be what the music teacher had in mind. Either the prop must be used or the rules of propriety broken by not using the piece.

Actions. A few simple pantomime actions can illustrate the words to humorous songs and those with compound repetition, such as "The Twelve Days of Christmas." There is one limitation to this device, however; too much literal pantomime can make the number look like a kindergarten rendition.

Music teachers sometimes become so accustomed to watching the smooth actions of professional singers that they expect the same enthusiasm and naturalness from the students. In most cases, however, the teachers will need to coach them on their actions. At least they should check them out before the performance.

Limitations to Consider in Staging

The type of prop and action is limited by the facilities available. These conditions should be taken into account.

Size of the Stage. The amount of available space should be figured with the curtain closed, because the area in front of a curtain is generally not usable as part of the stage setting. Room must be allowed for the risers and piano. If the singers are seated, more space will be needed.

Size of the Offstage Area. This consideration determines the ease with which students and props can be moved on and off the stage. Unused props should be out of the line of traffic.

Amount and Quality of Stage Equipment. Before planning extensive staging, teachers should know what stage equipment is available and if it is in working order. In some schools the lights and switches are handled carelessly by many students and teachers, and it is difficult to keep the stage equipment operational.

Practice Facilities. The amount and type of staging that can be undertaken are influenced to some extent by how much practice the group can schedule on the stage. If the stage is in the gymnasium, the presence of other classes may hamper practice. If the rehearsal room is large enough, it is wise to chalk or paint on the floor the exact area of the stage so that the students can become accustomed to working in the available space.

Staging Instrumental Music

Although bands and orchestras cannot as easily add visual interest to their programs as can vocal groups, there are some steps that can be taken to increase the visual appeal of an instrumental concert. A few of these suggestions are similar to those outlined for vocal groups.

Dancing. Instrumentalists need not descend into the pit to play a number that includes dancing. They can leave enough room at the front of the stage for the dancers, or if the stage is too shallow, a few of the players can move to one side to give the dancers more space.

Scenery and Stage Setting. Instrumental groups can use a backdrop as well as many of the props and flags mentioned for choral programs. Although instrumental music does not have a text to provide specific meanings, there are many descriptive works that suggest visual treatment. In the field of geographical description alone, the possibilities range from "The Great Gate of Kiev" to national anthems and folk tunes from around the world.

Instrumentalists need not always sit in the same arrangement. The use of seated instrumental risers enables all players to be seen more easily by the audience.

Featuring Sections.   Jazz bands regularly feature sections and soloists. This technique adds interest to the program and permits individuals to be recognized for their efforts. Separated placement is especially desirable for antiphonal music. While the following device has been encountered almost too frequently, it is a crowd pleaser: The piccolos stand, then all the brasses stand during the trio of "Stars and Stripes Forever." The same type of thing can be done occasionally with other music. In one school system the flutists from every school learned a charming folk melody, then joined together to perform it with band accompaniment.

In addition to small ensembles, which should be a part of the instrumental music curriculum, teachers may form a novel group such as a German band or a "jug and bottle" band. One or two numbers, presented just for fun that have not demanded a large amount of rehearsal time, may be worth including in the concert. The players may put on appropriate hats and in this way add more flavor to the musical rendition without a complete change of costume.

Musical Variety.   Instrumental teachers can look for a few novel works that are skillfully written and musically interesting. Such pieces are not easy to find. The *Toy* Symphony of Haydn, *Peter and the Wolf* by Prokofiev, and "The Typewriter" by Leroy Anderson are examples. Some of these works are educationally valuable because they demonstrate the qualities of instruments so well. Other pieces contain unusual actions, as in Haydn's *Farewell* Symphony or Johann Strauss's "Clear Track Polka," in which the conductor can add extemporaneous holds and rubato.

Vocal Soloists and Choral Groups.   Not only does a vocal soloist provide variety at an instrumental concert, but the combination of voice and instruments can be an impressive musical experience as well. Also effective are some finale numbers that involve a large chorus. As a further bonus, this type of presentation brings the vocal and instrumental departments together in a cooperative venture.

BUSINESS ASPECTS

Some musicians do not like to work at publicity, printed programs, and the sale of tickets, but these matters must be handled properly or unnecessary complications will result.

Printed Programs

The printed program is a vital part of the concert because it is closely examined by the public. Before hearing the students, the audience looks at the program and gains an impression of their work. Other music teachers see the program, even though they may not hear the concert. Programs are mailed to relatives of the students, pasted in scrapbooks, hung on bedroom walls, and looked at months and years after the actual performance.

Because the printed program is a permanent item and has a way of getting around, it must include the names of all the students who participate in the concert. If the students are listed by the part they sing or the instrument they play, the lists appear shorter, and each individual seems more important. Above all, the teacher must *make certain that no name has been left out and that all names have been spelled correctly.* If an error or omission is discovered after printing, the correction should be announced publicly at the concert.

Everyone who has assisted the music teacher in some way should be acknowledged on the printed program. This includes stores from which equipment has been borrowed, teachers and departments who have given assistance, administrators who have helped in scheduling, and the school custodians. Such acknowledgments go a long way toward maintaining good relations in the school. Soloists, accompanists, student officers, and members of student committees also deserve special mention. Such recognition makes the program considerably more valuable for many students, and if they have made extra contributions, they should be recognized.

The printed program can educate the audience about the music being performed. Although it is easy to list only the name of a work and its composer or arranger, a mere list of names does little to enlighten the audience. They derive more learning and enjoyment from a performance for which the music has been explained somewhat.

So it is good use of teachers' time, limited as it is, to write brief but informative notes about each piece. Here are two samples:

Liberty Bell March, John Philip Sousa

This is one of the many marches written by America's "march king." It follows the usual march form, with two strains (each repeated) and then a trio in a different key, which is also repeated. It glides along in 6/8 meter and contains several contrasts of loud and soft phrases.

O Domine Jesu Christe (O Lord Jesus Christ), Palestrina

The outstanding composer of music for the service of the Roman Catholic church was Giovanni Pierluigi da Palestrina, who lived in sixteenth-century Italy. One of his best-known compositions is the motet "O Domine Jesu Christe." The text is a prayer to Jesus, with special recognition of his suffering on the cross. It concludes, "I pray that through your wounds my soul may be redeemed." The music is polyphonic, which means that all four parts are equal in melodic importance. The music is restrained in character.

Because understanding the music is a prerequisite to writing helpful program notes, a few able students might be given an opportunity to prepare the written material. The purpose of this effort is not primarily to lighten the teacher's work load but rather to help the students better comprehend the music they are performing.

Outside pages or covers for programs are available from various firms. There are color pictures from which to choose, and the rest of the folder is blank to accommodate the printing or xeroxing. Original designs by skilled art students also make attractive programs.

The teacher should start working on the program two weeks before the concert. It takes time to have it set in type and be duplicated or printed. It is desirable to have the programs five days before the concert so that copies can be sent out as invitations and publicity.

Tickets

Tickets are not required when admission is free. They can still be made, however, and distributed for publicity purposes. Making tickets is simple and relatively inexpensive. If there are different price levels, each should be represented by a different color of paper. The ticket should state the following information: name of event, presented by whom, where, on what date, at what time, and the price of the ticket. It is wise to print more tickets than the number likely to be sold.

The policy of reserving seats has good and bad points. It has advantages for the reserved-seat holders (they don't have to arrive early to get good seats) and for the organization (a little more can be charged for the ticket). The disadvantages can be considerable. Each ticket must have two parts, one to be taken at the door and another to be kept by the holder as a receipt. Both the stub and the seat need to be numbered. A problem arises when the concert is given in a gymnasium and temporary chairs are set up. Also, sometimes there is a mix-up on reserved seats.

Tickets to school programs should be sold by the students themselves. Giving the students tickets to sell is also one of the best methods of publicizing the event. As an incentive, some teachers offer prizes to the two or three students who sell the most tickets. This device is not always effective, because about the second day of the ticket sales someone, perhaps a boy with a newspaper route, walks into class and says, "Well, I've already sold forty tickets, and I've got promises for twelve more." At that moment everyone else gives up. What seems better from the standpoint of motivating the students and filling the auditorium is to offer students one free ticket for every five that they sell. They can do whatever they want with the ticket—give it away or sell it and keep the money. This method makes a small reward accessible to all. Tickets should be available at the door on the night of the performance.

The bookkeeping of ticket sales is no small item. The easiest method is to give each student a fixed number of tickets, possibly three adult and two student tickets. Dispensing extra tickets can be recorded. Students should be told to account for all tickets given to them, and they should understand that they will have to pay for tickets that they don't return. When students are told this, they seldom lose tickets. All ticket collections should be suspended during class periods the final week before the concert. Financial activities consume valuable time, and most of these business matters can be handled outside of class.

Publicity

The best publicity for a concert is to include in the program as many students as possible. When a son or daughter comes home from school and announces, "We're having our concert in two weeks—can you come?" the parents are as motivated as they are ever going to be. It is a mistake for school music teachers to set great store in formal publicity efforts.

If posters are to be made, it is best to assign this project to students who are taking art classes. The public has grown so accustomed to printed signs stuck in store windows that another sign is seldom noticed. The creations of the students are more eye-catching than commercially printed signs. Besides, the signs made by the students usually cost only the price of the materials used.

In many communities, radio stations will broadcast announcements of school events such as music programs as a public service.

Local newspapers should be provided with notices of the event. The willingness of newspapers to publish material about school concerts varies. Many small-town papers are hungry for news and will publish anything given them, including pictures. Larger papers are less likely to print complete write-ups. However, many metropolitan newspapers publish local editions, which contain news of interest to only one area of their circulation. Some newspapers run a school supplement once a week.

All copy prepared for a newspaper should be double-spaced. Below is a sample story written newspaper style.

> *The first concert of the season will be presented by the Centertown High School Orchestra at 8:00 P.M. Friday, October 28, in the school auditorium, 1201 Center Avenue. The concert is free to the public.*
>
> *The seventy-piece orchestra will be conducted by James G. Smith, supervisor of instrumental music in the Centertown schools. Featured soloist will be senior Dina Eidelstein, concertmistress, who will be heard in the first movement of the Mendelssohn Violin Concerto. Completing the program will be Schubert's* Rosamunde Overture *and the Prelude, Chorale, and Fugue by Bach.*

The story should contain any items of interest about the concert, teacher, or soloists, and should be given to the newspaper several days before publication is desired.

The school newspaper is an important vehicle for publicity. Although it contains little that the students don't already know, it is significant because of the teenagers' desire to be recognized.

One of the most effective means of publicizing the program to the student body is to present, if possible, a preview or "teaser" assembly, from ten to thirty minutes in length. The idea is to show the students the best of the coming program so that they will attend the performance and, more important, talk favorably about the music organizations. The portions of the regular program with the greatest student appeal should be presented. If the students like what they see and hear, they are more likely to attend the concert.

TRIPS AND TOURS

The value of trips and tours for performing groups is controversial among educators. Much of the controversy has arisen because of the occasional misuse of trips. Some teachers have received kickbacks from the expense fees charged students. In other cases an "invitation" to a fair or a bowl game parade (which is usually sent *after* the school has expressed an interest in attending the event) has necessitated a tremendous effort to raise $50,000 or more to make the trip. In some states such situations have precipitated the establishment of codes and regulations by school principals' organizations or by state extracurricular supervisory boards.

What are the characteristics of a properly handled trip by a school organization? They do not differ much from the points cited for worthy performances.

The trip must be an educational venture for the students. Performing should be only one aspect of the undertaking. The students may listen to other music groups, see a musical, or visit a museum. The students should be impressed with the fact that the trip is an educational event, not merely a vacation.

In keeping with the Code of Ethics, no admission can be charged for any performance while on tour. Some school groups present goodwill concerts in the evenings in churches or school auditoriums and then take a collection. The amount received generally is quite modest. Many goodwill concerts are poorly attended, and the collection may not cover even the cost of publicity and other items.

The trip must be well planned and managed. Arrangements must be made for every meal and overnight stop. One teacher carefully planned each phase of the journey but forgot to arrange for a place for the bus drivers to stay.

Of more importance than meals and lodging is preparing the students for the trip. The vast majority of students behave themselves, but there are a few who look upon trips as a chance for a little hell raising. Nothing can ruin a trip and eliminate the possibility of future trips faster than misbehavior. A few teachers and schools have found themselves in trouble because students got lost from the group, committed petty shoplifting, took drugs, damaged property, or threw objects out of bus windows.

What can be done to ensure proper deportment? First, the students should be informed that the trip is a privilege—it is up to them to prove they deserve the privilege and can handle it. Then, with the school administration and student officers, the teacher should establish policies regarding behavior and penalties for misbehavior. These areas should be covered: staying with the group, smoking, room checks, and behavior on buses and in public places. Students should know that if they misbehave, the penalties will be stiff. All warnings and regulations should be stated in writing and presented to the students and parents, in case of later challenges or misunderstandings.

A sufficient number of parents and teachers should accompany the group as chaperones.

The roll should be called or checked by monitors each time before the buses move on.

Limits should be put on the amount of baggage that each student may bring.

Financing the trip must be kept to a minimum and handled in a sensible manner. The trip should not require an agonizing financial effort. There should be no need for a year of activities such as tag days, collections, car washes, sales of baked goods, candy, records, and so on. A trip that requires a huge effort to finance is out of place in the public schools.

Money-raising projects should be considered carefully. Often they require much work, and after all the expenses have been paid, there is not much profit. It is true that magazines, candy, and greeting cards are items that do not require an effort to make, but customers pay a lot for what they get. If other school groups also sell goods to the community, the field can get crowded.

Caution should be exercised in any money-raising project. Because the class-room, equipment, and teachers' salaries are already being paid for by the public through taxation, school organizations should be restrained in seeking money. Discretion is needed to help maintain the good will of the community and to impose reasonable limits on the financial aspirations of the group seeking support.

One successful method of financing is outright solicitation. Surprisingly, many people prefer this to buying candy or magazines they don't want. Funds can also be derived from selling tickets to music concerts. Except in the case of a musical requiring expensive costumes, scenery, and royalties, the outlay for a program seldom exceeds the income from tickets. This money can be applied to the cost of the trip, or at least held in reserve in case the actual expenses run over the estimate.

The schedule of the trip should disrupt the normal school routine as little as possible. The trip should not be so long and strenuous that the students come back exhausted. The number of performances should be limited to not more than three in one day—one in the morning, one in the afternoon, and one at night. Professional groups almost never perform more than one or two programs a day. Scheduling more than three performances involves the risk of falling behind schedule, hurried meals, and general tension.

When possible, trips should take place during a school vacation time. When students are removed from classes for trips, a sensitive situation is created. The other teachers are a bit envious of music teachers. They receive frequent public recognition for their work and here they are again taking time for a trip. In addition, the other teachers are inconvenienced by having students miss their classes. The best way for teachers to approach the situation is to explain carefully in a faculty meeting the purpose of the trip and the manner in which absences from class will be handled. The most successful procedure is to have the students get a signed statement from each teacher that their class work is of passable quality and that all possible assignments have been completed in advance. Students who cannot meet these requirements in their classes should not be permitted to go on the trip.

If these conditions are met, a trip can be a very worthwhile experience for the students. Never do they have such singleness of purpose or put so much into their performance. The students feel as they never have before: "We're really doing things in music!" The social contact, the experience in planning, the musical events heard and seen—all of these can make an important activity.

CHECKLIST FOR PROGRAM PLANNING

The following time schedule is helpful in planning a major performance. Items concerning costumes and scenery can be ignored for the less extensive concert.

September

Select and enter dates on master calendar of school activities. If school does not have a central calendar, clear dates with athletic and drama departments and with school administration.

Three to six months before performance

1. Select music.
2. Establish a budget for performance—music, costume rentals, programs, and so on. Have it approved by administration, if necessary.
3. Secure performance rights on music. Procure music.
4. Make arrangements for costumes.
5. Try out soloists or leads.

Two to three months before performance

1. Establish rehearsal schedule containing approximate dates for learning specific portions of the music.
2. Begin study of the music.
3. Schedule the learning of spoken lines by leads and understudies.
4. Make decisions regarding scenery and props.

One to two months before performance

1. Construct scenery and props.
2. Prepare publicity and program materials.
3. Arrange for tickets and ticket sales. Order tickets.

Two to four weeks before performance

1.   Have program printed or reproduced.

2.   Arrange for ushers, stage crew, and after-performance cleanup.

3.   Put scenery in place and rehearse with it.

4.   Arrange for warm-up and dressing rooms.

5.   Arrange for piano to be tuned on day of performance, if possible.

One week before performance

1.   Mail out complimentary programs and tickets.

2.   Plan rehearsals to consist of complete "run throughs."

3.   Set aside one rehearsal for looking over different music; let the students relax and rest.

4.   Check stage equipment and public-address system.

5.   Check to see that all small props have been secured.

6.   Arrange for curtain calls or acknowledgment of applause.

Performance

1.   Hold a brief warm-up session in which the students perform the first few measures of each number in a thoughtful and careful manner. Check the tuning of instruments.

2.   Make sure everyone is in place and equipment is functioning before starting.

3.   Start on time.

4.   Relax and enjoy the program (as much as possible).

After the performance

1.   Return all rented or borrowed music, equipment, and costumes.

2.   Thank custodians, secretaries, teachers, administrators, and merchants who contributed to the program.

3.   Finish collection of money from ticket sales.

4.   Initiate procedures with proper school personnel for payment of bills.

5.   Deposit, with proper accounting, the income from ticket sales.

Questions   1.   What do these performance-related incidents reveal about the teacher's understanding of music education?

(a)   Ruth Takamoto has five sections of eighth grade general music. For a PTA program on music, she chose the best twenty-five girls from the five classes to sing. "After all," she says, "there are a lot of kids in those classes who have precious little ability."

(b) Eric Holm is rehearsing his high school band. The first horn bobbles a note. "If you do that in the concert," Eric says sternly, "I'll clobber your grade, so help me. The audience cannot excuse mistakes."

(c) Lynne Golds wants her choir's performance of the latest Broadway musical to be as nearly professional as possible. As a result, her singers rehearse only that music for three months in preparation for the performance.

2. Suppose you are asked to have your students provide fifteen minutes of after-dinner music at a service club luncheon. The performance is strictly for entertainment. Should you not accept the engagement? Why or why not?

3. Which performances are acceptable under the Code of Ethics with the American Federation of Musicians?
    (a) an appearance by the band at a Memorial Day observance
    (b) a performance in connection with the opening of a new Sears store
    (c) a performance at the swearing-in ceremony of city officials
    (d) an airport appearance by the band when the national vice-presidential candidate comes to town
    (e) a performance by the school stage band at a dance held in a private club paid for by a group of families
    (f) a performance by the choir at a hospital benefit dinner

4. Should the group learn different music for a school assembly, an evening concert, and a performance at noon for a service club? Why or why not?

Projects 1. Plan a thirty-minute performance demonstrating the various activities of a general music class. Balance the amounts of time allotted to each portion, and mention points you want the audience to learn from the presentation.

2. Plan a program using two choral groups, one instrumental group, one small vocal ensemble, and one small instrumental ensemble to go on one stage with no halfway curtain but with a good orchestra pit. Arrange the appearances of the groups so that maximum efficiency can be achieved, and state how many numbers each will perform.

3. Think of a simple staging idea for each of the following:
    (a) a group of songs from Latin America
    (b) "Black Is the Color of My True Love's Hair"
    (c) "This Is My Country"

4. Write program notes for two of the following works:
    (a) "How Lovely Are the Messengers" from *St. Paul* by Mendelssohn
    (b) *Water Music Suite* by Handel
    (c) "Simple Gifts" arranged by Copland
    (d) "El Capitan March" by Sousa

5. Select three band numbers, one featuring the clarinets, another the trombones, and another the percussion.

6. Plan a choral or instrumental concert, and write up a four-paragraph publicity story about it that could be given to a newspaper.

7. Write a script for the narrator of a program that includes a series of six works based on American folk music.

8. Set up a sample budget for the presentation of a musical comedy. Include royalties; rental of orchestra parts, costumes, and scenery; and the cost of programs and tickets. Then, assuming a seating capacity of 500 in the audience, compute the minimum ticket cost for one performance and then for two performances.

Suggested Readings

Guidelines for Performances of School Music Groups. Reston, Va.: Music Educators National Conference, 1986.

Jipson, Wayne R. *The High School Vocal Music Program.* West Nyack, N.Y.: Parker, 1972. Chapter 12.

On Stage. Owatonna, Minn.: Wenger, 1980.

Tumbusch, Tom. *Complete Production Guide to Modern Musical Theatre.* New York: Richards, Rosen, 1969.

CHAPTER 14

Computers in Music Education

Developments in ... computer-assisted instruction should be applied to music study and research (Choate, 1968).

This statement was written in the late 1960s as a part of the Music Educators National Conference's Tanglewood Declaration. At that time music educators had no idea how important computer-assisted instruction, and the uses of computers in music education, would become. Today the computer has become an increasingly effective tool for music educators.

HISTORY OF COMPUTERS IN MUSIC EDUCATION

The use of computers as a teaching tool began in the late 1960s for voice analysis and instrumental music instruction (Diehl and Radocy, 1969; Kuhn and Allvin, 1967). Studies in those days utilized large "mainframe" computers. The units themselves were very large (often room-size) and very expensive.

The situation did not change until computers became much less expensive and much smaller. The microcomputer of today can be purchased for as little as a few hundred dollars and can come in the size and weight of a portable typewriter. These changes made computers accessible to almost all schools and millions of individuals.

This chapter is largely the product of Dr. Russell L. Robinson, Associate Professor of Music, University of Florida.

The availability of computers, in turn, encouraged people to write programs for them and to develop related equipment for music. It is this aspect of computer technology that is most important to music teachers, and it is also the one in which improvements are being made and new technology is being developed at the fastest rate. While the basic process of the computer has not changed over the years, its flexibility and applications have grown enormously.

Prior to computer-assisted instruction, sequenced instruction was utilized through programmed instruction. However, it was not until the invention and proliferation of the microcomputer that music educators were able to explore fully the many uses of these instructional machines. Microcomputers of all makes (IBM, Apple II's, Macintosh, Tandy, etc.) are virtually everywhere today—in homes, schools, and businesses. As they have increased in these areas, they have also increased in the music classroom. Most secondary schools and many school music departments have computers either within their rooms or available to them for faculty and student use.

WHY COMPUTERS IN MUSIC EDUCATION?

Computers and their related equipment have become so important in music education because they can offer the following benefits:

1. *Individualize instruction.* Teachers have little choice except to teach "to the middle of the class." That is, there will almost always be some students for whom the material is too difficult and some for whom it is too easy. The former group of students needs extra practice and individual tutoring. Computer materials can provide such help. The latter group needs enrichment; they are bored with going over material they already know. Computer programs can benefit them by letting them move ahead to the extent that their time and interest permit. Such individual attention is especially important in music classes and rehearsals because music teachers usually see more students per week than do most teachers or they see students in large groups, which severely limits individual attention a teacher can give.

2. *Provide interaction.* Computers are not unique in their capabilities for individual instruction. In a sense, a book can do that. But computers can do something that even workbooks can only begin to do: interact with the student. A computer can tell immediately if a wrong response was given, in what way it is wrong, and what to do about it. It can keep track of the student's progress and "speak" to him or her by name. In other cases, a computer can play back what the student has created on a keyboard. It can retain and perform one part while the student plays another. Computers can render what a student played almost immediately in notation, even though the student hardly knows

notation. Computers can also tell a teacher when he or she has used up all the funds in the music account!

3. *Reduce technical barriers.* In the past many people were limited in expressing themselves musically because they could not play an instrument or put their musical thoughts down on paper. A lack of technical knowledge and skill was a nearly insurmountable obstacle between them and making or creating music. Computers have almost eliminated that obstacle by taking care of most of the technical aspects. A person can plunk out a tune with one finger, and then, through working with the computer, play it back in a variety of tempos, timbres, and accompaniments.

4. *Save time and effort.* Computers can accomplish tasks in a fraction of a second that would take a person minutes or even hours to do. One wonders what Bach and Brahms would have done had they been able to put their ideas into sound and notation as quickly as is possible with a computer and related equipment! And one doesn't have to be a Bach or a Brahms to appreciate the ability of computers to keep records; one computer file can replace at least five handmade card files. Furthermore, computer files are much easier to keep up to date.

MUSIC TEACHERS AND COMPUTERS

In the film *2001: A Space Odyssey* a computer named Hal gains control over everyone on the spaceship. While such science fiction makes for interesting reading and movies, it is far from reality. No computer is going to take control of a teaching situation. People create computers, write the programs that they follow, and decide when and if they will be used.

Teachers should think of computers as complementing their work, not competing with it. Computers can expand what a teacher is able to accomplish. For example, no teacher can work with every student individually for more than a moment or two. However, a teacher can assign a program to a student who needs extra help on a topic in music, and then the computer can handle that instruction of the student for that aspect of the course. The teacher, then, is free to help other students or work on something else. In a sense, a computer is a tool. Tools such as a hammer or a screwdriver help people build things. However, they must be used appropriately (a screwdriver isn't used to pound in a nail) and at the right time (a board isn't nailed before it is cut to size).

Tasks that can be taken over by computers should be. With all the work that music teachers could do for students, it is only sensible to let computers assume some of the burden, especially of the more routine aspects of the job. When this happens, teachers become no less important and needed; instead, they become more effective and efficient in their teaching and its related duties.

DEFINITIONS AND COMPUTER JARGON

As with any other area in education, computers have certain terms and words (jargon) that you will need to know in order to understand the computer and its uses. You probably remember the first time someone said "tritone" or "augmented sixth chord." Just as music theory has its own jargon, computers have their own as well.

Computer keyboard Much the same as a typewriter keyboard with the addition of some keys, for example, "apple" keys, left, right, up, and down arrow keys, escape, reset, keypads, and function keys. If you know how to type it will help, because the basic typewriter keys are the same on all systems.

Memory This is how much information the computer will hold. An Apple IIe comes with 128K. "K" represents 1024 bytes of memory. A byte can hold approximately 1 character, or byte, of data (like the letter "a"); therefore, 128K = 131,072 bytes of memory. The Apple IIGS comes with 528K; other systems come with "megabytes" of memory (read on).

Megabyte 1024 kilobytes, or approximately 1000K (two to the twentieth power), or approximately 1,000,000 bytes.

ROM (read-only memory) The information in this memory never changes. It includes functions that remain the same and cannot be destroyed when the computer is turned off or when different programs are used. ROM is similar to the memory in a pocket calculator, which will perform the function (e.g., square root) because that information is always in the memory.

RAM (random-access memory) (also known as read/write memory)   These commands and functions change from program to program. The user and programmer have control over changing these commands. RAM allows the user to store information and run programs.

Diskette or disk A 5¼-inch "floppy" disk used to store information/programs for later use. It can hold 143,360 bytes of information, or about 70 pages of text. A 3½-inch disk can store 800K (819,200 bytes, or 400 pages of text). A 3½-inch diskette although stored in hard plastic is still a "floppy" disk.

Hard disk A storage device permanently housed in a sealed drive that can hold the equivalent of dozens of 3½-inch disks. A 20- or 30-megabyte hard disk is typical.

DOS (disk operating system) DOS controls disk-related activities, and it is the reason why some computers are not compatible with other computers. They use different disk operating systems. Even within systems there are different disk operating systems.

Booting The process of putting DOS into internal memory or RAM so that you can use it. You may insert the disk (not a blank disk but one with DOS on it) into the disk drive and turn on the power. This is called a cold boot. Or you may boot a disk or DOS when the system is already on. This is called a warm boot.

Hardware Computer components that one must have to run and execute programs—keyboard, disk drive, monitor, printer. Sometimes disk drives and printers are called "peripherals."

Software Programs that are written for execution with the hardware. Programs are generally written on floppy disks.

Program The set of commands that execute a certain function or interaction. These can be written by the user, written for a specific piece of software, or adapted to the user's needs.

Computer-assisted instruction (CAI)   Computer programs that are either interactive or informational to help the student achieve a desired objective.

Digital The basic system of information that the computer uses to send and receive information. The mode of information is binary—that is, 1 and 0. In the Apple system there are eight binary bits to a byte of information, or eight 1's and 0's that make up the unique information for the computer. Languages are simply translators for the computer to digital code.

Interface A device to link peripherals to the computer or perform specific functions. In the Apple II system this is done by simply opening up the computer and putting interface cards into the proper slots. Typical interface devices are a printer interface to hook up a printer, a graphic interface to allow for pictures to be printed, and MIDI interface.

MIDI (musical instrument digital interface) A system that allows digital music information to be communicated between the computer and synthesizers and other peripheral devices. This process requires a MIDI interface card in the computer, which is explained in the Performance and Composition section. The uses of MIDI systems include sequencing (sound-on-sound recording to disk), musical performance, computer-assisted instruction (CAI) using a MIDI keyboard, and music printing.

COMPUTER-ASSISTED INSTRUCTION IN MUSIC

Research in music education has suggested that computer-assisted instruction is an effective mode of instruction, especially for "drill and practice." Drill and practice involves those types of learning skills that students learn at varying rates. Examples are lines and spaces, key signatures, chord recognition, and interval recognition. A considerable amount of ear-training software has also been developed. This section discusses a few basic programming techniques, followed by a review of some CAI software in music education.

Writing Your Own Programs

Although you do not have to be able to write instructional programs to run a computer or to use it in your teaching, there may be times when a specific task you want to teach cannot be found in an existing software package. What do you do then? You could take the idea to a software company—or you may be able to write it yourself with a few simple programming techniques. There is another advantage to having a knowledge of programming: You learn that the computer does only what it is told and realize that you have command over the computer rather than the instruction being totally controlled by the software.

A Few Preliminary Programming Definitions

BASIC (Beginners All-purpose Symbolic Instruction Code) A computer language that allows programming with English commands and converts them into binary code that the computer microprocessor understands.

Applesoft Apple's own version of BASIC. Every make of computer has its own slight differences in BASIC language.

Variable A symbol. It can be just a letter that represents a number such as X, or it can be a "string" that represents a word or a name like X$.

String A variable that is alphanumeric representing non-numbers such as names or words. Strings are always followed by $, for example, X$.

Line numbers All programs in BASIC use line numbers, and commands are executed in order of line numbers.

A Few BASIC System Commands

CATALOG   Lists all files on the diskette, and tells what language they are written in, the number of sectors used (256 bytes = 1 sector), and the name of the program.

LOAD   Loads a specific program from the disk into the computer's internal memory.

Example: LOAD MUSIC

LIST   Displays the program currently in memory line by line.

Example: LIST

SAVE   Saves the program currently in internal memory on the disk for later use.

Example: SAVE followed by name of the program

LOCK   Protects saved programs from being erased. If a program is saved with the same name as a previous program, the previous program will be erased and replaced by the new program if it is unlocked. LOCK prevents this possible accident. When catalogued on the Apple IIe or IIGS, locked programs will have an asterisk (*) next to them.

Example: LOCK HELLO

UNLOCK   Unlocks locked program.

Example: UNLOCK HELLO

Some BASIC/Applesoft Program Commands

NEW   Clears the internal memory to write a new program. This should be typed only when beginning a program because it erases previous programs from internal memory.

PRINT   Prints characters to the screen; words that are to be printed or exact character display must be enclosed in quotation marks.

Example: PRINT "YOUR NAME"

INPUT   Accepts the character or characters from the keyboard as a response from the person executing the program for future analysis.

IF/THEN   A conditional command. "If something happens then this will happen." A real-life example: "IF I put my hand in the fire THEN I will get burned." IF/THEN specifies the condition. Often it is used with other statements in BASIC:

Example: IF X = 1 THEN PRINT "CORRECT"

GOTO   Tells the computer to go directly to a specific line number. Disregards skipped lines.

REM   Performs no function except to help the programmer remember what and perhaps why he or she did something in a program.

Example: REM X is the variable for number of sharps

Writing a Simple BASIC Program

Every system has a unique way of initializing a blank diskette. A blank diskette cannot be written to or read from until you have initialized it into a format compatible with writing and reading BASIC commands. After you have done that, you are ready to write a program.

Suppose you were going to write a simple program to print your name and your name is Joe Smith. The following commands would execute that program:

```
NEW
10 PRINT "JOE SMITH"
20 END
```

The output of that program would appear as:

```
JOE SMITH
```

If you wanted to ask the user what his or her name was and to say "Hello" and their name, the following listing would execute that operation:

```
NEW
10 PRINT "WHAT IS YOUR NAME? TYPE IN YOUR NAME AND
PRESS RETURN"
20 INPUT N$
30 PRINT "HELLO" ;N$
40 END
```

If Joe Smith was our user, the output of that program would appear as:

```
WHAT IS YOUR NAME? TYPE IN YOUR NAME AND PRESS RETURN
```

[user types in his name as JOE SMITH]

```
HELLO JOE SMITH
```

Note: The reason you used N$ and not N for the name is because Joe Smith is a person's name, not a number. If you are using numbers for variables, you simply use a letter such as N or X.

What if you wanted to ask a student "How many sharps are in the key of G?" and see if he or she knew the right answer? The following program would execute that operation:

```
NEW
10 PRINT "HOW MANY SHARPS ARE IN THE KEY OF G?"
20 PRINT "PRESS A NUMBER AND HIT RETURN"
30 INPUT X
40 REM X REPRESENTS THE STUDENT'S RESPONSE OF HOW
MANY SHARPS
50 IF X = 1 THEN PRINT "CORRECT"
60 IF X <> 1 THEN PRINT "INCORRECT, TRY AGAIN":
PRINT:GOTO 10
70 END
```

Remember, the REM statement does not serve any programming function but allows you to "write yourself a note" within the program so that you won't forget what X means. The <> stands for "does not equal." You could say in this particular instance:

```
IF X > 1 THEN . . .
```

The output of this program would be the following if the student answered correctly:

```
HOW MANY SHARPS ARE IN THE KEY OF G?
PRESS A NUMBER AND HIT RETURN
1
CORRECT
```

The output of this program would be the following if the student got two incorrect answers and then answered correctly:

```
HOW MANY SHARPS ARE IN THE KEY OF G?
PRESS A NUMBER AND HIT RETURN
2
INCORRECT, TRY AGAIN

HOW MANY SHARPS ARE IN THE KEY OF G?
PRESS A NUMBER AND HIT RETURN
3
INCORRECT, TRY AGAIN

HOW MANY SHARPS ARE IN THE KEY OF G?
PRESS A NUMBER AND HIT RETURN
1
CORRECT
```

From these simple examples, you can see how easy it is to write a short instructional program using BASIC language. There are also access programs that allow you to incorporate sound with your programs. Lists of supplementary books and materials are included at the end of this chapter to give you additional information on programming techniques and applications. If you had computer courses when you were in middle and high school, this material on programming probably is familiar to you.

PUBLISHED INSTRUCTIONAL PROGRAMS

Since the early 1980s CAI programs have proliferated at a rapid rate. Software companies have consulted music educators to determine the instructional strategies of the programs. Two companies appear to have the majority of the music instructional software on the market today: Electronic Courseware Systems and *Micro-Music Software*—Temporal Acuity Products. Although other companies will be mentioned later, the following overview of instructional software is a guide to the libraries of these two software companies.

SELECTED COMPUTER-ASSISTED MUSIC INSTRUCTION PROGRAMS FOR THE APPLE COMPUTER

Programs Available from Micro Music Software—Temporal Acuity Products

Note: All programs in this section require a DAC board (digital analog converter) for the Apple IIe unless otherwise indicated. A DAC board is available from *Micro-Music* and allows for sound to be isolated through headphones. Programs with an asterisk (*) are available in Master Edition for Apple IIe, Apple IIGS (with or without a DAC board), or use with a MIDI synthesizer.

Program	Description
*Arnold	An ear-training program for tone recognition and melodic memory skills. Major melodies designed for third grade through adult. Difficulty increases with melody length, leaps, range, and tempo.
*Catch the Key	Part of Moore Music Series. Drill and practice in the recognition of key signatures. Game and tutor modes.
*Chord Mania	Designed for one or two players. Aural and/or visual. Student may choose drill parameters. All combinations of sonorities with inversions. Game format like "Beat the Clock."
*Chordella	Aural discrimination of triads and seventh chords.
*Composers and Their Works	Several levels are provided. Multiple-choice, recall, and spelling are all options. No DAC board required.
*Count-Me-Out	Rhythm counting program.
*A Decent Interval	Visual and aural identification of intervals.
*Diatonic Chords	Traditional chord dictation. Students begin with bass line, then soprano line, then chord and inversion. Covers diatonic triads, sevenths, and secondary dominants and inversions.
*Doremi	One to four notes of a major scale recognized by solfeggio syllables. Branches

Program	Description
	when student makes mistake. Third grade through university.
Drake Musical Aptitude Test	Allows diagnosis of musical aptitude (musical memory and rhythmic memory). Teachers may compare their students with national norms.
*Foreign Instrument Names	Same format as Composers and Their Works.
*General Music Terms	Same format as Composers and Their Works.
*Harmonious Dictator	Using figured bass symbols, student hears and responds to chord progressions and inversions. Game format. Starts with I–V and difficulty increases as student progresses with correct responses. Progress report provided at end of each session.
*Harmony	Harmonic dictation with figured bass symbols.
*Hearing Melodic Patterns	Melodic dictation in major and modes and treble and bass clef.
*Interval Mania	One or two players. Much like Chord Mania in game format. All intervals are utilized with student or teacher choosing intervals to be used in each practice session.
*Italian Terms	Same format as Composers and Their Works.
*Jazz Dictator	Identification of chord progressions in jazz style. Progresses sequentially through diatonic progressions, borrowed chords, and secondary dominants.
*Just Between Notes	Interval tutorial with aural, visual, and instructional exercises.
*Key Signature Drills	Aural-visual or just visual recognition. Student identifies keynote and mode.
*Melodious Dictator	Student hears and notates single-line melodies. Begins with two-note pattern with major and minor seconds and in-

Program	Description
	creases to seven-note pattern with all possible intervals. Student notates with keyboard and corresponding staff notes.
*Mode Drills	Recognition of five church modes. Any chromatic pitch may be the tonic. Incorrect responses are compared to correct ones. Student may instruct self by selecting specific modes.
Micro-Brass Series	Fingering program for trumpet, French horn, baritone, and tuba. Uses a valve simulator.
*Music Symbols	Same format as Composers and Their Works.
*Pick the Pitch	Part of the Moore Music Series. Recognition of notated pitches in different clefs and key signatures. Student chooses parameters and may choose game or tutorial format.
*Pitch Drills	Note-name drills for treble, bass, and grand staff. Also drills for transposing instruments.
*Rhythm Drills	Develops rhythmic memory with drills ranging from whole to sixteenth notes. Elementary school through college.
*Rhythmic Dictator	Systematically sequenced. Random-generated rhythms. Summary of student progress. Format similar to Harmonious and Melodious Dictators.
*Rhythm Machine	Aural and visual discrimination program of rhythms.
*Rhythm Write	Flash card design with students writing on paper.
*Scale Lab	Scales, intervals, and melodies with three 5¼-inch and one 3½-inch disks.
*Sebastian II	Error-detection program. Student identifies mistakes in aural melody from visual representation. Errors of rhythm, pitch, and tempo. Fourth grade through college. Option for teacher to create own melodies for error detection.

Program	Description
*Sir William Wrong-Note	Error detection of single note in single chord. Student identifies aurally the part that was different from visual representation and then the exact wrong pitch. User may select types of chords.
*Sketch the Scale	Writing of all scales (major, minor, chromatic, pentatonic) in all keys and clefs.
*Standard Instrument Names	Same format as Composers and Their Works.
*Theory Sampler	Five programs in one. Various sequential theory programs.

Programs Available from Electronic Courseware Systems

Note: Programs with an asterisk (*) are also available for IBM-compatible systems. Programs that say MIDI are available for use with a MIDI-compatible keyboard for input and sound.

Program	Description
*Aural Skills Trainer	Identification of intervals and chords. Student record keeping included.
*Clef Notes	Note identification in treble, alto, tenor, and bass clef.
*Double-Reed Fingerings	Addresses specific fingering problems and unique problems with double-reed instruments. Student record keeping included.
Ear Challenger	Melodic memory game. Aural-visual. Student must remember a series of pitches.
*Early Music Skills	Music-reading skills such as lines and spaces, steps, skips. MIDI.
*Elements of Music	Music notation for children through adults. Major and minor keys and notes from staff and keyboard. Tests, progress reports, and instructor file.
*Functional Harmony: Basic Chords	Disks 1 through 4 provide tutorials in harmonic analysis from major and mi-

Program	Description
	nor keys in root position to secondary dominants and borrowed and altered chords.
*Hear Today . . . Play Tomorrow	Four sections: "Find That Tune," "Ear-Training Skills," "Melodic Dictation," and "Descending/Ascending Intervals." All are multilevel with appropriate branching and student record keeping.
*Keyboard Tutor	May be used with or without a MIDI keyboard. Matches notes to keys and keys to notes; keys; whole steps and half steps. MIDI.
*Listen!	Interval and chord recognition and perception. Reinforcement provided. Score page also utilized.
*Music Appreciation: A Study Guide	Correlated to *Music Through Experience*. Both music terminology and music history are quizzed and reviewed.
*Music Composer Quiz	Multiple-choice and random questions with ability for instructor to create own questions.
*Music History Review: Composers	Reviews Renaissance to twentieth century and is correlated to *History of Western Music* by Grout and Palisca.
Music Flash Cards	Disk 1—notes, rhythm values, and equivalents; Disk 2—major and minor scales, modal scales, and key signatures; Disk 3—intervals and basic chords. Evaluation at end. Drill and practice format.
*Music Terminology	Five separate programs (Glossary, Categories, True/False, Multiple Choice, and Fill-In) teach and assess knowledge of 100 music terms.
*Musical Stairs	Interval identification in treble and bass clef. Uses piano keyboard. Designed for younger students.
*Note Speller	Teaches names of notes in treble and bass clef. Words are created four to seven letters in length. Scoring based on time required for recognition.

Program	Description
*Patterns in Pitch	Companion to Patterns in Rhythm. Two parts, composer and dictator. Major and minor keys employed.
*Patterns in Rhythm	Designed to increase rhythmic memory by composing and dictating rhythms. Student record keeping included.
*Perspectives in Music History	Music history data and correlations between 1400 and present with graph and quizzes.
*Playing and Reading Music	Three-disk set to teach keyboard reading and playing skills. MIDI.
*Tap-It	Teaches beat and tempo as students tap to rhythm patterns.
*Tune-It II	A pitch-matching program using a stringed instrument representation. Student record keeping included.
*12-Bar Tunesmith	Uses major scale to help young children compose and play simple melodies.
*Spell and Define	Teacher may input words and definitions for student drills.
*Super Challenger	Pitch-memory program utilizing major, minor, and chromatic scales. MIDI.

Programs Available from Alfred Publishing Company

Program	Description
Basic Band Computer Tutor	Correlated to *Alfred's Basic Band Method.* Offers individualized instruction on common band instruments.
Basic Piano Theory Software I and II	Correlated to *Alfred's Basic Piano Theory.* MIDI compatible.
Music Made Easy	Self-teaching approach to music fundamentals. Diskette with workbook.
Practical Music Theory	Three volumes of music theory tutorials. Sequenced from easy to advanced. Spiral-bound workbook and two diskettes for each volume.
Music Achievement Series	Computer testing series that tests the mastery of the concepts in the Practical

Program	*Description*
	Music Theory program. May also be used as a diagnostic tool. Disks store student data for up to fifty students.

As a music educator, you should be careful in your software selection and purchases. You must consider which systems are available in your school. If your school is equipped with all IBM equipment and that is what is available to you for use, examine software available for that system. If Apple systems are available, contact the person in charge of the computer lab (usually a staff person has been appointed) and find out the availability of the lab for your use. Many teachers have found that a computer in their room "on loan" is of more use than taking a whole class to the lab.

Software companies generally have a means for teachers to preview programs before buying them. Because of the limited budgets that music teachers always seem to have, a purchase of the wrong computer software would be a serious mistake. Seek out funds or grants available to school systems for instructional technology. If only the math and science teachers request such funds, music probably will not be considered in the request. Music teachers must make their budgetary needs known.

MUSICAL PERFORMANCE AND COMPOSITION WITH COMPUTERS

MIDI—Musical Instrument Digital Interface

Computers are being used increasingly by music educators and students in the areas of performance and composition. Because the musical information in synthesizers is processed digitally and computers translate words or music into digital information, it is logical that the two systems would eventually link together. An early attempt at this was the Passport Designs Soundchaser system, which was a four- or five-octave keyboard interfaced with the Apple II computer and a large interface card that held the synthesizer information. With the rapid growth in synthesizer use and production, a standard communication device was needed to link any synthesizer to the computer without having a different linkup device for each synthesizer. Hence, MIDI (Musical Instrument Digital Interface) was developed by the industry as a standard way of communicating information about musical "events" such as note, volume, timbre, expression, and rhythm to and from the synthesizer to the computer and among synthesizers.

Since its inception in the early 1980s, MIDI has allowed musicians to use the computer and synthesizers for performance and composition in ways that were only dreamed of before. A MIDI interface is the piece of hardware needed to link a MIDI-compatible keyboard to a particular computer system or another MIDI keyboard. A MIDI keyboard or synthesizer has one to three MIDI input plugs located on the back of the synthesizer. The inputs are labeled "MIDI In," "MIDI Out," and "MIDI Thru." Although the same synthesizer may be "MIDI'd" to different computer systems, you must purchase a MIDI interface for your particular system. For example, an Apple IIe MIDI interface card will not operate on an IBM or a Macintosh. This point may seem trivial, but purchasing the wrong interface card for a system could be a costly mistake.

Sequencing

Using the MIDI system, it is possible for you to play in several "tracks" (or parts) separately, and then to play them back all at the same time using the synthesizer and computer, much like a multitrack tape recorder. This is called *sequencing*. Using software like *Master Tracks* with the Apple (or *Professional Performer* for the Macintosh, or *Texture* for the IBM), you could record up to sixteen tracks of sound-on-sound.

This type of sequencing and the sound output may be limited by the synthesizer itself. For example, if you have a synthesizer that has many different preset sounds, yet will only play one at a time, you can enter your tracks with different sounds. However, when you play all of your tracks back at once, you will hear only the sound that is "on board" at that time. If you wanted four pianos that would be fine, but if you wanted brass, strings, and percussion, you would need a synthesizer or sound module capable of playing several voices at the same time. This capability is called "multitimbral."

Many inexpensive synthesizers now have eight-voice multitimbral output. What does that mean? Generally, it means that you are limited to eight vertical events simultaneously. For example, if you play five notes with the piano sound, you have three sounds available over the rest of your tracks. However, technology is always changing. Now many dedicated synthesizers (synthesizers without keyboards, only used to access sounds) have thirty-two voice capability with eight timbres. In other words, you can have thirty-two vertical events utilizing up to eight different timbres.

One of the biggest advantages of computers for secondary-school music educators is the use of sequencing in creating music. No longer are students limited by their pianistic skills. They can actually input their "tunes" and chords very, very slowly. Once the tunes are in, they can be played back at whatever tempo is desired. Unlike tape recorders, there is no change in pitch when the tempo is changed on a computer. If you slow a tape recorder down to half the speed, pitches will sound one octave lower. Because pitch and tempo are recorded on the computer as two separate pieces of information, you hear the pitches in the correct octave regardless of tempo. The user also has the ability to input tunes in simple keys and transpose the playback to more difficult keys. This does not affect the tempo because pitch and tempo are two separate pieces of information.

Converting Sequences to Notation

With the Apple II systems, converting sequences to notation may not be an easy task, and the end product may not be very good. With *Master Tracks*, software called *Polywriter* and *Polywriter Utilities* can be used to convert sequences to notation. More desirable software is the *Professional Performer* and *Professional Composer* system for the Macintosh. Converting from sequences with this software provides the desired notation with more control over output.

Notation and Composition

Although musical notation is possible with the Apple II system, the best systems for professional notation are the Macintosh and the IBM. Using the *Professional Composer* system for the Macintosh or *Finale* from CODA Music Software, copy-ready manuscript is quick and relatively easy to learn. Similar output is possible with *Music Printer Plus* from Temporal Acuity Products, created for the IBM. An added feature of *Music Printer Plus* is that it reads and plays through the MIDI interface directly from notation. If one writes a crescendo or ritardando, these notations can be realized on playback, as will the notes.

The *FINALE* program has been billed as a second-generation sequencing and notation program. The transition from sequence to notation is the least cumbersome of any system yet to enter the market.

MUSIC PROGRAMMING, COMPOSITION, AND PRINTING SYSTEMS

Programs Available from Micro-Music Software— *Temporal Acuity Products*

Program	*Description*
BASMUSIC	Allows single-line melodies to be input into programs written in BASIC for use with the DAC board.
Designing Computer-Based Instruction for the Arts	For the serious student/teacher interested in designing courseware for the arts, especially music using the Apple IIe. All parameters of instruction, record keeping, graphics, and sound generation are addressed.
Envelope Construction	Excellent program for learning and understanding timbre and acoustics. Allows manipulation of time, amplitude,

Program	Description
	and harmonic context. Each harmonic is displayed with a three-dimensional graph. May be used to produce sound with Envelope Shaper program.
Envelope Shaper	Used to orchestrate music composed with Music Composer. Various instrument sounds, tempos, octaves, and transposition are possible.
Music Composer	Allows you to compose, play, display, enter, build, edit, save, and hear music in four voices through the use of the DAC board.
Music Printer	A quality music printing program that allows notation in single or grand staff plus lyrics. Has transposition, full scores, and complete editing capabilities. Copy-ready dot matrix for the Apple IIe or IIGS.
Music Printer Plus	Desktop music publishing for the IBM utilizing the IBM Music Feature Card. Notes may be entered with the IBM mouse or from a MIDI keyboard. Compositions may then be played back via MIDI.

Programs Available from Passport Designs

Program	Description
Passport MIDI Pro Interface	This is the MIDI card required for the Apple IIe computer. Also available for the Apple IIe, IIGS, and Commodore 64. Includes tape and drum sync for using multitrack tape recorders and drum machines.
Master Tracks Pro	A sequencing (sound-on-sound) program for the Apple IIe series. All sequencing and editing techniques are available.
Polywriter	Allows you to write music from the MIDI keyboard.

Program	Description
Polywriter Utilities	Allows you to print the sequences written with Master Tracks Pro. You need this to convert sequences to notation with Polywriter.

Programs Available from Mark of the Unicorn

Program	Description
Professional Composer	A complete music-writing program for the Macintosh system. Desktop music publishing. Any format from single line to orchestral score. Parts may be transposed, extracted, and played with a few keystrokes. Input is from the computer keyboard. Can be converted to Professional Performer.
Professional Performer	Sixteen-track sequencer for the Macintosh. Complete control over all facets of recording. Easily converts sequences to notation.

Program Available from CODA Music Software

Program	Description
Finale	A high-level (and somewhat higher priced) performance/sequence software package. Conversion from sequences to notation is done almost automatically.

MANAGERIAL USES WITH COMPUTERS

John Bradley, choral teacher at New Hope High School, begins the year with the following tasks:

1. He needs to write to each of his choir parents telling them of the students' schedules, programs, concerts, festivals, and fund-raising events for the entire year.

2. He needs to update his music library. His files are not in order. He needs to have an alphabetical listing of all his music by title and composer. He also needs them separated by style period and by voice classification. All the music is in file cabinets only arranged alphabetically by composer.

3. He needs to redo his choir robe inventory. Every time someone checks out a stole or robe it takes too much time to find the check-out card and erase or write over the previous person's name.

4. His choir parents and students are going to have to have at least one fund-raising project to fund their trip to a festival this year. He does not want to take class time to figure each student's account, daily totals, and weekly reports to the office.

When John Bradley anticipates all of these managerial duties before the year even begins, it is enough to make him (a) demand a secretary or (b) wonder why he went into teaching. It is true: Managerial and organizational tasks of secondary music teachers have been ever-increasing and it seems, unending. Any and all of the above four tasks that John is faced with are not uncommon for music teachers, not to mention typing and preparing programs and daily lesson plans.

What is a music teacher to do? The computer is a valuable time-saving tool for today's music educator. Each one of John's tasks may be assisted by the use of computers.

Word Processing

The computer can assist John with task #1 above using a procedure called *word processing*. As many of you already may know, this is a system that allows you to write letters and programs and to see them on a computer monitor or screen before they are printed on paper. This allows you to correct mistakes in the letter before they are printed in final copy.

Word processing also allows you to delete large blocks of text ("I really don't need to say all of that to my choir parents, but how do I take it out?"), move blocks of text ("I should have put all of the dates right up front, not at the end!"), correct misspelled words ("I spelled 'received' wrong every time. Do I have to go back and change each one?"), and personalize each letter of a form letter ("I don't want it to say 'Dear Parent:' on every letter. The letters should say 'Dear Mr. and Mrs. Petterson,' 'Dear Mr. and Mrs. Jones,' etc."). With some word processing programs, it is possible to merge data base files with your word processing files so that each letter is automatically personalized.

There are generally two types of printing available for word processing: dot matrix and letter quality. Dot-matrix printing produces letters and symbols through a series of tiny dots. This type of printing is also capable of producing graphics or pictures. Letter-quality printing is essentially connecting an electric typewriter to a computer. The print is determined by the particular "daisy wheel" printing font or type selected. On newer dot-matrix printers there is usually a "near letter quality" selector that compresses the dots even tighter or has the printer make two passes at each character. A third type of printer is now available for all computer systems: laser printers. Although expensive, they produce publishable-quality printing.

Data Base

The second and third tasks that John Bradley finds himself faced with may be assisted by the computer through a process called *data base*. This is a system that allows the user to input information and to sort, catalog, and retrieve that information by a number of different means. If John wanted to set up his choral music by all of the searching parameters that he needs, he would have to have a separate card catalog for retrieving his music by (1) composer, (2) title, (3) style, and (4) voice classification. That's four separate card catalogs! By inputting the information to the data base in the following manner, he can retrieve any or all pieces of music by any combination of the categories and even alphabetize any of the categories.

Sample Choral Music Data Base Fields or Categories

Title:

Composer:

Arranger:

Voicing:

Style period:

Date of Purchase:

Year performed:

Season:

Copies:

By looking at these categories, you can see the amount of information one may retrieve and imagine the amount of time saved in retrieval. Some possibilities for retrieval and listings include:

1. Alphabetize by title
2. Alphabetize by composer
3. All SATB music alphabetized by title or composer
4. All music purchased since 1980
5. All music purchased before 1955
6. All Baroque Christmas music for SATB voices

Retrieval and listing of information in these and other ways can be a real time-saver for beginning the year, for performing music throughout the year, and for end-of-the-year inventory. With data bases, listings and reports may be printed out at any time. A word to the wise: Put in all categories you think you will need before inputting the information for each entry. Many data base programs do not allow you to add a category after information has been put into those categories without deleting all information.

Spreadsheet

It would be a joy if John Bradley and other music teachers never had to raise money for trips or equipment. The truth is that you will be lucky if you don't have to raise some funds. Better to be prepared and try to avoid it than to find out you have to raise money without ever having thought about it. *Spreadsheet* is a process using the computer that allows you to calculate, recalculate, and keep track of individual items automatically. It is designed for corporations and small businesses to keep track of and project their profits and losses. Because spreadsheet is more difficult to learn than data base, it will suffice here to give just a few of the options that would be available to John with a simple spreadsheet program.

First, he (or an assistant or a volunteer) could keep track of each student's daily totals on sales. Then, at the push of a button, the office can be given a printed account of how much money was turned in that day, that week, and what is left to sell.

The computer can save you time in these and other managerial areas. In fact, after you have used a computer once, you will wonder how you ever managed without it! Keep in mind, however, that you should never take instructional time for managerial tasks, especially not for fund raising.

Word processing, data base, and spreadsheet are utilized with all computer systems. The nice feature is that once you learn word processing (and data base and spreadsheet) with one system, it is much easier to go to another system, much like learning one musical instrument in the brass or woodwind family and then learning another instrument in the same family.

Word Processing Programs

Note: All programs commercially available.

Program	Description
Appleworks	Part of the Appleworks trilogy (Word Processor, Data Base, Spreadsheet). A highly versatile word processor. Easy to understand and use.
Magic Window II	A good program once it's learned. Sometimes limited in features.
Microsoft Word	The state-of-the art word processor for the Macintosh. Every conceivable word processing option.
PFS:Write	Features all of the advantages of an expensive word processor, yet in the moderate price range. Easy to use.

Data Base and Spreadsheet Programs

Note: All programs commercially available.

Program	Description
Appleworks	A simple-to-use data base and spreadsheet. Not the most powerful, but has many nice features. Power may be increased by increasing to 512K on Apple IIGS. Also has Appleworks word processor. Also, an Appleworks GS version is available, which requires 1.25 megabytes.
Apple Gradebook	A complete grading system. Very adaptable. Automatically calculates class averages and standard deviations. Special end-of-term features. Accounts for different weights of tests.
DB Master	A very powerful program. Somewhat complicated yet manageable after the user becomes familiar with the program.
PFS:File	An easy data base with excellent capacity. A good generic data base.

Programs Available from Micro-Music Software— Temporal Acuity Products

Program	Description
Octavo Filing System	Files choral music. Parameters include season, voice ranges, and level of difficulties.
The Uniform Master	Band-uniform management system. Two hundred uniform capacity. Data for five uniform components. Assigns according to height, weight, and sex. Nine printout formats provided.

Program Available from Electronic Courseware Systems

Program	Description
Computerized Gradebook	All the features described in the two previous programs but in addition will

Program   *Description*

assign grades. Also includes password
security. Up to fifty names with ten assignments for each class.

OTHER TECHNOLOGICAL AIDS

Marching-Band Show Design with the Computer

An area that has seen increasing use of the computer by instrumental music teachers
is the writing of marching-band shows. Although there continues to be value in
sketching out shows with "grid" paper and perhaps colored pins for different
sections, the computer has proven to be a time-saver for today's instrumental
music teacher. The two computers best suited for this purpose appear to be the
IBM and Macintosh systems. Programs such as ADVANTAGE Showare (for Macintosh) and the PYWARE Charting Aid System (for Apple and IBM) allow the
user to plot players, use predesigned forms, mirror the band, see from the stands,
watch the band actually move (known as "flow"), and print the shows for the
entire band, section, or individual player.

Two Electronic Devices

Although they are not computers but use computer technology, two other technological devices should be mentioned. They are the Pitch Master and Tap Master
from Temporal Acuity Products. The Tap Master is a device to teach rhythmic
sight reading. It comes with a series of tapes from elementary to advanced levels.
The intermediate tapes are suggested for starting at the middle or high school
level; starting with the beginning tapes is not necessary. Students tap their responses
on the Tap Master, and their scores are recorded on a digital readout.

The Pitch Master is a sight-singing tool. The student sings into a microphone
along with recorded music, and the device keeps track of right and wrong notes.
As the student sings correct pitches, a reinforcing tone is heard. There are three
sets of tapes in sequential order, and teachers may also make their own tapes to
meet individual curricular needs.

Purchasing the "Right" Computer

Certainly, at this writing the Apple II (IIe and IIGS) computer has become the
instructional or educational machine, while the IBM and Macintosh have become
the office and desktop publishing systems respectively. In music, the Apple II
series has the largest share of the computer-assisted instruction software. However,
the IBM and Macintosh computers have considerable software for music printing

and performance systems as well as their managerial systems. As stated earlier, the majority of computer software for instruction is still written for the Apple II series computers. There are at least two reasons for this: (1) The Apple II was the first home computer and proliferated very quickly in the early 1980s. (2) The Apple II series (with the exception of the IIC) allows for the installation and removal of interface cards that are integrated circuits with computer chips to generate sound, graphics, and other special applications.

The Macintosh computer has become the graphics and desktop publishing machine, and its function for music printing and sound generation has been explored by music software companies. Although the IBM has become the office machine, it has also found many uses in music for music printing, sequencing, and file management. Some instructional software is available for both the Apple and IBM systems.

You must be judicious in purchasing hardware (and software) so that you and your school purchase equipment that will best meet your needs. "Purchasing a computer is like choosing a stereo system: You will need to do lots of research and watch many demonstrations before you can make an appropriate selection" (Rudolph, 1989, p. 63). Which system should you buy? The answer depends on what your computer uses will be.

With the information in this chapter (and, it is hoped, a computers in music education course), you should have some answers to the question "How will I implement the use of computers in my music teaching?" Computers can never replace your music teaching, but they can be used as an effective tool to assist your teaching. As Paul Lehman states, "Any teacher who can be replaced by a computer should be" (1986, p. 79).

The following are some suggested uses in your secondary music classroom:

1. *For slow learners.* Perhaps they don't grasp a concept about rhythm, key signatures, or major and minor chords. Outside class instruction with an appropriate CAI program may be of great benefit for these students and keep them from feeling lost.

2. *For very able students.* These students may be bored easily if you teach to the "middle" of the class. Having a MIDI setup in a practice room would allow them to be creative in composition or sound synthesis.

3. *In middle or high school general music.* The students can create, notate, and perform class compositions. In this way a more comprehensive approach to musical concepts is possible.

4. *In high school music theory class.* Transcriptions of compositions to MIDI sequences can also assist the areas of ear training and notation.

5. *For student assistants* to help with writing program notes using the word processor. They can submit them to you for the winning program design.

6. *In piano lab.* A large monitor can be used to teach notes or chords on the keyboard using MIDI instructional programs. The class can answer questions individually by inputting the answers on the MIDI keyboard.

As computer technology increases, many new uses of computers in music education will undoubtedly be explored. Because technology and computers are constantly changing, it is recommended that this chapter serve as a springboard for continued learning in this area. As you work with computers, you will find your own uses of computers to help you teach more effectively and perhaps save time with managerial tasks so that you have more time for other types of instruction. You should continue to keep abreast of music technology through workshops and classes and to use computers as an effective means to becoming a better music educator.

Questions   1.   Given John Bradley's need to inventory his choir robes (see task #3, p. 312), how would you design a data base for the robes? What search parameters would be necessary?

2.   If you had to decide now what your first music teaching job would be in a secondary school, what computer and software would be best suited to that situation? In what five specific ways can the computer help you do your job more effectively?

3.   If you wanted to use computers for your music classes, what are four strategies you could use to make a computer or computers available to the students? These strategies could include cooperative efforts with your fellow teachers, administrators, district music supervisor, and booster organizations.

Projects   1.   Based on the information in the section on data base, design and structure a data base for band-instrument inventory. Include all necessary fields and at least six ways you could search and list information.

2.   Write a lesson plan or unit plan for using a MIDI setup and computer to teach creative composition to a high school general music class. Include a listing of the necessary MIDI equipment and software.

3.   On page 317, six specific uses of computers in secondary music classes are suggested. Write four more, and then share these ideas with other members of the class.

Resources   ADVANTAGE Showare
476 Severn Way, Suite A
Lexington, KY 40503
Phone: 606-276-1113

Alfred Publishing Company, Inc.
1535 Morrison Street
P.O. Box 5964
Sherman Oaks, CA 91413

CODA Software
Box 448
Owatonna, MN 55060

Electronic Courseware Systems, Inc.
1210 Lancaster Drive
Champaign, IL 61821

Electronic Musician (Published monthly)
6400 Hollis Street #12
Emeryville, CA 94608

Keyboard Magazine (Published monthly)
20085 Stevens Creek Road
Cupertino, CA 95014

Maestro Music, Inc.
2403 San Mateo N.E., Suite P-12
Albuquerque, NM 97110

Mark of the Unicorn
222 Third Street
Cambridge, MA 02142

Micro-Music Software, Temporal Acuity
Products, Inc.
Building 1, Suite 200, 300
120th Avenue N.E.
Bellevue, WA 98005

Music Systems for Learning, Inc.
311 East 38th Street, Suite 20C
New York, NY 10016

Passport Designs
625 Miramontes
Half Moon Bay, CA 94019

Pygraphics
P.O. Box 639
Grapevine, TX 76051
Phone: 1-800-222-7536

Technology for Teaching: Column appears
every month in *Music Educators Journal*;
published by MENC.

Suggested Readings

Blackman, J. M. "The MIDI Potential." *Music Educators Journal,* 73, no. 4 (1986): 29.

Chopp, J. M. "The Computer: Integrating Technology with Education." *Music Educators Journal,* 73, no. 4 (1986): 22–25.

Diehl, N. C. "Computer-Assisted Instruction and Instrumental Music: Implications for Teaching and Research." *Journal of Research in Music Education,* 19, no. 3 (1971): 299–306.

Hair, H. I. "Teaching Music with the Computer: Guidelines for Teachers." *UPDATE: The Applications of Research in Music Education,* 3, no. 2 (1985): 9–12.

Hofstetter, F. T. "GUIDO: An Interactive Computer-Based System for Improvement of Instruction and Research in Ear Training." *Journal of Computer-Based Instruction,* 1, no. 4 (1975): 100.

————— · *Computer Literacy for Musicians.* Englewood Cliffs, N.J.: Prentice-Hall, 1988.

McGreer, D. M. "The Research Literature in Computer-Assisted Instruction." *UPDATE: The Applications of Research in Music Education,* 3, no. 1 (1984): 12–15.

Moog, R. "M.I.D.I. (Musical Instrument Digital Interface)—What It Is, What It Means to You." *Keyboard Magazine,* July 1983, pp. 19–25.

Peters, G. D. "Vibrato via Video." *Electronic Education,* 5, no. 2 (1985): 14–15.

Placek, R. W. "Choosing the Best Software for Your Class." *Music Educators Journal,* 72, no. 1 (1985): 49–53.

Robinson, R. L. "Uses of Computers in Music Education: Past, Present, and Future." *UPDATE: The Applications of Research in Music Education,* 5, no. 2 (1987): 12–16.

Rudolph, T. E. *Music and the Apple II: Applications for Music Education, Composition, and Performance.* Drexel Hill, Penn.: Unsinn Publications, 1984.

Shrader, D. L. "Microcomputer-Based Teaching." *College Music Society,* 21, no. 2 (1981): 27–36.

Strausbaugh, W. G., and W. R. Higgins. *Techniques of Applesoft Programming.* Scottsdale, Ariz.: Gorsuch Scarisbrick Publishers, 1985.

Wittlich, G. E., J. W. Schaffer, and L. R. Babb. *Microcomputers and Music.* Englewood Cliffs, N.J.: Prentice-Hall, 1986.

References

Choate, R. A., ed. *Documentary Report of the Tanglewood Symposium.* Washington, D.C.: Music Educators National Conference, 1968.

Diehl, N. C., and R. E. Radocy. "Computer-Assisted Instruction: Potential for Instrumental Music Education." *Bulletin of the Council for Research in Music Education,* 15 (1969): 1–7.

Kuhn, W. E., and R. Allvin. "Computer-Assisted Teaching: A New Approach to Research in Music." *Bulletin of the Council for Research in Music Education,* 11 (1967): 1–13.

Lehman, P. R. "The Last Word: To Explain in a Thousand Ways." *Music Educators Journal,* 72, no. 6 (1986): 79–80.

Rudolph, T. E. "Technology for Teaching: Selecting a Personal Computer." *Music Educators Journal,* 76, no. 1 (1989): 63–66.

PART 4

To Whom: The Students

So far in this book the questions "why," "what," and "how" have each been the topic of one or more chapters. A fourth essential question in the teaching process is, "Who is being taught?" The special interest of this book is the student in secondary school—the teenager. "To whom" concerns teenagers and their characteristics, and it is the subject of Chapter 15. Closely related to the matter of understanding adolescents is managing classes of adolescents. Chapter 16 suggests methods for doing this. ⚐

CHAPTER 15

Teenagers and Music

The problems of today's youth have not suffered from lack of news coverage. In fact, the problems have often been blown up out of proportion to their prevalence (Bandura, 1971, p. 194). Teachers and parents often find discussions about youth contradictory, inconclusive, or not applicable to the specific questions they encounter.

What do music teachers need to understand about adolescents, their motivation, their interests, and their physical and social development?

TEENAGE PROBLEM AREAS

The main area of difficulty for teenagers is the *transition from childhood to adulthood*. This "betwixt and between" situation is a trying time because they are unsure where they stand in relation to these two stages of life, and adults (teachers included) are never sure which form the teenagers' actions will take. This situation has several consequences. One is that most teenagers adopt contradictory views. They reject and accept the adult world—at the same time.

The tensions and uncertainties of teenagers' in-between status encourage reliance on peers, which in some cases is greater than their dependence on parents. The need for acceptance by one's peers is very strong during adolescence and accounts for the fact that teenagers conform to fads in dress, grooming, and behavior, even when they don't particularly like or agree with these fads. Joining an exclusive club or gang is appealing because such groups afford a sense of security.

The importance of peer acceptance naturally causes tension between adolescents and adults. Sometimes parents feel helpless to exercise any guidance, especially when confronted with the declaration that "everybody does it." Teenagers generally do not even want to be singled out, because this is a form of separation from their peers. It partially explains why teenagers do not appreciate students who try too hard to win a teacher's approval.

Involved with the process of becoming an adult is the *development of a self-image.* By early adolescence young people become aware that they are individuals with their own personality. The ability to mentally stand off and ask "Who am I?" develops during these years. And so does much sensitivity about appearance and capabilities, which in turn encourages tension.

Adolescents are confronted with new social situations, especially as they learn to get along with members of the opposite sex. The *emergence of sexual desires and feelings* is another powerful and often bewildering force that occurs during adolescence.

CONDITIONS AGGRAVATING ADOLESCENT ADJUSTMENT

Several conditions in contemporary American society make a smooth transition from childhood to adulthood more difficult. One is that adolescence in a highly developed society lasts far longer than it does in simpler societies. In New Guinea, for example, a ceremony is conducted at the advent of puberty. Before the ceremony the person is a child, and after it, he or she is suddenly formally an adult. There is no in-between stage. Such a clear-cut definition is not possible in civilizations generally requiring a high level of education for widely different and complex jobs, ranging from replacing an automobile transmission to interpreting tax laws. Young persons who are physically grown must still live for years in a state of dependency on their parents and society. It is not surprising that the situation sometimes rankles both adolescents and adults. The delayed assumption of responsibilities also postpones marriage for many years after the development of sexual desires and this frustration intensifies the problem of adjustment.

Another aggravating factor in adolescent development is the pluralistic roles of male and female in American society. For example, "woman's place is in the home" was at one time, by consensus, an accurate description of a woman's role. Today this belief is more the exception than the rule. A young woman can choose from a wide variety of roles. In fact, the role and influence of the family have diminished in contemporary American society. Clearly defined social guides are also lacking in many other areas—sex, substance use, religious belief and practice, economic well-being, and so on.

A third aggravating force is society's mixed concept of adolescents. Some adults perceive young people as primarily pleasure seeking, while others think of them as violence-prone, in need of firm control and discipline. Some see the giggling, awkward, but good-hearted youngster depicted in the movies and on radio during the 1930s and 1940s. Still other adults, perhaps to compensate for their own aging in a culture that greatly values physical beauty and youthful vigor, admire everything youthful and ascribe to adolescents their having the purest and wisest of insights, motives, and understanding, even of life's most complex problems. The fact that none of these stereotypes is true of more than a small minority of teenagers has not prevented people from holding such views. Unfortunately, expecting trouble from teenagers encourages a self-fulfilling prophecy. So pervasive is the expectation of trouble that one adolescent psychologist reports:

> *I have often been struck by the fact that most parents, who are experiencing positive and rewarding relationships with their preadolescent children, are, nevertheless, waiting apprehensively and bracing themselves for the stormy adolescent period. Such vigilance can very easily create a small turbulence at least. When the prophesied storm fails to materialize, many parents begin to entertain doubts about the normality of their youngster's social development (Bandura, 1971, p. 196).*

Finally, the adolescent is affected by all the social and world problems that affect adults—unemployment, racial tension, international conflict, pollution of the environment, substance abuse, and the changing mores relating to sex and marriage.

The Culturally Disadvantaged Adolescent

Research in the area of social and ethnic minorities becomes dated rapidly. What was true thirty years ago of children of East European immigrants is not very applicable to the black or Hispanic students of today. The recent tendency of some persons to view almost everything in life from a racial standpoint presents the schools and society with problems of unprecedented complexity and seriousness. If they are to help the culturally disadvantaged student, music teachers should be familiar with the most objective and rational scholarly works on how best to educate students who are not middle class and white.

Several points need to be kept in mind about culturally disadvantaged students. First, such students are often not *just* from a lower socioeconomic group or *just* from a broken home. They often bear multiple disadvantages, two of the most common being poor health and a low level of aspiration. Often it is the combination of difficult circumstances that causes students to fail in school or become social problems.

Second, it is reassuring to realize that many culturally disadvantaged students eventually lead happy and productive lives. It is only a small percentage who commit serious crimes or who give up in their attempt to function within society.

Third, the disadvantaged teenager thinks more in terms of a person-to-person relationship with teachers and less in terms of the total school and its curriculum.

Finally, disadvantaged students come from all races and areas. Many such students are black, many are native American, many are Hispanic, and many are white. As many disadvantaged people live in the rural areas as live in the cities. Many disadvantaged students reside in the southern states, but every region has such students.

Admittedly, attempts to generalize about people are never true for all persons in a classification, but valid generalizations contain enough fact to be helpful if not treated as stereotypes. Disadvantaged students often exhibit the following tendencies: They find it harder to adapt to the routine of school life (being on time, for example), find it more difficult to learn, are less able to handle abstractions, have a shorter attention span, are less verbally able, lack curiosity, have a limited range of experience, and tend to live for the moment with little thought for the future (Lindgren and Suter, 1985, pp. 109–15). Some of these characteristics affect what these students will do in music. For example, they are usually less likely to read music, to understand abstractions, and to persevere in learning the music for a program that is scheduled well in the future.

There are some advantages—and certainly some compensations—when teaching disadvantaged students. Because these students have fewer material comforts and enriching out-of-school activities, music usually means more to them. It is not just another nice activity that competes with ballet lessons and summer trips, as it is to some upper-middle-class students. Furthermore, the "rags to riches" experience of many popular performers provides motivation for many disadvantaged teenagers. And no music teacher should overlook the rich ethnic music background of these students. Although no music curriculum should be confined to a particular type of music, no music teacher should ignore (or disparage!) the richness that ethic types of music add to American culture.

The Teacher's Role in Adolescent Adjustment

Understanding teenagers' nature may not solve all the problems that arise, but if it makes teachers more patient and sympathetic, that attitude in itself often leads to improved learning in the students. Understanding adolescent psychology can help focus attention on the real reasons for students' actions, not simply on the symptoms of their difficulties. For example, one high school faculty attempted to discourage student smoking through an educational campaign about its harmful effects. But like most teenage smokers, the students had begun smoking because they felt it marked the attainment of adulthood. They were unconcerned about health conditions thirty years in the future. The faculty might better have concentrated on the connection in the students' minds between smoking and being mature.

Because adolescents do not feel secure about their status, they are extremely sensitive to condescension and patronizing attitudes. They want to be regarded as adults, even though they may at times slip back into childish behavior. They want (and need) teachers who are honest and straightforward with them and who take time to consider students' ideas seriously. Adolescents want no favoritism, no tricks, and no evasiveness.

In addition to being understanding and fair, teachers should be adults. Sometimes it is tempting for them to be "one of the gang" in an effort to be liked by their students. Not only does this stance rob teenagers of the leadership, guidance, and adult model they need, but in the long run it doesn't work. If adolescents sometimes have trouble trusting adults in general, imagine how much less they can trust an adult who tries to act like a teenager.* The act is phony, and they know it. Adolescents realize that they need to have parents and teachers—adults—as well as their own teenage friends.

Teachers should be leaders, not in the sense of being aloof and dictatorial but rather in the sense of being able to direct, persuade, and inspire. If teachers drop that role and become just another member of the group, the students lose confidence in them.

Teachers should realize that they cannot, and should not, do everything in the way of music for their students. Because some degree of independence is important to adolescents for establishing their self-image as adults and competent persons, they need to have a type of popular music that is theirs, a type of music that they know more about than music teachers do. To rob them of the satisfaction of knowing "This is ours" or "We did it ourselves" is to deny them something valuable.

Teenage Musical Development

It is easy for musicians who have had training at the collegiate level to overestimate the musical background and interest of most adolescents. Most music teachers had private instruction in voice or on an instrument before entering high school, and they continued private study and played or sang in several high school performing groups; they were among the 50 percent of high school graduates who went on to college. At this stage they are already well above average musically. In college they majored in music and probably went on for a master's degree in music. One would have to search among hundreds of people from the general population to find someone with as much background in music.

Little wonder, then, that it is often hard for music teachers and their students to understand each other. True, some students are exceptional, but most of them are musically far behind their teachers. Music teachers have developed a concept of tone quality for a good singing voice or a cello, but very few teenagers have. Where have the students had the chance to hear good tone? How many programs of art music have they heard? How many different performances have they participated in?

Even the way words are used often differs between students and teachers. Some music teachers talk about "covered tones," "intonation," "light sounds," and so on. Such terms must be clarified if they are going to mean anything to the students. Good communication between music teachers and students is possible *if* the teachers realize that most of the students live in a different "musical world" from them.

---

*It should be pointed out that to adolescents, any teacher is by definition an adult, as are most people more than a few years older than them.

Physical and Vocal Development

Particularly in the seventh and eighth grades, girls are often physically and mentally more mature than boys. This condition exists to some degree throughout high school, although boys tend to catch up by their early twenties. Individual variations are striking, especially in the seventh and eighth grades. Differences in height of a foot or more are not uncommon. Because growth can occur rapidly, especially in boys, there is a tendency toward physical awkwardness and a limited level of endurance.

Less well understood are the changes that occur in the voice. When a boy reaches puberty, the voice box enlarges to about twice its former size. Because the vocal cords double in length, the pitch of the voice drops about one octave. More boys experience voice change at thirteen years of age than at any other, with a lesser but equal number changing at ages twelve and fourteen, and an even smaller number at eleven or fifteen (Cooksey, 1977, pp. 9, 13). In most cases the voice change occurs at approximately the same time as other bodily maturation. With the change in the size of the vocal apparatus, boys experience difficulty in regaining muscular control over their voices. They are about as awkward vocally as they are in other physical movements. In a real sense they must learn to use their voices all over again. Because the changing voice is marked by instability and inconsistency, some boys for a period of a month or two can sing either a treble or a bass part with equal ease. The teaching of boys whose voices are changing was discussed in Chapter 11.

Girls' voices change also, but because there is no drastic change of pitch, there is no particular vocal problem. Most girls in early adolescence have voices that are light and fluty in quality, with limited volume. There is usually a widening of range with maturity. The voices of both boys and girls deepen and become richer in quality as they grow older.

MOTIVATING TEENAGERS

Motivation as an aspect of human behavior was mentioned in Chapter 5. People naturally want to know and to be successful and informed. However, are there factors that are special for students in the secondary schools? To some degree, there are. One of these factors is the enormous importance of conformity to adolescents. Teenagers, especially in the early teen years, are very inclined to "follow the crowd," to be influenced by peer behavior The importance of groups to them was mentioned earlier in this chapter.

Another difference relates to the formation of self-image, which was also mentioned briefly earlier in this chapter. Music teachers need to work on forming an association in the students' minds between knowing and liking music and the kind of person the students want to be. The influence of role models is very important in determining human behavior.

Eileen Morgan, music teacher at Dalton Middle School, makes displays featuring prominent men and women who have an interest in music. She posted a picture of a successful model holding a violin that she played in her school days, and another of a well-known professional football player performing his own composition with a symphony orchestra. Eileen hopes the pictures contribute to the motivating ideas that "successful" people know music and that music is for men as well as women.

The students' attitudes toward music ability can have a significant effect on the effort they put forth in music classes and rehearsals. Many persons believe that either you have talent or you haven't. People with talent need hardly lift a finger—music will just pour from them; if a person does not have talent, then no amount of effort will make a difference. Of course, such an idea is wrong, and music teachers should let their students know that it is wrong. Effort is essential for achievement in music; there is no substitute for plain hard work, even for people with much natural ability.

Group Motivation

In a discussion of motivation in music distinction should be made between a performing organization such as a band and a class such as music theory. Students in band develop a sense of belonging that students in theory classes do not experience. A theory class does not present its efforts before the public, and it is not evaluated as a group; the students succeed or fail on an individual basis. But an orchestra succeeds or fails primarily as a unified ensemble, with each person bearing responsibility for the group as well as for his or her own improvement. Both theory class and performing organizations should derive their motivation from the attraction of music and from the excitement and satisfaction of learning it.

Teachers of musical organizations can use several techniques to involve the students more fully in the welfare of the group and to provide additional nonmusical motivation.

1. Give awards for service rendered. This practice recognizes the faithful and lets the rest of them know that good service is valued. There is divided opinion about the use of awards. Some educators feel that students should give a course their best efforts not because they will receive an award but rather because the course seems worthwhile to them. Also, awards can lose effectiveness if they are distributed too freely and too often. Nevertheless, in our society public recognition is so much a part of life that teachers usually find awards advantageous. True, awards are a form of extrinsic motivation. If they are not overemphasized they can be regarded not as a mere motivating device but as a means of recognizing those students who under any circumstances would do better-than-average work.

2. Have a group uniform for public performances.

3. Let the students invest in the group. This gives them some equity in the success of the organization. One choir has each new member buy a stole with the school letters embroidered on it. The stoles are worn with the robes for performances, and each year a service bar is added. The stoles give the choir a better appearance and hence a morale boost. Most students in band and orchestra have purchased an instrument, so they already have a sizable investment in music.

4. Invite the graduates of the group to come back and sit in on rehearsals when they can. One choir has a particular number that it performs at every spring concert. All the choir alumni in the audience are asked to come up on stage and sing with the group during that number.

5. Make sure that names of all members are printed in the concert programs. Double-check to make certain that they are spelled correctly and that no names have been omitted.

6. Involve as many students as possible in the operation of the organization—setup committee, uniform committee, library committee, student officers, and so on. What teacher would object to being relieved of some of the routine duties! Occasionally teachers complain that the students do not do a good enough job and that a few students do not take any assignment seriously. In the first case, it should be remembered that the students are younger and generally less capable than the teacher. They need much guidance and frequent supervision to see that they are doing their jobs properly. As for the students who cannot fulfill their obligations, it is wise to talk with them in private about the situation. If they are not interested, let them resign and have the group elect someone else to replace them.

7. Help the students plan a Parents' Night, when their parents come for an informal orientation to the organization. Hold a potluck supper, after which the group can perform some music. The numbers need not all be learned and ready for performance, as parents frequently enjoy seeing the stages of learning to perform music. The group might even try sight-reading a number. Then students can explain about awards, committees, and other features of the organization.

8. Make a recording of the group. Several record companies custom-make a standard microgroove disc, complete with a printed label, from tapes supplied to them. If desired, the company can improve the sound of the finished product by adding a small amount of reverberation, a technique used in most commercial recordings to add life to the sound. No company can make a good recording from a bad tape, so get the assistance of a professional recording engineer who has high-quality equipment. The group members can buy the finished records. More important than the keepsake value of the recording is the obvious incentive this gives the students to produce a good performance.

Group Morale

An effective means of increasing interest and ego involvement on the part of the members is to develop group spirit. Persons have made tremendous efforts and sacrifices for a group, team, or nation. Group consciousness is a major reason for the use of uniforms, emblems, and organized cheers—all symbols of solidarity. In musical performance *esprit de corps* can have an effect on the musical results that are achieved, and the musical result, in turn, is a strong influence in building group feeling.

Morale, motivation, and group success are valuable in achieving good performing organizations in which a high level of learning takes place. Teenagers hunger for a favorable response from their peers, and few are unmoved by an appeal for group success. Teachers should realize that they are on firm ground psychologically when they tell a group: "Look, no one wants to be a member of a group that's the laugh of the school. The way for you to succeed is to learn the music so that the audience will enjoy hearing it." Teachers should realize, too, that the vast majority of teenagers do not want the less motivated students to detract from the group's efforts.

Because "success" is crucial to the motivation and morale of teenagers, it is necessary for them to understand what constitutes "success." How they arrive at an evaluation of the group's work is a matter of much importance. Three opinions influence the students' evaluation of their performing ability. The first, though perhaps not the most important, is the opinion of the teacher revealed through comments and reactions. The students are interested in specific comments; they want to know how well or how badly they did. For instance, "It was quite good (very good, rather good), but we still need to be more careful about our attacks and entrances."

Second, the students would not be human if they did not value the response of the audience and the audience's remarks to them after the program. Because of the importance of peer groups, the musicians are particularly sensitive to the audience's response at a school assembly. Wise teachers make an effort to receive a positive opinion from this diverse group, a point discussed in Chapter 13.

In time, a third evaluation should become more important, and that is the members' own opinion. As the year progresses the students should be given information on which to judge their own work. This information is an integral part of their education in music. They should learn to notice poor attacks, faulty intonation, and inappropriate tone quality when they happen.

THE TEACHER'S ATTITUDE

A significant factor in the morale of a performing group is the general spirit established in the class or rehearsal by the teacher. Because the subject of music is so closely intertwined with feeling, a music group requires a higher degree of pupil-teacher rapport than almost any other organization. Teachers cannot help being aware of the feelings of their students, and the students, in turn, are quick to assess teachers' attitudes and moods. If they are unenthusiastic, so are the students.

Students will not try to improve if they are criticized constantly. Everyone is sensitive to criticism, music teachers included. Therefore, teachers should adopt an attitude of "honest optimism." They should honestly evaluate the playing or singing; no good is accomplished if they tell a group their work is fine when it is not. Optimism is essential, too, because teenagers need encouragement, and teachers should set goals for the group. There is no need for teachers to become overwrought if one section can't master a particular place in the music. The students will get it in time, if the task is a reasonable one. Certainly they should not be punished over the passage: "Listen, we're going over this until you do it right!" It is much better to be good-natured and say: "Go home, get a good night's sleep, and eat a good breakfast. Then when you come to class tomorrow, it will seem easier!"

It is important to be diplomatic in criticizing student musicians. In fact, it is a good idea to preface a criticism with a compliment: "Trombones, your tone was good at letter B, but the intonation was off. Check your pitch on that E natural; you were flat the last time you played it." Teachers should impress on the students that although their performance has good points, it can be better still. They should encourage students to improve and yet not frustrate them with ideals that are beyond their reach.

Much of the classroom atmosphere depends on a teacher's attitude toward the students' mistakes. Most adolescents are not sure of themselves and are genuinely afraid of making an error. As a result, when they feel inadequate, they will fake their way along. Teachers should let them know that mistakes are part of being human. It is wise to encourage openness about errors. A teacher might say something like this: "Don't be ashamed of making a mistake; we're ashamed only of those we make over and over. If you're going to make a mistake, make it a *good* one; then we can correct it. Don't fake in rehearsal and save your error for the concert. It's too late to do anything about it then." Such a statement is psychologically and educationally sound, because it leads to the correction rather than the suppression of errors.

The natural tendency for teachers is to be irritated and impatient with student mistakes. It is easy to forget that the football player who drops the touchdown pass in the end zone feels worse about his error than any of the spectators. On the other hand, there are some instances in which students make the same mistake many times. If they are unwilling or unable to rectify their errors, they need private assistance.

Good rapport between students and teacher is achieved primarily through the attitude of the teacher. In neither of the illustrations that follow does the example represent a single act that won the students over forever. Rather, the incidents were typical of the teacher's actions throughout the year.

At the conclusion of a general music class, which had been excellent in every regard—learning had been going on, participation had been high, singing had been enthusiastic and of good quality—Roberto Sanchez found that he had less than two minutes left; not enough time to start something new. It was nearly 12:30 and the students would leave directly for the cafeteria.

"Let's read the menu," he suggested. A boy was asked to go to the bulletin board, which contained the week's menu along with other school announcements. "Wait till I set the proper mood, Jeff," and he began to improvise on the piano the most pompous, booming fanfare he could muster. One would have thought a king was coming. Finally, the climactic, final chord. Jeff began to read, "Onion soup," then more thunderous piano music, "Weiner on a bun," more music.

*   *   **

The class was attempting to play a tune on the melody bells, with eight class members each holding one pitch of the octave. At a point that required one student to play her note twice, Sharon Worthington said to the player, "Mary, hit the A twice."

"Oh, no," Mary said quietly, "It's the G that should be struck twice."

Mary was right; the teacher had inadvertently given the wrong note. "Good grief!" she quipped. "First mistake I ever made in my life! Mary's right. Judy, it's your G that's struck twice."

In the first instance the teacher stopped taking himself so seriously and sent the students from the room with a relaxed, positive feeling. In the second case, instead of becoming tense and embarrassed or making excuses, the teacher let the error pass for what it was: a simple mistake.

A touch of humor helps immensely to maintain a relaxed feeling in the rehearsal room. Good humor does not always mean telling jokes and engaging in humorous antics. It is an attitude of having fun while you work. Start at "letter G as in ghoul" or "E as in extraterrestrial." Humor can be worked into the directions given to the group: "Sopranos, you should hand the phrase over to the altos on a silver platter. But you know what you did last time? You tossed it to them on a trash can lid."

Another factor in teacher attitude that influences rapport involves the cohesiveness between teacher and students. Never should teachers allow a "wall" to develop between the students and themselves. There should be no teacher versus students; teachers should not even think in terms of two separate interests. Rather, there should be a feeling of "we're doing this together." Inclusion, not separation, will achieve the best results. The students should be included in the plans, hopes, and operation of the class.

A pleasant, optimistic outlook on the part of teachers does not negate the need for firmness and consistency in dealing with young people. Consistency in this relationship gives students a sense of security and confidence. If they never know what a teacher's reaction is going to be, they will never be sure how they should act.

The attitude of the teacher is not the only factor that contributes to a pleasant atmosphere within the group. There should be a ban on destructive criticism by the students, especially in performing organizations. Some adolescents go through a stage of making smart and cutting remarks, even when they are uncalled for. Bad attitudes can easily "snowball" from a few people to many in a short time. Students who persist in talking negatively should be handled as behavior problems. On the other hand, teachers should not be afraid of constructive suggestions from students. They should be invited to express their thoughts about class activities, as long as their comments are sincere and responsible. What should be avoided is the pointless, chronic complaining that a few students like to indulge in.

Finally, teachers can now and then talk about good attitude. This suggestion does not imply long lectures or pep talks but rather some occasional statements about the meaning of group endeavor. Say to the students: "You should be proud to be a member of the band. You don't have to go around the school beating on your chest and shouting 'I'm in the band!' But you should feel glad that you're in it, and when you know you're doing good work, don't be afraid to say so." It doesn't hurt to tell the performers: "There are sixty-five people in band, right? So when you hear the applause at the end of a number, one sixty-fifth of that applause is for you. Enjoy it."

SECURING ADEQUATE MEMBERSHIP

A problem that concerns only elective performing organizations is recruiting and maintaining adequate membership. It is fine for a textbook to state that a sixty-five piece band should have twenty B-flat clarinets and two bassoons, or that the choir should have a tenor section about the size of the soprano section. But this does not mean that teachers on the first day of school will find the prescribed membership in band or choir. What can they do about incomplete membership?

Music teachers should be clear in their own minds, and make clear to the administration and other teachers, the reason for seeking students for music groups. It is *not* to build a little "empire" for themselves. Rather it is to have a group of sufficient variety and size to provide a better musical experience. An orchestra without violas and bass viols is just as incomplete as a football team without guards and tackles. The quality of the tenor section in a mixed choral group can significantly affect the kind of music that is sung and studied.

A singing group can be built much more quickly than an instrumental organization, which requires specialized instruction encompassing several years. The problems and their solutions, however, are basically the same for both vocal and instrumental organizations.

The most effective way to get new students to join is to have a successful organization. The activities and attitudes of present members are the best advertisement. Students who consider joining a music group are influenced in most instances by three things. First, they want to know how the present membership feels about the group. If they hear grumbling, they are not likely to join. Second, the students' own impression, gained from hearing the group perform, helps them determine how well they think they would like the activity. If the choir sings only sacred numbers, and they don't care for that type of music, they probably will not enroll, no matter how enthusiastic the members seem to be. Third, the impression students gain about the teacher is important. Many high school students do not differentiate between liking music activity as such and liking the teacher. They gain their impression of a teacher from what they hear about that person and what they see of him or her in the halls and in assembly performances. So if the teacher walks around school with a long, glum face, students will assume that being a member of a music group is similarly dreary.

What can be done by a new teacher who starts the first week of school with only a small, incomplete enrollment of students who enrolled the preceding spring? Here are some suggestions:

1. Meet with the school principal or head counselor. Try to get his or her approval for schedule changes for students who might want to enroll in a music course. In many cases it is not possible to change the schedules of a sizable number of students after the school year has started. School schedules operate under restrictions in terms of other classes; for example, a section of biology can take only so many students. For this reason a teacher may have to live with an undesirable situation for a semester or a year.

2. If it is possible to effect schedule changes, obtain schedules of all students and list those who have time for an additional course. As much as new teachers may wish to succeed, they must not proselyte from the classes of other teachers!

3. Check the records to discover students who were members of music organizations in previous years but who are not now enrolled.

4. See personally those students who are able to enroll. Be enthusiastic, but don't plead. Some students wait until they have a chance to "size up" the new teacher before committing themselves.

5. Ask the present members for leads on likely prospects—students who have shown some inclination toward music.

6. Solicit recruiting ideas from the members.

7. Arrange a short, private audition for every new member. The audition allows you to assess the student's abilities and gives you a chance to meet each student personally.

8. Make the first rehearsal of the group a successful and pleasant experience. Accomplish something the first day, even if it is only singing or playing some very simple music. Save beginning-of-the-year routines for later (assigning music, robes or uniforms, and checking class lists). Be enthusiastic about the music organization!

9. Keep up the membership drive for no longer than five days. Then start to make the existing group into the best possible organization.

Some of the suggested steps may seem to encourage membership in the organization by any student regardless of his or her musical ability. Actually, few students who express an interest in joining a music group are innately incapable of profiting from the experience. Most of them need encouragement in undertaking music study because they have doubts about their ability.

Recruiting Boys

So often music teachers, especially in vocal music, bemoan the lack of boys. "If I only had more boys," one choir teacher complained. "Right now I have only four, and one of them has an unchanged voice." In many schools there is a shortage of boys in the ranks of string players and even in band. Getting boys into music, and keeping them there, is a special challenge. Male teachers may have an easier time involving boys in music. Yet there are many women who have successfully recruited entire boys' glee clubs, so the sex of the teacher is not the determining factor.

Sometimes boys feel that music is not quite manly. Fortunately, this attitude has decreased considerably in the last forty years, but remnants of it still exist. Overcoming such an attitude is one important step in recruiting boys. Teachers can point out many well-known male musicians. There are fine men's choruses, outstanding bands in the military services, which present excellent male vocalists.

The idea that music and singing are not appropriate for boys is only part of their attitude problem. Many boys sincerely feel that they are unable to sing. This is probably a reaction to the change of voice and the accompanying uncertainty and frustration it causes. Boys should be given encouragement and understanding. Specific advice on helping boys vocally has been included in other chapters of this book.

In some schools boys have been attracted to singing by the appeal of a barbershop quartet. Barbershop singing is traditionally done by ear. Today, however, a sizable number of arrangements are available, which are best learned by having everyone sing the melody (always in the second tenor) in unison on a neutral syllable. The S.P.E.B.S.Q.S.A. (Society for the Preservation and Encouragement of Barber Shop Quartet Singing in America), Inc., offers aid in organizing and training such groups.

For some reason a group of boys who sing with a big, strong tone can capture an audience, even though they are singing a simple unison song with not much polish. The boys may be in a group of their own, or the male sections of the chorus may sing alone. In either case the group should appear before an audience at a reasonably early date, because a long wait before performing allows interest to wane. It is best to begin with simple music in unison or two parts. After a successful performance everyone will be convinced that boys can and should sing. The more exacting work in parts should come after morale and interest have been established.

Both choral and instrumental music teachers usually welcome a member of the school's football or basketball team. The younger boys look up to athletes, whose entrance into the group seems to place the stamp of approval on music— an approval that can weigh heavily with the rest of the student body. The blessing of athletes in music can be a mixed one, however. These boys are putting their best time and effort into their sports activities, and music is usually in second place. Then, too, they are the object of so much attention that some of them are a bit harder to deal with. Teachers are glad when they get boys from the school teams in music, but their success does not depend on them.

Working with Boys

Care should be used in selecting music. Boys do not take readily to songs they feel are frilly and meaningless. By contrast, the boys in one high school choir became fond of the work "In Solemn Silence" by Ippolitov-Ivanov. It is a slow, chordal piece—a prayer to God that the sufferings of war may pass. Although not the type of work one usually thinks that high school students would like, it had a message they could comprehend, and they sang it with dignity and understanding.

Talk to boys in concrete terms. Instead of directing them to try "a more intimate style," tell them to sing the passage as they would a romantic popular ballad. Rather than say, "Boys, that sounded just lovely!" shout out, "Hey men, that's the way to do it—with some polish!" When boys talk at the wrong time in class or misbehave in any way, there is usually no subtlety to it. It is right out where everyone can see it, so don't be subtle about reprimanding them. Instead of squeaking out, "Boys, you behave yourselves now," bark out in a firm voice, accompanied by a forcefully pointed finger (and a twinkle in the eye), "John Jones, cut it out!" Be honest, unafraid, make yourself understood, and you'll get along fine.

The adolescent years are a challenging time in anyone's life. The transition from childhood to adulthood in present-day American society is not easy. Fortunately, music teachers can contribute significantly to teenagers' education and well-being. They need to understand them and teach them in a way that builds on (but not stops with) their needs and interests.

Questions   1.   Because teenagers are especially concerned with personal status, what might a music teacher do in the following situations?
   (a)   to help a student feel more at ease during an audition for a choral group
   (b)   to tell a student his tone is poor without hurting his feelings
   (c)   to encourage the student who worries a great deal about making an obvious mistake during a public performance

2.   What type of attitude does each of these statements indicate? How would each affect teenage students?
   (a)   "What's the matter, Pete! Is your third finger frozen? Let's play E flat next time!"
   (b)   "Altos, that was nice, except for one thing—you didn't sing the dotted quarter followed by the eighth correctly."

(c) "Whew! I've heard better tones from a New Year's Eve noisemaker!"

(d) "Sherman, I know it's hard to play low on a brass instrument and play it soft and in rhythm at the same time. But that's what the music calls for. Would you do some careful, thoughtful practice at home on that place?"

(e) "This melody you turned in doesn't seem up to your usual standard, Jennifer. Did you really write this?"

3. Think of instances in which you have observed a music teacher develop good rapport with the students through something he or she did or said. What points did these instances have in common?

4. Teenagers are sometimes impressed with a group if they feel that it is exclusive or difficult to get into. Should "snob" appeal be used to build up music organizations in the public school? Why or why not?

5. At what age do most boys' voices change? Do girls' voices change? If so, in what way?

6. What are the differences between intrinsic and extrinsic motivation? What are some techniques teachers may use to motivate students in music?

References   Bandura, Albert. "The Stormy Decade: Fact or Fiction?" In *Contemporary Adolescence: Readings,* edited by Hershel D. Thornburg. Monterey, Calif.: Brooks/Cole, 1971.

Cooksey, John M. "The Development of a Contemporary Eclectic Theory for the Training and Culturation of the Junior High Male Changing Voice," Part II. *Choral Journal,* 18, no. 3 (November 1977).

Lindgren, Henry Clay, and W. Newton Suter. *Educational Psychology in the Classroom.* 7th ed. Monterey, Calif.: Brooks/Cole, 1985.

CHAPTER 16

Music Teaching and Student Discipline

For some reason there is a tendency among prospective teachers (and some experienced teachers, too) to think of the teaching process and the handling of student discipline problems as two separate and distinct matters. Methods classes cover topics such as teaching students to perform music or write chords, but if they mention student behavior at all, they switch to discussing the means of keeping the students "in line." The teaching of music is approached in a positive tone, while the handling of classroom discipline is dealt with in a negative way. Such a view is unfortunate, and it tends to keep teachers from working to correct classroom conditions that encourage misbehavior.

Some educators are willing to manipulate classroom situations so that students learn subject matter, but they think that managing a situation so that the students learn necessary social skills is somehow not quite right. Such a belief is hard to understand, because unless sufficient social skills are learned, little learning of subject matter can take place. The two types of learning are very much interrelated.

DISCIPLINE AND TEACHING

Almost everyone believes that students ought to behave in school, but why? When all is said and done, the reason students need to behave is so that they can learn. It's just that simple. Yet students and teachers sometimes forget this basic fact. Students find it easy to fall into the habit of thinking that behaving in school is the teacher's idea. In other words, the focus of class behavior is diverted from creating a situation in which learning can take place to one in which students respond to teacher-created rules. And when that happens, often the response of the students is to make a game of violating those rules. This situation can be partly overcome if the class members get to help in the formulation of the class conduct guidelines. In that way the students will understand the guidelines better and feel that they are fair.

Teachers should keep the reasons for classroom discipline in mind for their own sake, too. True, teaching is easier and more enjoyable when class behavior is good, but that is not the main purpose of good classroom discipline. A greater goal is involved here: student learning.

DEVELOPING DESIRABLE CLASSROOM BEHAVIOR

How do teachers, experienced or inexperienced, go about developing classroom situations in which students can learn and be productive? Here are some suggestions, which are offered in no special order.

Work on building a desire to learn in the students. What is pointed out in Chapter 5 about children's curiosity is true. However, is there enough curiosity to motivate students through the over one thousand hours of school each year, year after year? It appears that there isn't. Students may be curious and want to learn generally, but that does not mean they care about learning to play recorder in general music class in a particular week in February. And how can the students' desire to learn be increased? Start by making sure that your teaching follows the guidelines suggested in Chapter 5. Well-taught classes in which the students see the point of what they are doing are much more likely to encourage students to learn. Also apply the information provided in Chapter 15 about motivating students in music classes.

Reward and reinforce the students in their learning and, equally important, *withhold reinforcement for undesirable behavior.* Rewards need not be tokens or pieces of candy, especially at the secondary school level. They can be words or looks of approval and the granting of activities and privileges. For example, music teachers in the elementary school usually find their students eager to play the instruments for accompanying songs. Teachers can reward those students who make a good effort in their singing and behave themselves by giving them the first chance to play an instrument. In the high school band an instrumentalist who wants to be the "class clown" has invalidated his or her chance to play first chair, even if that person is the best player in the section. The student in this instance should be told that a reward is being withheld because of undesirable behavior. An association needs to be formed in the students' minds between good behavior and advancement in the group.

One example of how teachers can employ reinforcement to improve the behavior of a class is reported in a study by Hall et al. (1968). A seventh grade class was being disruptive—talking, throwing things, and so on—when it should have been working. It met daily for forty-five minutes: It had a five-minute break and then a forty-minute session. Observations of the class revealed that only 47 percent of the time were students behaving as they should. The teacher was approving of some aspect of behavior about six times per session and disapproving about twenty times during that time span. First, the teacher increased the amount of time given the school work and decreased the attention given misbehavior. Also, the amount of approval and disapproval were made about equal. The results were an increase in appropriate student behavior to about 65 percent, but the noise level remained high. Next, the teacher placed a chalk mark on the board when students disturbed the class, with each mark reducing the break time by ten seconds; twenty-four marks eliminated the break entirely. The appropriate behavior increased to about 76 percent and the noise level dropped.

The teacher then tried doing away with the chalk marks, but the class behavior became worse; studying decreased and the noise level increased. So the chalk marks were reinstated, and this time the rate of appropriate behavior increased to 81 percent, and it stayed there for the remainder of the study.

Among other things, the study demonstrated the fact that class management does not lie in adopting an either-or position regarding approval or disapproval. Both have their place, if used correctly. Teachers need to develop the right "mix" of approval-disapproval and seek the right amount of leadership, a point depicted in the cartoon on page 345.

Although the reinforcement of poor behavior is not intended by some teachers, it is unwittingly encouraged when they yell at or in some way give recognition to students who are doing something they shouldn't. Although the words do not compliment the misbehaving students, they are giving them some attention, which is seen by them as better than being ignored.

Work on correcting specific actions. It does not help when a teacher accuses students, for example, of having a "bad attitude." That is so broad a charge that the students would not know what to change—even if they wanted to. What are the actions of the student that indicate a "bad attitude"? Being late for class? Talking at the wrong times? Slouching instead of sitting up straight? Writing obscenities on the pages of the music? Refusing to take part in class? Particular actions can be changed; general or vaguely stated impressions cannot.

In many ways, working on specific behavior problems is similar to teaching subject matter. Objectives are stated, a teaching procedure enacted, and the results assessed according to observable actions.

Be positive. Teachers should spend as much time and effort trying to catch students doing something right as they do in trying to catch them doing something wrong; they should be at least as quick to praise students for the good things they do as to criticize them for the undesirable things they do.

Some music teachers have been so well schooled in the goal of perfection that they find it hard to praise the less-than-perfect efforts of school students. These teachers should not give up their high standards, but they should be much more ready to be positive about what the students have achieved.

THE PROBLEM

The kids in your class are disrespectful and unmanageable . . .

THE WRONG APPROACH

THE MAD APPROACH

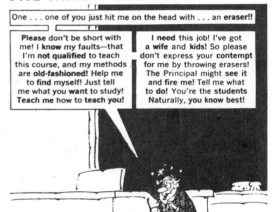

Somewhere between the "wrong" and the "Mad" approach there must be a "right" approach. © 1969 by E. C. Publications, Inc. Reprinted by permission of MAD.

Devote more attention to the many students who are neither the best nor the worst in the class. The best students receive plenty of attention. They play solos, answer questions in class correctly, get to sit in the first chairs of sections, and the like. Teachers enjoy having such students (and there is nothing wrong in that), and this pleasure is probably evident in the teachers' actions. The worst students often get a lot of attention, too, but in different ways. They get yelled at, kept in for recess or after school, have private conferences with teachers, and get special visits to the principal's or counselor's office. One of the ironies of teaching in the schools is the amount of effort teachers expend on the pupils who least want to learn. In the meantime, the large group of "average" students gets the rather limited amount of the teachers' attention that is left over after the best and worst students have been taken care of. This situation is wrong; teachers should probably give priority to the majority of their students who are neither very good nor very bad.

Be consistent. It is difficult to do, but teachers should try to be consistent from day to day and from situation to situation in dealing with students. The same student actions should produce the same response from the teacher, regardless of who the student is or what the day is. For example, if two students on two different days forget to bring their instruments to school, they should be treated in the same way. Inconsistent teacher actions have an unsettling effect on the students, because they don't know what to expect.

> *Marsha Martin was determined that there be no horseplay in chorus rehearsal. On Monday Jim Norton, a weak bass, was caught tossing a bit of paper at another bass. She immediately asked him to leave the room, and he was given an hour in the school's after-school "quiet room."*
>
> *On Wednesday Peter Ott, the only good tenor, was caught flipping a little piece of dried mud from off his shoe at another chorus member. Ms. Martin just glowered at him and said, "Now look! Let's leave the horsing around to horses." Peter was given no penalties.*

Mean what you say. Teachers who do not intend to follow up what they say should not say it in the first place. Students are quick, very quick, to discover idle threats. From the first day on teachers must mean what they say, or else they will be in for a long year.

> *The chorus students at Webster High School soon discovered that Jana Movesian's threats didn't mean a thing. When they came into class, they stood around the room in small groups, talking and laughing. Some students sat down in the wrong seats. Finally, after shouting and pleading, she got the chorus seated. She then started to talk about the day's work.*
>
> *Some members of the chorus began to converse with one another, and Jana barked out, "If you people don't stop talking, I'm going to assign extra homework!" The talking stopped for a few moments, then started again. She raised her voice so that she could be heard above the sound of shuffling feet and conversation. Finally, after more admonitions to be quiet, the chorus started singing, almost ten minutes after the hour began.*
>
> *A few students had not bothered to pick up their folders, and Jana noticed that they were just singing along without music. The song stopped. "Where's your folder?" she asked Joe Hinman.*
>
> *"Guess I left it in my locker," Joe replied lazily.*
>
> *"Listen, you people who forgot your folders," she said, "tomorrow I'm going to check each one personally for his folder. If you don't have a folder, I'm lowering your grade." The students weren't worried. She had made the same threat before but had never carried it out.*

Involve the students in developing the guidelines for class behavior. Charles Madsen and Clifford Madsen make these suggestions about developing guidelines:

1. *Involve the class in making up the rules.*
2. *Keep the rules short and to the point.*
3. *Phrase rules, where possible, in a positive way. ("Sit quietly while working" instead of "Don't talk to your neighbors.")*
4. *Remind the class of the rules at times other than when someone has misbehaved.*
5. *Make different sets of rules for varied activities.*
6. *Let children know when different rules apply (work-play).*
7. *Post rules in a conspicuous place and review them regularly.*
8. *Keep a sheet on your desk and record the number of times you review rules with the class (1981, p. 185).*

The suggestion about posting rules depends somewhat on the age of the students. It is more effective with younger students. The more mature groups in high school tend to resent the idea that they need much instruction on acceptable class behavior.

In the teaching of secondary school students, *be alert to whether the misbehavior is serious or just "pulling the teacher's leg."* Usually it is the latter. It is hard to put into words how you can tell, but with a little experience you can sense a certain look in the eyes and a lack of conviction in the voice of the students when they are just trying to get away with something, often for no other reason than to add a little zest to what they consider a humdrum day.

Do not be afraid that reprimanding a student will cause you to be disliked by the class. Inexperienced teachers are often reluctant to be effective in managing classrooms, partly for this reason. This worry is unjustified. If the students have participated in making the rules, the action of the group will support the teacher in maintaining order. The majority of the class wants the students who don't behave dealt with, because the majority feel that if they behave themselves, so should everyone else. Even the student who is being reprimanded seldom resents being put in line, although he or she is not overtly pleased at being singled out for misbehavior. Furthermore, teachers should remember that they will be seeing the students for many classes for a school year, so the students will have plenty of time to find out what a teacher is like; they will not base their judgment on the handling of just one or two incidents.

Appeal to the students' desire to be adults. Encourage the formation of an association between maturity and proper behavior in class, which is what the teacher is trying to do in this example:

> *Ray Johnson found that this reminder was effective with his students: "Look, you're big boys and girls now. You know the rules that we all worked out together for conduct in band. So do what you know is right. If you act like adults, you'll be treated as adults, and everything will be just fine. When you act like children, everyone, including me, will treat you as children. It's up to you. Now let's get to work on this music."*

Remain calm and rational, even if things go badly. No matter how disgusted, disappointed, or exasperated you may become, do not lose your temper. You should be adult enough to avoid the trap of acting childish. Firm, clear, reasonable, and unemotional directives achieve control without harmful aftereffects. Also, by remaining uninvolved personally and emotionally, you will be better able to deal with the problem.

Finally, *make a distinction between disliking as a person the student who misbehaves and disapproving of the things he or she does.* Try to have the students realize that you make this distinction.

> *Jim Baker found it necessary to penalize his principal second violin for persistently talking out of turn in rehearsal. "Look, Bill," Mr. Baker said, "personally I like you and you're a good fiddler. But in orchestra there are rules about talking and we all agreed on them. You seem to have trouble following them. I don't like this, and neither does the rest of the orchestra. Not only aren't you learning anything, but you're keeping the others from learning. So I think you'd better put in an hour after school. There are some bowings to mark in the violin parts. Why, I'd have to penalize my own mother if she talked as much as you do."*

The position taken by the teacher in the example is a good one, for several reasons. First, it is direct and easily understood. Second, it separates the student as a person from his actions. Third, it tells the student why his behavior is unacceptable. Fourth, it derives its authority from "we" or the group, not from the demands of the teacher. Fifth, the talk ends on a note of humor, letting the student know that the teacher has not become overly involved in the events that happened in class.

Special Suggestions for Music Teachers

Are music classes more susceptible to student behavior problems than are other areas? In some respects they have fewer such problems. Many students like music better than they do their other school subjects, and in secondary schools many performing organizations are elective, often only by the permission of the teacher. Therefore, student interest is higher and students with serious behavior problems are not present. Music classes are often active, which means that the students are kept busy at constructive activities, which in turn means that they have less opportunity for deviant behavior.

In other ways music classes are more prone to behavior problems. Music lacks the concreteness of some academic subjects in terms of work to be covered and tested. An eighth grader may be held back in school for failing English but not for failing music. In the secondary schools music classes are sometimes very large, especially the performing groups. Having more students means a greater chance for students' misbehavior.

Here are some suggestions that apply to the teaching of music groups:

Maintain eye contact with the class. Minor behavior problems are sometimes encouraged by teachers whose attention is focused more on their music than on the class. If a teacher hovers over the music and does not look at the class, the changes are that some students will lag in participation and behavior. In other cases, music teachers cannot tear themselves away from the piano. The piano is either a "crutch" to help them through their teaching or a "fortification" standing between them and the class. Whatever the reason, if the music or the piano is such an attraction for a teacher, he or she should deliberately teach part of each class without using the piano or looking at music.

Learn the students' names. Teachers of elementary and junior high school general music classes usually see a great many students each week. For this reason they have many names to associate with the faces they see. However, part of the preparation for teaching such classes should be the learning of the students' names. Sometimes class pictures are available from the previous year, and they may help in learning names. If such pictures are not available, the teacher simply has to work harder at learning names. For the first class or two in the fall, music teachers in elementary or middle school can request that the students wear name tags.

Names are important because students feel more free to misbehave if they think that the teacher is not sure who they are. Also, if teachers want to praise the good work of student—and it is hoped that they will—then saying the student's name is essential. It is not very effective to say, "You with the green shirt, you did a good job of singing with us that time."

Problem Areas for Music

There are areas in which policies have to be made for almost every music class. Here are some suggestions that may serve as guides in dealing with these areas.

Talking. It is difficult for most people to sit for a half hour or more without talking to someone. Anyone who has observed a meeting of teachers will quickly realize that they are no different from anyone else in this regard. Complete silence is, therefore, not a reasonable expectation of American school students. What the students need to learn is that there is a time for talking and a time for keeping silent. The times for talking that the class can consider in setting up rules might be (1) during changes of music or activity, (2) before class starts, and (3) any time that the teacher is not trying to teach, such as when conferring with an individual student. Uncontrolled talking should be prohibited at other times.

The two spots that appear to cause the most trouble with talking are when teachers work with one group of students and leave the others sitting with nothing to do, and when they stop a group to make a suggestion on the performance of the music. *Teachers should not give suggestions or directions to the class if some students are talking.* The students who miss the directions will make the same errors again, and the teacher will need to repeat the directions especially for the talkers. In classes of much size, the students should raise their hands and be recognized before speaking. That procedure makes for a more orderly class and offers the students a more equal chance to be heard.

Inability to Participate.   Students are sometimes present but unable to sing because of colds or laryngitis. Instrumental teachers have to deal with broken or forgotten instruments, cut lips, and sprained fingers. These situations should be handled in basically the same way: The students should report their afflictions to the teacher *before* class begins. Then they should sit in their regular places and follow the class activities, learning as much as possible without actually participating.

Sometimes students in secondary schools who cannot participate will ask permission to do homework during music class. If doing homework under such circumstances is allowed, it is surprising how many students develop throat problems or broken instruments on days in which there are important examinations in other subjects! Unless students are allowed to practice music in their other classes (which of course they are not), then students should not study other subjects in music class.

Attendance.   Usually there are schoolwide policies and procedures for handling excessive tardiness and unexcused absences. When this is so, music teachers need to do little about these problems.

Problems with attendance may arise in conjunction with out-of-school performances. Music teachers, who for the most part have been taught throughout their lives a sense of obligation and responsibility, are distressed when a few students fail to appear for a performance. Legally, students can be required to be present, and grades lowered or other penalties administered, *if* two conditions are met. One is that the students enrolled in the music course know that out-of-school performances are involved. This situation is not true for performances in which an entire fourth grade sings at a PTA meeting for example; it applies only when the students have elected the class. The other condition is that the students be notified a reasonable amount of time in advance of the performance. Ideally teachers should hand out a list of the performances for the group or class the first week or two of the semester. If these conditions are met, then teachers cannot allow missed performances to pass without notice. Failing to show up for a performance mocks the efforts of the rest of the students who did appear. Again the class should help formulate the penalties, which will probably vary according to the nature and importance of the performance.

A situation that appears to be increasing at the secondary school level is a time conflict between school activities for some students on days of performances. As school calendars become more crowded, students run a greater chance of conflicts with athletic events, school plays, or field trips. Music teachers need to work with the school administration to keep such conflicts of dates to a minimum. If conflicts do arise, the student should, with everyone's knowledge, alternate his or her presence equally between music and the other activities. Because a student is on the swimming team does not mean that he performs with the music group *only* when there is no swim meet.

Other Problem Areas. Chewing gum and making music do not go together. Students should be asked to dispose of their gum before class begins. To get this practice started, teachers can designate a different student each day to pass around the wastebasket.

All students in music classes, but members of performing groups especially, should maintain good posture. It increases alertness and improves behavior. Slouchers can be reminded that they are starting to look like a question mark or a pretzel. Good-natured remarks by teachers usually bring about better posture. In most classes slouching can be corrected by having the class stand; this suggestion includes instrumental groups as well as choral.

MAINTAINING CLASSROOM CONTROL

The following suggestions about what specifically teachers might do in handling discipline situations should be viewed in light of all that has been said earlier in this chapter about good teaching procedures and the motivation of students. Without effective teacher methods the procedures for handling behavior situations will be of limited value. The suggestions are offered because prospective teachers like the security of knowing some things they can say and do in various situations.

Students have an uncanny way of knowing when teachers are confident in what they are doing, and they are especially discerning when teachers are hesitant. Teachers should make sure that the rules have been clearly established, that the class understands them, and that students are dealt with in some manner when they violate the rules.

Handling Minor Disturbances

It is often wise not to make an issue of a small offense. Everyone makes small infractions of rules on occasion. When motorists are caught overparking the time on the meter, they get a ticket. They are wrong and they know it, but they don't want to be treated like criminals. Students feel the same way about their small offenses.

There are many ways to pass out mild reprimands for rule infractions. The following illustration describes how one case *might* be handled.

> *Helen Oliver was telling the Girls' Glee Club about the procedures they would follow at the concert for getting on and off the stage. Denise turned and whispered to her neighbor. Helen stopped talking for a moment, looked at Denise, and said in a firm voice, "Denise." She waited a moment more for her to stop whispering. Denise stopped, and Helen went back to explaining the stage procedures for the concert.*

Most small violations can be handled in a similar manner. With less sensitive students it is necessary to be blunt, but most students will respond to a short reminder.

What does a teacher do if a student continues to talk even after a reminder? This situation probably will not happen, but it can. Here is how it might be handled:

> *Leon Russell was working with the tenor section. One of the basses turned around in his seat and started to talk and laugh with one of his friends. Leon said, "Jack, sometimes I think you should've joined a speaking chorus instead of a singing one." Before Leon could finish working with the tenors, Jack resumed his talking and laughing. Leon then said in a firm voice, "Jack, you were just told to stop the chatter. Now do it!" He kept looking at him until Jack turned around and gave him his full attention.*

What would happen if Jack still persisted in violating the rules? The teacher would have no choice but to deal wth him outside the class. The ways of doing so will be discussed shortly.

Another type of situation involves no particular individual but rather a sizable portion of the entire group.

> *To Sandra Babcock, it seemed as if the whole general music class was talking and not yet ready to work. She held up her hand and said in a clear voice, "A moment of silence, please." She waited about fifteen seconds for the group to quiet down, meanwhile catching the eyes of several students and looking directly at them. After a few seconds of silence she said, "Ah, what a wonderful sound—silence." Then she immediately started to work on the day's activities.*

How much better this solution is than standing in front of the group and shouting for attention, making everyone tense and irritable. For the technique to be effective teachers must wait for real silence, and by their manner they must insist on it. Their duty is to keep a cool head, get the attention of the students, and give firm, clear requests. They should put the group to work as soon as possible and make their own remarks pertinent to teaching the class.

Handling Persistent Rule Violators

If a student persists in violating standards of conduct in spite of good, positive teaching and the employment of reminders and mild reprimands in the classroom situation, the teacher should deal with him or her outside of class. Usually a friendly private conference is the most effective means of working with such a student. It does not bring any additional class attention to the troublemaker, and attention in some form is frequently what is wanted. Furthermore, it avoids embarrassing the student in front of the other students.

Teachers should keep in mind several points when speaking with a student in such a conference.

1. Be friendly, honest, and unhurried. Remember to make a distinction between disliking the student as a person and disapproving of what he or she has done. Sarcasm, ridicule, and anger are ineffective.

2. Approach the student positively. Something like this is usually effective: "Look, Mandy, you could be a lot of help to the chorus. We need singers who know their parts and can sing on pitch. You could be a big plus in chorus, if you wanted to be. Why don't you spend your energies building up the group, rather than seeking attention for yourself by talking so much?" Such an approach is better than emphasizing the negative by saying, "Don't do this, and don't do that."

3. Give the student a chance to talk. A conference is a two-way affair; both parties should have the opportunity to express themselves. Ask the student if there is anything that can be done to help him or her behave better in the future. Sometimes a change of seat in the group will largely solve the problem.

Sometimes students will try to talk their way out of a situation, even when they are clearly at fault. Some of these statements are so predictable that they have become almost "time honored." One defense basically asks, "Why are you picking on me?" The answer teachers can give is the obvious truth: "You were doing something you shouldn't, and that is why you got caught." Another standard defense essentially says, "I wasn't the only one; others were doing it, too." The previous teacher response is appropriate here also, with the added comment that if others continue doing it, they will be in trouble, too. Some persistent perpetrators of small offenses offer a justification that runs, "All I did was ask Sherri a question (pick up Aaron's music, take a comb out of Miguel's pocket—a great variety of actions fit the statement), and I got in trouble." The teacher response can simply be that the question should have been asked of the teacher. In addition, the teacher should point out that the student is being called in because of the accumulation of many small infractions of the rules that the class had developed and agreed on.

Handling Serious Problems

If a private conference with the student does not work, then more forceful action is required. It is best to work with the principal or counselor on serious behavior problems. Often a student who is causing a problem in music is also a problem in other classes. The principal or counselor can study the situation and suggest a course of action. In some cases this action may involve calling in a parent or a temporary suspension of the student from class. Also, the student might be assigned to do something constructive for the music department after school hours, or the poor behavior might be reflected in the student's grade. However, the lowering of a grade has little effect on students who don't care about what grades they receive.

Should a problem student in an elective secondary school course be permanently removed from the course? Yes, under certain conditions. One condition is that the teacher and the school have tried to work with the student and can demonstrate that fact with written records, if necessary. The second condition is that the benefits to the individual are outweighed by the negative effect of the student on the group or class. Teachers have an obligation to the majority of students, who do behave properly; they deserve the best instruction in music that can be offered in the available time and facilities. One or two students should not be permitted to spoil it for everyone else.

Although the extremely serious school disruptions—threats of physical violence, knife pullings, fights—are rare in music classes, a word should be said about them. Under no circumstances should a teacher attempt to wrestle a weapon from a student or hold two combatants apart. Besides inviting injury, physical intervention complicates the determination later of what really happened. Instead, send a fleet-footed, responsible student for the principal or school security officer if the school has one. Do not panic outwardly or lose self-control. Meanwhile, in the most determined, forceful tone of voice possible, tell the student or students to stop fighting or put down the weapon. Surprisingly, this command will sometimes work. But in any case, unless the teacher issues a clear directive, during a later investigation it may not be possible to establish the point that the teacher did all that was reasonably possible to maintain control. Again, such violent behavior problems are rare, but for a number of reasons they have been increasing in the last thirty years. A little forethought helps in handling a potentially dangerous situation that might arise.

For teachers who demonstrate a positive approach combined with consistency and reasonableness in handling student behavior problems, the amount of effort required for such matters seems to go gradually away. What was a major concern becomes an occasional minor challenge.

***

Questions

1. Why is it necessary for students in music classes to behave properly?

2. What factors present in most classrooms contribute to good student behavior? What factors contribute to undesirable behavior?

3. Suppose that you are a secondary school choral or instrumental teacher. You receive a telephone message that a member of the group cannot be present for the big spring concert because the student has to work that night at a local fast-food establishment. What reasons can you give the parent as to why the student should be present? Can you require that the student be present for the performance?

4. For each of these incidents, decide what teachers can do to prevent it from occurring and what teachers should do if it does happen.

    (a) Bob, a sophomore, is somewhat of a "show off." A student running errands for the principal's office enters the room with a notice for the teacher. Bob shouts to the girl bringing the note, "Patty! Baby!"

    (b) Linda is a quiet freshman in the clarinet section. As the teacher is explaining a point, he notices that Linda is talking quietly to her neighbor.

    (c) Howard has caused trouble in the eighth grade general music class before. Feeling that he is seeking attention, the teacher assigns him a report to make to the class, with the hope that this would provide him with attention and the class with useful information. While giving the report, Howard talks and talks, uses the occasion to be a "clown," and is clearly not interested in giving a real report.

(d) The seventh grade general music class is attempting to adapt an Autoharp accompaniment to a song. Tony is usually reasonably well behaved. However, as he holds the instrument waiting to play the chords the class decides on, he can't resist strumming lightly on it.

(e) The ninth grade girls' glee club is practicing its music for a performance at the annual Mothers' Recognition Dinner. As the teacher walks by frivolous, talkative Diane, he notices that she is looking at a *Glamour* magazine in her folder.

(f) A nearby store is featuring inexpensive plastic water pistols this week. Nearly every boy entering Ms. Hixson's seventh grade general music class has a loaded water pistol in his pocket.

Project 1. While observing teachers in school situations, notice the following:
(a) the proportion of approval/disapproval actions of the teacher
(b) whether or not class begins on time
(c) what behavior the teacher reinforces and how it is reinforced
(d) the existence of behavior guidelines for the class
(e) how matters such as talking and gum chewing are handled
(f) whether the teacher maintains eye contact with the students

Suggested Readings

Cangelosi, James S. *Classroom Management Strategies: Gaining and Maintaining Students' Cooperation.* New York: Longman, 1988.

Gibson, Janice T. *Discipline Is Not a Dirty Word.* Lexington, Mass.: Lewis, 1983.

Ramsey, Robert D. *Educator's Discipline Handbook.* West Nyack, N.Y.: Parker, 1981.

Strother, Deborah B., ed. *Effective Classroom Management.* Bloomington, Ind.: Phi Delta Kappa, 1985.

References

Hall, R. V., et al. "Instructing Beginning Teachers in Reinforcement Procedures Which Improve Classroom Control." *Journal of Applied Behavior,* 1 (1968): 315–28.

Madsen, Charles H., Jr., and Clifford K. Madsen. *Teaching/Discipline.* 3d ed. Boston: Allyn & Bacon, 1981.

PART 5

Plans and Results

I shot an arrow into the air,
It fell to earth, I knew not where.

These lines from Longfellow describe in a poetic way what many teachers do: They lead an activity, but they are not specific about what they are trying to accomplish and they don't know the results of their effort. Shooting an arrow skyward implies a lack of clarity about what, if anything, was to be achieved. Not bothering to find out where the arrow landed implies a lack of interest in assessing the results. Unlike poets, teachers should know where their "arrows" are aimed and where they land. Chapter 17 is devoted to the aiming and assessing of the results of the "educational arrows" of music teachers.

Because all music educators are members of a profession, they need to be informed about and conscious of the larger field. Chapter 18 seeks to encourage such an awareness. ⚡

CHAPTER 17

Planning and Assessing Music Teaching

At first glance it may seem odd to talk about planning and assessment in the same chapter. Planning is concerned with organizing for instruction, while assessing involves finding out how much the students have learned. The reason they go together is that they are actually two sides of the same coin, so to speak. Planning concentrates on what will be learned and how it will be learned, and assessment centers on how well the students learned what was planned.

USING OBJECTIVES

The key to both planning and assessing is the formulation of objectives—statements of what the students should gain from the instruction. Without clearly defined objectives, both planning and assessing will be ineffective and largely a waste of time. It is, of course, possible to have effective planning without any assessment of whether or not learning took place, but the opposite is not possible: Teachers cannot assess learning if no objectives have been spelled out to assess.

Objectives are most useful when they are stated (1) specifically and (2) in terms of what the students should be able to do to indicate they have learned. Here are three examples of objectives that meet the two criteria just mentioned:

George Edwards is teaching his seventh grade general music class about major and minor chords. He wants the students to be able to recognize by ear the difference between major and minor triads.

Aaron Feldman wants his band members, among other objectives, to tell the difference between harmony and counterpoint when they hear them in a band composition.

Lori Petrosky is teaching her high school fine arts class about the main features of romanticism—its fondness for nature and the "long ago and far away," its trusting of emotions instead of intellect, and the like—and wants the students to recognize those characteristics in works of art, music, and literature.

These objectives can be stated in actions or behaviors that the students do to show that learning has taken place. All that is needed is to answer three questions: (1) What will the students do? (2) under what conditions? and (3) with what degree of success? Here is how the three teachers just mentioned might assess the objective they had selected:

George Edwards: "The students will indicate by answering questions after a triad has been played or by raising their hands during the playing of the music that they recognize the difference between major and minor triads."

Aaron Feldman: "Nine out of ten band members will be able to answer correctly in rehearsal whether the music they are playing at the moment is basically a melody accompanied by chords or counterpoint."

Lori Petrosky: "Given a short romantic poem not previously studied in class, most of the students will be able to locate and list in writing three characteristics of romanticism in the poem."

Figure 17.1 presents visually the three essential components of a behavioral objective.

You may have noticed that one of the teachers established a standard or criterion level for student learning: Nine out of ten were to answer correctly. The setting of a level is done arbitrarily by the teacher as a goal for his or her teaching and in some cases for the students to complete a portion of a course. Specifying a standard is not an essential part of assessing learning, but it can be a valuable guide to teachers and students. Teachers can use the criterion level in making decisions about what should be done in future classes or rehearsals. Students can use criterion levels in completing tasks that are part of a larger program of study. Many students find the learning of a program bit by bit much more effective than dealing with large chunks of learning.

A clear statement of objectives in terms of what the students should be able to do is not just an intellectual exercise. It is necessary for good teaching, and in many ways it represents an important change of emphasis from the way teachers have usually thought about planning and assessing. With behavioral objectives the attention is shifted from what teachers do to what students are able to do. This change is more the way it should be because, in the end, schools exist so that students learn, not to provide employment for teachers (as desirable as that may be).

Furthermore, looking for student actions to indicate the amount of learning prevents teachers from simply assuming that their students have learned. Too often

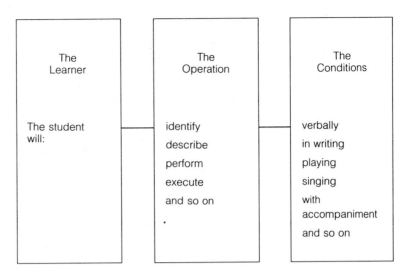

Figure 17.1   *The three essential components of a behavioral objective.*

teachers have had objectives that were so general that no one could tell if the students had achieved them or not. Having students understand this or that point may be a desirable objective, but teachers must be specific about what the students will be able to do as a result of the instruction and not trust their luck that learning has taken place.

PLANNING

Because planning precedes assessing in terms of when it takes place, it is logical to begin with it. Some points concerning planning merit explanation: why it is needed, how much of it do music teachers do, how it can be done, and what aids exist in making plans.

Need for Planning

The reasons for planning in teaching any subject may be so obvious that they are sometimes overlooked. The main reason planning is done is to enable teachers to know what they are trying to accomplish and how they will accomplish it. Without planning, teachers are not clear about what they want to teach or the methods they will use to help the students learn.

There are other benefits of planning. One benefit is the feelings of confidence and security it encourages, which usually helps a teacher be more effective. Another benefit of planning is that time and effort are not wasted because of uncertainty and confusion. Time is usually wasted when teachers try improvising in front of a class. Making up instruction on the spot seldom helps students learn.

Amount of Planning by Music Teachers

Many music teachers, especially those who direct performing groups, do not do much planning; in fact, a few teachers seem to do none at all, except for the setting of some dates for performances and other nonteaching matters. Planning is not a popular topic in the music education profession. If planning has the benefits just described, then why do music teachers not do more of it? There are several likely reasons. One is that some music teachers see the function of school music as the providing of entertainment instead of the education of students. As long as the students seem to be having a good time, these teachers are not worried about learning. Although they may not be aware that they have made such a fundamental decision, by their actions, as Chapter 3 points out, they have indicated their beliefs.

Some teachers wonder if anyone cares whether or not the students in their classes learn much about music. Sometimes, or so it seems, the principal is favorably impressed if there are few complaints about music class from the students and almost never is anyone sent to the office for disciplinary reasons. Other music teachers and some parents want a performing group to win high ratings at contests or present entertaining performances, and they don't care about other aspects of music education. In other words, the rewards (or reinforcement, to use a psychological term) to teachers for teaching students about music are not strong in many situations.

Many music teachers carry a heavy teaching load. They hurry from one class to another for six hours a day, and after school they have special rehearsals or help students. There simply is not much time or energy left for planning by the end of the day.

It is clear that there are aspects of music teaching that cannot be fully planned for. When teaching a song in two parts to a general music class, no one can predict exactly how well the class will sing the song or the places where mistakes will occur. Therefore, the teacher must make some on-the-spot decisions, regardless of the amount of prior planning.

Some music teachers are suspicious of planning because they think it might encourage teaching that lacks flexibility and spontaneity. This might be true if teachers were unwilling to make any changes in their plans or allowed their plans to shackle their enthusiasm and adaptability. Clearly, if it seems wise to alter a plan and it appears that the students will learn more if a change is made, then no teacher should hesitate to change what has been planned. Although some plans may be altered before they are used, the original planning was not a waste of time. The unused planning was a foundation on which the teacher built a better lesson; it provided something for the teacher to work from, which is better than stumbling about without objectives and ideas of how to achieve them.

Aids in Planning

It is not a sign of weakness or incompetence to take advantage of books and curriculum guides in planning, especially if you are not an experienced teacher. Music teachers in the secondary schools see five and sometimes six classes a day, and elementary music specialists often teach music at six different grade levels and see each classroom twice a week. That amount of teaching requires a lot of planning. A new teacher has no reservoir of ideas from previous years, so an even greater effort in planning is required. Any help that a teacher can utilize in planning and teaching should not be avoided.

Several sources are available that provide suggestions and ideas on which teachers can build. Some school districts have developed curriculum guides or courses of study for parts of their music curriculum. Some of these guides are useful, but others are very general and of limited value to teachers. Many states publish curriculum guides, some of which can be a source of ideas for teachers. Elementary and middle school music specialists can take advantage of the ideas offered in the music series books. These books contain not only materials and lessons but also suggestions and teaching aids. Teachers need not use everything in a book or guide; they can choose what will be useful to them and omit portions that are not of value.

Planning for Different Types of Classes

Music classes tend to divide into two types. One type is the general music classes found in the elementary and junior high or middle schools. The other type consists of rehearsals of performing groups and is found mostly in the secondary schools. The general music classes study music through a variety of activities such as singing, listening, creating, discussing, and reading.

An important difference between general music classes and the rehearsals of performing groups lies in the much greater amount of on-the-spot judgments and decisions that teachers make when rehearsing. There is also a difference in that rehearsals of performing groups do not usually entail the wide variety of musical learning that is found in general music classes.

Long-Range Planning

Where does a teacher start in planning for an entire school year? Because this is no easy task, the beginning teacher should feel free to take ideas from any source—books, curriculum guides, and other teachers. And there should be no hesitation about coming up with one's own ideas. But what kind of ideas? Ideas about what you want the student to learn, to be able to do.

At the beginning these ideas may be general and vague. They need to be honed and sharpened so that they can be stated clearly and in terms of student actions. For example, suppose you have an idea that you would like to see the students understand and read music notation better. That is a perfectly good but vague notion. The next step is to state the idea in specific terms so that you can express more clearly what you want them to know about or do with notation. It might be that among other things you want them to become conscious of the size of intervals in a melody. You hope they notice that adjacent intervals sound closer than wide intervals, and you also hope that the students can identify the basic intervals such as thirds and fifths when they see and hear them. What began as a general idea has now become more specific.

Although it may not be easy to "fill in the blanks" for classes meeting a couple of months in the future, teachers should attempt to plan for an entire semester or school year. Long-term planning allows for thinking through the sequence in which topics will be presented. Without such plans, gaps or duplication probably will occur. For example, one teacher was teaching about the jazz influences in music and wanted to have the students learn about blue notes. When he got to the point where he wanted to explain how the third, fifth, and seventh notes of the scale are lowered, he realized that the students did not know the pattern of the major scale.

Planning for a course or a school year concentrates on the main topics and their order of appearance. Making detailed lesson plans for classes that will be taught three months in the future probably is a waste of time, because changes will be needed by the time the plans are to be taught. For these reasons, prospective and beginning teachers should think of long-term planning as the first step. They should expect to make changes in them; in fact, they can expect to make quite a few changes.

Sometimes inexperienced teachers plan for much more than can be covered adequately. The extra material presents no problem, as long as it does not frustrate the teacher or cause him or her to skim over topics in an effort to cover the content. It is better to have more ideas than can be used than it is to have too few and run out of things to teach.

Unit Planning

In a sense, planning for a group of classes or rehearsals is halfway between planning for a course and planning for just one class. Unit plans have elements of long-term planning in that they cover three or more classes, but they are much more specific about what will be taught and how it will be taught. It is at this point that the objectives become more specific. Sometimes the plans for a small number of classes or rehearsals can be written at the same time.

The idea of unit planning makes it possible for a topic to act as a unifying thread for a number of classes. A topic is not treated in just one short presentation but rather is developed and studied in enough depth to help the students remember it better.

The unit idea can be overdone, of course. Conceivably, an entire year could be spent on music of Russia, with all theoretical learnings, songs, recordings, and class activities revolving around that single topic. Instead of aiding learning, such an excess could become excruciatingly boring.

One guideline that music teachers should follow in developing or selecting units is that they be centered on something to do with music. Rather than selecting a group of songs about rivers or lines from plays, both of which are nonmusical topics, units in general music classes should be about sound, types of music, uses of music, playing or singing, and so on. The difference between building around a musical or a nonmusical topic may seem like hairsplitting, but it can lead to quite different types of lessons. In the case of the nonmusical topic, music is included when appropriate for the topic. In the case of a musically centered unit, other information is included as it pertains to the music being studied.

Because class situations vary greatly, and because each unit has its own particular requirements, it is impossible to provide a model plan that can be used for all units. Essentially the unit should focus on some phase of music and integrate as much as possible the activities of singing, listening, creating, discussing, and reading. It is neither possible nor desirable for every unit to encompass in each class period the wide variety of activities that could be included. Some topics suggest singing, while others invite discussion and study. Teachers should not strain to achieve subject matter integration where it does not logically exist. If a unit does not in itself suggest appropriate songs, then the class can work on songs that are not directly related to the unit and that will not detract from the unit. When possible, videotapes, books, bulletin board displays, field trips, and appearances by outside authorities should be integrated into the unit of study—not forcibly, but as a logical extension of the learning experience.

The rehearsals of performing groups can also be planned in units. If, as is hoped, the course of study consists of more than preparing for one public performance after another, then units can be formed around types of music, forms, or technical problems. For example, a unit for studying choral music could be formed about particular aspects of works from Russia or the Renaissance, a unit of band music developed around overtures, and a unit for orchestras created around types of bowing. While such learning is going on, the group is also rehearsing some of the music for performance.

Lesson Planning

When all is said and done, lesson planning is merely the process of organizing the things a class will do to learn music. Although several approaches can be used to develop lesson plans for teaching music, certain guidelines should be considered:

1. Consider what most of the students know and what would be worthwhile for them to learn in music. Finding out the students' present knowledge or skills may involve giving a test. However, because of practical limitations of time and energy, music teachers cannot do this very often. Furthermore, after a teacher has taught a group of students for a while, he or she should have a

rather clear idea about what the students know and can do musically. In performing groups each performance of music provides the teacher with information about what the group can do. Observing student responses to questions and other learning activities provides some information in music classes. Although teachers need not give formal pretests often, they should consciously look for and consider where the students are in terms of the subject and what has been covered in previous classes.

2. Select two or three specific topics or skills to teach in music classes—or one specific topic or skill in each rehearsal. Students, especially those in elementary and middle school, become restless and their attention wanes if any one activity is continued for too long a period of time. One activity is satisfactory for rehearsals because a lot of time is spent playing or singing.

3. State the points to be studied specifically. An objective such as "to learn about music composed in the Renaissance style" is too vague and too broad. An objective such as "to identify aurally and in notation the points of imitation in Renaissance madrigals and motets" is much clearer and more manageable.

4. Formulate the objectives for the class or group in terms of what the students should be able to do as a result of the instruction. Unless the students can provide evidence of how much they have learned, it is hard for a teacher to determine what should be taught in subsequent classes. Behavioral objectives can apply to skills; for example, "The group will learn to sing Palestrina's 'Sanctus' with a light tone and accurate pitch." Other objectives can apply to cognitive learning with a criterion level added if the teacher so desires; for example, "Ninety percent of the students will be able to locate in the notation three examples of imitative entrances in 'Sanctus' by Palestrina."

5. Select appropriate materials. The teacher who wishes to teach about Renaissance madrigals should try to secure the most authentic version of each madrigal that is available and to play recordings of madrigals being sung in an authentic style.

6. Decide on how the content is to be taught. Suppose that a class is learning to identify A B A form. There are several ways in which this could be done. If the class knows a song that is in A B A form, they could sing it through and identify the different sections. A recording of a work with clearly delineated sections in A B A could be played. The students could create a simple piece in three-part form using classroom instruments. They might think of ways to represent visually the different sections of a piece of music, such as with different symbols or colors for the various sections of the work. Each of these ways—and many others—is appropriate under the right circumstances.

7. Assess the results of each portion of a class or rehearsal. Assessing learning is discussed in the second half of this chapter.

These seven guidelines are based on the basic questions raised in Chapter 1 about teaching: What? To whom? How? With what results? Lesson plans should contain the "in action" answers to those four basic questions. Of course, there is a fifth question that underlies all teaching: Why? The reasons for knowing music are basic to all planning and teaching, but they do not need to be restated for each lesson.

The exact manner in which a lesson plan is put down on paper is not of major importance, but planning for the main points to be taught is. What follows is a sample plan built around the basic questions of what, how, and with what results. In the sample plan these questions are indicated along the left-hand side of the page by the words "Objectives," "Materials," "Procedures," and "Assessment of Results." Notice that the categories are used for both of the main topics to be presented in the lesson. Estimates of the amount of time to be consumed by a topic are also included. Such estimates provide a teacher with some guidance on how much time to spend but should not be followed slavishly. The "If time permits" heading allows for some latitude in using time and saves a teacher from the uncomfortable position of completing the planned lesson with ten or more minutes of class time remaining. As you become more experienced in teaching, it may not be necessary to write plans in as much detail as the one presented here. Often one-word cues are enough. The amount of detail in plan is a matter on which teachers have their own individual preferences.

Sample Lesson Plan for General Music

Objectives	1. Learn about the music and words of typical ballads.
	2. Become informed about the gestures used in conducting, the conductor's score, and interpretations and how they differ.
Materials	1. *Music and You,* 7, and recordings.
Procedures	1. Ballad (15 minutes):

    (a) Review "Henry Martin" (*Music and You,* p. 41), by singing the song again. Give the class the seventh and eighth verses.

    (b) Ask if most songs they sing express feelings or tell a story. Discuss the text. Does it tell a story? Is it happy? Does it repeat lines or words? Does it contain any words they don't understand?

    (c) Ask about the characteristics of music. Does it need much accompaniment? Does it have several verses to the same melody? Does it contain any portions that are similar or the same? Is it highly expressive music? What's unusual about the rhythm?

    (d) Listen to the recording of "Henry Martin."

    (e) Sing the song again with improved expression and style.

Lesson Plan

Aspects of music to be taught through materials or activity	Materials and/or activities	Method or procedures to be used to teach topic or skill	Actions of students to be observed for evaluation of amount of learning

Figure 17.2   *Example of lesson plan in which the information is to be written in columns.*

2. Conductor (25 minutes):
   (a) Read and discuss the pages on conducting in *World of Music* (pp. 89–94).
   (b) Discuss the musical decisions of conductors. Point out how the size and style of gestures give an idea of the style of the music.
   (c) Study the page of the score of "O Fortuna" from Orff's *Carmina Burana,* and explain any words the students don't know.
   (d) Play the recording of the two versions of "O Fortuna." Which is faster? Louder? How does the tone quality differ between them?
   (e) Ask if one version is better than the other or just different. Discuss personal preferences and their validity.
3. If time permits (5 minutes): Review "Frog Went A-Courtin'" (*Music and You,* p. 122). Compare with "Henry Martin." Discover what chords are used in the accompaniment.

Assessment of Results

As a result of the lesson, the students will be able to:
1. Describe the characteristics of storytelling, strophic form, rather detached quality in the ballad, and find similar measures. (Check for participation in singing.)

2. Describe how conducting gestures reflect style of music, describe the basic pattern of an orchestral score, and state differences between two versions of "O Fortuna."

Lesson plans can be arranged in several different formats. One has just been presented. Another example, shown in Figure 17.2, presents a different type of format in which the information is to be written in columns according to the portion of the teaching process.

Lesson plans should not be like scripts for a play that teachers read almost line by line to a class. Such plans are very time-consuming to prepare, and few people can read a lecture to a class and make it seem interesting and vital. Some materials available to teachers do provide ready-made questions and lines to read to the class; these are the actual content of a lesson, not plans for a lesson. There is a difference between a plan and something to read.

Planning for Rehearsals

To prepare for rehearsals, teachers must decide (1) which pieces will be studied, (2) which places in the music should receive special attention, and (3) what should be accomplished or learned in conjunction with the music. In addition, teachers need to study the score and parts to the music they don't already know. The teacher studies the music prior to class or rehearsal to analyze it, to learn the score, to work on any special conducting techniques, and to decide on the best interpretation of the work. Also, the study should anticipate spots that are likely to be difficult for the group. When the students reach a troublesome passage, teachers should be quick to come up with the alternative fingering for G on the trumpet, a bowing technique that will help the strings to coordinate the bow with the left hand, or a suggestion for getting the woodwinds to play a particular rhythmic figure correctly. *No teacher or conductor should be caught unprepared for such problems in the music; plans should have been made for overcoming them.*

No single outline of activity is suitable for all rehearsals of performing groups, of course. The methods and content will vary according to what the students have learned previously, the closeness of a performance, and the type of music being studied. Many teachers begin rehearsals with a combination warm-up and technique-developing routine. This portion of the rehearsal should be varied from day to day and be relevant to the other activities in the course. In singing, for example, attention can be centered on producing the sound correctly or singing in tune. In instrumental music, playing techniques can be stressed, or a scale or exercise can be played to practice correct fingerings or bowings. This type of work should be brief—not longer than five or seven minutes.

To close a class, the students can review something they do well or put together something on which they have been working. The idea is not to leave the group hanging in the middle of learning a piece of music when the period ends. Between the opening and closing of the rehearsal, the group can begin studying new music, review familiar works, perfect its current repertoire, and learn aspects of music theory and literature relevant to the music being rehearsed.

It is probably possible to get by without spending time in planning for teaching. However, music educators should set their goals higher than just getting by. If students in music classes and performing groups are to learn the most they can in the time available, teachers need to plan carefully for what they will do.

ASSESSING

"What did the students learn?" has become an important question, for a number of reasons. First, teachers have become increasingly aware that they need to have evidence on how well their students are learning. Without such evidence, they have no solid basis for making educational decisions. Second, federal, state, and local school agencies have grown more concerned about the results of education. To put it bluntly, the taxpayers want to know what they are getting for their money. Giving a lot of attention to the immediate, visible results of learning may be shortsighted, but it is understandable.

A third reason for securing evidence of learning is that it helps teachers in planning subsequent instruction. A teacher whose band has not learned to play dotted eighths and sixteenths correctly should be aware of that fact and try different methods to teach the playing of this pattern. At least the original approach should be tried again, perhaps more thoroughly than before. Unless past results are confronted and assessed, planning for the future is an exercise in guesswork.

It is surprising how careful some teachers are in preparing for a class and how careless they are about finding out what is really learned in that class. It is easy to assume that learning is taking place. Also, sometimes teachers think that if the students do not learn, it is the students' fault. And then, some music teachers are unsure of how or what to evaluate, and some teachers may fear that evaluating student learning will show that the teachers have not taught as much as they thought they had.

Ways of Assessing

Doing assessment well is not easy, because it is not possible to measure many aspects of learning directly. For example, the concept of *musicianship* is not something that can be weighed, seen, or held in the hand. It exists only as a concept or mental construct in people's minds. To most people, actions such as performing the music accurately, phrasing at suitable places, and changing dynamic levels carefully and sensibly are indications of it. However, no two people mean exactly the same thing when they use the word *musicianship*. This situation presents a problem, because people look for slightly different things in musicianship. What, then, can be measured about musicianship or any mental construct? The answer is *indicators*. Indicators of musicianship probably include keeping a steady tempo, performing in tune, phrasing at the right places, using an appropriate tone quality, and so on. It is very unlikely that a student who plays with poor intonation, breaks up phrases, and seldom varies the dynamic level will be considered musical. Although seeking evidence about indicators of something does not solve all the assessment problems (for example, some people may not agree that keeping a steady beat or knowing where a breath should be taken are valid indicators), such evidence is far more valid in assessing learning than is trying to deal with general ideas.

Assessing the effectiveness of instruction does not mean giving one test after another. It is not necessary to involve all the members of the class in every evaluation situation. A sample of four or five students selected at random to answer questions or in other ways indicate what they are learning is usually enough to provide a good idea of how much learning is taking place.

Tests and Testing

Because grading is involved in most courses, and because school administrators, boards of education, and parents want reports on student achievement, teachers usually need to construct and give tests. Their informal observations of student learning are valuable for their own use, but inadequate for purposes of grading. So a more formal assessment of students is needed, in addition to the evaluation of instruction.

What is being discussed here is the evaluation of achievement—what the students have learned—and not aptitude. Admittedly there is a rather close relationship between the two types of tests—achievement and aptitude—but the correlation is not so high that the two can be used interchangeably.

As was pointed out in Chapter 5, the nature of instruction, and therefore evaluation, differs somewhat according to the type of learning—cognitive, psychomotor, or affective. The discussion of testing is, therefore, divided into these three types.

Cognitive Tests.   One type of cognitive test is the essay examination. It gives the students latitude in organizing their responses and expressing their ideas fully. But different test graders vary in their assessment of the answers, and even the same grader will vary from one time to another. Also, verbally adept students have an advantage over the less articulate students on this type of examination. For many instructors, the essay examination is simply not feasible because the grading can be too time-consuming when large numbers of students are involved.

The true-false examination is generally unsatisfactory. The 50 percent chance of guessing the correct response requires that many items be written to cancel the effects of chance and achieve significant results. Furthermore, it is difficult to write true-false questions that probe an area in depth.

The completion question requires the students to fill in the correct word. For example, "The stick held by the conductor is called a _____." Completion questions are satisfactory when a precise term is required. The question should be worded so that there is no ambiguity about the correct answer. For example, the question "A feature of Baroque music is _____" could be answered by the words *continuo, harpsichord, metrical rhythm,* or a number of other terms. Such a question should be avoided.

The multiple-choice question has several advantages. It can be scored easily either by hand or by machine, so a large number of tests can be graded quickly. Its chance factor is usually one in four or five—much lower than the true-false item. With imagination and planning, teachers can write multiple-choice questions to test general understanding as well as specific facts. A correct response does not depend on a student's ability to verbalize an answer.

A multiple-choice question consists of two parts. One is the statement, called the "stem," which applies to all the choices. For example: "In sonata form the first large section is called . . ." The stem must be short. The choices to complete the stem are called "foils" or "distractors." If teachers have trouble inventing enough logical foils for four or five choices, they can write foils such as "None of the above," "All of the above," "True of both (a) and (b)," and so on. In the preparation of such a test, there is a tendency to put a disproportionate number of the correct choices in the last distractor, which causes an undesirable overbalance on it. Apparently there is a subconscious desire to withhold the right answer until the students have read the other choices. In addition, the correct choice often contains the most words because it must be accurate; the wording of the incorrect foils seldom matters. Here is a typical multiple-choice item:

The song "Scarborough Fair" is from:

(a) the Appalachian Mountains

(b) France

(c) England

(d) the western United States

(e) Mexico

The difficulty of an item can be varied by adjusting the specificity of the question. For example:

"Scarborough Fair" is:

(a) a ballet

(b) an aria

(c) a broadside

(d) a ballad

(e) an art song .

is a much more demanding question than

"Scarborough Fair" is:

(a) an opera

(b) a ballet

(c) a folk song

(d) a church hymn

(e) none of the above

A statement or question employing a negative in the stem is useful when you can't think up enough logical foils. An in-depth examination of an area can be accomplished through a series of multiple-choice questions. Sometimes several questions can be built to refer back to a single descriptive paragraph or musical example.

The most important criterion of a test is whether it is valid—whether it tests the students on the real content of the course. If the general music class spends most of its time singing, and the band spends most of its time getting ready for public appearances, it is hardly fair to test the students on the keys of Beethoven's symphonies, as this information is not a logical outgrowth of their experiences in the course.

No matter which tests are favored, the teacher should include questions that involve varying degrees of complexity and comprehensiveness. There is a big difference between these two questions: "What does the word *accelerando* mean?" and "Which of these two musical examples is most representative of the Renaissance polyphonic style?" The first question is confined to a specific musical fact, one that can be learned by rote without much understanding. The second requires pulling together knowledge, experiences, and comparative judgment for evaluating music. The first type of question is certainly acceptable; factual knowledge has its place in any subject. But the rudimentary level of comprehension should not be the only one tested, as was pointed out in Chapter 5.

The most notable published achievement test is the *Music Achievement Test* by Richard Colwell. It uses a recording and is designed for evaluating students in upper elementary grades and junior high school. The Music Achievement Test includes subtests on pitch, intervals, major/minor, meter discrimination, auditory-visual discrimination, feeling for tonal center, tonal memory, melody, pitch, instrument recognition, and identification of style, texture, and chords. Its reliability is high, and its validity has been established by correlations with other tests, by performance ratings of students made one year after taking the test, and a variety of teacher ratings of students. The norms were developed from a sample of 9600 students, a far greater number than was used in standardizing any other music test.

Psychomotor Tests   Music teachers are often concerned with the development of skills. Administering ear-training examinations, adjudicating at contests and festivals, and deciding who will be first-chair clarinet are three examples of situations that require the teacher to evaluate technical skills. Often this area is not handled in as capable a manner as the testing of cognitive achievement.

The problem in assessing skills properly is apparent in the contest situation. Adjudicators must rely solely on their impressions of one performance. Even when an adjudication form is available, it calls for general observations about various aspects of the performance—tone quality, technical proficiency, and so on.

Most of the rating forms are general categories of technical skills required in performance, which does encourage more consistent reporting. They do include some space for the adjudicator's comments and criticisms. However, merely listing grades for each category is not particularly informative. For example, what does a grade of B on technique mean? That the group was not together? Some notes were missed? Some rhythmic figures were not executed properly? Some articulations were incorrect or sloppy? The tempo slowed down in the difficult places? Teachers and students can assume that B is better than C but not as good as A, and that's all. In some respects, adjudicators might have given a more useful report if they had been provided a blank sheet of paper on which to write comments.

Sometimes adjudicators vary widely in their assessment of a performance. For example, in one contest the same band received a first division rating from one judge, a third division from another, and a fifth (the lowest possible rating) from the third judge. Some states allow adjudicators to confer about their ratings so that such embarrassing disagreements can be avoided. Differing opinions are not confined to contest adjudicators, either. Varying evaluations of performing ability occur regularly among juries of applied music teachers who hear individual performances of college music majors.

The probable cause for varying ratings by teachers and adjudicators is not that they are incompetent but rather that they are each listening and looking for different things—the problem of mental constructs mentioned earlier in the chapter. For assessments to be useful, they must be made on specific points that are agreed on by the panel or jury and should be specifically stated, preferably in writing.

Within the class or rehearsal room, assessment should also consider specific aspects—the more specific, the better. How can this specificity be accomplished? One method is to tape-record a performance and replay the example enough times to hear everything thoroughly. This involved procedure is used in research studies, but it is too time-consuming for most teachers to undertake. The answer to the dilemma between the need for accurate assessment and limited time is to select a sample of the music and aspects of performance.

Suppose that in the "Hallelujah Chorus" from Handel's *Messiah,* the teacher decides to test the basses by concentrating on three phrases from the bass part. (The students may sing more than the three phrases. They need not know the exact places selected for adjudication.) One of the phrases is:

And He   shall   reign   for - ev - er   and   ev - er

From this phrase the teacher might choose three places for precise assessment: (1) the tone quality and pitch of the high D, (2) the accuracy and evenness of the two eighth notes, and (3) the diction and tone quality of the last note of the phrase. Other aspects could have been chosen, of course, but these three can be used to secure some solid evidence for assessment. Because these three places occur several beats apart, which allows the teacher time to think, it is possible for their quality to be assessed during a live performance.

A published test employing some of the ideas advocated here is available for specific instruments: the *Watkins-Farnum Performance Scale* by John Watkins and Stephen Farnum. The test consists of sixteen graded levels of achievement. Reliability is rather good. Validation was made by correlating an overall ranking with the test scores. The correlations are high, from .86 on some brass instruments to .68 on drums. The test is carefully developed and norms are provided. The most common complaint of teachers who have used this test is the complicated scoring process. Actually, teachers can pursue the idea of specific, precise assessment without using this particular test by carefully developing their own performance examination.

A word of caution needs to be given about employing tape recordings for evaluation, especially when large groups are involved. Even the finest equipment under the best conditions cannot reproduce exactly what the human ear hears. In some cases the recording is a distortion of the actual sounds. School recording equipment and recording conditions are usually not the best, and they do not faithfully reproduce some aspects of the music, especially timbre and overall balance. Ideally, one could evaluate those aspects during live performance and then use the tape recording to check for wrong notes, phrasing, and the like.

The tape recorder can be a valuable aid in hearing students individually without consuming a lot of rehearsal time. The recorder can be set up in another room, with its volume level, treble and bass setting, and microphone placement properly adjusted before the auditions begin. Each student individually goes into the room, pushes the "record" button, announces his or her name, plays or sings the assigned music, then stops the recording and returns to class. The teacher can listen to the audition tape at a more convenient time.

How should test of skill development be scored? The rating system used in some state contests assigns a specific number of points to the grade given in each category. The points are then totaled to determine the overall rating. The practical result in some states is that as long as the student or group shows up and performs, it is impossible for that entrant to receive the lowest overall rating. This fact may reduce anxiety for the participants, but it undermines the integrity of the ratings. A more serious flaw in assigning points is that they tend to blur valid distinctions among performers. For example, if a group does well on almost everything, but has terrible intonation, it can still be placed in the highest rating. In actual practice, adjudicators adjust points in other areas so that this does not happen. But adjusting points to achieve the correct overall rating is evidence of the weakness of such a point system. Another weakness is that each piece of music is different: In one work the tone quality and expression may be most important, while in another it is the execution of the notes. If points are assigned to areas of performance, they need to be reapportioned for each musical work in order to be valid.

The best answer is to assign points to the specific places selected. Returning to the phrase from the "Hallelujah Chorus" cited earlier in this chapter, the teacher-adjudicator should determine how many points can be earned by the best possible execution of the three places selected. Then points should be assigned—so many for the timbre on the high D, so many for the accuracy of its intonation, so many for not sustaining the r sound on the final note, and so on. As in all testing, some subjective judgment is involved in assigning points. However, by observing skills as objectively and systematically as possible, teachers can assess performance as accurately and fairly as they do cognitive learning.

Affective Assessment. Assessing attitudes presents obstacles not found in assessing factual learning or skills. First, is it possible to test attitudes? Either students know what a diminished seventh chord is, or they don't. But if asked, "Do you enjoy the sound of a diminished seventh chord?" the students can give the answer they think the teacher wants to hear. Furthermore, words are not always indications of true belief and practice. Some people profess honesty, but cheat on their golf score and income tax.

Second, there also remains the question of whether beliefs and values *should* be graded, a point mentioned in Chapter 4.

To be valid, the assessment of attitudes should be separate from grading students. Freeing the assessment of attitudes from grades encourages the students to respond honestly by removing the influence of rewards or penalties from their answers. To assure the students that they may express their attitudes freely, teachers can suggest that written responses to questions of attitude be made anonymously.

Assessing students' attitudes accurately requires skill both in gathering information and in interpreting it. Although music teachers are not expert researchers, they still can gain insight into how students' attitudes are being affected by observing the choices students make regarding musical activities. Do they go to concerts voluntarily? Do they seem to listen to music or just daydream? Did more students attend concerts this year than last? What records do they check out of the library? Has there been a significant change during the year? What songs do students ask to sing? Do they read about musical events in newspapers and magazines?

Questioning students directly can also provide information, but the questions should be subtle. Asking "Do you like Benjamin Britten's music?" is too obvious an approach. Teachers will find out more by asking "Would you like to hear Britten's *A Ceremony of Carols* again?" or "Would you like to hear other music by Benjamin Britten?" or "'This Little Babe' from Britten's *A Ceremony of Carols* is (a) a sissy piece, (b) weird and dull, (c) okay but not as good as many other pieces I know, (d) different but interesting to hear." Another way to ask questions about choices is: "Suppose you've won the lucky number drawing at the music store. You can have *free* any five records of your choice. Which would you choose?" Many variations of this question are possible: "Which composer would you most like to meet? Why?" "Is 'This Little Babe' from Britten's *A Ceremony of Carols* a piece that people will listen to a hundred years from now? Why or why not?"

A somewhat different type of questioning asks students to register their feelings on a scale from *strongly disagree, disagree, neutral, agree,* to *strongly agree.* The statement might be this: "Benjamin Britten's *A Ceremony of Carols* is fascinating music." In this type of item, the wording of the statements should vary. Students circle their choices from the five possible responses.

The projective question is another testing technique: "'This Little Babe' from Britten's *A Ceremony of Carols* sounds like _____." The problem with this type of question is the interpretation required of the answer, especially in the case of students who are not articulate. Playing pairs of musical examples and then asking the students which of the two they prefer can also be used to assess musical attitudes. Several unpublished tests are based on this technique. Unless a teacher can devote considerable time to developing such a test, the results will not be valid.

None of the techniques described here can provide conclusive data about students' attitudes, but each can indicate whether the students are becoming more receptive to and interested in music.

GRADING STUDENTS

Music teachers often consider grading students as a necessary nuisance and feel justifiably that any grading system is inadequate to reflect what a student is accomplishing in music class. Therefore, teachers sometimes tend to consider grading a rather insignificant, routine duty. The students look at grades with interest and concern, even though, paradoxically, grades as such are not a primary motivation for most teenagers. Because many students are sensitive about grades, and because what is learned in music class is less often subjected to concrete examination in written form, it is important that the manner of giving grades be seen by the students as fair and understanding. If grading is handled brusquely or carelessly, it can hinder the establishment of good relationships between students and teachers.

Teachers should establish clear-cut criteria for grading that are consistent with the overall evaluation procedures of the school. So that later misunderstanding is prevented, these standards can be written down and given to each student. The criteria may or may not carry definite point or percentage values. Assigning a certain number of points for effort, for deportment, for technique, and the like gives students a sense of concreteness, but the objectivity is more apparent than real.

Teachers should make clear to the students that the elements forming a grade are interrelated—that effort is usually related to accomplishment, for example. Here are some criteria for a performing organization that consider both effort and ability:

Grade of A

1. Continues to improve in performing music.
2. Has shown much willingness to assume responsibility and better the organization.

3. Has shown much ability to perform a part with accuracy and a good sense of ensemble.

4. Has shown much understanding of the music performed by the organization.

5. Has learned all assigned music and earns high grades on tests.

6. Has shown much initiative by individual practice and study outside of school time.

For a B grade the words *good* or *above average* can be substituted for *much*. The C grade can use *average* or *some* as modifiers, and the D grade can use *below average* and *little*. Attendance is not cited in the criteria because it is assumed that the school has a policy concerning unexcused absences and makeup work.

The purpose of grading is to provide parents, students, and teachers with an accurate picture of the student's work. A single grade cannot do this. If the report card allows for only a single grade, which is often the case, music teachers can give students and parents a clearer understanding of the evaluation by providing supplementary information. A narrative paragraph is often helpful. Another possibility is a form on which teachers check statements about singing, completion of assignments, progress during the marking period, concert attendance, aspects of playing, or whatever is significant for the class. The supplementary sheets should be mailed to the home if teachers want to be sure they are received; students are unreliable couriers, even of favorable reports.

Music teachers face two dilemmas in grading: one between pupil growth and a fixed standard, and the other between musical accomplishment and class deportment. Marks can be determined in relation to some standard, with an A or 100 representing perfection in this system, or they can be decided in relation to the progress and effort that the student has shown. Both methods are valid when applied to the right situations. In college a grade should represent fulfilling some standard. In the elementary schools, however, the concept of rigid standards is not appropriate. It is somewhat unfair to grade a child with many musical advantages by the same standard as another child with an impoverished musical background. Still, by the time students reach secondary school, teachers cannot ignore the existence of some standard of achievement.

A report on the student's musical achievement and his or her contribution to the entire group is especially pertinent in performing organizations. A girl may be the best soprano in the choir, but if her behavior impedes the progress of the group, determining her proper grade is difficult. If the school does not have a dual marking system—one for academic achievement and one for citizenship—her overall grade should reflect her inappropriate behavior.

The value of the curve as a basis for establishing music grades is doubtful, especially for performing groups. First, it is not possible to measure precisely the amount and quality of music learning. It is possible to measure the speed of people's typewriting but not their understanding of a musical phrase. Second, grading rigidly on the curve automatically sentences a certain number of students to low grades, and this is not fair. Third, in high school performing groups that have achieved a fairly high level of advancement, students of lower ability have already been eliminated (especially in instrumental music) by the normal attrition, or they have been placed in less advanced groups. If students are learning well, they deserve to earn reasonably high grades. Although the curve can be considered in determining marks, it should not be followed rigidly.

Some music teachers set up a "point system." Under this system a student receives a specified number of points for each rehearsal attended, each solo appearance, every hour of practice, each private lesson, and so on. When the student earns enough points, he or she receives a specified grade or award. Point systems are based solely on quantity of work and therefore lack validity for purposes of grading, although they are appropriate for determining awards based on service. The teacher may consider the number of points earned in determining a grade if he or she evaluates quality as well as quantity.

Many teachers have students in performing groups audition as a part of class work and grading. These auditions can be held privately, apart from the rehearsal period, or during rehearsal by using a tape recorder outside the classroom. Some teachers prefer to have the students become accustomed to performing publicly, and so the students perform by twos or threes, or alone, in front of the others. Teachers can easily pick out the individual performances in small groups. Students are often stimulated to better efforts by the knowledge that they will have to perform in front of their peers.

Some teachers promote self-assessment by the students. Young people are surprisingly objective in rating their efforts, and others are more critical of themselves than teachers are. The exact wording of the points on which they are asked to assess themselves will vary with the age and development of the group. The students can be asked about the amount of effort they put forth and their achievement in musical areas. Educationally speaking, there is a strong case for self-assessment: It helps the students acquire the ability to judge their own work. Whether self-assessment should become involved with grades given by teachers is another matter. Such involvement might undermine the success of self-assessment. However, if students and teachers understand and accept this technique as a valid part of the grading process, it can be useful. But self-assessment should not force the students to testify against themselves.

Questions
1. How can teachers present well-planned lessons and at the same time allow for some flexibility and spontaneity in their teaching?

2. What are the main differences between music classes and rehearsals with regard to planning? Should plans even be made for conducting a rehearsal? Why or why not?

3. What are the benefits of unit plans over planning for individual lessons?

4. Where can music teachers look for ideas to help in planning for classes or

rehearsals? Why should beginning teachers be especially interested in ideas and suggestions about what they might teach?

5. Which of the following statements are objectives adequately stated in behavioral terms?
   (a) The students will not throw paper in class.
   (b) The students will learn the song "Chester" by Billings.
   (c) Each singer will be able to sing his or her part in "Chester" in tune, with a clear tone, and at tempo, while the piano fills in the remaining parts.
   (d) The students will learn about the Baroque style.
   (e) The students will be able to describe verbally the pattern of the exposition of a typical fugue.

6. Why are educational objectives and assessment so closely related?

7. Name one music achievement test, and describe how it assesses learning in music.

8. What are the advantages and disadvantages of essay examination questions? Of true-false? Of multiple choice?

9. Describe some techniques for assessing students' attitudes and feelings.

10. How would you grade each of these students? (The school requires that you do so; therefore, you can't avoid it.)
    (a) Herb: very talented; first-chair trumpet for two years; loudmouth; makes cutting remarks about other students' playing; written work average.
    (b) Barbara: quiet seventh grader; can hardly be heard when she sings; written work below average but passable; shows little reaction to general music class.
    (c) B. J.: tries very hard in chorus and is improving, but singing only barely passable; written work passable; manager of group and takes care of risers, chairs, and so on. Little aptitude for music, but loves it.

Projects
1. Plan a unit of four general music classes for grades 7 or 8. Assume class periods last for about forty-five minutes. Plan several different topics and/or activities for each class. Allow for some student involvement in each class. Use either format presented in this chapter.

2. Plan a unit of four rehearsals for any performing group from grades 7–12. Assume rehearsal periods last about fifty minutes. Plan one or two points to teach in each rehearsal in addition to playing or singing pieces of music. Use either format presented in this chapter.

3. Administer the Watkins-Farnum Performance Scale to an instrumentalist friend.

4. Write objectives in behavioral terms for this chapter.

5. Examine and evaluate tests you have taken in this and other courses in terms of validity and reliability.

Suggested
Readings

Colwell, Richard. *The Evaluation of Music Teaching and Learning.* Englewood Cliffs, N.J.: Prentice-Hall, 1970.

Klotman, Robert H. *The School Music Administrator and Supervisor: Catalysts for Change in Music Education.* Englewood Cliffs, N.J.: Prentice-Hall, 1973. Chapters 9 and 10.

Labuta, Joseph A. *Guide to Accountability in Music Instruction.* West Nyack, N.Y.: Parker, 1974.

Lehman, Paul R. *Tests and Measurements in Music.* Englewood Cliffs, N.J.: Prentice-Hall, 1968.

Popham, W. James, and Eva L. Baker. *Establishing Instructional Goals.* Englewood Cliffs, N.J.: Prentice-Hall, 1970.

CHAPTER 18

The Music Education Profession

Music teachers are never alone in their work, even though they may be the only music teachers in a particular school or district. They are identified as "music teachers," whether they like it or not. Their work is affected to some degree by what others who teach music have done in the past and are doing now. This happens in several ways.

To begin with, teachers usually succeed other music teachers, and so they inherit a legacy from their predecessors. If, for example, the previous choral teacher devoted his or her main efforts on a big musical each year, it may be hard to wean the students and community away from the annual spring entertainment.

Another influence is that administrators and teachers are aware of what goes on in neighboring school districts, and they tend to make comparisons among schools in relation to enrollments, curriculum, number and length of class meetings, and the size and quality of the performing organizations. There is an unfortunate tendency on the part of some school board members and administrators to be guided more by what similar schools are doing than by what is best for their particular situation. More than one music teacher has been asked: "Why should we start a string program (add more classes of general music, buy some quality instruments for general music classes in the middle school—the same sentiment can be applied to many matters) when Duxbury and Westfield don't have one?"

Also, all school music teachers are involved in the same general type of work. Like it or not, the same conditions and public attitudes affect everyone who teaches music in the schools. If a school music program succeeds and music is made stronger, music education in general benefits. And, unfortunately, every teacher or program that fails hurts music education a little bit.

WHAT IS A PROFESSION?

Music education is often spoken of as a profession, but is it? What characteristics should a type of workers possess in order to earn the distinction of being a "profession"? Four factors seem essential for a profession. One is that their jobs require extensive education and preparation, usually a baccalaureate degree from college and often several years of additional study. A medical doctor graduates from college and completes three or four years of medical school plus several more years of internship and residency. Music teachers do not have as much training, but they usually hold a college degree plus at least one year of graduate study. So they qualify in terms of amount of education.

A second characteristic of a profession is the responsibility for making decisions. An architect plans—makes decisions about—the design and construction of a building; the electricians, plumbers, bricklayers, and other workers carry out specific tasks according to the blueprints of the architect. Music teachers make decisions about how and what students learn in music classes, but they are usually also responsible for carrying them out. Nevertheless, they do make decisions about how something is done.

A third characteristic of a profession is the commitment to their jobs possessed by the membership. Most professionals do not think of their work as only a 9-to-5 undertaking. They work more than the minimum number of hours, and they work when no one tells them to work. Nor is it unusual for them to take some work home with them from the office. Most music teachers (but not all!) possess a real sense of commitment to their chosen work. In fact, their deep sense of commitment sometimes causes problems for them if the public and school administrators do not view the teachers' work as particularly important and do not support it well. That situation can cause frustration and conflict.

Finally, a profession has an organization that is mainly concerned with the advancement of the profession, not with the welfare of its members. This is the main difference between a union and a professional association. A union's main obligation is to improve the pay and working conditions of its members; a professional organization seeks to provide for its members' continued growth in carrying out their work and to advance their profession. This is not to say that unions are wrong or bad (because they have an important role in society) but only that the nature of a professional association is different.

The professional organization of school music teachers in the United States is the Music Educators National Conference (MENC). Although it engages in a wide variety of activities, its two main efforts are professional in-service conferences and publications. In recent years MENC has also spoken for music education to various legislative and governmental agencies at the federal and state levels. To the degree that MENC is successful in promoting music education, all music teachers and students benefit. And the success of MENC depends on how well music teachers are united in supporting it. Smaller, specialized groups within music education such as choral directors and elementary music specialists in one method or another cannot speak for music education as a whole. Teachers who feel attracted to a specialized organization should still retain their commitment and membership in MENC. If they do not, the profession becomes more fragmented and easier prey to the wolves of poor financial and educational support. As Abraham Lincoln quoted from the Gospel of Mark, "A house divided against itself, that house cannot stand."

THE PROFESSION IN THE PAST

There has been music in America since the first Indians migrated to this hemisphere thousands of years ago. European music came with the first settlers to Jamestown and Massachusetts, but it is not clear when professional instruction in music started. The first music instruction books were the product of John Tufts, a minister, who in the early eighteenth century wanted to teach the churchgoing colonists to sing psalms and hymns. He devised a tetrachord system of notation in which the octave is broken into two identical halves. Tufts chose the tetrachords E F G A and B C D E, which he identified by the first letters of the syllables *mi, fa, sol,* and *la* (Lowens, 1964, Chapter 3). His system was later adapted into "shape notes" in which each of the four shapes of note head indicates a syllable. Shape notes are still seen occasionally in the notation of some hymnals, especially in the southern states.

Tufts's efforts were followed by the "singing school movement" in which music teachers traveled from one town to another to give lessons for a few weeks. The singing school was primarily to teach church music. One of the leaders in this movement was Lowell Mason, who in 1837 was able to persuade the Boston Board of Education to initiate singing in the school curriculum. New York had instituted music in the common school program a few years earlier in 1829. Mason was a strong advocate of the ideas of the Swiss educator Johann Heinrich Pestalozzi, as were other educators of that era.

Prior to the twentieth century, education consisted mainly of a common elementary school for children; high school education was mostly preparation for college. Only a small percentage of teenagers attended school, and their education was limited and routine by today's standards. Teachers were poorly prepared and paid and were generally treated as second-class citizens (Brenton, 1970, Chapter 4). Along with many other subjects, music received only rudimentary treatment at best.

The first organization of music teachers, called the National Music Congress, assembled in 1869. This organization grew into the Music Teachers National Association, which created a committee on public school music in 1884. Shortly before the twentieth century the leadership in school music passed to the Music Section of the National Education Association (NEA). The present MENC began in 1907 in Keokuk, Iowa, as a meeting of music supervisors. Two years later the group met again and adopted the name Music Supervisors National Conference, which was not changed to Music Educators National Conference until 1934. The first issue of the *Music Supervisors Bulletin* was published in 1914, and the name was changed to *Music Supervisors Journal* in 1919 and later to the *Music Educators Journal.*

The first elementary basal series music books were published by Edwin Ginn in 1870. The emphasis in these books was on music reading, and it remained so for at least the next half century. The first instrumental groups appeared early in the twentieth century in Winfield and Wichita, Kansas, and in Richmond, Indiana. They were orchestras and were initially combined school-community efforts. Bands became significant in the 1920s, and the first group method books for winds were also published in that decade.

Music education as we know it today did not develop until after 1920 with the growth of the high school, a point mentioned in Chapter 4. Even by 1940 music education did not reach into many schools; that would not happen until the 1950s and 1960s. By the end of the 1970s it was clear that the rate of growth had slowed down considerably. However, in spite of some distressing local situations, more school music programs continue to report increases than decreases in staff and students enrolled.

Has the growth of music education been a steady, smooth climb from its small beginnings? In a pig's eye it has! For some reason, music educators have had a tendency to think that their programs were only a step away from elimination when, in fact, they were thriving. In the early 1930s one of the leaders of music education, Jacob Kwalwasser, advised his students that music education had been a great experiment; but now the depression was here and music probably would not last in the schools, and they should plan pursuing work in their teaching minor area or another field (Sur, 1982). In 1958 the National Defense Education Act was passed by the U.S. Congress. It contained support for the physical sciences, foreign languages, and a few other related educational areas such as counseling, but nothing for the arts and humanities. Also this was the time of the shock caused by *Sputnik*. The great fear was that the sciences would greatly reduce the arts in the schools, and many music educators were filled with pessimism. Yet when the data finally came in for the years 1958–63, they turned out to be some of the best ever for the growth of music education (National Education Association, 1963, p. 12). So while at the time of this writing, things do not appear as bright as they did a decade or two earlier, it is reassuring to know that doubts about the future of school music have a long tradition among music educators—all while the profession was continuing to grow. Fortunately, the trend for music education seems to be on a slow but steady rise after reaching a low point in the early 1980s.

CONCERNS AND OPPORTUNITIES

Music education programs in some places are being threatened with cutbacks and reductions, and their preservation has become a major concern of many music teachers. And other concerns from previous decades also are present. Music educators are questioning the adequacy of what is being offered. Is it affecting a large enough share of the students? Is it meaningful to the students? Are too many hours spent in entertaining the public at the expense of what the students are learning? In addition, other long-term problems remain: the rather high rate of turnover among music teachers, the tendency for many music teachers to have a "looking out for No. 1" attitude, the limited musicianship of some persons currently teaching music, and the excessive amount of attention given to the portions of the music curriculum that the public sees, to say nothing of all the problems that affect education in general.

What should you, as a future teacher of music in the schools, do about the situation? Here are some suggestions to consider:

1. Be committed to your ideals and goals, yet be flexible in achieving them. Granted, this sounds like asking someone to be rigid and flexible at the same time, which is inconsistent. The answer to the dilemma lies in being firm in what you want to accomplish as a teacher but flexible in how you achieve those goals. No one can expect to have his or her way all the time, or even most of the time; accommodations and maybe an occasional retreat will have to be made. For example, you may want to have your students perform a certain piece of music, but there is little to be gained if they do not like it at all or are unable to perform it. It is better to put it away for another year when circumstances should be more favorable. However, do not lose sight of the "big picture" of what you are trying to do. It is easy to lose perspective when you become immersed in the day-to-day activities involved with teaching, and this temptation should be resisted.

2. Keep in mind a view of music education that is greater than just your individual teaching assignment. There really is more to being a music educator than meeting your classes, even though that does require a great deal of ability and energy to do successfully. For instance, unless you and your colleagues educate the school administration and community about the purpose and progress of the music program, there may be fewer classes for you to teach in a year or two. Remember that the more unified music educators are in educating the public and school administrators, the more effective they will be. Try to work with music teachers you hardly know and even those you do not like personally. Like it or not, you are all in the same profession.

3. Continue learning and growing professionally. This point was made in Chapter 2 but it is so important that it bears repeating. Although you may have had excellent training in your undergraduate years (and the "benefits" of reading this book!), that preparation is only a good start toward becoming a good music teacher. There is much more to learn, far more than could be learned in only four or five years and a semester of student teaching. As a part of growing professionally, learn about and evaluate carefully new ideas and practices in teaching music. Examining new practices does not mean that you

must adopt them. Some of these practices should be rejected or modified in their application to your teaching situation. The real criterion is not the newness of a method or proposal but rather the contribution it can make toward educating students in music. Try to strike a happy medium between one who jumps on each new bandwagon and adopts the latest buzzwords and one who has closed his or her mind to any new thoughts.

4. Try not to let a few weak or cynical colleagues discourage you from becoming a good teacher. Keep in mind the fact that every profession, even medicine and law, has members of whom the profession isn't particularly proud. Because it is a large profession and its admission requirements not as high as those of some professions, teaching may have a greater number of them. The thing for you to do is make sure that you do not end up being cynical or ineffective (which is one reason for continuing to grow professionally) and make yourself into the best teacher possible. You can do something about your own teaching; there is little you can do about teachers with low aspirations or abilities. So work with them when you must, as was suggested in point 2 of this discussion, but do not let yourself be dragged down or disenchanted by them.

5. Enjoy teaching music for what it offers young people and society, without becoming overly concerned about the modest financial rewards that teaching provides. In the long run, it is far more satisfying and important that you work at something you enjoy and believe in than to make more money doing something you don't enjoy and don't think is worth much to humanity. For the reasons presented in Chapter 1, teaching can be interesting and enjoyable. For how many types of work can the same thing be said to be true? Not very many. Yes, every job, including music teaching, has its good and bad points. Modest financial rewards is perhaps teaching's worst feature. However, there are other personal benefits, such as fewer days of work each year than in most occupations and after tenure is achieved a higher degree of job security, in addition to the satisfaction and enjoyment. However, if making money is your main goal in life, then a reexamination of your choice of occupation seems called for, because teaching will probably not provide a high enough income to satisfy you.

THE FUTURE

The profession of music education not only has a long and distinguished past but also is alive and vital today, and it is seeking to improve and to do better in the future. To the first sentence in this book—". . . you have chosen a profession that is interesting, challenging, and important"—should be added the word *dynamic* or *vigorous*. This vitality is a good sign, and it bodes well for the future of music education. Not only does it attract the type of person who seeks a continuing challenge, but it also ensures that music education will progress and keep pace with education and society as a whole. Music education cannot afford to rest on its laurels, and if the current scene indicates anything about the future, the profession is in no danger of standing still.

An active and dynamic profession that is seeking to do an even better job produces differences of opinion. And so it is in music education. A kaleidoscope of opinions can be found on almost every aspect of music teaching. To beginning teachers, the lack of agreement may seem confusing. They may wonder why a committee of recognized music teachers cannot be formed, perhaps under the auspices of MENC, and write comprehensive and detailed publications on the best way to teach a particular topic. The answer is that music education, because it is trying new practices and considering divergent views, can achieve only general agreement. Experimentation and differing ideas are not necessarily bad. In fact, they generally indicate intellectual curiosity and professional vitality.

Music education will continue to evolve in the years ahead. Twenty years from now it will not be exactly what it is today. There may be diversions and even regressions, but if the first ninety years of the twentieth century are indicative, there will be continued growth. Generally the changes will be evolutionary, not revolutionary. Real progress in human affairs, education included, seems to come in small increments.

One piece of dismal news is the impending shortage of teachers. According to the National Center for Educational Statistics, the supply of teachers easily exceeded the demand in the 1970s. By 1984, however, the demand began to exceed supply, and it has or will increase each year until by 1992 it exceeds demand by 750,000 teachers for that one year alone, to say nothing of the accumulating shortage from previous years (*A Nation Prepared,* 1986, p. 27).

At first glance, a shortage of teachers may seem beneficial, because it should have the effect of promoting higher salaries. But there is a negative side to this situation. It means that schools have few, if any, candidates to choose from, a fact that affects the smaller and less affluent school districts especially. Many school students are not going to receive the music education they deserve unless good teachers can be employed. The teacher shortage also will encourage states to try sidestepping regular certification procedures in the hope that a lot of uncertified but capable teachers will appear from somewhere. The fact that this hope is unrealistic has to date not discouraged proponents of the idea.

Two major trends in American society are favorable for the future of music education. One of these is the increased emphasis on education (sometimes not matched in financial support) in general, and the other is an increasing interest in the fine arts, especially music. Partly because of the vast sums of money it requires, but more because of society's need for it, education receives much support from local and state sources. Not only are more people going to school, but they also are staying in school longer, and many others are returning to school in adult education programs.

As for the fine arts, greater leisure and economic affluence have enabled artistic interests to develop throughout the population. Radio, television, and the electronic reproduction of music have contributed to the trend. Certainly the great American experiment in mass education can also claim some credit for the increasing interest in the fine arts. For the first time in the long history of the human race, society has the means, the time, and the financial resources to make great music and other arts available to practically everyone. Evidence of this trend is seen in the number of community orchestras, the number of musical instruments purchased, the sales of recordings and sound-producing equipment, the money spent for musical events, and the establishment of fine arts centers and arts councils in many cities and almost every state.

The future of music education will partly be what music educators make of it. The challenges and opportunities are there. To be more complete and accurate, the sentence that opened this book should now be further expanded to read ". . . you have chosen a profession that is interesting, challenging, important, and dynamic, and one with a promising future."

References   Brenton, Myron. *What's Happened to Teacher?* New York: Avon Books, 1970.

Lowens, Irving. *Music and Musicians in Early America.* New York: Norton, 1964.

Music and Art in the Public Schools, Research Monograph 1963-M3. Washington, D.C.: National Education Association, 1963.

A Nation Prepared: Teachers for the 21st Century. New York: Carnegie Forum on Education and the Economy, 1986.

Sur, William R. Letter to the author, April 1982.

APPENDIX

The Music Code of Ethics

The Music Code of Ethics was originally adopted over thirty years ago, and it was slightly revised and reaffirmed in 1989 by the Music Educators National Conference, American Federation of Musicians of the United States and Canada, AFL-CIO, American Association of School Administrators, National Association of Elementary School Principals, and the National Association of Secondary School Principals.

Music educators and professional musicians alike are committed to the general acceptance of music as an essential factor in the social and cultural growth of our country. Music educators contribute to this end by fostering the study of music among children and by developing a greater interest in music.

This unanimity of purpose is further exemplified by the fact that a great many professional musicians are music educators and the fact that a great many music educators are, or have been, actively engaged in the field of professional performance.

The members of high school instrumental groups—orchestras and bands of all types, including stage bands—look to the professional organization for example and inspiration. The standards of quality acquired during the education of these students are of great importance when they become active patrons of music in later life. Through their influence on sponsors, employers, and program makers in demanding adequate musical performances, they have a beneficial effect upon the prestige and economic status of the professional musicians.

Since it is in the interest of the music educator to attract public attention to his attainments, not only for the main purpose of promoting the values of music education but also to enhance his position and subsequently his income, and since it is in the interest of the professional musician to create more opportunities for employment at increased remuneration, it is only natural that some incidents might occur in which the interests of the members of one or the other group might be infringed upon, either from lack of forethought or lack of ethical standards among individuals.

In order to establish a clear understanding as to the limitations of the fields of professional music and music education in the United States, the following statement of policy, adopted by the Music Educators National Conference and the American Federation of Musicians and approved by the American Association of School Administrators, the National Association of Elementary School Principals, and the National Association of Secondary School Principals, is recommended to those serving in their respective fields:

I. MUSIC EDUCATION

The field of music education, including the teaching of music and such demonstrations of music education as do not directly conflict with the interests of the professional musician, is the province of the music educator. It is the primary purpose of this document and the desire of all the parties signatory hereto that the professional musician shall have the fullest protection in his efforts to earn his living from the playing and rendition of music; to that end it is recognized and accepted that all music to be performed under this section of the "Code of Ethics" herein set forth is and shall be performed in connection with nonprofit, noncommercial, and noncompetitive enterprises. Under the heading of "Music Education" the following are included:

1. *School functions* initiated by the schools as a part of a school program, whether in a school building or other site.

2. *Community functions* organized in the interest of the schools strictly for educational purposes, such as those that might be originated by the parent and teachers association.

3. *School exhibits* prepared as a courtesy on the part of a school district for educational organizations or educational conventions being entertained in the district.

4. *Educational broadcasts* that have the purpose of demonstrating or illustrating pupils' achievements in music study or that represent the culmination of a period of study and rehearsal. Included in this category are local, state, regional, and national school music festivals and competitions held under the auspices of schools, colleges, and/or educational organizations on a nonprofit basis and broadcast to acquaint the public with the results of music instruction in the schools.

5. *Civic occasions* of local, state, or national patriotic interest, of sufficient breadth to enlist the sympathies and cooperation of all persons, such as those held by the American Legion and Veterans of Foreign Wars in connection with their Memorial Day services in the cemeteries. It is understood that affairs of this kind may be participated in only when such participation does not in the least usurp the rights and privileges of local professional musicians.

6. *Benefit performances* for local charities, such as the Red Cross and hospitals, when and where local professional musicians would likewise donate their services.

7. *Educational or civic services* that might be mutually agreed upon beforehand by the school authorities and official representative of the local professional musicians.

8. *Student or amateur recordings* for study purposes made in the classroom or in connection with contest, festival, or conference performances by students. Such recordings shall be limited to exclusive use by the students and their teachers and shall not be offered for general sale to the public through commercial outlets. This definition pertains only to the purpose and utilization of student or amateur recordings and not to matters concerned with copyright regulations. Compliance with copyright requirements applying to recordings of compositions not in the public domain is the responsibility of the school, college, or educational organization under whose auspices the recording is made.

II. ENTERTAINMENT

The field of entertainment is the province of the professional musician. Under this heading the following are included:

1. *Civic parades* (where professional marching bands exist), ceremonies, expositions, community concerts, and community-center activities; regattas; non-scholastic contests, festivals, athletic games, activities, or celebrations, and the like; and national, state, and county fairs (see section I, paragraphs 2 and 5, of this document for further definition).

2. *Functions for the furtherance,* directly or indirectly, of any public or private enterprise; functions by chambers of commerce, boards of trade, and commercial clubs or associations.

3. *Any occasion that is partisan* or sectarian in character or purpose.

4. *Functions of clubs,* societies, and civic or fraternal organizations.

Statements that funds are not available for the employment of professional musicians; or that if the talents of amateur musical organizations cannot be had, other musicians cannot or will not be employed; or that the amateur musicians are to play without remuneration of any kind, are all immaterial.

This code is a continuing agreement that shall be reviewed regularly to make it responsive to changing conditions.

INDEX

A

ABC method, 6
Accompaniment, 168–169
Accompanist, selection of, 233–234
Administrators, school and fundraising, 20
Adolescents:
    and adjustment, 326–327
    disadvantaged, 327–328
    motivation of, 330–332
    musical development, 329
    and negative statements, 336–337
    problem areas, 325–326
    and teacher attitude 334–337
    vocal development, 330
Aebersold, Jamey, 264
Aesthetic experiences, 33–34
    in music appreciation course, 126–127
Affective assessment, 376–377
Alfred Publishing Company, 306–307
American Association of School Administrators,
    17
American Federation of Musicians, 17
American Symphony Orchestra League, 38
Amplification, use of, 188
Appreciation course, music, 120–129
    content, 120–121
    introducing works, 128
    listening in, 121–126
    recognition of styles, 127–128
    testing in, 128–129
    textbooks, 129
"April Is in My Mistress' Face" (Morley),
    162–166

Arrangements:
    choral, 170
    instrumental, 171
Assessing learning, 370–379
    affective changes, 376–377
    cognitive learning, 371–373
    methods of, 370–371
    psychomotor learning, 373–376
Attitudes:
    assessing, 376–377
    in curriculum, 55–56
    learning of, 98–99
Ausubel, David, 10

B

Baker, David N., 264
Balance, 185
Band Music Guide, 172
Bandura, Albert, 327
Behavior modification, 84
Benton, Myron, 10
Besson, Malcolm, 102
Beyond the Classroom: Informing Others, 17
Binion, W.T., 264
Blend, 183–185
Bloom, Benjamin, 80, 91
Booting, 295
Bowing, 253–254
Breath:
    in singing, 216–217
    in wind instruments, 246–248

Broudy, Harry, 56
Bruner, Jerome, 82, 83, 84

C

CODA Music Software, 311
Code of Ethics, 17, 274, 286, 390–392
Cognitive learning, 80–88
Cognitive tests, 371–373
Computers:
    BASIC programing, 297–300
    composition and printing, 309–311
    data base, 313
    definition of terms, 295–296
    history, 292–293
    instructional programs, 300–307
    managerial uses, 311–316
    marching band shows, 316
    MIDI, 307–308
    and music teachers, 294
    in music teaching, 296
    purchase of, 316–317
    sequencing, 308–309
    spreadsheet, 314
    uses of, 317–318
    values of, 293–294
    word processing, 312
Concepts, 51–52
Concise Introduction to Music Listening, A,
    (Hoffer), 129
Conformity, and teenagers, 325
Copyright law, 172–174
Creating music:
    in general music, 112–114
    in theory courses, 136–137
Creativity, 53
Credit, for music study, 69–70, 70–71
Cross, Neal M., 130
Curriculum:
    areas of, 62–69
    attitudes in, 55–56
    enriching rehearsals, 65–66
    and fund raising, 20–21
    general music, 94–99
    implementing, 71
    intellectual understandings, 51–52
    jazz groups, 69
    marching bands, 68–69
    nonperforming classes, 63–64
    orchestras, 67–68

    performing groups, 64–65
    and popular music, 62
    selection guidelines, 57–60
    skills in, 53–54
    small ensembles, 67
    and music teacher, 56–57
Cykler, Edmund, 131

D

Dewey, John, 32
Diction, 221–223
Digital, 296
Dimensions of Musical Thinking, 80
Discipline:
    and attendance, 350
    development of, 343–348
    and minor disturbances, 351–352
    for music teachers, 348–349
    and participation, 350
    of persistent violators, 352–353
    reinforcement in, 343–344
    serious problems, 353–354
    and talking, 349–350
    and teaching, 342–343
Discovery learning, 85
Disk, 295
Distributed practice, 89–90
"Domine Jesu Criste, O" (Palestrina), 283
DOS, 295
Dykema, Peter, 36
Dynamics, 185–188

E

Ear training:
    in music appreciation, 123
    in music theory, 133–135
Ebbinghaus, Hermann, 87
Ehret, Walter, 220–221
Electronic Courseware Systems, 300, 304–306
Embouchure:
    on brass instruments, 250–251
    on double-reed instruments, 249
    on flute, 249–250
    on single-reed instruments, 248–249
Evaluation, and group morale, 334

F

Fainting, 276
Falsetto voice, 224–226
Fine arts:
  combined courses in, 118–119
  course, 129–131
  infusion in subjects, 119–120
Forcucci, Samuel L., 102
Foster, Robert E., 264
Fund raising, 19–21
"Funkie Winkerbean," 9

G

Gehrkens, Karl, 36
General music:
  creativity activities, 112–114
  goals of, 97–99
  in high school, 95–97
  listening in, 111–112
  planning in, 114–115
  singing in, 106–111
  small group instruction in, 105–106
  status of, 94–95
Ginn, Edward, 385
Grading students, 377–379
Graduation requirements, 69–70
*Guidelines for Performances of School Music
  Groups,* 270

H

Hall, R.V., 343
Hard disk, 295
Hardware, computer, 296
Heine, Richard W., 264
History of Western Music, A (Grout), 178
Hopper, Dale F., 264
Humanities course, 129–130
Humming, 194

I

Improvising, 112–113
Instruction, computer-assisted, 296

Instrumental

Instrumental music, teaching of:
  beginning instruction, 238–245
  equipment, 260–262
  fundamentals for winds, 246–252
  guiding students in, 239–240
  instruction books, 241–242
  musical qualities in, 244–245
  organizing instruction, 240–241
  percussion, 255
  practicing, 245
  rhythm in, 245
  rote procedures, 243–244
  score preparation, 262–263
  string instruments, 253–255
  substituting instruments, 260
  transferring instruments, 258–259
Instrumentation, 255–257
Interface, 296
Interpretation:
  authenticity in, 178–179
  balance, 185
  blend, 183–185
  deciding on, 177–179
  dynamics, 185–188
  feeling and technique, 195–196
  legato, 190–191
  obstacles to teaching, 179–180
  performance practices, 178
  personal judgment in, 179
  phrasing, 191–193
  rhythm, 180–183
  staccato, 189–190
  sustained tones, 188–189
  timbre in vocal music, 193–194
  of vocal music, 193–195
Intonation:
  in choral music, 206–209
  environmental factors in, 202
  illusions in, 198–199
  instrumental, 202–206
  methods of tone production, 200–201
  and musical experience, 199–200
  psychological factors in, 201–202
  on string instruments, 204–205
  on wind instruments, 203–204

J

James, William, 85
Jazz band, 263–264

Jazz groups, 69
Johnson, John Paul, 228
Judd, Charles, 85

K

Kwalwasser, Jacob, 385

L

Lamm, Robert C., 130
Langer, Suzanne, 32
Lasker, Henry, 132, 133, 135
Learning:
    affective, 91
    applying guidelines, 91–92
    cognitive, 80–88
    intuition in, 85
    memory in, 86–88
    motivation, 81–82
    in music, 49–56
    psychomotor, 88–90
    reinforcement in, 84
    sequence in, 84
    skills, 53–54
    structure in, 82–84
    transfer, 85
    types of, 78–79
Legato, 190–191
Liberty Bell March (Sousa), 283
Lincoln, Abraham, 384
Listening:
    in general music, 111–112
    in music appreciation, 121–126
    role of memory in, 125
    by students, 148–149
    by teachers, 149–150
Locke, John, 83
Lopez, Raymond, 58
Luh, C.W., 87
Lyon, D.O., 89

M

Machlis, Joseph, 129
Mad, 345
Madsen, Charles and Clifford, 347
Marching bands, 68–69

Mark of the Unicorn, 311
Mason, Lowell, 384
Maturation, 79–80
Mayer, R.F. 36, 264
McKenzie, Duncan, 226, 227
Megabyte, 295
Memorization of music, 234–236
Memory, computer, 295
Mendez, Rafael, 246, 247
Meyer, Leonard B., 61
Micro Music Software-Temporal Acuity
    Products, 300, 301–304, 309–310
MIDI, 296
Motivation, 81–82
Music:
    avocational value, 38–39
    evaluation of, 60–62
    and fine arts, 31
    and mental health, 38
    nature of, 2
    nonmusical values of, 36–39
    value of, 31–33
Music Achievement Test (Colwell), 373
Music, adapting, 174
Music Educators National Conference, 9, 17,
    19, 292, 383–384, 384–385
    professional certification program, 22
Music in General Education (Ernst and Gary),
    97–99
*Music in the High School: Current Approaches to
    Secondary School General Music,* 96–97
Music in Our Schools Month, 19
Music, selection of, 167–171
    instrumental, 170–171
    sources, 172
    vocal, 168–170

N

National Center for Educational Statistics, 388
National Defense Education Act, 385
National Education Association, 384
Nonmusical outcomes, 56

O

Observable behaviors, 7
Orchestras:
    need for, 67–68
    selecting music for, 171
"Over the Sea to Skye," 107–110

P

Parent organizations, 20
Passport Designs, 310–311
Percussion, 255
Performances:
    adjusting to conditions, 274–276
    assemblies, 273
    checklist for, 288–289
    enhancing instrumental programs, 281–282
    enhancing vocal programs, 278–281
    guidelines for, 269–272
    informality in, 273
    music for, 172
    outside of school, 273–274
    planning for, 272
    printed programs, 283–284
    publicity, 285–286
    reasons for, 268–269
    tickets, 284–285
Pestalozzi, Johann Heinrich, 384
Phrasing, 191–193
Piaget, Jean, 79
Piano:
    in accompanying singing, 234
    in orchestra, 171
Pitch Master, 316
Planning:
    aids in, 363
    amount of, 362
    criterion levels in, 360
    in general music, 114–115
    lesson, 365–369
    long-range, 363–364
    need for, 361–362
    objectives in, 359–361
    for rehearsals, 369–370
    for types of classes, 363
    unit, 364–365
Popular music, in curriculum, 62
Practice, individual, 245
Profession, music education, 382–387
    characteristics of, 383–384
    future of, 387–389
    history of, 384–385
    opportunities in, 385–387
Program, computer, 296
Psychomotor learning, 88–90
Psychomotor tests, 373–376

R

RAM, 295

Range:
    boys' high notes, 224–226
    and intonation, 206–207
    in selecting music, 168
    in singing, 220–221
Reading music, 155–161
    counting in, 157–159
    functional, 157
    patterns in, 159–161
Recordings:
    in assessing learning, 375
    and group morale, 332
Recruiting, 337–340
    of boys, 339–340
Rehearsal procedures, see Teaching music
Rhythm, in instrumental classes, 245
Roe, Paul, 217
ROM, 295

S

SAB music, 170
SATB music, 143
School Music Program: Description and Standards, The, 63, 71
Schopenhauer, Arthur, 33
Scores:
    condensed, 262–263
    simplified for listening, 124
Seating:
    of choral groups, 232
    of instrumental groups, 257–258
"Semper Fidelis March" (Sousa), 140–143
Simpson, Elizabeth, 88
Singing:
    aural approach, 219–221
    boys' voices, 224–229
    diction, 221–223
    foreign languages, 195
    in general music, 106–111
    girls' voices, 224
    need for methods of, 212–213
    physical actions in, 214–218
    range, 220–221
    short notes, 190
    slurring, 194–195
    softly, 186–187
    styles, 219–220
    in theory classes, 135
Small ensembles, 67
Software, 296
Sousa, John Philip, 256
SPEBSQSA, 339

Spera, Dominic, 264
Spohn, Charles, 264
Springer, George H., 265
Staccato, 189–190
Stein, Keith, 247
Students:
    disadvantaged, 327–328
    and popular music, 102–103
    and/or subject, 39
Student teaching, 15–16
Suzuki, Shinichi, 83
Swanson, Frederick, 226, 227
Syntax, musical, 50

T

Tanglewood Declaration, 292
Tap Master, 316
Tatarunis, Alphonse M., 102
Teacher Education in Music: Final Report
    (Klotman), 9
Teacher, music:
    and adolescent adjustment, 328–329
    and amount of planning, 362
    appearance, 10
    attitudes, 334–337
    characteristics of, 11–12
    and colleagues, 12
    and community, 16–17, 19
    and computers, 294
    continued growth, 22–24
    and educational goals, 29–32, 39–40,
        56–57
    efficiency, 12
    and ego, 8–10
    and extroversion, 10–11
    and fund raising, 20
    and general music, 96, 99–105
    knowledge of teaching, 13
    and mouthing words, 236
    and music merchants, 17–18
    and performing groups, 64
    personality, 8–10
    and playback of classes, 23–24
    and popular music, 62
    preparation, 12–13
    preprofessional experiences, 14–16
    and private music teachers, 18
    and profession, 385–387
    and professional musicians, 17
    and public relations, 42–44
    and recruiting, 337
    and school administrators, 40–42
    and self-evaluation, 22–23
    and supplementary employment, 24
    working with boys, 340
Teacher rating forms, 23
Teaching music, procedures for:
    aesthetic awareness, 34–36
    beginning instrumentalists, 238–245
    boys' changing voices, 226–229
    choral music, 143–145
    components of, 3–7
    defined, 2–3
    ear training, 133–135
    general music, 100–105
    indicating entrances, 146
    instrumental performances, 140–155
    intonation, 203–209
    isolating difficult places, 146–147
    keeping students occupied, 147
    listening in appreciation course, 122–126
    memorization, 234–236
    musical interpretation, 179–193
    musical qualities, 140
    musical understandings, 161–166
    music reading, 155–161
    pace in, 152–155
    preparation for, 139–140
    providing individual attention, 150–151
    rehearsal enrichment, 65–66
    reviewing learned music, 148
    saving time, 151
    singing, 214–220
    verbal commentary in, 145
Tenor part:
    clefs, 234
    extending range, 224–226
    in selecting music, 168
Text, in selecting music, 168
Theory course, 131–137
    content, 132
    creative work, 136–137
    ear training, 133–135
    keyboard experience, 133
    singing in, 135
Thinking in music, 52–53
Thorndike, E.L., 85
Tiede, Clayton, H., 265
Tonguing, 251–252
Tracey, Hugh, 83
Transfer of music learning, 37–38
Trips, 286–288
Tufts, John, 384
Turk, Rudy H., 130

U

Understanding of Music, The (Hoffer), 124, 129

V

Validity, curricular, 58
Vibrato:
    effect on intonation, 205
    on string instruments, 255
Voices:
    change, 226–229
    classifying, 229–231
    names of parts, 231–232

Vowels:
    and diction, 222–223
    and intonation, 201

W

Watkins-Farnum Performance Scale (Watkins
    and Farnum), 375
Westerman, Kenneth, 222
Wilson, Harry R., 225
Wold, Nilo, 131
Wolff, Karen I., 38